S0-CEZ-343

BROOKLYN
A State of Mind

To Sheela and Joels

Michael Robbins

BROOKLYN
A State of Mind

Edited by Michael W. Robbins
Designed by Wendy Palitz

Workman Publishing, New York

Copyright © 2001 Michael W. Robbins and Wendy Palitz

All rights reserved. No portion of this book may be reproduced—
mechanically, electronically, or by any other means, including
photocopying—without written permission of the publisher. Published simultaneously in Canada by Thomas Allen & Son Limited.

Library of Congress Cataloging-in-Publication Data
Brooklyn: A state of mind / edited by Michael W. Robbins
and designed by Wendy Palitz.
          p.cm.
ISBN 0-7611-2203-6—ISBN 0-7611-1635-4 (alk. paper)
1. Brooklyn (New York, N.Y.)—Description and travel. 2. Brooklyn
(New York, N.Y.)—History. 3. Brooklyn (New York, N.Y.)—Social
life and customs. 4. New York (N.Y.)—Description and travel. 5.
New York (N.Y.)—History. 6. New York (N.Y.)—Social life and cus-
toms. I. Robbins, Michael W.
II. Palitz, Wendy.
F129.B7 B6525 2000
974.7'23—dc21   00-043528

Workman books are available at special discounts when
purchased in bulk for premiums and sales promotions as well as
for fund-raising or educational use. Special editions or
book excerpts can also be created to specification. For details, contact the Special Sales Director at the address below.

Workman Publishing Company, Inc.
708 Broadway
New York, NY 10003-9555

Printed in the United States of America
First printing, June 2001
10 9 8 7 6 5 4 3 2 1

To Patrick, third-generation New Yorker
and first-generation Brooklynite "troo and troo."

Acknowledgments

Many people contributed in many important ways to the development of this book, including, of course, all the writers, photographers and illustrators whose work appears here, as well as those who sat for interviews and shared with us their enthusiasm for Brooklyn.

We want to thank the many institutions with repositories of Brooklyn information, lore and art, and their many professionals who were so generous with their time, resources and helpful suggestions: Brooklyn Historical Society (Carol Clark, director, and Anne Myerson, curator); Brooklyn Information & Culture (JoAnne Meyers and Mona Smith); Brooklyn Navy Yard Development Corporation (Richard H. Drucker); Brooklyn Public Library, the Brooklyn Collection (Julie Moffat and Judy Walsh); Brooklyn Museum of Art (Barbara Millstein, curator); Brooklyn Academy of Music (Elena Park, Kila Packett and Amy Hughes); Brooklyn Chamber of Commerce (Joe Chan); ConeyIsland USA (Dick Zigun and Sarah Russick); Municipal Archives of New York (Kenneth R. Cobb, director); and the Museum of Modern Art, Film Stills Archive (Mary Corliss).

In addition, we want to single out those who went the extra mile in helping shape the whole work with their ideas, insights, stories, suggestions, support and encouragement—the true friends of this book: B.J. Altman; Kevin Baker; Mel Brooks; Steve Byers; Russell Christian; Seymour Chwast; Bill Costello; Patricia Curtis; Margaret A. Daly; Cezar Del Valle; Joe Fodor; Genia Gould; Stanley Greenberg; Monique Greenwood; Nora Guthrie; Ted Hardin; Robin Holland; Michael Kamber; Ivan Karp, OK Harris Gallery; Sean Kelly; Marc Kirkeby; Anne Kostick; Jason Lampkin, 40 Acres & a Mule Productions; Mara Faye Lethem; David Levine; Phillip Lopate; David McCullough; Brian Merlis; Arthur Miller; Dan Morgenstern; Minda Novek; Arlene Palitz; Carolanne Patterson; Linda Perney; Mary Placek; David Plowden; Ida Pollack; Henry Hope Reed; Buddy Scotto; Willie Shahwan; David Sharps, Hudson Waterfront Museum; Richard Snow, *American Heritage*; Glenn Thrush; Alison Tocci, *Time Out New York*; Dorothy Weiss; Randy Weston; Sol Yaged; and Kara Yeargans.

Two others... and they know why: Roger Cohn, *Mother Jones*; Alan Sussman, Verandah Media.

And thanks to all at Workman Publishing, and especially Susan Bolotin; Lynn Strong; Paul Hanson; Lydia Buechler; Anita Dickhuth; Kevin Davidson; Ina Weisser; Nicole DuCharme; Heather Conway-Visser; and Sally Kovalchick.

Title spread (Coney Island): Kim Iacono; this spread (Williamsburgh Bank Building): Mara Faye Lethem.

Contents

page 171

page 357

6. The Look

7. The Waterfront

page 11

8. Made in Brooklyn

9. Almost Lost

page 351

Preface

This book began, appropriately for Brooklyn, with *talk*, with a conversation my wife, Wendy, and I had with Peter Workman. The subject was a completely different book idea, but in the midst of the discussion Peter broke in with a question to us: "Do you love Brooklyn?" Yes, of course, we answered, and started to rhapsodize about the neighborhoods, the characters, the food. Peter waved us off. "But do you really, *really* love Brooklyn?" Yes, we answered again, but more warily this time, sensing that something was up.

What was up was the scarcely formed notion that we ought to do a book on Brooklyn, not just the sort of history/nostalgia book that had already been done several times over, but something fresher and livelier, more in keeping with the kind of incredible place Brooklyn has been and still is.

We started with the premise that Brooklyn is a unique city, at once familiar and exotic, at once a part of New York City and a place with its own distinct identity (even its own dialect), at once an earthly real place and a kind of mythic realm. It is, in our experience, the most diverse and colorful community in America, with a very rich past, a perky present and almost certainly a hot future. We all agreed in that first conversation that Brooklyn is alive with stories and tales, rumor and his-tory, amazing events and fantastic characters—without knowing specifically what the stories would turn out to be, or which voices and visions would finally end up in the book. But we were confident that if we started seek-ing those stories and voices, we would find them.

Most books go through an evolutionary process as they come into being, with the original motivating idea or guiding premise changing in response to newly dis-covered facts, to conversations with knowledgeable con-tributors and subjects, to hard questions from people who don't initially understand why anyone would do such a book, and to fresh reflections on how to bring order to so vast and chaotic a subject. Our book evolved more than most—in part because we had to get the first thirty stories before we could begin to see what kind of book it might really be. By the time we had a hundred or so stories in hand, we began to believe that we were working on a book that would be like no other, that may be a new way to attempt what is surely an impossible task—to capture the life of a whole city. Not through an almanac of facts, or a narrative of political or economic events, but in a book that is like an exhibition: a gather-ing of authentic voices and tales and details and images that altogether conveys a true sense of a place that's at once fabulous and real.

So the book, like Brooklyn itself, is hard to categorize. It is not a guidebook, not a coffee-table book, not an anthology (this is, with the exception of a *Holiday* piece by Arthur Miller, all original writing), not a formal history, certainly not an encyclopedia (though it ranges far and wide) and not another nostalgia trip. What it is: a large illustrated collection of true and original stories about life in Brooklyn past and present.

On the subject of time: a lot of fantastic things have happened in Brooklyn over the past century or so, and millions of people claim roots here. (For years now, we've been hearing that one American in three . . . or five . . . or seven was either born and raised in Brooklyn or has family here: a notion that's impossible to verify.) And although Brooklyn nostalgia is practically a cottage industry, it was neither our motive nor our main focus. Brooklyn did not freeze forever the day the Steeplechase or the *Eagle* shut down, or the day Jackie Robinson stole his first base or the Dodgers left for Los Angeles or at any moment in the past. Instead, Brooklyn has continued to thrive and develop, and renew itself. On this very day it is a diverse, energetic, zesty and appealing city in its own right, full of enthusiastic residents who simply would not live anywhere else. Many people love Brooklyn for what it is right now, and through this book we've tried to address that fact.

Many of the stories that appear on these pages came by way of interviews of the subjects of the stories, conducted by the bylined writer or by one of us. However the stories reached us, we have all worked to preserve the voice, the point of view, the attitude of the subject. This is a book *of* Brooklyn and we were determined to let the Brooklynites have their say.

If we started over again tomorrow, collecting more Brooklyn tales and images, we could come up with another 125 stories and hundreds more great photographs without repeating ourselves. Brooklyn, after all, is a very large city (with a population of about 2.3 million, it would be the fourth-largest American city were it still independent). That tells us there must be at least "eight million stories" here. Maybe it's more like eighty million: one of our neighbors, Willie Shahwan, a lifelong resident of Brooklyn, has hundreds of stories of his own. And we can only imagine how many Willie Shahwans live in the scores of Brooklyn neighborhoods. In the manner of listening to such stories, this is a book to browse through. Of course, we hope that people will eventually read it all and look at every image. But from the beginning, we never saw this as the kind of book anyone would read cover to cover in linear fashion.

Although this is not an encyclopedia, everyone who's worked on this book has struggled to make it as accurate as one, cross-checking dates, verifying events, comparing accounts—all with an eye toward making this a book to be trusted. The extent of its accuracy is attributable to the efforts and care of its contributors and the many other people named in the acknowledgments. Any faults or lapses or errors must be attributed to me.

—*Michael W. Robbins*

Bob Day

My Hometown

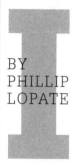

BY
PHILLIP
LOPATE

I sing of Brooklyn, the fruited plain, cradle of genius and stand-up comedy, awash in history, relics of Indian mounds, Dutch farms, Revolutionary War battles, breweries and baseball. In Brooklyn, miles of glorious town houses and brownstones— among the most architecturally satisfying residential neighborhoods in America— coexist not far from dismal slums with some of the highest infant mortality rates in the country. Brooklyn is home to millions of immigrants, many of whom never learn to speak proper English, so surrounded are they by Brooklynese, a curious dialect. Brooklyn is my hometown.

There must be some mercury in the water that brings on a need to recount or show off. Brooklyn breeds writers, performers, gangsters as effortlessly as Detroit turns out convertibles, coupes, hatchbacks. Bernard Malamud and Norman Mailer, Barbara Stanwyck and Barbra Streisand, Woody Allen and Al Capone, the Miller Boys (Arthur and Henry), Mel Brooks, Judge Samuel Liebowitz and the Amboy Dukes, Red Auerbach and Spike Lee, all came up in the encouraging yet fanatically competitive atmosphere of Brooklyn schoolyards. Even more numerous have been the illustrious, born elsewhere, who took to the hospitality of Kings County: Marianne Moore, Walker Evans, Hart Crane, Richard Wright, Truman Capote, Carson McCullers and Thomas Wolfe.

It isn't that, as Thomas Wolfe put it in his famous story, "only the dead know Brooklyn," although a good chunk of the borough is taken up by cemeteries. No, it's that the place is so large, so various and, for all its ostentation, so diffident that even a homeboy like me is hard-pressed to characterize it. When you've said that it's the most populous borough in New York City, that some 2,300,000 people live here on eighty-one square miles at the southwestern tip of Long Island, you haven't begun to describe it. When you note that it's a patchwork of neighborhoods and zero in on Crown Heights, Greenpoint, Bedford-Stuyvesant, Bay Ridge, Bensonhurst, Flatbush, Gravesend, you're perhaps a little closer to the essence of Brooklyn, though not much. A friendly place (I knew more about the people on my block a few months after returning to Brooklyn than I did about the occupants of the next building after ten years in Manhattan), the contradiction remains that Brooklynites can be so inviting to newcomers within their neighborhood, yet so xenophobic and murderously guarded toward strangers from ten blocks away. This phenomenon of neighborhood-as-fortress, plus an overall urban design that is more amoebic and organic than Manhattan's grid, helps to account for the borough's elusiveness.

If, as the pop song goes, there is a "New York state of mind," what might be a "Brooklyn state of mind"? I'll give it a shot. The Brooklyn state of mind is combative, wry, resilient: troubles are nothing new, but you relish daily life, in all its plainness and peculiarity. From Washington's strategic retreat to the present, often it consists in making a virtue of setbacks. Brooklyn Dodger fans became famous for their fortitude and obstinate belief in "next year." It is no accident that when the Dodgers finally did win a World Series, they quit the borough almost immediately for the sunny, celebrity climes of Los Angeles. The Brooklyn aesthetic is that not of the winner but of the stoic. Brooklyn likes a beautiful loser. Perhaps the defining loss was municipal identity: in 1898, when corpulent Brooklyn was the third-largest metropolis in the country, it amalgamated with spindly Manhattan (and three other boroughs,

Queens, Staten Island and the Bronx, but that's another story) to form our modern New York City. In amalgamating with Brooklyn, Manhattan became the python that swallowed the elephant. I am not one of those who rues consolidation. I rejoice that Brooklyn feeds the greater whole. There are those who will not accept her diminished status, who still speak of Brooklyn as a city. (Perhaps they even have in mind a symbiotic rivalry along the lines of the Twin Cities, Minneapolis/St. Paul.) I am a realist: I consider it a borough. But what a borough! I will go so far as to say that the spicy character of Brooklyn derives in large part from its "codependent" relationship with Manhattan. Having relinquished its municipal birthright, it haunts the island like a doppelgänger, or a conscience. Manhattan is the tower, Brooklyn the garden. Manhattan is Faustian will, Brooklyn is domestic life. Manhattan preens, disseminates opinions; Brooklyn is Uncle Vanya schlepping in the background to support his peacock relative.

As self-supporting as Brooklyn can be, it is also a colony: for over a century, millions of men and women have commuted every day to make a living in Manhattan. Like my father and mother, who spent their vital essence as garment center clerks, riding the subway in together every morning, coming back at night, the *New York Post* (then a liberal rag) under my father's arm, ready to be relinquished to me or my brother for the sports pages. Before the *Post*, it was the *Brooklyn Eagle*, a surprisingly well-written local paper, but lacking, as we would say today, an edge.

You cross the bridge from Manhattan into Brooklyn and you immediately feel it: the decompression, the increase of sky. It's like you've gone from a tense verticality to a semi-prone position, scuttling past three- and four-story houses. Everything is more casual: the way people dress, their presentation of self, their not trying to come off as world-beaters. Even the sluggards have fewer airs, less ideology or ambition about their inaction than Manhattan dropouts: the furniture in a Carroll Gardens coffeehouse seems like living-room throwaway. There is, in short, a touch of the amateur, the voluntaristic, the homemade about the place. Charles Siebert puts it beautifully when he writes, in these pages, of the "paradoxical sense of Brooklyn as a country-city, the embodiment of what I think of as the 'urban pastoral,' a place at once teeming and tame, multipopulous and personal, fast-paced and yet somehow plodding."

BROOKLYN HAS CYCLES OF RESURGENCE AND DISAPPEARANCE in the Manhattanite's (and, for that matter, the average American's) consciousness. I would argue that it tends to be most vivid to the outside world during periods of economic boom, like now. In the era of World War II and its aftermath, when more battleships were built in the Brooklyn Navy Yard than in all of Japan, Brooklyn became the symbol of democratic, pluralistic tolerance and common decency, in short, the values for which we were fighting against the Fascists. Every platoon in the war movies had its William Bendix GI who swore Flatbush was the greatest spot on oith. In the 1945 film *Anchors Aweigh*, the earthy dame with the heart of gold is called, simply, "Brooklyn." When the boy-meets-girl pair in *The Clock* (also 1945), with a weekend in New York to fall in love and commit, need a glimpse of domesticity to inspire them, they go out to Brooklyn and encounter a gruff, kindly milkman (played by James Gleason) and his family.

This highly flattering, slightly condescending mythology of the borough as adding the leavening pinch of soul to Gotham's glamour grew out of a national love affair with white ethnicity (primarily Italians, Jews, Irish) at just that moment when these groups were starting to leave the city, to be replaced by African-Americans, Hispanics and Asians. For reasons involving racism and compunction, it has been much more difficult to cast the newer, darker-skinned faces of Brooklyn in the role of America's Everyman. White journalists who had routinely filed amusing stories about curbstone "characters" (think of A.J. Liebling's deft sketches of cigar store owners and tummelers) were hesitant to draw the portrait of minority entrepreneurs or streetcorner society in such comic, local-color terms, and minority journalists were in no mood to patronize their own. What needs to be said, however, is that there was always some truth to these loving, Ralph Kramden caricatures, side by side with the condescension. There is something earthy and appealing about folk Brooklyn. Much of what continues to keep Brooklyn a vital, colorful place, as numerous sketches in this book demonstrate, stems from the artisanal care of small specialty businesses (Junior's cheesecake, custom carousels) or the communally sanctioned loneliness of obsessives who live for some hobby or sport (like Joe Durso, the handball wizard captured brilliantly in Joe Glickman's profile).

We Brooklynites all have our nostalgia, even those who fight sentimentality to the death. With me it's not nostalgia for egg creams or the *Brooklyn Eagle* or stoopball, or even the 1950s Dodgers. What I miss about the Brooklyn I grew up in is the working-class atmosphere: that sense of an industrial giant that manufactured thousands of goods and employed millions of people who did not require college degrees, but could work with their hands and take home a paycheck and feel, if not happy, at least dignified about their situation as laborers. And all the cafeterias and candy stores and delis and trolleys that Brooklyn memoirists lament were really cogs of that functioning working-class culture. When several hundred thousand manufacturing jobs left Brooklyn in the 1950s and '60s, never to return, it broke the backs of the neighborhoods. Decades of massive disinvestment accompanied the deindustrialization process.

Now the money has started flooding back: Brooklyn is hot again. It's hard to imagine how Brooklyn could ever fall out of favor for long, given its magnificent housing stock and its close proximity to Manhattan's overheated real estate market. So the dailies and city magazines carry regular features about this or that area to explore: Williamsburg, Sunset Park, Fort Greene. But Brooklyn's new prosperity looks different, with its cutting-edge bistros and boutiques. It's no longer a relaxed working-class ambience; it's that thinner, self-congratulatory consumerist culture that was originally identified, disparagingly, as "yuppie" or "gentrification" but that now seems like some globally unstoppable, ubiquitous force.

At the same time, almost invisibly, a whole different, labor-driven Brooklyn is taking shape, fueled by massive recent immigration and heroic striving. As Ray Suarez has commented in an essay included here, "The America Factory": "Brooklyn works because it still has a job to do. When I returned to my alma mater, John Dewey High School, to give a graduation speech, the two top academic stars of the graduating class were born not here in Brooklyn but in India and Russia. They will push and scuffle and study and hustle, along with the Dominican grocery store owner and the Chinese needle-trades worker, the Israeli jeweler and the Guyanese transit motorman, and continue to build this borough, this ever-renewing work in progress."

Brooklyn spirit remains a mixture of pride and provincialism. That its citizens have very much to be proud of is an indisputable fact. But what's odd, for such a world-renowned place, is the still rinky-dink sound of its boosterism, the narrow perspective of its free newspapers (which reprint the police dockets and church bingo schedules like a small-town gazette), the up-from-mimeo, defensive character of its horn-tooting. Even the crooked pride taken in its stinky parts, like the Gowanus Canal, which until recently was a repository for dead bodies and olfactory insult. Brooklyn's provincialism, be it said, is not, or not entirely, a failure to achieve cosmopolitan worldliness; it is also a painstaking, willed achievement. For it's not easy to situate oneself next to the most au courant place on the planet and resist the smoothing of one's rough edges.

The book that follows is chock-full of Brooklyn character. No better case could be made for the uniqueness of the place. Its authors collectively walk a tightrope between celebration and irony, appreciating what is still innocent or unspoiled in the Brooklynite's perspective, but bringing to it their literary sophistication. The result is a masterful freeze-frame of a world in flux.

—*Phillip Lopate*

The Time Line 1900-2000

Most time lines concentrate on major political, economic and social milestones—who was president in a given year, or who invented the whatsis. But since Brooklyn is different from other places, this time line reflects that difference.

What you'll find here are the moments that helped Brooklyn become whatever it's in the process of becoming. Some are large, others small, and many of them are wacky—like Nathan's decision to use a decomposing whale to promote their hot dogs, or almost everything that ever occurred at Coney Island. Where else would anyone even think to display incubator babies or to re-create the Boer War? Where else but from Floyd Bennett Field (in Brooklyn, of course) would Douglas Corrigan have taken off the "wrong way" to Ireland and immortality?

Leave the global cataclysms for the history books. This is a time line for the Brooklyn state of mind.

THE BOROUGH Brooklyn enters the century as part of "greater" New York in an era of ambitious building: more bridges, more transportation, more amusements. Brooklyn's 1900 population is 1,166,582.

Composer Aaron Copland is born here on November 14, 1900

Luna Park: fantastic shapes and elephants for hire

Williamsburg Bridge, second East River span, nears completion

The ever-expanding St. George Hotel

Brooklyn Royal Giants form (and show off new uniforms) in 1905

The 00s

1900: Aaron Copland (*Appalachian Spring*) is born to Russian immigrant family; will attend Boys High School. Mae West born in Greenpoint.

1901: The St. George Hotel peaks with over 2,500 rooms as NYC's largest hotel; indoor saltwater swimming pool is big draw. Brooklyn Law School opens on Ryerson Street.

1902: Willis H. Carrier invents air conditioner. Pomeroy, local auto maker, starts and folds same year. Morris Michtom creates the first "teddy bear."

1903: Luna Park opens in blaze of electric light. Williamsburg Bridge erected in half the time of Brooklyn Bridge—and looks it. Prison ship *Jersey* found under mud in Navy Yard.

1904: Dreamland opens in Coney Island. Baseball teams like the snappily uniformed Royal Giants become popular.

Clara Bow, vampy "It" girl, born on July 29, 1905

Harry Houdini brings escape act to Orpheum Theater

Third East River span, Manhattan Bridge, is erected

Heraldic ceramic marks opening of Borough Hall IRT station

BAM opens with opera—and Caruso

1905: Silent-movie queen Clara Bow (*Mantrap, Dangerous Curves*) is born over Baptist church on Bergen Street.

1906: Escapist Harry Houdini (real name Ehrich Weiss) performs at B.F. Keith's Orpheum Theater on Fulton Street. Vitagraph builds big film studio in Midwood.

1907: Actress Barbara Stanwyck (Ruby Stevens) born here July 16. First broadcast of a song: Eugene Farrar's "Do You Really Want to Hurt Me?" on Navy Yard transmitter.

1908: Brooklyn Academy of Music opens current building on Lafayette Avenue, with Enrico Caruso as Faust. IRT subway opens.

1909: Traffic is still heavy, so a third span, the Manhattan Bridge, is built across the East River, with subway trains that make onlookers nervous and a design that inspires no poets.

The Brighton Beach Girl
1910

Music Hall Programme

Dreamland goes
up in smoke on the
night of May 27

The new Bushwick
Theatre: Beaux-Arts
rises in Bed-Stuy

The IRT (2, 3, 4) goes
under Grand Army Plaza

At the resort
hotels of
Brighton Beach,
musical revues
are popular

A little Gershwin... or two:
George and brother Ira with
piano class in 1910 outing

The 10s

1910: Boot and shoe workers stage walk-out. Giacomo Puccini, opera composer, walks across Brooklyn Bridge on sightseeing jaunt. Manhattan Bridge opens to foot and vehicular traffic.

1911: Dreamland, famous for "Fighting Flames" show, burns down for real. Bushwick Theatre opens.

1912: Casey Stengel joins the Dodgers. Ferry service begins across the bridgeless Narrows to Staten Island. Battleship USS *New York* is launched at Brooklyn Navy Yard.

1913: On April 5, Ebbets Field opens for exhibition game with Yankees and new era in Brooklyn baseball. Genevieve Ebbets throws out first ball; Dodgers win in bottom of ninth.

1914: Seventh-Day Adventist leaders anticipate world's end this year; decide to await Armaggedon in Brooklyn (nothing happens). Japanese Garden constructed at Botanic Garden.

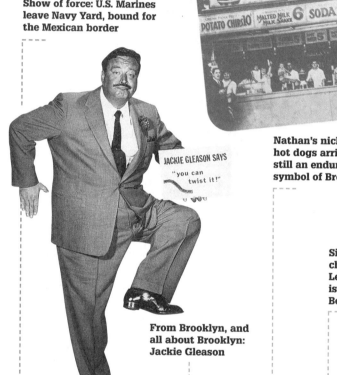

Show of force: U.S. Marines leave Navy Yard, bound for the Mexican border

DOWNS AND UPS In the decade of World War I, some famous places burn and some other famous places—and sons and daughters—are born. Immigration from Europe continues, and Brooklyn's population rises to 1,634,351.

JACKIE GLEASON SAYS
"you can twist it!"

Nathan's nickel hot dogs arrive— still an enduring symbol of Brooklyn

U.S. Mail plane makes an unscheduled stop near the Old Stone House

Silky chanteuse Lena Horne is born in Bed-Stuy

From Brooklyn, and all about Brooklyn: Jackie Gleason

1915: Navy Yard launches USS *Arizona* (sunk at Pearl Harbor, 1941). Sheepshead Bay Speedway opens; Stutz averages world-record speed of 102.6 mph for 315 miles.

1916: Jackie Gleason is born in Bushwick. Nathan Handwerker opens 5¢ frankfurter stand on Surf Avenue. Margaret Sanger starts America's first birth-control clinic, on Amboy Street.

1917: Singer Lena Horne born here June 17; will go to Girls High before Cotton Club. Puerto Ricans get U.S. citizenship; start big immigration to Brooklyn.

1918: Speeding BRT train jumps track at the Malbone Street (since renamed Prospect Park) Station at rush hour, November 1; kills 97 passengers.

1919: Brooklyn Army Terminal opens for shipping. Brooklyn trolley conductors and motormen go on strike. Sheepshead Bay Speedway closes.

THE TWENTIES roar, here and elsewhere, with Brooklyn spreading out, growing up, and Prohibition-era mobsters thriving. The population of Brooklyn reaches 2,018,356.

Barbara Stanwyck, front and center, debuts in *The Noose*

Mornings grow quiet as rubber tires appear on dairy wagons

Prohibition shuts down Fallon and many other breweries

Brooklyn leads the nation in new home construction

Norman Mailer moves in and never leaves

The 20s

1920: BMT Brighton subway line opens direct link to Coney Island. Frieda Loehmann opens her first discount designer clothing store.

1921: Spanish-American War-era cruiser USS *Brooklyn* decommissioned and sold. Dodger catcher and three-time Most Valuable Player Roy Campanella born November 19.

1922: Brooklyn Technical High School opens (two graduates will win Nobel Prize). New York State Barge Canal grain terminal opens in Red Hook.

1923: Norman Mailer, Brooklyn's most famous living novelist, is born this year; will move at age four to Brooklyn, where he'll write his great stuff.

1924: Brooklyn becomes America's busiest seaport. Fulton Ferry stops operating after 110 years. Immigration Act restricts heavy flow of Europeans to New York.

Cyclone, Coney's most
enduring ride, opens

Mobster Frankie Yale
memorialized in Holy
Cross Cemetery

Birth-control
pioneer
Margaret
Sanger (left)
goes on trial

Williamsburgh
Bank opens
for business—
in 1929.

Pet lovers on
parade at Grand
Army Plaza

1925: Poet Hart
Crane moves into
106-110 Columbia
Heights (riv vu),
already enchanted by
subject of his epic
The Bridge. Albee
Theater opens on
Fulton Street.

1926: Long Island
University, Brooklyn,
established. Washing-
ton A. Roebling,
Brooklyn Bridge
builder, dies.

1927: Cyclone opens.
Ex-slave Mrs. James
Hunt speaks about
the 1860 purchase of
her freedom by Henry
Ward Beecher's
congregation.

1928: Mobster
Frankie Yale (né Ioele)
murdered in his car
by Capone's mob in
first-ever hit with a
tommy gun. Fox
Theatre opens at
Fulton and Nevins.

1929: Williamsburgh
Bank opens in that
great year for banks.
Charged with operat-
ing a (then illegal)
birth-control clinic,
Margaret Sanger goes
on trial April 24.
Dodgers finish sixth.

THE DEPRESSION hits Brooklyn hard, bringing suffering, discontent and leftist politics. But things get modern as well, with radio broadcasts, daring aircraft feats and night baseball. The population of Brooklyn is 2,560,401.

Brooklyn College opens with five Georgian-style buildings on Bedford Avenue campus

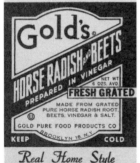

Vito Genovese rises to mob power by killing prior boss Giuseppe Masseria

Gold's Horseradish Co. starts in Hyman and Tillie Gold's apartment

Italo Balbo's seaplanes prepare to land at Jamaica Bay

The 30s

1930: Brooklyn College founded. Brooklyn becomes New York City's most populous borough.

1931: On April 15, Vito Genovese guns down soon-to-be ex-boss Giuseppe Masseria in Scarpato's restaurant. Floyd Bennett Field, Brooklyn's airport, is dedicated.

1932: Tillie and Hyman Gold get grater as gift, start a condiment business in their Borough Park apartment...Gold's Horseradish empire is born!

1933: On July 19, skies above New York fill with formation of 24 seaplanes, flying to Floyd Bennett Field under command of Italian air marshal Italo Balbo. Prohibition ends.

1934: Lundy's big seafood restaurant opens on Emmons Avenue. Mrs. Stahl's little knish stand opens on Brighton Beach.

Cruiser USS *Brooklyn* launched at Navy Yard

Classy pioneer pilot Amelia Earhart flies in and out of Floyd Bennett Field

Bush Terminal booms with eighteen piers in Sunset Park

Return of long-lost pet makes for big news in Brooklyn

Mayor Fiorello La Guardia delivers a campaign speech at Wallabout Market

Dodgers are shut out by Cincinnati Reds in Ebbets Field's first night game

1935: For a year, John Peterson wonders where his dog went; June 23, *Eagle* notes Prodigal Pom's return. Jackson Pollock show at Brooklyn Museum. Woody Allen born here December 1.

1936: USS *Brooklyn* is launched at Navy Yard November 30. The A train links Harlem and Brooklyn, inspires Duke Ellington.

1937: Brooklyn College opens and soon earns nickname "Little Red School House" as intellectual home of Marxists, Leninists and Stalinists.

1938: Lights on, lights out: first night game at Ebbets Field, June 15, is great for baseball, bad for Brooklyn, as Cincinnati's Johnny Vander Meer throws his second straight no-hitter.

1939: On August 25, in first-ever televised major league game, Dodgers lose to Cardinals at Ebbets Field. Brooklyn Public Library opens after years in the building.

Half-Moon Hotel in Coney Island: site of mob canary Abe Reles' last flight

Let the sun shine: workers remove elevated train structure from Fulton Street

Novelist Betty Smith checks out "the tree"

Parachute Jump from '39 World's Fair becomes Coney Island favorite

Short of gas and tires, but not beer: Trommer Brewery delivers with horsepower

The 40s

1940: The house at 7 Middagh Street in Brooklyn Heights becomes a salon as novelist Carson McCullers, poet W.H. Auden, novelist Richard Wright and others call it home.

1941: Jump I: Abe "Kid Twist" Reles shows he could sing (about Murder Inc.) but not fly: dies in a "fall" from Half-Moon Hotel window. Jump II: Parachute ride proves popular.

1942: Breweries revert to horse-drawn beer wagons. Singer Barbra Streisand born here April 24; will attend Erasmus Hall High School.

1943: Author Betty Smith launches coming-of-age novel (and borough's most enduring cliché), *A Tree Grows in Brooklyn.* Folksinger Woody Guthrie moves to Coney Island.

1944: Fire at Luna Park. Pfizer produces penicillin for wartime allies. *Arsenic and Old Lace,* Frank Capra's black comedy, is set in Brooklyn.

WORLD WAR II era is Brooklyn's peak as a manufacturing city, with Navy Yard and other facilities running full steam ahead. But there's still time for fun—and to confront issues like racism. The population of Brooklyn is 2,698,285.

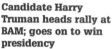

Manpower shortage ends; thousands of women leave Navy Yard workforce

Candidate Harry Truman heads rally at BAM; goes on to win presidency

Actor Danny Kaye (David Kaminsky) really *is* a kid from Brooklyn (East New York)

Dodger Jackie Robinson breaks major leagues' color barrier—and plays to win

Arthur Miller draws on Brooklyn roots for blockbuster *Death of a Salesman*

1945: World War II victory (Japanese surrender documents signed on Brooklyn-built *Missouri*) sends Navy Yard's women welders back home.

1946: Forgettable (except for its folkloric title) 1946 comedy *The Kid from Brooklyn* stars Danny Kaye, a Thomas Jefferson High School graduate. New York City Tech opens.

1947: On April 11, first African-American major leaguer, Jackie Robinson, debuts with Dodgers; despite racist abuse, becomes Rookie of the Year. Air Show draws 2.5 million to Coney Island.

1948: Underdog Democrat Harry Truman caps off his famous whistle-stop campaign with a rally at the Brooklyn Academy of Music—and goes on to win.

1949: *Death of a Salesman* opens at Morosco Theater to emotional reception; propels Brooklynite Arthur Miller to immortality. Polio epidemic hits in August; beaches deserted.

Junior's restaurant
opens on Flatbush

**Carmine
Persico,
future mob
boss, busted
at eighteen**

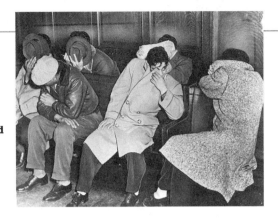

**Got milk? During 1953
milk strike, a Carroll
Gardens market
sneaks in truckload
of the white stuff**

**Barton's candy
factory on
DeKalb churns
out Kosher-for-
Passover
macaroons**

**Students protest
at Abraham Lincoln
High School over
programs, not wars
or rights**

The 50s

1950: Harry Rosen opens Junior's on Election Day; years will pass before he begins to make great cheesecake. Brooklyn-Battery Tunnel opens.

1951: *A Tree Grows in Brooklyn* opens on Broadway. Charlie Parker records jam session in Brooklyn. Giants' Bobby Thomson's homer breaks hearts as Dodgers lose pennant race.

1952: Carmine Persico nabbed on March 26 for numbers running; will eventually run Colombo crime family and then out of luck; in 1989 draws 100-year sentence for racketeering.

1953: Aircraft carrier USS *Hornet* recommissioned at Navy Yard. Dodgers win seventh pennant (lose Series to Yankees).

1954: Jerry Seinfeld born here April 29. Brooklyn Bridge reconstructed, tracks removed and roadways widened. Brooklyn Philharmonic founded.

Pencil (and eraser) maker Eberhard Faber leaves Greenpoint for Pennsylvania

BROOKLYN BREAKS OUT, with prosperity and big changes after World War II: new suburbs lure would-be home owners. Returning vets are restless with old ways. Biggest breakout: Dodgers finally win the World Series. The population of Brooklyn is 2,738,175.

Soviet spymaster Rudolf Abel busted in studio on Fulton Street

Bums no more! Dodgers finally beat Yankees to win World Series

Barbra Streisand graduates from Erasmus Hall with a 91 GPA

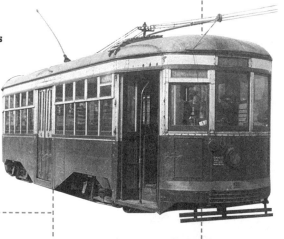

Last trolley makes final run on Coney Island Avenue

1955: Brooklyn Dodgers win their only World Series. *The Honeymooners,* with Jackie Gleason, begins TV broadcast. Brooklyn *Eagle* shuts down after bitter strike and 114 years.

1956: November 30, last #68 trolley rattles into oblivion. FBI tracks stolen microfilm to Soviet spy Rudolf Abel, posing as artist in Fulton Street studio.

1957: Ebbets Field goes dark after Brooklyn Dodgers play final game here and move to Los Angeles. New York Aquarium built in Coney on site of old Dreamland.

1958: Elvis Presley ships out from Army Terminal. Little Anthony (Gourdine), late of Fort Greene Projects, and the Imperials release mega-hit "Tears on My Pillow."

1959: Mergenthaler Linotype Co. moves to Long Island. Aircraft carrier USS *Independence* commissioned January 10 at Navy Yard.

Paramount Theatre, early home of rock and roll, is sold to LIU

Verrazano Bridge opens, spanning the Narrows

Jetliner crashes on streets of Park Slope

1962
THIS IS THE FORMER SITE OF EBBETS FIELD

Ebbets Field replaced by apartment building

Anchors away: the Navy Yard stands down

The 60s

1960: On December 17, a United Airlines DC-8 crashes on Sterling Place in Park Slope; 90 people die. Brooklyn-Queens Expressway completed. Ebbets Field demolished.

1961: Comedian Eddie Murphy born here April 3. Brooklynite Joseph Heller publishes *Catch-22*. Singer Bob Dylan hitchhikes to Brooklyn to meet Woody Guthrie.

1962: Jackie Robinson makes baseball Hall of Fame; Paramount Theatre sold to Long Island University to become a student union and gymnasium.

1963: Basketball star Michael Jordan born here February 17. Sun Ra and his Arkestra record three albums at the Tip Top Club.

1964: Verrazano Bridge opens. Reverend Galamison and Siloam Presbyterian Church push school reform. Steeplechase and Luna Park close.

A WATERSHED ERA Brooklyn's economy and its sense of itself change forever when the federal government closes down the Navy Yard—for years Brooklyn's largest employer. The population of Brooklyn is 2,627,319.

The other guys are the joke.

Reverend Milton Galamison leads parent boycott of public schools

Harvey Lichtenstein takes over BAM

Norman Mailer runs unusual campaign for NYC mayor

Mayor John Lindsay joins bicycle race at Grand Army Plaza

Shirley Chisholm, America's first African-American U.S. congresswoman

1965: Brooklyn Heights becomes NYC's first landmark district. Big change in U.S. immigration law brings many from the Caribbean to Brooklyn.

1966: Brooklyn Navy Yard stands down after 165 years of shipbuilding; the federal government will sell it to New York City.

1967: Harvey Lichtenstein assumes command of Brooklyn Academy of Music. Weeksville is rediscovered. First West Indian Day parade. Vietnam War protest at Brooklyn College.

1968: Shirley Chisholm, born in Brooklyn, becomes the first African-American woman elected to U.S. Congress.

1969: Norman Mailer runs for mayor of New York City; finishes fourth in a field of five. Medgar Evers College, a memorial to slain civil rights leader, opens in Crown Heights.

DECADE OF BELL-BOTTOMS, condo mania and disco: Brooklyn wins some and loses some. Local greats like Dodger Sandy Koufax reach the heights, while the whole city flirts with bankruptcy. The population of Brooklyn is 2,602,012.

Park Slope spearheads Brownstone gentrification

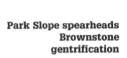

Bobby Fischer wins world chess championship

Raised in Weeksville, Mrs. Harriet Lane contributes oral history

People's Firehouse takeover is symbol of Williamsburg residents' activism

The 70s

1970: Hattie Carthan Center opens. Weeksville's Hunterfly Road houses declared historic landmarks. Kings Plaza Shopping Center opens (borough's first mall).

1971: Dodger immortal (and Lafayette High School graduate) Sandy Koufax reaches baseball Hall of Fame at age thirty-six—youngest ever.

1972: Brooklynite Bobby Fischer wins world chess championship. Gateway National Recreation area created from Floyd Bennett Field and other shoreline odds and ends.

1973: Park Slope Food Co-Op starts up; will become the largest in the U.S. Coney Island native Arlo Guthrie releases album *Last of the Brooklyn Cowboys.*

1974: Takeover of city-closed Williamsburg firehouse ("People's Firehouse"), leads to widespread activism. First Atlantic Antic street fair held.

Lundy Brothers' legendary restaurant shuts down after forty-five years

Schaefer, one of borough's biggest breweries, moves out

Ex-Lax Building, jokes aside, converts to condos

NYC Transit Museum opens at Schermerhorn Street station

John Travolta electrifies Bay Ridge in *Saturday Night Fever*

Howard Golden begins longest run as borough president

1975: President Gerald Ford announces his opposition to any federal assistance to financially challenged NYC. *Daily News* headline reads "Ford to City: Drop Dead."

1976: Schaefer and Rheingold move their breweries out of Brooklyn. NYC Transit Museum opens downtown.

1977: Fulton Mall built in effort to stabilize decaying downtown. *Saturday Night Fever* puts Bay Ridge, disco and John Travolta on entertainment map. Bargemusic begins in barge at Fulton Ferry.

1978: Howard Golden wins his first borough president election. *Flatbush Follies* revue reopens Loew's Kings –for one night. Ansonia Clock works in Park Slope turns into apartments.

1979: The old Lundy's seafood restaurant on Emmons Avenue folds. Ex-Lax Building on Atlantic Avenue converts to condos.

OLD & NEW The Brooklyn Bridge centennial is a reminder of the borough's maturity as mermaids parade on the Coney Island boardwalk and the Next Wave breaks at the Brooklyn Academy of Music. The population of Brooklyn is 2,230,936.

Durable ragtime pianist Eubie Blake plays at BAM benefit

Brooklyn Bridge Centennial fireworks display

First Mermaid Parade is held, inaugurating a truly Brooklyn tradition

Merce Cunningham's "Roratorio" at BAM Next Wave Festival

The 80s

1980: Norman Mailer, still writing in Brooklyn Heights, wins second Pulitzer Prize. Hotel Margaret, Brooklyn Heights 1889 landmark, is destroyed by fire.

1981: BAM starts Next Wave Festival of performing arts. Ken Burns' documentary film on the Brooklyn Bridge airs.

1982: Ancient vaulted railroad tunnel discovered under Atlantic Avenue. It was there all the time.

1983: For 100th anniversary of the Brooklyn Bridge, the Grucci family puts on a memorable East River fireworks show. Pianist Eubie Blake, same age as bridge, dies at 100.

1984: Brooklyn Army Terminal shuts down after sixty-five years of shippin' 'em out.

Cher as "moonstruck" Carroll Gardens poster girl

Two-year renovation brightens 1848 Borough Hall

Al Sharpton leads protest of Yusef Hawkins murder

Spike Lee shoots riotous films in hometown Brooklyn

Majestic Theater reopens as deliberate "ruin"

Steinhardt Conservatory opens at Botanic Garden

1985: East Brooklyn Churches coalition completes Nehemiah Homes, 1,000 new single-family houses in Brownsville.

1986: *Brighton Beach Memoirs* opens, Neil Simon's comic film of Jewish family crises in the 1930s.

1987: Downtown MetroTech Center built. Nabe movie *Moonstruck* shot in Carroll Gardens; Camerari's Bakery, closed in 1999, lives on in film. Majestic Theater, 1903, restored.

1988: One Pierrepont Plaza opens as borough's first skyscraper since 1929. Jazz vocalist Betty Carter starts Jazz Ahead! program in Fort Greene.

1989: Sixteen-year-old African-American Yusef Hawkins is shot to death by white Bensonhurst toughs. Borough Hall (old Brooklyn City Hall) reopens after restoration.

THE BOROUGH enjoys a decade of growing prosperity: crime is down, construction is up, beer is back, major bad guys get put away, terrific restaurants open all over, and in the media Brooklyn appears cooler than ever. The population of Brooklyn is 2,300,664.

Local at last: "Brooklyn" opens brewery in Williamsburg

Renovated Wildlife Center reopens in Prospect Park

Flatbush-bred attorney Ruth Bader Ginsburg appointed to U.S. Supreme Court

Leaving Brooklyn: John Gotti, mob boss, sentenced to life in ... Illinois

Accidental death of African-American child sparks Crown Heights riot

The 90s

1990: The killers of African-American youth Yusef Hawkins (shot while responding to used-car ad in Bensonhurst) all acquitted of murder.

1991: Racial tensions in Crown Heights: African-American child is killed by auto driven by Hasidic Jew; in ensuing riot, a visiting Hasidic Jew is killed by African-American youths.

1992: Hudson Waterfront Museum opens in barge on Red Hook waterfront.

1993: Brooklyn native Rudolph Giuliani defeats David Dinkins in NYC mayoral race. *Brooklyn Bridge,* television sitcom about borough life in the 1950s, folds after two seasons.

1994: Genovese don John Gotti, convicted of racketeering, is sentenced to life. *Crooklyn,* Spike Lee's film of African-American family life (shot in Park Slope), is released.

Brooklyn actor Jimmy Smits plays *NYPD Blue* Brooklyn detective

Marriott, first major Brooklyn hotel since St. George, opens downtown

Smell not: Gowanus Canal cleans up

Smith Street gets hot, bringing floods of foodies.

"Sensation" vigil at Brooklyn Museum

1995: Lundy's renowned seafood restaurant reopens on site of the original. *Smoke,* film comedy based on Paul Auster stories of nabe characters, gets warm reception.

1996: Brooklyn Beer opens new brewery in Williamsburg. A fixture on Fulton Street since 1879, Gage & Tollner restaurant is restored.

1997: Patois bistro kicks off Smith Street restaurant boom. In *NYPD Blue,* hunk actor Jimmy Smits (who grew up here) plays a detective who lives in Brooklyn and keeps pigeons on roof.

1998: Marriott Hotel opens on Adams Street and is soon booked solid. (No surprise: how many urbs with 2.3 million people were hotel-free?) Rose Cinema opens in BAM.

1999: "Sensation" exhibit at Brooklyn Museum of Art lives up to its name when Mayor Giuliani, who dislikes one painting, tries to evict the museum. Peewee Reese dies at eighty-one.

A Mythic Place

Brooklyn is one of those rare places in the world that has achieved mythic status, alongside others that are at once locales and legends: Hollywood, Paris and maybe Texas. It exists as an ordinary reality of streets and apartments and glowing signs and restless people. But it has another existence—as a fabulous realm the mere mention of which stirs laughter, memories, respect and, occasionally, fear. It can be seen, of course: you can gaze at the real Brooklyn Bridge, cross the real Flatbush Avenue or stare at real Brooklynites (though not for long). But Brooklyn remains an oddly invisible city: One can ride clear across it and form no sense of the incredible events that have unfolded here, or of what is happening now behind those walls and faces.

While Brooklyn is legally a "borough" (New York's word for one of its five political divisions), it is to most of the world and to all Brooklynites a fabulous city unto itself. It has long loomed large in the world's imagination, perhaps because all the world is here: Brooklyn's people are the most diverse in America. Still, all Brooklynites have much in common—accent, urban smarts, pride, toughness of character, the *attitude.* And above all, the recognition that they live in a mythic place.

**Previous spread: Prime time
at Ebbets Field with a
packed and rapt crowd, 1954.**

Previous spread: AP/Wide World; this page: Brooklyn Historical Society

Being from Brooklyn

It's not a borough, it's a country

INTERVIEW WITH
JERRY DELLA
FEMINA

Brooklyn people have "street smarts." Sure it's an overused term, but the fact is, people from Brooklyn almost never get mugged. They have that ability to size up whoever is walking toward them—that Brooklynite way of sensing what other people are all about. Once I had a boss who came from Brooklyn, and he always knew when I was looking for a job. He'd say, "Are you looking for a job today, kid?" and it drove me crazy. I'd say, "No no no," and he'd say, "C'mon, you are looking for a job today." Then two or three months would go by and I'd have an interview, and he would look at me and say, "Are you going to an interview today?"

Finally I said, "I'll admit I'm going for an interview if you tell me how you always know." And he said, "Your shoes. The only time you shine your shoes is when you have an interview."

That is *so* Brooklyn—looking at something or someone and not just seeing them but figuring out how they affect you and how to deal with it. It's an interesting sense, and everyone from Brooklyn has it. I think it's passed on in families.

We Brooklynites really did come from a time when sizing up other people, understanding what they were doing, what they were up to (and it might not even be

bad), was important. In some cases it was life-saving: I grew up in an area where some people turned out to be gangsters. And you knew when you talked to them—first of all you tried *not* to talk to them as often as you could—but you really knew. One guy named Joe G. was a psychopathic killer, and you *knew* when you played ball with him that when he said he was safe on second . . . he was safe on second. It could be that you tagged him out on first, but he was safe on second.

I am always hesitant to say I came from a bad neighborhood. I think there was a *time* when my neighborhood was a bad neighborhood, but I find that the more people accomplish in life, the poorer their neighborhood becomes. One thing I want to hear is someone who has accomplished something great say, "Oh, I came from a wonderful neighborhood."

Occasionally I go back to my old neighborhood. What I love about Brooklyn is that it doesn't really *change*. The specific people change, the look changes, but the work ethic doesn't change. The sensibility doesn't change.

In my part of Brooklyn, which was the Gravesend section, people are still the same. For example, they still won't talk about the Mafia. I wrote this book about the neighborhood called *An Italian Grows in Brooklyn*, and my own mother wouldn't read it. She really didn't like that I said things about the Mafia in Brooklyn. In fact, she was terrified: "You just don't do that. You don't talk about these people." I remember

Russell Christian

4

once using the word "Mafia" in front of my grandmother and she slapped me. "You can't say that," she said. "Somebody will hear." I pointed out that we were alone in the house. There probably isn't even that much of a Mafia left anymore, but these people don't care, it is just not to be discussed.

Joe G. was finally killed by the Mafia, and it was like a movie. They took a dead fish and put it into what was clearly his clothing and threw it in front of his girlfriend's house. She lived across the street from me, and the arrival of the dead fish was an *event*. And this is not just out of *The Godfather*—this is long before that movie. In that neighborhood, you did get a sense of knowing who a person was and what was going on.

I lived in the middle of West Seventh Street. We still own the house. In the 1940s Mr. Kahn, the gentleman who owned the house, offered to sell it to my mom for $2,000. She pointed out to him that $2,000 was more money than there was in the entire world. And of course we couldn't afford it, so we rented for all that time. Over the years we just paid rent and then it got to a point where Mr. Kahn was going to sell a whole string of houses and we were in danger of losing our home. But by then it was no longer $2,000—I think now it was like $6,000. My mom put down the smallest down payment she could, took loans from Household Finance and every financial company in the world and managed to buy the house with a thirty- or forty-year mortgage. She got very sick a while back and I didn't want her to be in a house where she has to walk up the steps to do anything, so I moved her into Manhattan on East End Avenue. But I knew that if I ever sold the house in Brooklyn, she'd think she was going to die. So we still own the house.

The house is very narrow, with two floors exactly

alike. And in that house there was my mom, my dad, me, my brother, my grandmother, my grandfather and my uncle. In the movie *Radio Days*, which was about living in Brooklyn, the thing that Woody Allen did so brilliantly was to show how we were able to live in these tight places. My brother and my uncle slept in the bed in the side room. My grandmother and grandfather slept in the middle room. My mother and father slept in the front room. And these were tiny rooms—the house itself was tiny. Yet we never got in each other's way. We never brushed against each other, never pushed each other. It was almost like someone was doing choreography: we were able to weave through one another, going from one room to the one bathroom without making contact.

The streets were wonderful. On hot summer nights in Brooklyn, everyone came out and put their chairs outside on this tiny narrow street. The kids would play ball, "kick the can" and "Johnny on the pony." We did not have play dates. What we *did* have was this incredible community of people who were all very much like us.

And there was music. I played the mandolin (every little Italian boy plays the mandolin, except if they're blind, in which case they play the accordion). There was always one man who could play the guitar, and sometimes we would play together. I was a little kid and everyone was so amazed that there I was, playing the mandolin when I was eight, nine or ten. It was during the war years, but there was a real sense of peace. In those days, if you were alive and you had a job you were a success. You had very few things. You had food, which was important because it was about showing love. And there was great planning around food and great talk of food, and great thinking about food and planned meals and family dinner time.

Brooklyn is where the family really hung on the

 It seemed to me the sun was always shining in Brooklyn, drying clothes, curing rickets, evaporating puddles, inviting children out to play, and encouraging artificial flowers in front yards." **Anatole Broyard**

longest and was the most important—it's not just the Brooklyn Italians, it's the Brooklyn Jews, the Brooklyn everybody. It was about family then, because family was all you had. Consequently we spent our time visiting each other, enjoying each other. The family feeling, the work ethic and the great fun gave everybody from Brooklyn this incredible leg up on people from other places.

It's always a mistake to think that Brooklyn is a borough. Brooklyn is a *country*. There is this country called Brooklyn, and people respect it. It is a country to the rest of the world, a place where people are different from them. We had our provinces, our different sections, Italian, Jewish, black and Irish, and kids fought "gang wars," but in comparison to today it was relatively benign. And everyone was proud of where they came from, proud of their high school.

There is still absolute awe when people hear someone is from Brooklyn. (I used to think that came from the movies, but there aren't movies anymore where somebody says he's from Brooklyn and people applaud.) I know all these people who, when they talk about themselves, always talk about Brooklyn. Brooklyn is a great place to be from. It really does help you. If I go to a meeting and someone says he's from Brooklyn, there is an immediate kinship.

Jerry Della Femina is a restaurateur who also writes a column for the East Hampton Independent.

ONLY IN BROOKLYN Billed as "the eighth wonder of the world" at its opening in 1883, the Brooklyn Bridge is both a marvel of engineering and a work of art.

Michael Kamber

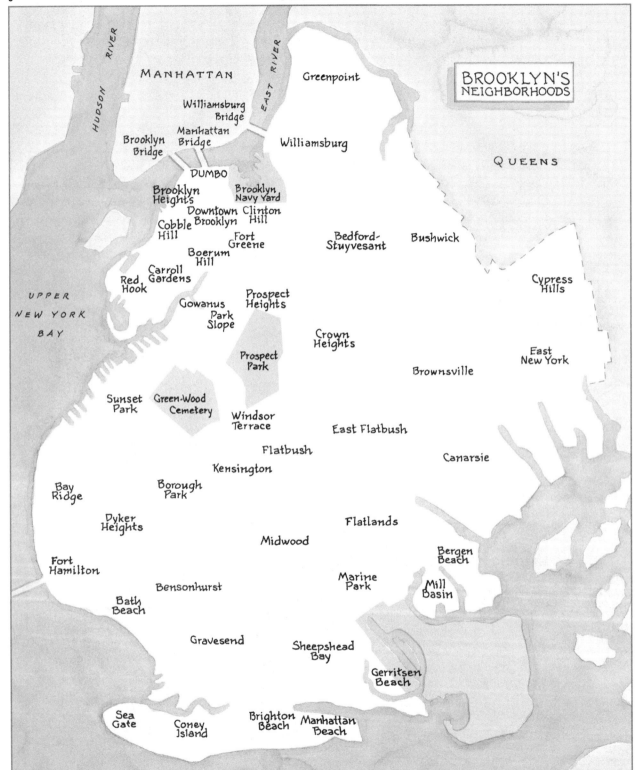

MANHATTAN

HUDSON RIVER

EAST RIVER

Greenpoint

BROOKLYN'S
NEIGHBORHOODS

QUEENS

Williamsburg
Bridge

Manhattan
Bridge

Brooklyn
Bridge

Williamsburg

DUMBO

Brooklyn
Heights

Brooklyn
Navy Yard

Downtown   Clinton
Brooklyn   Hill

Cobble
Hill

Fort
Greene

Bedford-
Stuyvesant

Bushwick

Boerum
Hill

Carroll
Gardens

Red
Hook

UPPER
NEW YORK
BAY

Gowanus
Park
Slope

Prospect
Heights

Crown
Heights

Cypress
Hills

East
New York

Brownsville

Prospect
Park

Sunset
Park

Green-Wood
Cemetery

Windsor
Terrace

East Flatbush

Flatbush

Canarsie

Kensington

Bay
Ridge

Borough
Park

Dyker
Heights

Flatlands

Midwood

Bergen
Beach

Fort
Hamilton

Marine
Park

Mill
Basin

Bensonhurst

Bath
Beach

Gravesend

Sheepshead
Bay

Gerritsen
Beach

Sea
Gate

Coney
Island

Brighton
Beach

Manhattan
Beach

David Cain

The America Factory

Keeping up with the times

BY RAY SUAREZ

Brooklyn *worked*. It functioned successfully as a city. It grew as America did, from a sleepy string of farm villages into a bustling, teeming place that loomed large in the nation's imagination. Now the question is: "Does Brooklyn *still* work?" The answer for me is a simple one and lies in understanding what Brooklyn does: it teaches all kinds of people to become Americans.

Brooklyn took an economic beating in the 1960s, '70s and '80s. Factories closed. Docks fell silent. Families nourished by the borough and nourishing it in return pulled up stakes and headed out to Long Island, northern New Jersey and other places across the country. Schools crumbled. The subways decayed. New York City as a whole, which Brooklyn had joined in 1898, swooned and flirted with bankruptcy.

Without the deep institutional inheritance enjoyed by Manhattan—the corporate headquarters and tourist attractions—Brooklyn found it much harder to ride out the financial storms. Fundamentally a working-class place, the borough couldn't simply fall back on its wealth or trust that rich and powerful friends would ride to its rescue. In those recent, troubled decades, Brooklyn began to have less in common with Manhattan and more in common with the cities that had long since passed their historic industrial prime: the Detroits, the Clevelands and Milwaukees, the Buffalos and Youngstowns.

Unlike those foundry towns and smokestack jungles of the industrial Northeast and Great Lakes, Brooklyn was so big and diverse that it could, in effect, be many different places all in one. Across its eighty-one square miles it has immigrant ghettoes and a fishing village. It is a gracious town of upscale shopping and lovingly restored silk-stocking row houses and blue-collar settlements filled with long blocks of massive apartment buildings. It's a college town. It's a bedroom suburb of Manhattan. It's a seaport. It's home to factories and warehouses. Its art museum makes the headlines, and its great concert hall presents edgy and exciting music, theater and dance.

At the one hundredth anniversary of the creation of Greater New York, some writers and historians specu-

A young Brooklynite embraces the best of both worlds.

David Grossman

lated that Brooklyn got a raw deal when it hitched its wagon to Manhattan's star. Today it must be admitted that Manhattan's overheated prosperity and prices create opportunities that Brooklyn could not make for itself. The push factor of Manhattan housing costs has reinvigorated and expanded the gentrified neighborhoods around the borough's northern shores: Brooklyn Heights, Cobble Hill, Boerum Hill, Carroll Gardens and Park Slope. Artists spilling over from the frantically escalating apartment and loft market across the river (and migrating with newly minted diplomas from nearby Pratt Institute) are remaking the old neighborhoods east and west of the Brooklyn Navy Yard.

A common dream scenario of mayors across the country striving to save their decayed old cities is that, somehow, recovery and gentrification will be led by a vanguard of prosperous consumers—yuppies and artists, gays and empty nesters. It's happened in some urban places, but it's not what has been happening in Brooklyn. Wander under the thundering D train, a stone's throw from the Atlantic Ocean in Brighton Beach. Wait

A Bay Ridge bakery caters to local Scandinavians.

at "the Junction" of Nostrand and Flatbush Avenue, where Midwood, East Flatbush and Flatbush collide. Pick a sunny Saturday afternoon and stroll along two of Olmsted and Vaux's gifts to Brooklyn: Ocean Parkway and Eastern Parkway. Come up from underground on Fourth Avenue in Sunset Park for a plate of rice and beans and roast pork. And everywhere, keep your eyes

open. What you'll see in all these places is the new Brooklyn, built on the foundations of the old. You'll see the jitney-style cabs familiar to shoppers in Kingston, Jamaica, and in the Bahamas. You'll see shop signs in the Cyrillic alphabet telling thousands of new Russian Brooklynites about the goods and services available—in a mix of the mother tongue and a roughly rendered Russo-English argot invented just for the occasion.

In short, what is making Brooklyn work at the turn of the century isn't all that different from what made it work in 1929—a happy amalgam of geography and politics, urban form and national immigration policy. When families just years out of the shtetls of the Czar's western possessions were ready to move on, they often made Brooklyn their first American stop. When Southern Italians looked for green space and undeveloped land for truck gardens, they found it in Brooklyn's leafier southern neighborhoods. The Irish arrived, built schools and churches, and swelled the ranks of the civil service along with the sons and daughters of their immigrant peers. But when the 1920s economy came bursting out of a postwar recession, the pace of immigration picked up again. And the renewed flow from the Old World reawakened the deep American suspicions of immigrants, of their alien languages, religions and political beliefs. So, during the late 1920s, Congress effectively shut the door on one of the greatest flows of people in the history of mankind. The country took a breather, took the time to accommodate the human tide that had come ashore from Europe. Then, after the stock market crash in 1929 and the worldwide economic depression, World War II shut down European immigration.

Consider Brooklyn again, in 1950. The grandchildren of immigrants in many cases no longer spoke the Yiddish, Sicilian, Norwegian, Polish and German they had heard on the streets and in church or temple. The yearning to assimilate had been reinforced by a great wartime surge of patriotism, and a fear of what was un-American. To be sure, a statue of Our Lady was still carried once a year through the streets by the men of the parish. You could still smell Grandma's cholent cooking on Friday

Ted Hardin

afternoons, a meal that would sit on a warming dish all day Saturday to avoid breaking the Shabbat proscriptions against kindling a flame. But Brooklyn no longer struggled to absorb a flood tide of poverty-stricken Europeans. Instead, Puerto Ricans, U.S. citizens since 1917, began taking up residence in the streets left behind by earlier immigrants who moved out to the new suburbs sprouting just over the city line, courtesy of housing and highway subsidies from Uncle Sam.

It was only in the mid-1960s, when Congress reconsidered the formulas governing immigration, that Brooklyn began once again to assume its traditional mission of being the great place where immigrants learned to become Americans—the America Factory. This time the undersubscribed pro-European quotas vanished, and the golden door was opened to Asia, the Caribbean and Latin America. The tiny apartments that once contained dreams nurtured in Kraków, Cork and Calabria would now do the same for people from Guangzhou, Port-au-Prince and Santo Domingo. The largest immigrant groups in Brooklyn in the 1990s came from Haiti, the Dominican Republic, Guyana and the English-speaking islands of the Caribbean. Neighborhoods once home to the vast common run of struggling human-

Specialty food stores are a common sight in ethnic neighborhoods.

ity as well as the petty gangsters, hoods and indigents are once again home to all of these—but the accents and skin tones have changed. When we make a new generation of war movies for a new generation of wars, the platoon from Brooklyn won't be Rizzuti, Weinstein and Holochek, waiting for a scrap of news about the Dodgers. That Brooklyn belongs to history. The new platoon will include new and different names, new accents, different complexions. Those new-generation GIs will still be homesick for a place that fundamentally looks the same and lives a similar day-to-day life.

Yes, Brooklyn works because it still has a job to do as the way station beside "the golden door." When I re-

turned to my alma mater, John Dewey High School, to give a graduation speech, the two top academic stars of the graduating class were born not here in Brooklyn but in India and Russia. They will push and scuffle and study and hustle, along with the Dominican grocery store owner and the Chinese needle-trades worker, the Israeli jeweler and the Guyanese transit motorman, and continue to build this borough, this ever-renewing work in progress: at once the new and the same old Brooklyn.

Ray Suarez is the author of The Old Neighborhood: What We Lost in the Great Suburban Migration *and a senior correspondent for the* NewsHour *on PBS.*

Michael Kamber

A GLOSSARY OF BROOKLYNESE

Brooklyn has always been a borough of immigrants, and for immigrants the "th" sound in English is a bitch. As a vocal noise, "th" is practically unique to the ancient Anglo-Saxon language, in which it had its very own letter of the alphabet, known as the "thorn." The French, for example, when attempting to pronounce this sound, make do with "z." ("Is zat so?") But in Brooklyn the letters "th" at the end of a word (as an ultimate fricative consonant) are invariably pronounced like a "t":

    bath = bat
    both = boat
    Smith = Smit
    with = wit
    tooth = toot
    truth = troot

When the letters "th" come at the beginning of a word, Brooklynites sometimes pronounce them as "t"...

    three = tree
    third = toid
    thrill = trill
    thing = ting
    throw = tro

but more often as if they were a "d":

    that = dat
    them = dem
    there = dere
    this = dis
    those = dose
    they = dey

Sometimes in ethnic Brooklyn pronunciation of the short "o" is "hypercorrected" into a cross between a drawl and a whine:

    coffee = cwawfee
    dog = doowahg
    God = Gwodd

or,

    walk = wooawk
    talk = tooawk

The letter "r" is seldom pronounced anywhere in the Northeast, from New Hampshuh to Hahvud to New Yawk. In Brooklyn, "more" is "moowuh," "door" is "doowuh," and "her" is "huh." "Brooklyn" itself comes out (something like) "Bwookn," while "Canarsie" is "Cnawsee." Furthermore, the vowel sound that precedes the unpronounced "r" sound is pronounced "oi":

    Bensonhurst = Bensonhoist
    bird = boid
    first = foist
    girl = goil
    heard = hoid
    murder = moiduh
    nerve = noive
    perfect = poifect
    world = woild
    certain = soitun

No one really knows why this is so. In *The American Language*, H.L. Mencken attributes it to the influence of Yiddish. Anyway, and perversely enough, in Brooklyn the "oi" sound itself is pronounced "er":

    boil = berl
    Greenpoint = Greenpernt
    noise = nerse
    oil = erl
    oyster = erstuh

Thus, when Dodger knuckleballer Hoyt Wilhelm dropped to his knees after being struck by a line drive, the Ebbets Field crowd gasped as one, "Hert's hoit!"

—Sean Kelly

The Brooklyn Accent

Fugehdabboudit!

BY BURKHARD BILGER

Alan Rodin left Brooklyn for Chicago and graduate school, some twenty-five years ago, convinced that the world was his oyster: "De woild is my erstuh," he would have said back then.

Born and brought up in Bensonhurst, Rodin had graduated from Brooklyn College with an inverse correlation between good grades and poor speech. He was the bearer of a peculiar stigma, one that evokes both pride and discomfort: he spoke *Brooklynese*. According to a nationwide poll, Brooklynites have the worst diction in the country, yet everyone seems to want to imitate them. When Jimmy Cagney played the role of a Chicago gangster, he put on a Brooklyn accent; when Henry Winkler became The Fonz, he spoke Brooklynese even though *Happy Days* was set in Milwaukee.

As for true Brooklynites, they cling to their dialect even as they disown it. As one woman in Sheepshead Bay put it: "I was set up on a blind date with this guy, but once he stahted tawkin' I knew it wasn't gonna woik. He said things like 'toidy-tree' and 'erl' and 'batroom.' I just couldn't sit dere and conversate with someone like dat."

Linguist William Labov notes in *The Social Stratification of English in New York City* that Brooklynese is determined less by location than by class. You can hear it spoken in all five boroughs as well as out on Long Island and in New Jersey, but almost exclusively among the lower classes. The cheaper the department store, Labov found in his fieldwork, the more likely customers are to say "fawth flaw" rather than "fourth floor." "New York City working-class speech," as he calls it, is unusually parochial. Most city dialects spread into the sur-

rounding countryside for a hundred miles or more. "But the boundaries around New York speech," says Labov, "are the same as they were in the Revolutionary War, when British troops occupied the city."

That cramped space, and the mass of immigrants within it, has turned New York into a linguistic witch's cauldron. In the late 1600s, Dutch and Belgian settlers, forced to speak their conquerors' English, probably gave Brooklynese its "muddas and faddas," "deses and doses" —though some language experts attribute the d/th swap to the Germans and Irish. After the Revolutionary War, Yankees who relocated from New England encouraged Brooklynites to drop the "r's" from the ends of words, yielding nuggets like "watuh" and "drivuh." Then in the 1850s Irish immigrants continued the New York vendetta against "th" sounds. In their mouths, "think" became "tink" and "thumb" became "tumb." Over time, the "oi" sound in the middle of words became similarly endangered, giving us "liar" for "lawyer."

Finally, Southern settlers gathered up all those orphaned "oi's" and found new homes for them in words like "noive" (nerve) and "woim" (worm). If not for such charity, an anonymous author might never have written "Da Brooklyn National Antem":

Da spring is sprung
Da grass is riz
I wunnuh weah
    da boidies is?
Da boid is on da wing—
    dat's absoid!
From what I hoid
    da wing is on da boid.

Russell Christian

No Brooklyn Accent for Arlo

My mother, Marjorie Mazia, the wife of Okie folksinger Woody Guthrie, said, "I will not have my children speaking with a Brooklyn accent!" Especially not my brothers Arlo and Joady. Mother had a school for modern dance, and she hired this drama teacher who was also a speech teacher—a big, fat Englishwoman named Irene Mailin. The three of us were her first pupils, and she made us repeat words over and over, trying to pronounce them with-out a Brooklyn accent. I remember my brothers riding along in the car on the Belt Parkway, saying "Don't! Don't! Don't!" sometimes in a Brooklyn accent and sometimes not.

The trouble was, both Arlo and Joady *liked* their Brooklyn accents and did not want to give up saying "Toidy-Toid and Toid" for "Thirty-Third and Third." And even now, when you listen to Arlo's records, you can hear this accent. For years everyone has been saying, "Oh, your brother has this flat Okie drawl just like Woody's." But it isn't that. Arlo picked up his Okie drawl from Ramblin' Jack Elliott, who was living with us at the time in Coney Island.

Arlo's got that twang all right, but the way he pronounces the words is pure Brooklyn. He's got a Brooklyn accent that's overlaid with an Okie twang. Listen to his records. —*Nora Guthrie*

According to linguist Margaret Mannix Flynn, who spent decades at Brooklyn College studying Brooklynese, Italian immigrants taught Brooklynites to sing their words a little—to add a dash of rhythm to their flat Nordic syllables. Some say Brooklyn's Jewish settlers went even further, refining the dialect's combustible mixture of velocity and lilt, its ability to halt a dizzying line of dialogue with a semantic squeal of the brakes: "Shuddup awready, cantcha see I'm woikin' ovuh heeeah?"

These days, a new Brooklynese is emerging from a fusion reaction with Black English and Spanglish, further fueled by borrowings from the Caribbean, Eastern Europe, the Far East and Russia. As Robert Hendrickson notes in his book *American Talk*, some immigrants are reinforcing old borough habits. Haitians, for instance, have a familiar penchant for "dis" and "dat." Others are adding new sounds to the mix: Puerto Ricans prefer "sheep" to "ship"; Trinidadians stress their word endings as if punching a backbeat. Those who bemoan the death of the dialect, in other words, just haven't been listening to the right people.

Or maybe they've been talking to Alan Rodin. Rodin is back in Brooklyn now, and when he walks down the streets of Flatbush, he greets people in smooth, rootless English, projecting and articulating like some cornbelt politician. Give him a few sentences and he'll guess where you were born from your accent. Then he may preach you a sermon on the joys and agonies of reinventing yourself through language.

Rodin is the premier example of the reformed Brooklynese speaker. Now a freelance speech coach and a professor at Brooklyn College, he teaches lawyers, politicians, college students and child actors. He rides in limousines with public figures, coaching them on their prepared speeches. "For some people, it's like getting a nose job or a breast augmentation," he says. "They don't want it known. When I call their offices, their secretaries don't know who I am."

Some 60 percent of Brooklyn College's incoming freshmen are asked to take Speech 10, popularly known as "How to Lose Your Brooklyn Accent," before they graduate. For most of them, as it was for Rodin, changing accents is a matter of professional life or death. "It marks you. It's like a badge," a student from Bensonhurst explains, pronouncing the last word "bee-adge." "Some people might consider you ignorant if you speak that way."

Rodin strides into his classroom, on a typical morning, and scrawls the following sentence on the blackboard: "Pa poured water on the poor dog's paw." He then asks each student to read the sentence aloud. The class comprises some thirteen ethnic backgrounds, but you wouldn't guess it from the voices. "Pa poowuhd watuh on the poouh dawg's poowuh," they each say: six distinct vowel sounds all reduced to blasts on the same foghorn.

Surviving in Brooklyn, Rodin concludes, takes two dialects. Speak with a Brooklyn accent in Bensonhurst and you may not get mugged; speak without one and you may get a job. With a Brooklyn accent, a teacher might not get certified; without one, Ed Koch might never have been elected mayor. Like a used-car salesman, you have to size up your audience and tailor your talk accordingly. "Okay, let's say I get stopped by a policeman," Rodin says. "Which way do I have a better chance of getting a ticket: if I say, 'Yo! Officuh! Wuz I speedin' or what?' or if I say, 'Pardon me, Officer, was I speeding?'" The students laugh, shaking their heads.

Part stigma, part secret handshake, Brooklynese has long divided Brooklynites against themselves. Movie and sitcom stereotypes have only heightened an age-old dilemma: Which is more worthy of allegiance, cosmopolitan culture or local culture? A sense of place or a sense of broader belonging? And is it worth trying to have both, as Rodin suggests, at the risk of having neither? "I'm not putting a value judgment on it," Rodin says. "But the fact is that language matters."

Eli Wallach: A Brooklyn Accent Saves the Day

"When I was a kid, I went to school at the University of Texas—directly from Erasmus Hall High School in Brooklyn—because it had the lowest tuition in the country (and also because I couldn't get into City College). When I arrived in Texas, it was like going to another planet. This was in the 1930s. At Texas, I was constantly called on by my professors. Not because they wanted my answers to their questions, but because they wanted to hear my Brooklyn accent.

I was born and raised in Red Hook's Little Italy. On Union Street. Once I was supposed to play a gangster onstage, and I couldn't figure out how to play him. My character was Albert Anastasia—the one who was shot in the barbershop. I went to California and they said to me, "Well, we have his brother on tape, Tony Anastasia, appearing before Senator Kefauver's committee investigating organized crime. And here's the tape." Rudolph Halle was the prosecutor, and he says, "Mr. Anastasia, where do you live?" Tony Anastasia says, "I livuh at Wunnuh Sixty-Sevenuh Union Street." I immediately said, "Shut off the machine." I was born at 166 Union Street. So I knew how to play Anastasia. I had full knowledge of how to play him."

Stage, screen and television actor Eli Wallach is a founding member of the Actors Studio. His major films include Baby Doll, The Magnificent Seven *and* Godfather III.

Brooklyn Public Library–Brooklyn Collection

For Rodin, the holy grail can be best glimpsed in the speeches of Martin Luther King, Jr.: a soaring eloquence one moment, an honest folksiness the next. "When Dr. King spoke in Montgomery or Selma, I wouldn't have understood him," Rodin says. "But when I listened to his 'I have a dream' speech, I thought it was the most eloquent thing I had ever heard. It cut across cultures."

In the end, such linguistic harmony may be even harder to achieve than racial harmony. Even Rodin admits that his own standard speech can sound a bit affected, and some "d's" and "oi's" can slink in among his carefully tailored syllables. When he says "because," you can still hear Brooklyn sounding among the vowels.

"How to make it second nature, that's the hard part," he says. "I've had students who could master it in two weeks and others who, well, after a term, I just wanted to give them their money back."

As the students file out, Rodin has each of them say "hot chocolate and coffee." Most of them do well with the hot chocolate, dampening the echo chambers in their mouths. But when it comes to the coffee they give up. No amount of self-consciousness and deliberation can defeat two centuries of urban identity. "Cawwwfeee," they all say, then shrug with a bittersweet smile:

"Fugehdabboudit!"

Burkhard Bilger is a senior editor at Discover.

BROOKLYN ON FILM

In Love with a Wonderful Bridge

The Brooklyn Bridge, the borough's most famous and enduring icon, has been celebrated in literature, music, the fine arts—and on film. Moviemakers across the span of film history have paid tribute to its ageless appeal from a variety of perspectives—over, under and facing the bridge.

New Brooklyn to New York via Brooklyn Bridge, no. 1 (1899), is a rare nineteenth-century "actuality" film. Mounted on the front of a locomotive, a camera traverses the bridge. It captures the formal beauty of the suspension cables whizzing by, provides glimpses of strolling pedestrians and reveals faint images of children scrambling across the railroad tracks.

In *Under the Brooklyn Bridge* (1953), artist Rudy Burckhardt films an affectionate portrait of children who dive into the East River and swim from the foot of the bridge. In the background, Burckhardt frames the majestic span and simultaneously

captures the extensive commerce that was once conducted in the harbor and the river in the shadow of the bridge.

Ken Burns' documentary *Brooklyn Bridge* (1981) recounts the epic struggle of the Roeblings, father and son, to build this great bridge, highlighting their engineering ingenuity.

Donna Cameron at Work (1991), a video documentary by Mike Kuchar, reveals the method by which Brooklyn artist Donna Cameron visually deconstructs and reconstructs the bridge. She uses still photographic images of the bridge's span and her process culminates in the creation of abstract moving images of the suspension cables. These abstract rhythmic patterns then appear in Cameron's own experimental film *Tyger, Tyger* (1990).

The bridge's appeal has been most vividly personified by Frank Sinatra in the feature film *It Happened in*

Brooklyn (1947). In this movie, Sinatra portrays a soldier recovering from an illness at the end of World War II. As his nurse grills him about his girl back home, she grabs a photo out of his hand and realizes that his "girl" is actually the Brooklyn Bridge. Upon being discharged from the army, Sinatra's character proceeds directly to the object of his desire, where he sings to, dances on, and cavorts with his beloved bridge.

–Jon Gartenberg

Everett Collection

The Accent Onstage

Don't mess with a good thing

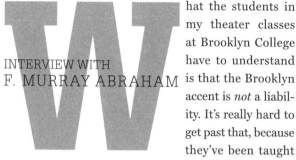

INTERVIEW WITH
F. MURRAY ABRAHAM

What the students in my theater classes at Brooklyn College have to understand is that the Brooklyn accent is *not* a liability. It's really hard to get past that, because they've been taught that accents—and it's an international class, so there are all kinds of accents there, from Israeli to mainland Chinese—put them in a certain stratum or class. Or an accent *types* them. They must learn that a Brooklyn accent is a salable commodity, something that is *charming*. And also that an accent is culturally valuable to maintain, especially in a world that is becoming increasingly homogeneous. In terms of individuality, it's imperative to maintain accents.

Now, the only problem I see with a true Brooklyn accent is the same as with any dialect: it's hard to understand unless you tone certain things down. Cockney, for example, is *impossible* to understand, so in the theater you have to use it wisely. But a true accent is not something one can simply drop—or learn very quickly, either. It's something one has to adapt to, and that's a problem when working with students who are taking only one course with you, or studying with you for only one session.

What you do, with an accent, is fall into a pattern of speaking that really almost dictates how you think. So if you start trying to monitor the way you sound, you interrupt your thought process and begin not to trust your instincts or speech patterns. And in acting terms that's the *worst* kind of thing because it's unreal; it's something practiced and sounds sticky and stiff. You're constantly looking at yourself, listening to yourself—and that's not art at all. So what I have to do with my theater students is let them know that they have to be clear enough to be understood, but at the same time their instincts and speech habits still have to function.

The value of a Brooklyn accent is that it's something that people *enjoy*. It makes them smile. It's something they look forward to hearing. The word "Brooklyn" conjures up a very particular thing in many people's minds.

**As Salieri, Abraham won an Oscar.
In real life, he teaches drama.**

They couldn't tell you specifically what that particular thing is, but they do know that "Brooklyn" *means* something to them: it's colorful, it's interesting, it's quirky. And it's also reliable. When you say someone's from Brooklyn, you're talking about a family feeling, about someone who's a stand-up guy. If you were in a fight of some kind, or in any kind of trouble, you'd want a Brooklyn guy on your side. You don't want Brooklyn guys to be *against* you. Not only because they would be tough, and tenacious, but also because they would really fight.

There's something philosophical about the Brooklyn accent, by the way. There's a kind of richness and warmth to it—it's got *heart*. And you just don't expect that same kind of gritty character from someone in, say, Massachu-

Photofest

Joe Gilford on Jack

Yankel Gellman's mother, Saska, one of the only divorced women in the neighborhood, struggled alone as manager of a lunch counter, a midwife and, finally, a bootlegger. Her home-made still was in a bedroom and the smell of fermenting mash filled Yankel's house, infesting his clothes so he stank of bourbon at school. It wasn't enough that he was frail and homely. Now he was an eight-year-old who smelled like a drunk.

Some free amusements were available to poor Jewish boys, like climbing the framework of the El for a free ride to Coney, or getting up on a stoop to entertain the neighbors with impressions of Keaton or Chaplain.

Career choices for a poor kid from Brooklyn were slim—sports, the mob or entertainment. While laboring at a Garment District cosmetics wholesaler, Yankel spent his weekends seeing Jolson and Jessel at the Manhattan Paramount or Rivoli. The thrill of the stage, of laughter and applause, was too much for Yankel to resist and he joined the young entertainers who competed at the Brooklyn Fox or Loew's Pitkin in the weekend Amateur Night contests. Luck brought his idol, Milton Berle, to one of his shows. The master had found his pupil, and Yankel was

apprenticed to Berle for three grueling years on the road. He changed his name from Yankel to Jack. And Berle said "Gellman" sounded too Jewish, so they agreed on "Gilford."

After the end of Prohibition, many establishments sought to retain their clientele by providing music, comedy and dancing, and Jack found work at a progressive new night-club in Greenwich Village—Cafe Society—the first to be racially integrated.

He also developed a new form of comedy: rather than telling jokes, like Jessel or Berle, Jack gave his audiences a guided tour of his consciousness, with freely associated ideas and impressions. He did bits of a frustrated baseball pitcher, a losing tennis pro, a cowardly boxer. He imitated animals—a benign camel, a proud chicken. He offered lines like "I was an early fan of jazz. But it wasn't known as jazz then. Before coming up from New Orleans, it went by another name—Shapiro."

What started as a youthful escape for Yankel Gellman became a career. The leaps he took onstage were like those he risked in Brooklyn, rising to the top of a stoop at the age of twelve to lighten the struggles of his pals and neighbors with the comforts of laughter.—*J.G.*

---

setts, unless of course they're from South Boston. There's a rich mix of people in Brooklyn, and that's part of what you're talking about when you talk about the Brooklyn accent.

And I do absolutely have Brooklyn types in my theater class. The first thing my students do when they hear a Brooklyn accent is *smile*—because of what that accent means. But then to get past that and achieve some kind of distance, I ask each of them to duplicate

the accent. It gets pretty funny because some of the other accents in the class are pretty thick. What they do is what they *think* a Brooklyn accent is. And when they all go through that, it's amazing how it breaks the ice. The class becomes a unit very quickly. And we all have a good laugh.

F. Murray Abraham, winner of an Oscar for his role in Amadeus, *teaches drama at Brooklyn College.*

What's So Funny?

Only Brooklynites can laugh at Brooklyn

BY SEAN KELLY

Brooklyn has been the butt of jokes in bars, on radio and TV, in Borscht Belt resorts, in cartoons and headlines," moans Elliot Willensky, author of the elegiac *When Brooklyn Was the World*. Hey, Elliot, lighten up. You're confusing laughin' with and laughin' at. Brooklyn is a funny place and nobody likes laughing about Brooklyn more than Brooklynites.

It has always been true that for an easy snicker, any stand-up comic need only mention Podunk, Burbank or Brooklyn. Both Podunk and Burbank may, indeed, be "the butt" of jokes, since both are presumably populated by rubes. But there are no rubes in Brooklyn.*

Even when we were represented to the world by a major league baseball team known as the Bums (one of whom, Babe Herman, once stole second with the bases loaded), the joke was always about Brooklyn, not on it, since we—the Bums and their fans—were always in on the joke. And at their daffiest, the Dodgers were never funny/contemptible; they were funny/lovable. They were the underdogs, the ones whose side everybody always takes. They made us smile, because they filled us—against the odds, even against the Yankees—with a crazy kind of hope. At Ebbets Field, whenever the first Dodger pitch on opening day was called a ball, a chorus of unanimous resignation would ring out from the bleachers: "Wait 'til next year!"

*Interestingly, all three of the place-names that are surefire laughs (Podunk, Burbank and Brooklyn) contain the letter "k." Mel Brooks maintains that words containing the letter "k" are inherently funny. Mr. Brooks is from Brooklyn, and both his stage name and real name (Kaminsky) have a "k" in them.

The comic stereotype of the Brooklyn Bum—down-but-not-out, feisty, street-smart, fast-talking and on the make (he'll offer to sell you the Brooklyn Bridge)—got his first big laughs circa 200 B.C. in the works of the Roman playwright Plautus. The stock character of the tricky slave, known as *servus dolorosus* (translation, working-class con man), was the one who initiated and complicated the plot as he connived, by all means necessary, to win his freedom. And that's why, in our time, the comic spirit of Brooklyn has been best represented in a re-write of Plautus: the musical comedy *A Funny Thing Happened on the Way to the Forum*, in which the role of Pseudolus was originated by the incomparable Zero Mostel and then re-created by motormouth Phil Silvers, both great comedians born in deepest Brownsville.

In the popular imagination, Brooklyn gals are all similarly hard-boiled, smart-mouthed and proletarian. Indeed, the original model, Mae West of Greenpoint,

"Can we talk?"
—Joan Rivers

This page: Photofest; next spread left to right: Brown Brothers, Brooklyn Public Library, Corbis, Culver Pictures (both), Brooklyn Public Library (both).

lamented, "Just because I was born in Brooklyn, some people figure that the West family tree is a rubber plant." Mae was pragmatic but not ungenerous, as her signature line notes: "Come up and see me sometime. Come up Wednesday. That's amateur night." Her on-screen successor was Brooklyn-born actress Patsy Kelly, who started out as half of a vaudeville insult-comedy team—though hardly the straight woman. Renowned as the Queen of the Wisecracks, Patsy cracked wise in scads of low-budget film comedies. In *The Girls from Missouri*, she and Jean Harlow play showgirls entertaining in a retirement home. When one lecherous codger lunges at Patsy, she turns to Harlow. "Will you look at this?" she marvels. "Death takes a holiday!" Actress Rhea Perlman of Bensonhurst carries on the tough-talking Brooklyn broad tradition, but there are currently no serious contenders for the title Joan Rivers (born on Eastern Parkway) has proudly claimed: "the meanest bitch in America."

The aggressive linguistic skills of the Brooklynites are all the funnier because we're not supposed to speaka de English so good. We say dis and dat and dese and dose, not to mention badda-bing, badda-boom. We're ethnic: Italian, like Dom DeLuise of Bensonhurst; Jewish, like Alan King of Williamsburg; black, like Eddie Murphy of Bushwick; or Irish, like Mary Tyler Moore, who spent her childhood in Brooklyn Heights (an area, as her mother repeatedly reminded her, "distinctly superior to and separate from Flatbush").

For a former generation, Brooklyn boys were the valiant movie GIs who wisecracked even while dying. Frequently played by William Bendix, as in *Guadalcanal Diary*, they were sometimes actually nicknamed "Brooklyn." Next, they surfaced as the goofy TV sitcom Sweathogs of *Welcome Back, Kotter*. Illiterate? Sure. Delinquents? Maybe. But cute. Even Brooklyn's adult criminals are an amiable if not exactly admirable bunch—c.f. *Goodfellas* and *The Gang That Couldn't Shoot Straight*. And it was our real-life homegrown felon, Willie "the Actor" Sutton, who explained that he robbed banks "because that's where the money is."

Jokes—and jokers—are frequently exported from Brooklyn since we tend to produce more of both than we can consume domestically. To the Borscht Belt, the vaudeville circuit and beyond, the City of Homes and Churches has, over the years, dispatched many top bananas, tummelers and headliners, all of them "typically" Brooklyn: born to run off at the mouth.

In that roster: the venerable smart-aleck Joey Adams (from Brownsville); the furious and frenzied Jack Carter (Brighton Beach); the reprehensibly potty-mouthed Andrew Dice Clay (Sheepshead Bay); snarling

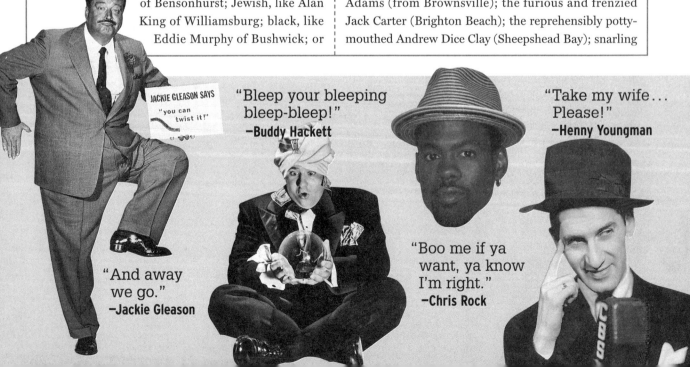

JACKIE GLEASON SAYS
"you can twist it!"

"Bleep your bleeping bleep-bleep!"
—Buddy Hackett

"Take my wife... Please!"
—Henny Youngman

"And away we go."
—Jackie Gleason

"Boo me if ya want, ya know I'm right."
—Chris Rock

put-down artist Pat Cooper (Red Hook); sputtering, indignant Phil Foster (Flatbush); short-fused Buddy Hackett (Bensonhurst); double-talking Danny Kaye (East New York), who played a prizefighting milkman in *The Kid from Brooklyn*; and the immortal Henny Youngman, King of the One-Line Zingers, who grew up in Bay Ridge.

Perhaps less typical of Brooklyn funnymen were the aggressive but inarticulate Three Stooges, two of whom —Curly and Moe—were from Bensonhurst. Being born in Flatbush was the first thing Woody "Manhattan" Allen had to be embarrassed about. He confessed to his biographer, Eric Lax, "Sometimes when I look in the mirror I say, 'You're Allen Konigsberg from Brooklyn. Shouldn't you be eating in the basement?'" But Mel Brooks shamelessly proclaims his Brooklyn origin. In a *Playboy* interview, he boasted, "We lived at 515 Powell Street, in a tenement. I was born on the kitchen table. We were so poor my mother couldn't afford to have me: the lady next door gave birth to me."

Chris Rock grew up on Decatur Street. He describes his area of Bedford-Stuyvesant as "the kind of neighborhood where the only people with money are drug dealers, people who hit the daily number, and people who got hit by a car, sued and got paid." He claims that as a lad he spent eight hours a day in the middle of Fifth Avenue "trying to get run over, disguised as a pothole."

But if there is one comic-Brooklyn archetype for the ages, it is the Great One, Jackie Gleason. Most of the characters he portrayed on-screen were pure blue-collar, in-your-face, against-the-odds *Brooklyn*: a pool shark, a fight manager, a frenetic television pitchman, a bumbling plumber, a garrulous bartender and, most memorably, the big-talking, short-tempered, luckless, lovable bus driver Ralph, who honeymooned with Alice at 328 Chauncey Street—the same street on which Gleason spent his own hilariously miserable Brooklyn boyhood.

Sean Kelly, a Canadian expatriate and longtime by-choice Brooklyn resident, is coauthor of How to Be Irish Even If You Already Are.

Some Classic Gags

"I was born in Brooklyn."
"What part?"
"All of me."

A cabbie has the ball game on the radio when a passenger gets in.
Passenger: "How're the Dodgers doing?"
Cabbie: "They got three men on base."
Passenger: "Which base?"

Army doctor: "Where are you from, son?"
Recruit: "Brooklyn."
Doc: "Any other defects?"

Q: When there's a Brooklyn father-son football game, who loses?
A: Blue Cross.

"Come up and see me sometime."
–Mae West

"Did I kid my best friend's mother about her heart condition?"
–Phil Silvers

"If you've got it, flaunt it!"
–Zero Mostel

Casey Comes to Town

New hope for Dodger fans

BY FRANK
GRAHAM, JR.

Most people my age are dead," the aging Casey Stengel once remarked. But before his demise he could boast of being the only man who played marquee roles in the fortunes of all four baseball teams that represented New York in the majors during the twentieth century—the Brooklyn Dodgers, the Giants, Yankees and Mets. He managed the Dodgers, Yankees and Mets, and was a World Series batting star for the Giants. But he started his major league career in Brooklyn, where his antics and syntax branded him forever as a member of the "Daffy Dodgers."

Stengel arrived in Brooklyn in 1912 at the age of twenty-two. He had been enrolled as a student at the Western Dental College in his hometown of Kansas City, and during the summers he had picked up money for tuition by playing minor league baseball. That's where he came to the notice of one of the Brooklyn Dodgers' roving scouts, who liked what he saw. Stengel signed up, then gave up drilling teeth for the delights of the national pastime. That September he was ordered to report all the way to Brooklyn.

Not to Ebbets Field, though. In those days the Dodgers played their home games in Washington Park,

In Casey's day, Brooklyn's major league team was known variously as the Superbas, the Robins (after manager Wilbert Robinson), the Kings and finally the Dodgers (after the earlier nickname "Trolley Dodgers").

Library of Congress

a distinctly substandard assortment of grandstands and fences thrown together by team president Charles Ebbets on leased ground between First and Third Streets and Third and Fourth Avenues in a neighborhood known as Gowanus, for the nearby industrial canal. Ebbets would not build his new ballpark until the following year.

Stengel, who had stayed overnight in a Manhattan hotel, set out to join his new team on the morning of September 12. With the aid of elevated and streetcar rides and the directions of friendly natives, he located Washington Park and convinced the gatekeeper that he really was a team member.

The start of a Hall of Fame career.

"C'mon in," the gatekeeper said. "The clubhouse is down there—and you'd better be good."

Stengel started for the Dodgers in center field. There wasn't much of a crowd in the stands that day, for it was late in the season and Brooklyn was mired deep in the National League's second division. But there were still plenty of spectators. Beyond the outfield wall and across the street rose an apartment building called the Ginney Flats, on whose network of fire escapes the residents gathered to watch their heroes. Those who had extra space rented it to neighbors at ten cents a head. Enterprising neighborhood saloonkeepers had adopted the practice of selling growlers of beer to the fans perched on the upper stories, the fans hoisting the brew from the street on ropes supplied by the publicans.

One result was that by game time the residents were really enthusiastic, even rowdy. While they usually defended the local heroes with loud words, and occasionally with their fists, a bad play by a Dodger might quickly alter their good spirits. From the sub-Olympian heights of the Ginney Flats, the mob alternately hurled cheers and maledictions at their favorites and were known to bombard enemy outfielders with spears fashioned from

umbrella ribs. In Stengel, they were to find a home-team player who could trade greetings and insults with them on even terms, and at times shout them down.

Sizing up these conditions, Stengel decided he'd better heed the gatekeeper's admonition— and be quick about it. He hammered out four straight base hits and twice stole second base. On his last trip to the plate, with a left-hander now pitching for the visiting Pittsburgh Pirates, their manager shouted from the dugout: "Okay, busher, let's see you cross over!" Stengel, a lefty who had never batted right-handed, cockily stepped across the plate and assumed a right-handed stance. Perhaps unnerved by this brash bush leaguer, the pitcher proceeded to walk him on four pitches.

"The next day the newspapers said I looked like the new Ty Cobb," Stengel recalled years afterward. "But pretty soon they found out I was nothing but the old Casey Stengel." Which, in the end, proved to be pretty good. Stengel became a regular outfielder for the Dodgers for the next five seasons, returned to Ebbets as a coach and later manager in the 1930s, and then crossed town to manage the Yankees from 1948 to 1960, guiding them to ten pennants and seven World Series appearances. And in 1966 he was elected to the Hall of Fame.

But it all started with an antic afternoon on the Gowanus Flats. The fans loved the young rookie from Missouri whose colorful antics had so enlivened what otherwise might have been just one more of the meaningless games they had to endure during that era.

Frank Graham, Jr., has written more than a dozen books, including Since Silent Spring, Where the Place Called Morning Lies *and* The Audubon Ark. *He served for five years as publicist for the Brooklyn Dodgers.*

Our Common Ground

The Dodgers were the only thing we could agree on

BY CARL
E. PRINCE

A panoramic photograph of the Ebbets Field scoreboard, taken in 1946 from the press box, shows some 2,000 fans looking up from the right-field grass, where they had all gathered after the Dodgers lost the last game of the season. Those most faithful fans were awaiting the outcome, posted inning by inning, of the final regular-season game between the St. Louis Cardinals and the Chicago Cubs being played in Chicago. If St. Louis lost, the Dodgers would tie them for first place and a three-game playoff for the National League pennant would ensue.

Every true Bums fan knows what happened: the Cards did lose to the Cubs on that Sunday, but then went on to beat the Dodgers in the playoff.

Whose side are you on, anyway? Fans' faces tell the story.

That photograph was valuable to me because somewhere on that hallowed right-field turf, I was among the fans who had left the bleachers at the end of the game to go and look up at the scoreboard. That was my first Dodger game, and I was only there because my dad had bribed or intimidated Jerry and Allie, two of my more than thirty first cousins, to schlepp me to the game. To us, it seemed a miracle that the Cards lost after the Dodgers blew their very first of many postwar October chances. The emerging "Boys of Summer" would manifest their presence in Ebbets that October day—and I was there.

Hilda Chester, the Dodgers' cowbell-toting number-one fan, stayed on while we waited. She had sat in her usual center-field seat, maybe one section over from my bleacher seat. The Dodger Sym-Phony swung noisily by, to my ten-year-old astonishment. And my sophisticated older cousins used me as their excuse to do the uncool thing and await the outcome of the Cards game on the grass. They too were unwilling to leave Ebbets Field until they knew that the Dodgers would live to fight another day.

I come from an extended immigrant family. My grandparents and the seven youngest of their nine children arrived in Brooklyn in 1919 from what had recently been Austria-Hungary. By 1946 these seven children, married and with many offspring, were scattered over the borough: Brownsville, of course, that Jewish shtetl, but also Brighton Beach and Coney Island, even one family in the Italian and Irish bastion of Bay Ridge. But only my Aunt Celia and Uncle Ben were situated in Flatbush, in an apartment on Empire Boulevard (I thought it was *Umpire* Boulevard, even after I learned to read), just two blocks from Ebbets Field. That's where my cousins would gather before weekend games. Aunt Celia

Brooklyn Public Library–Brooklyn Collection

A moment in history: Dodger fans jam right field to check the progress of the all-important Cardinals game.

adopted us all, making up ten or fifteen salami sandwiches to go, complete with ripe pickles, for a lunch in the bleachers.

The thrill of that on-the-field moment in 1946, the vivid memory of it, carried me from age ten until I was twenty-one and the Dodgers left Brooklyn in 1957. It carried me to nascent adulthood in a wave of tension-ridden family clannishness that I know now was too much of a good thing. Years later, after reliving that part of my boyhood by writing about my Dodgers as both a fan and a historian, I realized that provincial, isolated Brooklyn made *family* loom much too large in most of our lives. But in those days, everyone—young or old—was a Dodger fan. So the team provided a community of intense inter-

est that connected the generations of immigrant ethnics who dominated every Brooklyn neighborhood. My clan was no exception. The team was about the only thing on which we could all agree.

In October 1946, about the time that Ebbets Field photograph was taken, my family began to come apart. It started to unravel when my three oldest male cousins were discharged from the army. The three brothers of the older generation, my father included, believed the returning veterans would, of course, subordinate their ambitions to the family's common good—as had always been the case.

Baseball Hall of Fame Library, Cooperstown, NY; right: Brooklyn Historical Society

Loyalty pays off in 1955 when the Dodgers win the World Series championship against their longtime arch-rivals—the New York Yankees.

The three vets came home with some harrowing, half-told horror stories. My cousin Charlie spent eighteen months in Halloran Veterans Hospital on Staten Island, mostly recovering from his war wounds. He was a decorated platoon lieutenant in one of the first two regiments to cross the Rhine and hold the Remagen bridgehead.

These three Brooklyn men (not the boys their uncles or fathers still thought them to be) were flush with accumulated combat pay, plus the "fifty-two twenties" they got from Uncle Sam (twenty dollars a week for fifty-two weeks), and the vast educational benefits the GI Bill would provide. The uncles thought the money belonged collectively to the family and had several business ventures planned, using both the dollars and the returning cousins' labor. While we younger cousins puzzled at the obtuseness of our elders, the three veterans were angry and embittered to be asked—after three or four years of war service—to give up their postwar dreams for the generalized interests of a tight-knit, old-fashioned clan. My family, evincing all the provincialism and sense of us-versus-them isolation, was thus a microcosm of the borough itself. The three vets would not play the same old game, and if our parents did not understand, we younger cousins did.

The two veterans who had married during the war took their wives and left for the west coast, to go to school out there and remake their lives three thousand miles away from the family. The third quickly married and pioneered eastward, along with tens of thousands of other Brooklynites, buying one of the tract houses that had replaced the potato fields of Long Island. World War II irreparably and permanently changed the old ways. The generational deference that marked the immigrant clans disappeared for my family, as I suspect it did for most of the Brooklynites who fought the war.

The three vets led the second generation (the first *American* generation, after all) in fleeing the perceived clutches of a half-displaced, gritty and imperious foreign-born generation. The unique experiences of war, including the chance to see a wider world than Brooklyn, the alienation and the difficult return, the opportunities of the GI Bill, all played out in my family.

After October 1946, after that one moment caught in that panoramic photograph, we all still had the Dodgers, but we had a lot less of each other.

Carl E. Prince is the author of Brooklyn's Dodgers: The Bums, the Borough, and the Best of Baseball *and a professor of American history at New York University.*

You've got plenty: Jackie Robinson and Campy and big Newk, and Dodgerdom again watching everything you do. You won last year. Come on." **Marianne Moore**

And the Band Played On...

Joseph Laurice has created a small shrine to the Brooklyn Dodgers in his East Meadow, Long Island, home. His autographed balls, pennants and posters transport him back to the quirky, comfortable confines of Ebbets Field. But of all his memorabilia, he cherishes one piece the most: a big megaphone bearing a Brooklyn insignia and the autographs of many of the Dodgers. The megaphone was one of the "instruments" belonging to the Sym-Phony—a ragtag ensemble of musically inclined fans—who in the 1940s and '50s traipsed the grandstand aisles and danced atop the dugouts, inciting the crowd and entertaining the players.

Laurice is one of three surviving members of the original band that was founded by his younger brother, Shorty, who played the trumpet and bugle. His sidekicks performed on the bass and snare drums, trombone and cymbal. Some just whistled and jitterbugged down the aisles. And whatever their harmonic shortcomings, they made up for them in enthusiasm and sheer volume. They called themselves the Dodgers' Bums Band, until the legendary sportscaster Red Barber dubbed them the "Sym-Phony" since they weren't real musicians.

The band was unsparing in its musical commentary on what was happening on the playing field. "When the umps came out," Laurice recalls, "we played 'Three Blind Mice.'" If an opposing player struck out, Laurice and company would strike up "The Worms Crawl In, the Worms Crawl Out," then give a big boom on the drum the instant the hitter sat down on the dugout bench.

The other two surviving members of the original band, JoJo Delio and Louis Dallaja-

cono, still form the rhythm section of the renascent Sym-Phony. Delio performs on the cymbals and Dallajacono beats his bass drum, which is still emblazoned with the old Dodger logo. Three newer bandmates now play the saxophone, trumpet and trombone. The ongoing Sym-Phony band still serenades the Brooklyn streets, playing at block parties and neighborhood fairs. It is the exclusive band of the *New York Daily News*' streetball tournament and of P.C. Richards, a chain of electronics stores. "Whenever they open a new branch, we're there," says Dallajacono. In 1999, they showed up with Yankee Hall of Famer Phil Rizzuto and Yankee manager Joe Torre.

Perhaps the sweetest note struck by the Sym-Phony is its relationship with the Dodger players. "We played at a streetball tournament in Louisville, Kentucky, Pee Wee Reese's hometown in 1997," says Dallajacono. "The Chamber of Commerce told him his 'friends from Brooklyn' were there, and he made it his business to come see us. We were very close."

—David Seideman

Left: The New York Daily News; this page: Brooklyn Public Library–Brooklyn Collection

The Great Bridge

The bridge is now so familiar and successful, so accepted as a vital transportation link and a symbol of the city, that it almost seems natural—as if it had always been there.

But in its time, it was a bold leap into the future. In the years when it was dreamed of and planned and constructed, very few people, outside the Roebling family, were certain that such a bridge could be built—whether a span of such length could survive high winds or heavy loads, whether the caissons and masonry towers could be constructed, whether the whole enormous structure would stand proudly or twist and fall.

Some marvels of American engineering did precede it, but when the Roeblings' masterpiece was completed in 1883 it opened a great age of bridge-building in New York—though no subsequent bridge has matched it for engineering or aesthetics. When finished, it towered over other buildings in Brooklyn and Manhattan; only the Trinity Church spire reached higher.

The Brooklyn Bridge has inspired works of art in every medium from poetry to cinematography, and gradually the realization dawned that it is itself a work of art. And while it is so familiar to Brooklyn and Manhattan that it's almost possible to take it for granted when, say, hurrying across in a taxi, it does like any truly great work of art insist on making its powerful statement. So every crossing becomes an occasion, a brief brush with greatness, like shortcutting through the Chartres cathedral on your way home.

© Stanley Greenberg, courtesy Yancey Richardson Gallery

The Secret Life of the Brooklyn Bridge

PHOTOGRAPHS BY
STANLEY GREENBERG

What we see of the Brooklyn Bridge is limited to its exterior: the dark masonry towers with the Gothic arches, the great swoop of the suspension cables, the long arch of the roadway from shore to shore. But there is another aspect to the bridge, long hidden and seldom seen.

Those enormous spun-wire cables that drape across the twin towers and hold up the bridge deck must themselves be anchored securely, deep in the earth. Similarly, the long gradual approaches to the suspended deck are themselves very large masonry viaducts enclosing once useful spaces; the arches of the Brooklyn-side approach used to house the 300-horsepower steam engines that pulled the early cable cars to and fro across the bridge. Beneath those approaches and inside the anchorages are dark structural vaults, reminiscent of ancient catacombs, that have not known much daylight or many visitors since 1883. Now the city uses those vaults to store half-forgotten items like civil defense helmets and patterns for casting iron bridge parts.

Photographer Stanley Greenberg has an eye for such hidden, essential places. Using a large-format camera and a minimum of artificial lighting, he

Approach vault on the Brooklyn side.

has documented the bridges, tunnels, cathedrals, stations and piers that are part of the engineering that makes the city work. He's done so from the inside, the underside, the cellars, the shafts, the attics and other spaces usually seen only by construction and maintenance crews. In his photographs, Greenberg has illuminated the inner secrets of the Brooklyn Bridge to reveal the original dimensions of its structure, materials and beauty.

Stanley Greenberg's photographs appear in his 1998 book Invisible New York *and in the collections of the Metropolitan, Whitney and Brooklyn museums.*

Above: Manhattan-side approach vault, once used as a wine cellar for storing champagne.

Right: Carved wood pattern for cast-iron bridge component, one of hundreds of casting patterns stored in the approach chambers.

"It is an organism of nature. There was no question in the mind of its designer of 'good taste' or appearance. He learned the law that struck its curves, the law that fixed the strength and the relation of its parts, and he applied the law." **Montgomery Schuyler**

Interior, approach chamber, Brooklyn side.

" It took Cheops twenty years to build his pyramid, but if he had had a lot of Trustees, contractors, and newspaper reporters to worry him, he might not have finished it by that time. The advantages of modern engineering are in many ways over balanced by the disadvantages of modern civilization." **Washington A. Roebling**

Literary Lights

Why so many writers have worked in Brooklyn

BY CHARLES SIEBERT

Some fifteen years ago, I violated what for a writer is one of the cardinal tenets of the creative spirit by returning to my hometown to live. Not a soul noticed, not even me.

I grew up in Brooklyn, whose landscape and populace are both vast and varied enough to render an entire childhood a mere figment, yet another of the borough's notoriously crooked avenues to wander down. Just the other day, in fact, I found myself on Flatbush, eating lunch at Junior's, having waited in line all morning at the nearby courthouse to argue a parking violation.

I sat at one of the restaurant's front booths, looking toward DeKalb Avenue and the Brooklyn Hospital two blocks down, suddenly recalling that Junior's is where my father waited out each of my mother's seven bouts of labor. We were the prototypical postwar Brooklyn family.

I don't have much patience for chauvinistic outpourings from writers about any one place, and Lord knows, Brooklyn has gotten more than its share of these. But here, too, is an avenue worth exploring: the fact that so many writers over the years have either come from Brooklyn, or have come to call it their home. Any attempt at a comprehensive list would end up being overlong and incomplete, so allow me to use as my touchstone the sequence of named stones that make up the Celebrity

The house at 7 Middagh Street (fourth from left) was a unique 1940s literary salon.

Brooklyn Historical Society

Poet Hart Crane was obsessed with this view of the Brooklyn Bridge from his window at 110 Columbia Place.

Path at the Brooklyn Botanic Garden just across from my own longtime niche here on Eastern Parkway.

The path, honoring Brooklyn-born or -based notables over the years, begins with Walt Whitman and ends (the last time I walked it, at least) with Phillip Lopate. In between one finds the names of Hart Crane and Marianne Moore and Derek Walcott, of Thomas Wolfe and Isaac Bashevis Singer and Henry Miller, of Betty Smith and Truman Capote and Bernard Malamud and Alfred Kazin and Arthur Miller and Neil Simon and Woody Allen, and on and on.

That Brooklyn would spawn so many writers is not that difficult to understand. It can, in large part, be ascribed to the sheer density and variety of its population over the past 250 years, the onslaught of aspiring immigrants who've called Brooklyn "home"—a word one can't stress enough when attempting to conjure the ultimately indecipherable blend of experiences, influences and impulses that make a writer. Masses in motion, with millions of stories, Manhattan has these, too. But Brooklyn offers a greater measure of that necessary antidote to (or is it the fruitful antagonist of?) such constant stimuli: the stasis and sameness of home, neighborhoods with familiar characters going about the plain business of living and, finally, a more gradual pace and sense of tranquillity in which, to paraphrase Wordsworth, strong emotions get recollected.

Of course, these are not qualities that out-of-town writers look for in realty ads when they're deciding where in New York City they want to live. Brooklyn's own distinct history and burgeoning cultural life notwithstanding, there's no getting around the fact that the great number of writers and other artists who've taken up residence here have done so because of the cheaper rents.

I'd been living in Manhattan for a number of years before coming here, paying too high a price to satisfy that urge to be in the midst of what, upon reflection, seems to me little more than the sum of everyone else's urge to be in that same midst. When it came to my attention one fall day in 1984 that I could have my current sprawling, two-bedroom, high-ceilinged apartment with a glorious view of Manhattan for the same price I'd been paying to live in one of that view's dingier studio squares, I didn't hesitate. It was only on the backswing that I'd come to know and fully appreciate the more resonant, enduring qualities of the place my family had fled, along with countless others, for the suburbs back in the mid-sixties when I was ten years old.

"Brooklyn," said Thomas Wolfe, who wrote *Of Time and the River* while living on Verandah Place in Cobble Hill in the early 1930s, "is a fine town—a nice big country town—a long way from New York. You couldn't find a better place to work." "Indeed," wrote Walt Whitman, who thought of Brooklyn as a kind of ideal middle ground between the rural remove of his native Long Island and the ever-burgeoning commerce of Manhattan, "it is doubtful there is a city in the world with a better situation for beauty, or for utilitarian purposes."

Implicit in both observations is the paradoxical sense of Brooklyn as a country-city, the embodiment of what I think of as the "urban-pastoral," a place at once teeming and tame, multipopulous and personal, fast-paced and yet somehow plodding enough, that it will absolve a spiritually restless writer of any guilt about possible provincialism even as it allows him or her to delight in its very cozy, small-town, provincial feel. It is this sense of openness, of slight remove within the very press and pull of multitudes that one chooses to be a part of when living in a city—that is most often cited by writers who've found themselves drawn to this side of the East River.

For the countless writers who, like Wolfe, Crane, McCullers and Capote, have made the pilgrimage from their more provincial homes in the American hinterlands to what Capote called Manhattan's "tall dazzle" and that even more illusory, downright apparitional entity known as the New York literary scene, Brooklyn always seems something of a revelation. Over and over again, writers attracted to the lights of New York City wind up—like confused, half-baked, Oz-exiled Dorothys—in Brooklyn, a stone's throw from Oz and yet suggestive enough of Kansas, of "home," to spare them the tacit surrender of actually having to go back there again.

"It is strange in New York to find yourself living in a

real neighborhood," Carson McCullers wrote of her days in Brooklyn Heights in the early 1940s, when she lived at 7 Middagh Street in a group house whose other tenants included W.H. Auden, Christopher Isherwood, Jane and Paul Bowles, Richard Wright, Anaïs Nin and George Davis, literary editor of *Harper's Bazaar*. Comparing Brooklyn to Manhattan, McCullers wrote, is "like comparing a comfortable and complacent duenna to her more brilliant and neurotic sister. Things move more slowly out here . . . and there is always the feeling of the sea."

In many ways, Brooklyn's distinct identity vis-à-vis Manhattan is an accident of geology. With the opening of the Erie Canal in 1825, Brooklyn, like Manhattan, began to make the full-scale shift away from an agrarian, small-town culture toward becoming a modern, industrial-based urban center. But "Breuckelen," as the Dutch originally named it, a word meaning either "broken valley" or "land of brooks and marshes," simply didn't have the subsoil necessary to support the tightly clustered table of towers that has come to give Manhattan its iconic power—a skyline that, for all its vertical audacity, mirrors as well the island's dense understory of glacial schist.

"You have only to cross a bridge to know it," wrote James Agee, "... how even among the riverside throes of mechanisms and of tenements in the iron streets, this whole of living is nevertheless relaxed upon horizontalities, a deep taproot of stasis in each action and each building. Partly it suggests the qualities of any small American city, the absorption in home, the casualness of the measuredly undistinguished. . . ."

Home, visible sky, proximate ocean, the alternate weight of work and leisure—these are elemental attractions, ones offered by many cities in the United States and abroad, but by none at once so near to, and yet so distinct from, a place like Manhattan. That simple geographic equation is a big part of the appeal of living in a place like Brooklyn, the sense that you're getting the best of both worlds—the great, bustling metropolis and its own quasi-pastoral getaway just across the river.

Writers, it has been my experience, can get a bit pre-cious about choosing where to live. It's the result, I think, of both a restless disposition and a chronic lack of a regular job, that necessity which, for a vast number of people in the world, dictates what part of the world they end up living in. Writers, in other words, are usually more at liberty to entertain and indulge their innate sense of homelessness. Thus they tend to get as fine about the process of picking a place to settle down and do their work as they do about the work itself, there being some deep conviction that the quality of the former must inform that of the latter—everything from the slant of the late afternoon light through your windows, to the precise tenor and lilt of the sound rising daily from your street, to the proximity of that street to a good bar full of interesting, unexpected faces when the day's work is done.

My hunch is that for a goodly number of writers settling in Brooklyn is a matter not only of money but of timing. For me there was a time when I wouldn't have been able to stand it "out here," when the very proximity of Manhattan, twinkling there on the horizon, would have gnawed at me, filled me with the feeling that I was missing something. But there comes a point when you want to be free of that kind of aimless striving, free of your self, of vanity and all its attendant, outsize concerns with whatever rendition of literary success Manhattan is in the process of anointing at any given moment. It's like finally deciding that you're ready to leave a much-anticipated fancy party full of big shots because you've had enough of the pretense and bluster, yours and others', and just want to get away and back down to earth and business.

I think I knew I was coming back here long before I actually did. I'd been living abroad for the better part of a year and upon my return ended up taking a late-summer sublet in Greenpoint, to live out the last few months of my Manhattan subletter's lease. It was the top floor of one of those four-story, bronze-eaved walk-ups that defines most Brooklyn neighborhoods, my bedroom window hard by an elevated stretch of the Brooklyn-Queens Expressway, with the steady whir of traffic and the clanking of flatbed trucks all day along the shadowed streets below, taking their loads of scrap metal to the East River junkyards. It was a neighborhood of utility and rust, of tar roofs and factory smokestacks, and of endless, airy light. Italian and Polish and Puerto Rican families lived side by side, milled about their front stoops in the evening, had barbecues on the roof and flew pigeons from there as well. The place filled me with the same feeling I used to have as a child growing up in Flatlands, the sense that "we were of the city," as fellow native Brooklynite Alfred Kazin writes of his own childhood in Brownsville, "but somehow not in it."

I remember one early September evening in particular, finding a huge monarch butterfly trapped in my window. Before shifting the panes to set it free, I took the opportunity to stare at it, to actually see, through one dark yet diaphanous wing, the expressway traffic winding its way toward a faintly shimmering Manhattan skyline and, in the window just across the way from mine, the same man I'd been seeing there nearly every evening throughout the summer, dressed in the same white T-shirt, ribbed, sleeveless, stained, resting his bare arms on the sill—a tired man staring off within the wingspan of a life that had no memory of ever crawling. I felt, just then, fondly reacquainted both with the full weight of being human and with the inherent and deeply inviting loneliness of the work of writing about it.

Brooklyn tends to leave you alone, to stay off your back. This, to me, for such a big city, may be its biggest and most basic attribute: the way in which the low lay of the land and open light here, the surfeit of visible sky, puts the bold frenzy and built-in self-importance of city living in some perspective, isolates you on sidewalks or at windows, Edward Hopper–like, in your own thoughts and longings, beneath the wide, empty press of a day.

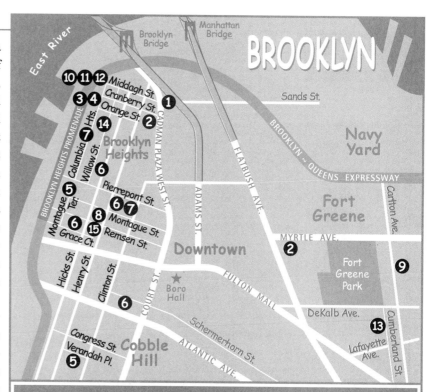

Where They Lived & Wrote

1. Thomas Paine lived at Sands and Fulton Streets.
2. Walt Whitman lived at 106 Myrtle Avenue; typeset *Leaves of Grass* in print shop at Cranberry and Fulton Streets.
3. Hart Crane wrote *The Bridge* at 110 & 130 Columbia Heights.
4. John Dos Passos lived at 106-110 Columbia Heights.
5. Thomas Wolfe lived at 40 Verandah Place; wrote *Of Time and the River* at 5 Montague Terrace.
6. Arthur Miller lived at 18 Schermerhorn and 155 Willow Streets; wrote *Death of a Salesman* at 31 Grace Court.
7. Norman Mailer wrote *The Naked and the Dead* at 102 Pierrepont Street, many other novels at 142 Columbia Heights.

8. Henry Miller grew up at 662 Driggs Avenue; later lived at 91 Remsen Street.
9. Richard Wright wrote part of *Native Son* at 175 Carlton Avenue.
10. Carson McCullers wrote *Ballad of the Sad Café* at 7 Middagh Street.
11. W.H. Auden lived and wrote at 7 Middagh Street.
12. Jane and Paul Bowles lived at 7 Middagh Street.
13. Marianne Moore lived at 260 Cumberland Street and wrote *What Are Years* and *Collected Poems* there.
14. Truman Capote lived and wrote *Breakfast at Tiffany's* and *In Cold Blood* at 70 Willow Street.
15. Norman Rosten lived and wrote at 84 Remsen Street.

Charles Siebert lives and writes on Eastern Parkway. He is the author of Wickerby: An Urban Pastoral.

Judy Sitz

Portraits of the Artists

DRAWINGS BY
DAVID LEVINE

Among the many literary artists who have chosen to live and work in Brooklyn are some true giants who have defined whole genres and styles. Artist David Levine, renowned as the house caricaturist for the *New York Review of Books*, chose to delineate five of them on these pages.

A Brooklynite through and through, Levine learned his stuff at Erasmus Hall and Pratt, and even now resides and enjoys morning coffee in the Heights. Beyond the lines of his famous caricatures, he is a versatile watercolorist whose work graces such collections as those in the Cleveland Museum of Art, the Library of Congress, the Metropolitan and—of course—the Brooklyn Museum of Art.

Thomas Wolfe

Thomas Wolfe
Prose Writer with the Soul of a Poet

Lived: 1900-1938

What he wrote in Brooklyn:
Of Time and the River

Where he wrote:
40 Verandah Place;
5 Montague Terrace

Inspirational habits:
Like the big guy in his short story "Only the Dead Know Brooklyn," favored exploring all kinds of places, from Red Hook to Bensonhurst. Apparently never forgot anything he saw–or failed to write it down.

Truman Capote
Creator of the Nonfiction Novel

Lived: 1924-1984

What he wrote in Brooklyn:
Breakfast at Tiffany's; In Cold Blood

Where he wrote:
70 Willow Street

Inspirational habits:
Roved the neighborhood streets, especially down along the East River via Water Street, wondering at the mysteries of a ghostly, seemingly unoccupied river-front hotel and "the silent miles of warehouses with shuttered wooden windows, docks resting on the water like sea spiders."

"I live in Brooklyn. By choice."
Truman Capote

Walt Whitman

Walt Whitman
The Good Gray Poet

Lived: 1819–1892

What he wrote in Brooklyn: Poems collected in *Leaves of Grass* and *Drum Taps*.

Where he wrote: 106 Myrtle Avenue; print shop at corner of Cranberry and Fulton

Inspirational habits: Spent time "sometimes riding, sometimes boating, but generally afoot, absorbing fields, shores, marine incidents, characters, bay-men, farmers, pilots" and racing up and down the hard sand at Coney Island, declaiming Homer and Shakespeare to the surf and gulls.

"There are worse crimes than burning books. One of them is not reading them."
Joseph Brodsky

Marianne Moore
A Realist of the Imagination

Lived: 1887-1972

What she wrote in Brooklyn: *Selected Poems*; *What Are Years*; *Collected Poems* (won Bollingen and Pulitzer prizes as well as National Book Award); *O to Be a Dragon*; more.

Where she wrote: 260 Cumberland Street

Inspirational habits: Watching baseball, especially as played by the Dodgers; worshiping regularly at her neighborhood church, the Lafayette Avenue Presbyterian; strolling in her tricorn hat and cape.

Joseph Brodsky
Russian expatriate; poet laureate

Lived: 1940-1996

What he wrote in Brooklyn: "Ode to Concrete," "Blues," "Love Song"; other late poems.

Where he wrote: Residence in Brooklyn Heights

Inspirational habits: After expulsion from Soviet Union in 1972, devoted to making poetry a more central part of American culture—"as ubiquitous as gas stations, if not as cars themselves."

Marianne Moore

Memories of Midwood

Growing up in a Brooklyn village

BY ARTHUR MILLER

Nobody can know Brooklyn, because Brooklyn is the world, and besides it is filled with cemeteries, and who can say he knows those people? But even aside from the cemeteries it is impossible to say that one knows Brooklyn. Three blocks from my house live two hundred Mohawk Indians. A few blocks from them are a group of Arabs living in tenements in one of which is published an Arab newspaper. When I lived on Schermerhorn Street I used to sit and watch the Moslems holding services in a tenement backyard outside my window, and they had a real Moorish garden, symmetrically planted with curving lines of white stones laid out in the earth, and they would sit in white robes—twenty or thirty of them—eating at a long table, and served by their women who wore the flowing purple and rose togas of the east. All these people, plus the Germans, Swedes, Jews, Italians, Lebanese, Irish, Hungarians and more, created the legend of Brooklyn's patriotism, and it has often seemed to me that their being thrown together in such abrupt proximity is what gave the place such a Balkanized need to proclaim its never-achieved oneness.

But this is not the Brooklyn I know or was brought up in. Mine is what is called the Midwood section, which now has no distinguishing marks but thirty years ago was a flat forest of great elms through which ran the elevated Culver Line to Coney Island, two and a half miles distant. My Brooklyn consisted of Jews, some Italians, a few Irish—and a Mr. Dunham, whom I remember only because he was reputed to carry a gun as part of his duties as a bank guard.

Children going to school in those days could be watched from the back porch and kept in view for nearly a mile. There were streets, of course, but the few houses had well-trodden trails running out of their back doors which connected with each other and must have looked from the air like a cross section of a mole run; these trails were much more used than any of the streets, which were as unpaved as any in the Wild West and just as muddy. Today everything is paved and your bedroom window is just far enough away from your neighbor's to leave room to swing the screens out when fall comes.

My aunts and uncles, who moved there right after World War I, could go to Manhattan on the Culver Line for a nickel (although my cousins always climbed around the turnstile, which was easy, so long as you didn't mind hanging from iron railings a hundred feet or so above the street), but they had to buy potatoes in hundred-pound sacks because there was no grocery store in four miles. And they planted tomatoes, and they canned fruits and vegetables, and kept rabbits and chickens and hunted squirrels and other small game. The Culver Line cars were made of wood, like trolleys hooked together, and clattered

Russell Christian

above the cemeteries and the elms, and I must say there was something sweet about it when you got aboard in the morning and there was always the same conductor who knew you and even said good morning.

I DON'T KNOW PRECISELY WHY, BUT BROOKLYN IN MY memory has always been full of characters and practical jokers. I suppose it is really a collection of villages which all seem the same to a stranger's eye, but are not; and the characters thrive and express their special ways in a village atmosphere. My father was one, and is the last of those Mohicans as he sits in front of his frame house of a Sunday afternoon, remembering, as he glances down the tree-lined block, the old friends and screwballs who lived in each of the houses and are now resting peacefully in the cemetery that spreads out two blocks away, their pinochle decks laid down forever, their battles done.

My father, a large, square-headed man who looks like a retired police captain and has that kind of steady severity, is likely to feel the need, from time to time, to "start something." Years ago, he sat down on the Culver Line one morning, and seeing a neighbor whom he regarded as particularly gullible, moved over to him and in his weightiest manner, began:

"You hear my brother-in-law got back from Florida?"

"Yes, I heard," said the neighbor. "What does he do down there? Just fish and like that?"

"Oh, no," my father said, "haven't you heard about his new business?"

"No. What?"

"He raises cockroaches there."

"Cockroaches! What does he do with the cockroaches?"

"What does he do with the cockroaches? Sells them!"

"Who wants cockroaches?"

"Who wants cockroaches! There's a bigger demand for cockroaches than for mink. Of course, they gotta be of a certain breed. He breeds them down there. But they're all pure-bred."

"But what good are they?"

"Listen," my father confided, lowering his voice. "Don't say I even mentioned it, but if you happen to see any cockroaches around, in your house, or anywhere like that, my brother-in-law would appreciate it if you brought them all to him. Because I tell you why, see—he's raising them up here now, right in his house, but in Brooklyn it's against the law, you understand? —but once in a while a couple of them escape, and he's bashful to ask people, but you'd be doing him a big favor if you happen to catch any, bring them to him. But be very careful. Don't hurt them. He'll pay five dollars for any purebred cockroach anybody brings him."

"Five dollars!"

"Well, listen, that's his business. But don't tell anybody I told you because it's against the law, you know?"

Having planted this seed, my father left the neighbor. A week or so later my uncle's doorbell rang, and there was the man, considerably insecure in his mind, but there nevertheless, with a matchbox full of cockroaches. For three whole days my uncle refused to play casino with my father.

THERE IS IKE SAMUELS, WHO RUNS—OR RATHER SITS outside—the hardware store. Ike's way with women who come in not knowing precisely what they want is something not easily described. I have watched him double-talking a *Hausfrau* for better than ten minutes, but when they come in with complaints he rises to a height of idiotic evasion that is positively lyrical. I was myself a victim of his for years, as a boy. We lived three blocks from his store, and often as I passed he would open his eyes against the sunlight where he sat in his rocker beside the door and say, "Raining on Ocean Parkway?"

For years I answered him seriously because he has a remorseless poker face and thick lenses on his eyeglasses that make a clear view of his eyes impossible. Out of respect, at first, I described the weather three blocks away; but later I began to doubt myself and came to wonder, now and then, whether it *had* been raining there while the sun shone here.

But that was the least of Ike Samuels. I happened to be in his store one morning when a woman entered. Like so many of them at eleven A.M., she had a coat on top of her nightgown—and in her hands was an electric broiler which Ike had repaired only a week before. She strode in, a large woman with lumpy hair that, in her anger at the broiler, she had neglected to comb, and she plunked the broiler down on the counter.

"You said you fixed it!" she began.

"What is the trouble?" Ike said.

"It don't heat! My husband came home last night, I put four lamb chops in, we could've dropped dead from hunger, it was like an ice box in there!"

Ike took off the top of the broiler and made as though to examine its works. There was a silence. He peered this way and that inside it, and I could tell he was winding up for a stroke that would resound through his whole day. Looking up at her like a detective on the scent, he asked, "What did you say you put in there?"

Suspecting, perhaps, that she had in fact done something wrong, she parried: "What do you mean what did I put in here?"

Like a prosecutor, Ike leaned in toward her: "Answer my question, madam; what did you put in this broiler?"

Her voice smaller now, off balance she replied, "I said—lamb chops."

"Lamb chops!" Ike rolled his eyes at the ceiling, where the mops and pails hung. "Lamb chops she puts in!"

Close to tears now, the woman began to plead. "Well, what's the matter with lamb chops?"

"What's the matter with lamb chops!" Ike roared indignantly. "Can't you read, lady? What night school did you go to? Look!" With which he turned the broiler upside down and pointed to the brass plate riveted to the bottom, on which were embossed the long serial numbers of the manufacturer's patents, and the Underwriter's Laboratory seal.

She bent over to peer at the tiny numbers and the few words. And before she could fix her eyes, Ike was upon her. "It's plain as day. 'No lamb chops,' it says; this is written by naval architects, graduate engineers from the Massachusetts Institute of Technology—'no lamb chops'—and you throw lamb chops in there. What do you want from me, lady? I fixed it for steak!"

Her eyes were distraught now, utterly bewildered. "But he likes lamb chops," she pleaded.

And now, having won the initiative, he came around the counter and escorted her to the door. "Now look, don't be discouraged. I'll do my best, and I'll fix it for lamb chops. I got a license for that, but you gotta have a double affixative on the forspice."

"Could you put one on?" she asked, exhausted.

"For you anything, darling," he said, and sent her on her way.

IT WAS A VILLAGE, EVEN DOWN TO FEEBLE-MINDED DANNY, who hung around Ike's store, and when you came by he would point at you and say, "Navarre 8-7135," because his pride lay in remembering everyone's phone number. If he overheard Ike talking about somebody's aunt, he would interject "Dewey 9-0518," which, in his mind, identified the aunt. "Ulster 5-8009 is getting married, Ike," he announced one morning. Asked who the bride was, he answered, "Navarre 8-6661." But he had his dignity, which he enforced. If they started kidding him, he would get off the barrel and leave, saying, "I gotta see a party."

It was a village, and while to the stranger's eye one street was no different from another, we all knew where our "Neighborhood" somehow ended, and the line of demarcation was never more than three blocks away. Beyond that, a person was somehow a stranger.

It was a village with village crimes. I don't recall a

Brooklyn Public Library–Brooklyn C

time when the cops had to be called. Everyone was so well and thoroughly known that the frown of his neighbors was enough law to keep things in line. When we stole from the candy store, when we played handball against the druggist's window and broke it, it was enough for the offended proprietor to let it be known to the parents. Although I must add that Mr. Dozik, the pharmacist, had it a little harder. The wall of his building was perfect for handball, and poor Dozik had to be all the time giving us water from his soda fountain. He tried putting up billboards that projected from the wall, but we played around them, until finally he had his soda fountain removed. Mr. Dozik is the first man in history to discover that boys cannot play handball where there is no cold drinking water.

He's still there as he was then—a kind of doctor who knows what ails everybody; a man who sewed up the arms, hands and ears of all my cousins and remembers every stitch.

It was a village with no stream, however, so my cousins and I would get up at four in the morning and climb around the turnstile of the Culver Line, and rickety-rackety down the two-mile track to Coney Island and fish off the rocks and bring home flounder or sea bass—even in winter, when the wind was raw off the ocean.

The above article, originally titled "A Boy Grew in Brooklyn," appeared in Holiday *magazine, March 1955.*

NOW & THEN Brooklyn's waterfront in the 1940s, with its gang-run unions, was a world apart from the "suburbs." Arthur Miller drew on his experiences there in *A View from the Bridge.*

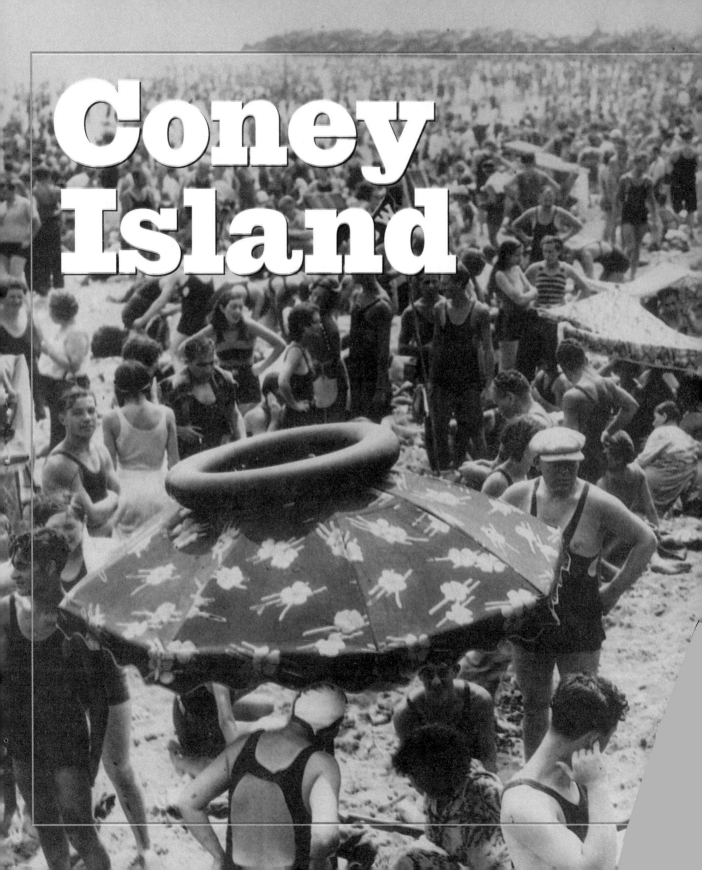

Coney Island

A worldwide symbol for letting the good times roll, Coney Island often comes as a shock to people who go there and find it's an actual place, an actual honky-tonk zone with an actual boardwalk on one of the biggest and best beaches on the Atlantic seaboard. It's real—and it's still fun. There are rides and attractions, a sideshow, and an annual parade that is one of the most outrageous in the country.

Brooklynite Henry Miller and poet Lawrence Ferlinghetti both wrote about a "Coney Island of the Mind." And no wonder: Coney has a powerful hold on the popular imagination. It's surely the most widely known part of Brooklyn.

Indeed, it may be better known around the world than the borough itself. And why not? Coney Island is a novelty in an all-too-serious world—a community that's entirely devoted to having fun.

Previous spread: Cooling it in the pre-air-conditioning era—the beach at Coney Island, July 1930.

Previous spread: Brooklyn Public Library–Brooklyn

The Original Fantasy Island

A world of ups and downs

BY KEVIN BAKER

Coney Island has always been a place where determinedly family fun and utter squalor intermingle. A place devoted to release and raffish good times. And there is still no place more synonymous with noise and summer and joyful chaos.

The mysterious, charming name comes from *konijn*, Dutch for "wild rabbit," which was about all the first European settlers found running through the five flat miles of grassy shoreline along the southern tip of Brooklyn. But in the America before air conditioning and airlines any local beach was a resort in the making, and by 1824 an inn and a seashell road had been built out by the water's edge. Both the masses and a host of leading American celebrities followed, including P.T. Barnum, who perfectly personified the schizophrenic nature of Coney entertainment.

Barnum's presence was auspicious, but nothing more. It's a wonder that he didn't see the potential in the place. Before long there was a maze of entertainments and hostelries, high and low, in the neighborhood

Luna Park with every lightbulb ablaze in the summer of 1905.

This spread and next: Library of Congress

48   B R O O K L Y N

just off the beach. Soon there were heavyweight championship fights on Surf Avenue, and gambling and brothels and shooting galleries in "the Gut" along Ocean Parkway, and a racetrack and swank hotels just down the surf along Manhattan and Brighton beaches.

There were numerous "miracles," including the invention of the hot-dog-in-a-bun by Charles Feltman in 1870 and the appearance of the World's Largest Ferris Wheel, courtesy of George C. Tilyou, in 1894. And if, in fact, Tilyou's wheel was about half the size of the one he had tried unsuccessfully to buy from the Chicago World's Columbian Exposition in 1893, and if it seems hardly likely that the idea of sticking a sausage in a fold of bread first occurred to someone on the shores of Brooklyn a scant 130 years ago— no matter. Coney Island has always depended in large part on a willing suspension of disbelief.

Tilyou proved the perfect impresario for the place. His family had moved to Coney at the end of the Civil War and he had grown up there, hawking souvenir bottles of salt water and cigar boxes full of sand when he was a teenager. In 1897 he opened up a huge fourteen-acre park and named it for a ride called the Steeple-chase, on which patrons rode mechanical horses up and down over long iron tracks. By today's amusement park standards, it was quaintly slow and easy—which was the point. The kicker came at the end, when patrons had to exit across something called the Blowhole Theater. As they did, jets of air blew women's dresses up, a deranged-looking dwarf in a harlequin's suit attacked everyone with a cattle prod, and previous patrons (victims?) sitting in bleachers known as the Laughing Gallery howled at the sight.

The suckers didn't mind, at least not too much. They had already got what they came for. The point of the slow-moving Steeplechase was that couples could take all the time they wanted to cuddle and clutch each other without having to worry about actually falling off their horse. It was such a hit that Tilyou soon surrounded it with an entire glassed-in park of attractions guaranteed to literally throw people together. There was the Mixer, the Soup Bowl, the Barrel of Love, the Human Pool Table and the Bounding Billows. Fake elevators came crashing back down to the floor, staircases split in two, spinning wheels hurled people around a floor. And if the Steeple-chase would be a tort lawyer's dream today, customers at

A 1910 panorama: Dreamland at center; water chutes at left, observation tower at right.

the turn of the century were satisfied just to be hurled together, no matter how many bones they jarred. "If Paris is France," crowed Tilyou, "then Coney Island, between June and September, is the world."

Yet something else was needed, some transcendent genius, if Coney Island was to be more than Atlantic City or Long Branch. It arrived in the form of Frederic Thompson. In 1903, just across Surf Avenue, Thompson and his partner, Elmer Dundy, put up Luna Park.

Fantasy Made Real

Luna was unlike any other amusement park ever built, before or since. It was twenty-two acres of lagoons and fantastic domes and minarets, arches and trellises, tinted in lush beach pastels of white and gold and orange. Nearly every conceivable type of architecture was there, piled right on top of each other like something out of a drawing by Dr. Seuss. From the walls hung drooping, lascivious carnival heads of wolves and clowns and pigs. Over the entrance were spinning half-moons and a dazzling bit of neo-Catholic iconography, a red heart with two cross-shaped daggers plunged into it and bearing the legend "The Heart of Coney Island."

Inside, visitors could ride live camels or elephants. They could watch belly dancers, or gold chariots, or diving elephants. They could visit villages in China and India or the Arctic wastes. They could even journey to the moon, as in one particularly silly futuristic ride that concluded with dwarfs handing the space travelers pieces of green Swiss cheese and singing popular lunar songs—and yet, in the dark, held some of the mysterious allure of the new movie theaters.

All the wild, abrupt, funhouse juxtapositions were deliberate, the handiwork of the alcoholic, fantastically creative Thompson. It was he who recognized that amusement park visitors "are not in a serious mood, and do not want to encounter seriousness. They have enough seriousness in their everyday lives, and the keynote of the thing they do demand is change. Everything must be different from ordinary experience. What is presented to them must have life, action, motion, sensation, surprise, shock, swiftness or else comedy."

And so it did. Thompson and Dundy (the businessman of the partners) raised around $1 million to build their grand creation, and on opening night they were down to their last $22. That evening 43,000 people

Pleasure-seekers on foot and atop elephant pass by the entrance to Dragon's Gorge.

poured into the park, and their fortune was made. Luna Park's strange and marvelous shapes were capped by the burgeoning new phenomenon of electricity. Everything was lit by some 1.2 million individual lightbulbs, transforming the park at night into glowing towers and spinning wheels of pure light. Luna Park was a cathedral of frozen fire, much more spectral and awesome and haunting than anything the gentler neon of later, feeble Disney imitations could produce. No one who saw it at night ever forgot the sight.

In Brooklyn, as in America, success breeds grandiosity, and the third and most ponderous of the great Coney Island trinity was soon to follow. In 1904 William H. Reynolds, a state senator who also developed Bor-

ough Park and Long Beach, Long Island, put up Dreamland across from Luna on Surf Avenue, long Coney's main drag. This was a vision taken almost wholly from the White City of the 1893 Chicago Columbian Exposition. It was very white and very beautiful in a sort of heavy, neoclassical way, with a great central tower and a lagoon, and it stressed the family attraction even more than its predecessors. There was an excessive sentimentality to its emphasis on the educational, its mock canals of Venice and fake Swiss mountains; its trip to Heaven and the laughable, admonitory tableaux of Hellgate, which included a girl being whisked down to hell for the terrible sin of admiring a hat.

Dreamland's immense tableaux reenacted such spectacular real-life events as the Johnstown Flood of 1889 and the Galveston Flood of 1900, a volcanic explosion in Martinique and an earthquake in Italy. And in the Grand Naval Spectatorium, all the navies of the world sailed by to raze a scale Manhattan (an act all of Brooklyn could relate to) before being sunk in turn by the American navy. This brought cheers from the patrons, many of them new immigrants though they were. One of the biggest Dreamland attractions was "Fighting Flames," in which every day a fake tenement was set on fire and its acrobat/tenants rescued by a fake fire department. People who lived in constant dread of being burned out in real life flocked to see it. For them, Coney Island was the pageant of their new lives in America, their best hopes and worst fears of the future played out on a vast, marvelous, three-dimensional screen. And thanks to the cosmic fortuitousness of its location, for so many immigrants steaming into New York Harbor, the first thing they saw was not the Statue of Liberty, or Ellis Island, but the stunning luminescence of Coney Island.

The Dark Side

Of course, there was always a subterranean luridness, a certain grasping under all the clean family fun and the high educational purposes. Coney Island had its own thriving Bowery, little better than its namesake in Manhattan, full of sordid saloons and shooting galleries and tattoo parlors. Even in the big parks, visitors who dared

Brooklyn Public Library–Brooklyn Collection

The Steeplechase slide offered lots of laughs—and lumps.

Brian Merlis Collection

On twenty-two acres in "the heart of Coney Island," Luna Park was a wonderland of fantastic architectural shapes and figures.

to rest were shocked off benches by mild electrical currents and propelled back to spending money. Entrepreneurs rolled barbed wire all the way out into the surf to protect the plots of land they had marked off.

There was worse: Coney Island also featured a working ward full of incubator babies. The doctor who ran it was legitimate, and most of the babies lived; he simply hadn't been able to get a New York hospital to take a chance on his invaluable invention. Yet there was something a little unnerving, something faintly obscene, about seeing an actual life-and-death struggle as commercial entertainment. Still worse were the Son-of-Ham shows, a standard carny attraction of the time in which patrons paid money to throw baseballs at the head of a black man. Other blacks, and Indians, Eskimos and Filipinos, were exhibited in their "natural" tribal villages. There was even a year-round city made up entirely of dwarfs and midgets, which was both a real place to live and an exhibit. Sex was also a major lure. Innocent sex, to our eyes. Men and women could come out and flirt, and wear those terribly risqué bathing suits of the time, and have their fillings rattled together on Tilyou's infernal machines. Smarmier

sex as well, in dozens of back-alley brothels.

Things began to get still sleazier, still more honky-tonk, once Dreamland burned down just before the season's opening in 1911, victim of an electrical blaze that started in Hellgate. The all-midget fire department joined Brooklyn's bravest in answering the wild nine-alarm blaze and actually fought the flames well, but it was too late. Dreamland was gone and the other parks went into a slow decline, the diving horses and elephants eventually replaced by pigs, the chariots by cockroach races.

The irony was that Coney Island was just reaching its salad days in attendance. The first subway line out to the beach was completed in 1920, and from then until the 1950s over a million people a day came out at the height of the season—even more in the fleeting, dreamlike years just after World War II. It was from this period that the famous Weegee photos were taken of the Coney Island beach, packed cheek-by-jowl with grinning humanity out for a breath of sea air. A small but vibrant full-time community sprang up as well, comprising mostly Jews and Italian-Americans. There were even periodic plans to immortalize the mostly wooden palaces of Steeplechase and Luna Park in stone.

But it was not to be. The archfiend was Moses—Robert Moses, who not only built Coney's most serious local rival, Jones Beach, out on Long Island, but also provided the highways to get there. Resenting, as always, any competition for his vision of a future defined by very tall buildings, wide highways and pristine, sterile beaches, he trashed much of the old Coney. The boardwalk, first built in the '20s, was pushed back, the beach enlarged and numerous small concession stands thereby put out of business. Much of the neighborhood was bulldozed, the old tenements and family homes replaced by enormous, ugly, Moses-style housing projects that betrayed New York's great tradition of class- and race-integrated, human-scale public housing.

Yet it's too easy to blame the decline of Coney just on Moses. It took fifty years of collective indifference on

Brian Merlis Collection

the part of a whole borough, a whole city, to bring down the most fantastic entertainment complex ever known. A series of fires had finished off beautiful Luna Park by 1946. Tilyou's beloved Steeplechase went out of business after the 1964 season, despite last-ditch attempts to keep the crowds coming by setting up whole banks of television sets tuned to different channels. But the rows and rows of TVs only meant the enemy was already within the gates.

The Comeback

Times change, tastes change, income levels change, and the changes of the sixties and seventies were especially rough on Coney Island. Those old Coney denizens who had not moved out to Long Island or New Jersey, who had not headed south to Fort Lauderdale or Miami Beach or who had simply died off; those who could not afford to vacation in Hawaii or Southern California were still not interested in spending their leisure time in a dreary, crime-ridden neighborhood where New York City had stashed some of its poorest, most unfortunate citizens.

But slowly, like so much else of Brooklyn and the wider city, Coney rose from the ruins. Feltman's, with its Ur-hot dog, was gone, but Nathan's Famous was still in business. A small, tenacious amusement park hung on, still surviving with rides still rolling. The New York Aquarium was moved out to where Dreamland once

On a hot summer weekend, a million people would hit the beach—and maybe even get to the water.

Brooklyn Public Library–Brooklyn Collection

stood. Some of the best basketball in the world was played on Coney, a bright spot of virtuosity, at least, on the grim playgrounds of the housing projects.

And now, at the start of a new century, there are raucous, annual parades along Mermaid Avenue that draw hundreds of thousands of spectators, the crime rate is way down, and on warm summer days the sands may not be as full as they were in Weegee's day but Coney still boasts one of the broadest and best beaches on the eastern seaboard. There are still swimmers, fishermen and crab fishermen out by the remnants of the old amusement park piers. The Cyclone coaster still runs and the old Parachute Jump is still standing, a testament to the wonder that was Coney and a monument

still easy to pick out for travelers sweeping down by plane over the rough, sandy edge of Brooklyn. There are plans for a multisport complex and a minor league baseball park, and while these things are probably frivolous at heart, while there is always a better use for such money, Coney always was frivolous—a painted, libidinous, spectacular bride for the City of Churches.

And if we don't know what to do with her this time around, more shame on us.

Kevin Baker is the author of Dreamland, *a best-selling novel about Coney Island and the raw New York of Tammany and the Triangle Shirtwaist fire. He was chief researcher for Harold Evans'* The American Century.

BROOKLYN ON FILM

Coney Island–
A Great Location

Coney Island has been prominently featured in films from the very birth of the movies at the end of the nineteenth century. Coincidentally, the early center of the film industry was New York City, and one industry pioneer, Vitagraph Company of America, had film studios in the Midwood section of Brooklyn. Vitagraph and other early studios frequently used Coney Island as a spectacular backdrop. Dreamland, Luna Park and Steeplechase Park all appear as locations in early feature films.

Most common in these early days were "chase" films, such as *Rube and Mandy at Coney Island* (1903), *Boarding School Girls* (1905) and *Cohen at Coney Island* (1909), in which the protagonists pursue one another among the attractions and spectacular rides. One film of the time, *Electrocuting an Elephant* (1903), in which an injured circus animal is actually wired up and put to death, shows not only the era's

fascination with electricity but a vastly different sense of what is acceptable entertainment.

Decades later, Coney Island still worked as a compelling location. *Little Fugitive* (1953), made by Morris Engel, a still photographer for *Life* magazine, the late Ruth Orkin (famous for her photographs of Manhattan street life and Central Park), and technician Ray Ashley, depicts a child-centered world. Mistakenly thinking he has killed his brother, a young boy escapes to Coney Island, where he indulges in the many pleasures of the amusement park, all the while fearful of being discovered and punished by the adult world. The film employed a child's perspective, with low-angle shots of scenes such as lovers embracing and the play of light and shadow beneath the boardwalk. It won an award at the 1953 Venice Film Festival and was one of the first independent American films to be released in theaters across the United

Little Fugitive, 1953

The Crowd, 1928

States. Stylistically, it bridges the 1940s expressionistic American film noir and the French New Wave.
         —*Jon Gartenberg*

MOMA Film Stills Archive

Postcards from Coney

The island of fire, in lurid color

BY RICHARD SNOW

One evening nearly thirty years ago, during the long hiatus between graduating from college and moving out from under my parents' roof, I was sitting in my room studying turn-of-the-century Coney Island postcards when my father walked by the open door. "Ah!" he said. "Here's something to fill any parent with pride—a son seeking not only the escapism of an amusement park, but the ultimate escapism of a vanished one."

Escapism? Sure. Vanished? Yes and no. Coney Island was still out there, of course, just as it is today. And it still had—still has—the Wonder Wheel and the never-surpassed Cyclone roller coaster. But the Coney that held me in its thrall was the place shown on the postcards I'd been collecting with increasing passion for the last couple of years: the incandescent city whose three great amusement parks—Luna, Steeplechase and Dreamland—shone so brightly that they drew the eyes of all the country, even of Europe.

But has even that Coney entirely vanished? In the fairgrounds outside Aspen, Colorado, a stand offers "Coney Island Hot Dogs"; a concession in Taos calls itself "Chimayo Coney Island." "Coney Island" signs still flash today in Detroit and Milwaukee, Chicago and Los Angeles. Not everybody knows what Coney Island is, but everybody knows what "Coney Island" means. Something racy, spectacular, exciting, tawdry and cosmopolitan. Frying meat and chowder and beer and oysters. Coney Island is the very machinery of exhilaration.

The people who built those stands, commissioned those signs, are using a tremendous ghost to sell their

From the 1890s:
Tilyou's "Pavilion of Fun."

beer and hot dogs. It's the ghost of Coney Island blazing at its turn-of-the-century zenith, of the place whose spectacles prophesied the imperial power that America was soon to become, the little finger of land at the foot of Brooklyn where the twentieth century took early shape in mirth and violence and torrents of electricity.

That Coney got under my skin long before I ever saw it. I was a Westchester County boy and had never set foot in Brooklyn when I became fascinated by Coney Island. I liked amusement parks, and early got the idea that Coney was their Rome. This may have been implanted by the June 1958 issue of *American Heritage*,

Collection of Richard Snow

izontal in a perpetual leap, the operator threw a lever and I rasped out into daylight to scale a gentle rise while the ribbed glass wall of the Pavilion slid back past my left shoulder. Then, my rival horses and their riders nosing ahead and falling behind, I careened around the park. It was fun, but nowhere near as exciting as the Dragon Coaster at Rye Playland in West-

On a single summer day in 1906, revelers mailed 200,000 postcards from Coney Island.

8962. TWILIGHT, DREAMLAND, CONEY ISLAND, N. Y.

COPYRIGHT, 1905, BY DETROIT PUBLISHING CO.

which had an article about George C. Tilyou called "The Master Showman of Coney Island." I remember staring at a painting of Steeplechase Park, a highly detailed aerial view, and at the jovially menacing Steeple-chase Man with his stove-polish hair and carnivorous grin—a symbol of all the liberations of summer. I was ten years old then. Two or three years into what could by then be called an obsession, I wheedled my father into taking me to Coney Island.

"The old Coney is gone, darlin'," O. Henry had one of his people say fully ninety years ago, and certainly that was true by the time my thirteen-year-old self finally arrived there in the blue-white dazzle of a summer Sunday. Nevertheless, there were enough lively remnants to give me a fair sense of what it had been: three roller coasters running and a fun house that Reginald Marsh had drawn, any number of concessions that invited you to lose money throwing baseballs at wooden milk bottles and, of course, the Steeplechase. Part roller coaster, part merry-go-round, it had sent its wooden horses off eight abreast when the park opened; now the tracks had dwindled to four, but otherwise the ride was unchanged. I climbed onto the back of a horse stretched almost hor-

chester. And yet I find that to this day I can spool that ride through my memory in something like real time. A year later, Steeplechase was gone.

I kept visiting Coney all through college, and the dwindling amusement zone always gave a good account of itself. But even as the old Coney disappeared, I discovered a way to retrieve it. I was poking around in a midtown antiques shop one day when I came across a postcard that showed Steeplechase Park, the Pavilion glowing and the horses running. I picked it up and turned it over. It was postmarked 1911. I bought it at once (paying, I later learned, about five times its worth) and then set out to find others. I had become a postcard collector.

I had happened on the fullest record there is of Coney Island's glory years. Americans sent a staggering number of cards to each other in those days, and 200,000 went out from Coney on a single day in 1906.

No attraction was too mere to have a card of its own, as I soon found. Along with operatic views of the parks—Dreamland with its sententious classical frostings, Luna basking in its much-celebrated tiara of electric lights—were palm-reading joints, shooting galleries, and a big concession that sold sausages, rib roasts, sides of bacon and lamb chops, all scrupulously faked in marzipan.

I joined the Metropolitan Postcard Club, and at the monthly meetings I began to piece together my lost Coney. Here was a series of cards showing the progress of the Boer War as replicated by 600 British and Dutch veterans brought to Coney by the showman William A. Brady; here was Dreamland's grandiloquence reduced to ashes by the 1911 fire; here was a visit to the moon and a more advanced successor, "A Trip to Mars by Aeroplane"; here were freaks and comic Negroes and motion-picture theaters, puzzled rubes and racing cars and miniature steam trains and immense restaurants: Stauch's, Henderson's, Feltman's (whose proprietor, Charles, has a reasonable claim to being the inventor of the hot dog since Nathan's Famous is the child of Nathan Handwerker, who started out slicing rolls for Feltman and in 1916 built the still-bustling place on Surf Avenue where his five-cent franks undersold his old boss's by a nickel). In short, here was a place that fascinated Americans because it was their country—their psyche—distilled into a few sexy acres of beachfront.

Along the way, I picked up other items: a shooting-gallery lion manufactured by William Mangels, who built amusement devices a few blocks from Steeplechase (and whose B & B Carousell is still spinning on Surf Avenue); a streetcar card advertising the season opening of Luna Park; combination tickets to Steeplechase and Luna; a poster celebrating "Barnum & Bailey's Great Coney Island Water Carnival."

It was always the postcards, though, that made me feel closest to the essence of the place—these pieces of pasteboard with pictures, some epic, some intimate, bought and sent by people who were at the moment as enchanted as I was by Coney and which, almost a century after they were mailed, arrived at my home.

I chased after the cards for years and wrote two novels about the world they showed (both manuscripts, objects of mild loathing to my agent and utter indifference to editors) before a daring publisher issued a book of the postcards, all of them printed in color. I never earned a dollar from this project, but it was intensely gratifying nonetheless. The book seemed to me somehow to ratify the time I'd spent grubbing through miles of cards, as though I'd visited a country that lay over the edge of time and had returned to draw a plausible map of it.

I've never stopped going to Coney. Whether by subway, with the great horizontal unfolding of the ocean thirty feet below your seat, or by car, when the spectral ribs of the Parachute Jump rise beyond the arc of the Verrazano Bridge, there is always a little click of surprise on alighting. You're in a different place. This may be as simple a matter as the fact that Coney runs east to west while Manhattan runs north and south, so that the light falls differently on everything. But perhaps it's something more. Perhaps in the weary gallantry of those well-used buildings still working to give people a good time, in the Cyclone's high lariats of track, in the sudden blue glint of sea and the carousel pumping forth a song that turns out to be "Tenting Tonight on the Old Camp Ground," and in the corrupt pink of cotton candy and the synthetic blaze of candy apples, there is still the tug of the old Coney, the numinous sense that these few blocks of catchpenny diversions are one of the great places on earth.

Richard Snow is editor in chief of American Heritage *magazine and the author of* Coney Island: A Postcard Journey to the City of Fire.

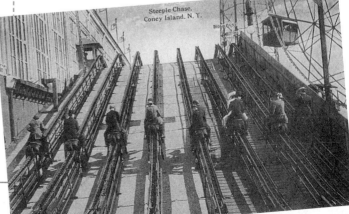

CHWAST'S
CONEY ISLAND

Days at
the Beach

DRAWINGS
BY SEYMOUR
CHWAST

When he was at Abraham Lincoln High School, illustrator Seymour Chwast spent a couple of summers working at the Skeeball alley, making change. "The price was nine balls for a nickel. Ladies got the first one free. And when I wasn't working," he says, "I'd walk down onto the beach and sketch people or just hang around there to pick up girls."

Seymour Chwast is a designer and a founder of Push Pin Studio.

"

There were
willing models
all over the
place. I would
see them
again and
again. Young
couples,
and mothers
with kids,
and a lot of
old, fat people
who didn't
move around
much."

Seymour Chwast

S. CHWAST

Woody's Home Place

A mecca for musicians

BY BRUCE
D. STUTZ

The important thing about my father's years in Coney Island," says Nora Guthrie, "was that after a life of wandering he had a place to call home, a desk to work on and shelves to hold his notebooks, diaries and artwork. Eighty percent of his archives come from his work done in Coney Island."

And that work was considerable. Woody Guthrie was a tireless composer/singer/poet/storyteller/artist/activist, and when he moved to Brooklyn in 1943 he was more prolific than at any other time in his life. His Depression-era dust bowl ballads had made him the country's most famous Oklahoma native. Now, in Brooklyn, he became—with Pete Seeger and the Almanac Singers, with Leadbelly and Brownie McGhee—the center of a renascent folk-music movement.

It was a long road from Okemah, Oklahoma, where Woodrow Wilson Guthrie was born in 1912, to the tiny row-house apartment at 3520 Mermaid Avenue (long since demolished in favor of a high-rise). Guthrie had been on his own since he was fourteen, traveling out west from one town, one job, to the next until he began performing in California, where he hooked up with his cousin Jack Guthrie. Failing at becoming "singing cowboys" since Woody, with his slight frame, had terrible luck with horses, they eventually ended up performing on the radio. When Jack left the show, Woody took it up, adding a woman singer to the soon-popular act and storytelling in a loosely constructed, good-natured patter. His wit, humor and seemingly boundless creative energy would keep him writing and restless the remainder of his life. When in 1941 the opportunity arose to come to New York with the Almanac Singers—Seeger, Lee Hayes and Millard Lampell—Guthrie took it.

During rehearsals for a folk/dance performance piece devised by Sophie Maslow, one of Martha Graham's premier dancers, Guthrie met Marjorie Greenblatt Mazia. She was also a Martha Graham dancer, the daughter of Russian-Jewish immigrants Isidore Greenblatt, who worked in the garment business, and Aliza Waitzman Greenblatt, a Yiddish poet. Although both Marjorie and Woody were married at the time, they became fast friends and soon—much to the Greenblatts' chagrin—lovers.

"I thought he was mad sometimes," Aliza Greenblatt wrote of Woody. "And

Woody Guthrie Archive (both)

Guthrie's friends, Leadbelly and Pete Seeger among them, filled his place on Mermaid Avenue with music in the 1940s. When not writing or recording, Woody reveled in family time (opposite) on the Coney beach.

there were times I was ashamed to admit that I even knew him . . . his pants held up by a string, his hair unkempt, his entire self unwashed." Despite all this, she finally had to admit that she liked him and admired his work—enough so that she and Woody would share poems and songs. Greenblatt would offer her work to him for criticism and he would write music to some of her poems.

Woody and Marjorie were married in 1945 and had their first daughter, Cathy Ann. Nora Guthrie says her father was captivated by the city life and its melting pot of immigrants. "When I walk along and look at your faces," he wrote in his poem "Voices"...

I set here in a Jewish delicatassen, I order a hot
* pastrami*
Sandwitch on rye bread and I hear the lady ask me
Would you like to have a portion of cole slaw on
* the side . . .*
And I told her I would take my slaw on a side dish
And would like to have a glass of tea with lemon
And she knew that I was speaking her words.

The first years in Coney Island were happy ones. Guthrie, in between stints in the merchant marine and the army, was writing and recording. He spent his time on the beach and boardwalk with Cathy Ann. According

Breakfast at Nathan's

Woody took us to Nathan's every morning. Mother had to mop the floor before she left to go to her dance school, but there were three small kids in the house and the deal was he had to get us out of the house for about twenty minutes while the floor dried. So he'd take us over to Nathan's. They did not serve breakfast there, but they were open early. So we had hot dogs and french fries—hot patooties—and I fell in love with the place. I took my husband there. Even now, when someone asks where I want to go for dinner, I tell them I want to go *there*." —Nora Guthrie

to biographer Joe Klein, the house was filled with music and musicians—as well as young troubled kids—making pilgrimages to see Guthrie and learn from him and enjoy the liveliness of the household. Guthrie worked especially closely with a Brooklyn kid, Elliott Adnopoz, who called himself Buck Elliott and eventually Ramblin' Jack Elliott.

"By all accounts," says Nora Guthrie, "it was a pretty hoppin' place with Sonny Terry, Brownie McGhee and Pete Seeger or Leadbelly dropping by." Guthrie was writing children's songs (*Songs to Grow On* was released in 1946) and reveling in family life for the first time. "He was fascinated," says Nora, "by the Yiddish culture,

the Russian immigrants, the beach and the bathers." He was also becoming much more involved in politics, especially in anti-Hitler politics, speaking often at the Frederick Douglass Club, the Communist party headquarters on Coney Island and performing for FDR benefits.

In February 1947, Cathy Ann was killed in a fire in the Guthrie apartment. It was a difficult time for the couple. Guthrie's older sister had also been killed in a fire when he was young, and his father nearly died in a fire. Guthrie began rambling again, finally pulled back home by the birth of his son Arlo in 1947, another son, Joady Ben, in 1948 and Nora in 1950. Guthrie buried himself in work. He began a new novel, wrote feverishly, turning out more children's songs, even Hanukkah songs, and began to see some of his work pay off.

When Guthrie received money for the Weavers' version of his dust bowl ballad "So Long, It's Been Good to Know You," Marjorie moved with the children to 59 Murdoch Court in Coney Island and opened the Marjorie Mazia School of Dance in Sheepshead Bay. Soon, however, her husband began to be affected by both his drinking and his incipient Huntington's chorea, the disease that had left his mother to die in an institution. He traveled often, and often aimlessly, around the country. Sometimes he would visit the family in Howard Beach, where they were now living. When he returned, things might be fine for a time but then quickly dissolved in his bouts of dementia. In 1954 Guthrie was hospitalized for Huntington's. Soon, musicians became interested once again in his music, and to singers such as the Kingston Trio and Bob Dylan, Guthrie became an icon of American music.

One of the last things Woody Guthrie did before he died, according to Joe Klein, was to listen to a recording of his son Arlo singing. It was "Alice's Restaurant." On October 3, 1967, Guthrie died. His family scattered his ashes in the water by the jetty that separates Coney Island from Sea Gate—Woody's favorite spot on the beach.

Bruce Stutz is a writer and former editor of Natural History *magazine. He is the author of* Natural Lives, Modern Times: People and Places of the Delaware River.

Brian Merlis Collection

A Whale of a Stunt

Even for Coney, this one was a whopper!

BY FRANK GRAHAM, JR.

Nathan Handwerker was a Brooklyn institution all by himself, an immigrant merchant whose hot dog establishment at the heart of Coney Island became known worldwide as "Nathan's Famous." Following what was a common pattern among immigrant families in Brooklyn, Nathan remained something of an old-world patriarch, keeping a tight and conservative controlling hand on the family business, while his son Murray—ambitious and thoroughly Americanized—was imbued with the spirit of hucksterism and hustle. He had, after all, been around Coney Island all his life.

Murray felt that the family hot dog business would benefit from some new-world hype. He approached the Dodger organization with his idea of putting on a "Coney Island Night" entertainment at Ebbets Field. Between the games of a twi-night doubleheader, Nathan's Famous would pay for a Coney-style show with clowns, stilt walkers, tumblers and pretty girls cavorting for the ballpark crowd. In return, of course, Nathan's would get its name mentioned over the public-address system. It seemed an agreeable and innocuous promotion, and it proved popular: even the big-league players themselves returned early from their clubhouse siesta to take in part of the show.

But for young Murray Handwerker and his family "Coney Island Night" carried a far weightier significance. It seemed that the success of the promotional show at Ebbets Field had done much to repair a breach in the Handwerker family and to rebuild Murray's confidence and self-esteem in the wake of an earlier promotional disaster. A year or two before the event, while patriarch Nathan was taking a summer holiday in Miami Beach, Murray had been given a rare opportunity to mind the store and was approached by a man who had somehow come into possession of—of all things—a whale. A very large and very dead whale. The man talked Murray into renting the remains of this leviathan for the purpose of installing them in a vacant lot next-door to Nathan's Famous—on the theory that the crowds thus lured to gawk at this unusual spectacle would naturally be inclined to buy quantities of hot dogs and cold sodas.

A deal was struck, and the dead whale was ensconced next door to Nathan's eatery. For a day or two, all went exactly as Murray and the unnamed huckster had anticipated. Crowds of curious passersby gathered near Nathan's, and some did purchase the famous hot dogs. But then, unexpectedly, a powerful heat wave descended on the borough. Sprawled out in the hot sun near the

Russell Christian

beach, the deceased—and decaying—whale began to exude a powerful odor. Eventually, an overpowering stench spread out over that area of Coney Island.

Pleasure-seekers, beachgoers and, of course, potential diners fled to other, far-distant attractions. Owners of neighboring businesses complained to the police, who branded the decomposing whale a public-health hazard and ordered Murray Handwerker to dispose of it. Immediately. At the height of the stench and the uproar, who should return from vacation but Nathan himself, the family patriarch who had built his

business not on hucksterism and hoopla but on selling quality meat at a fair price?

"Pop let me know what he thought about this cocka-mamie promotion," Murray said. "And he was *apoplectic* when he found out how much it cost me to hire a man to cut up the whale and tow it out to sea. The business didn't recover for weeks."

Frank Graham, Jr., long a resident of Brooklyn, was public relations chief for the Dodgers. He is the author of The Audubon Ark *and* Gulls: A Social History.

NOW & THEN Known as "the City of Fire" for its nighttime brilliance, Coney Island was a frequent victim of real-life conflagrations. This one, in 1939, threatened Steeplechase Park.

Brian Merlis Collection

The Cyclone

The mother of all roller coasters

PHOTOGRAPHS & TEXT BY MARA FAYE LETHEM

On June 26, 1927, a new word was added to the bedrock Brooklyn lexicon: "Cyclone." It cost Jack and Irving Rosenthal $100,000 to build their roller coaster, a behemoth of grace and terror. But from opening day the line of willing thrill-seekers went around the block, and at twenty-five cents a ride their investment was made back within weeks. Like most everything about Coney Island, the Cyclone is infused with a certain edgy magic. Besides being one of the last wooden coasters in America, it is also one of the few remaining solid links to Coney's heyday.

The Cyclone occupies a special niche in the lives of people growing up in Brooklyn: "My *mother* rode the Cyclone—and loved it," says Jerry Mendito, who has been overseeing the ride and enforcing the height requirement for the last twenty-five years. "The Cyclone is something Brooklyn parents tell their children about, something that you know as a little kid—there's a big coaster in Coney Island, and someday I'm gonna ride it. It's sort of like a hand-me-down. And if it wasn't for that first drop, I'd probably ride it a lot more." The Cyclone was the only coaster Mendito knew when he was growing up. "It spoiled me for the more modern sanitized rides," he says.

For me, the thrill of the Cyclone is its hint of greater hazard, of *anarchy*. Coney Island is no Disney World; if Mickey Mouse shows up here, I'll mug him myself. As a kid, I gladly paid to ride the Cyclone because it made me feel like I really could die. The staccato clacks as the chain pulled the cars up the first peak built the tension like a Bernard Herrmann score in a Hitchcock film. That creaky prelapsarian climb was excruciating. Then there's that brief moment at the apex, where you feel on top of the world, overlooking the whole boardwalk and beach and ocean. Then everything just falls out from under you as the train suddenly goes perpendicular.

It's actually 31.4 percent off the perpendicular, but you can't tell the difference from up there. The heavy hardwood-and-steel cars pick up enough speed from the first plunge to travel on their own momentum for

Let the good times roll: the start of a terrifying 3,000-foot run.

the six turns and eight drops that follow. Once the cars have been set in motion, there's only one other place on the compact figure-eight track where it's even

possible to stop the train—which has been clocked at sixty-eight miles per hour.

The 3,000-foot-long track is made up of layers of wood, supported by wooden trestlework and reinforced with steel supports. The cars travel its entire length in one minute and fifty seconds. One customer asked for his money back because he decided that he'd only been given half a ride. He *couldn't* have covered that block-long pile of twisted trackage in less than two minutes—or so he thought. "He went out and came back with a cop," says Mendito. "Fortunately, it was a cop who knew the ride. 'No way in the world are you getting half a ride here,' the cop told the guy. 'Once you're in there and it goes over that hill, you're coming home. You gotta go all the way.'"

Designed by Vernon Keenan and built by noted amusement inventor Harry C. Baker, the Cyclone is truly a feat of engineering. Recently I got an insider's look at its underbelly. I saw the huge bullwheel, thirteen feet in diameter, that drags the cars with what looks like a big bicycle chain up to the first peak. And that infernal clacking is actually caused by safety "dogs" that prevent any backsliding. I saw the three trains, each with three cars, dismantled for their winter repairs and even

Robert Harvey checks out the six turns and eight stomach-churning drops of the Cyclone's wood-and-steel track and the massive wooden trestlework that supports it.

climbed up the track itself with Robert Harvey as my guide. Harvey has worked on the ride for fifteen years and is quite fearless. He didn't ask me if I wanted to use a safety harness; he just promised to bury me underneath if I fell. But as I peered over the edge of the eighty-five-foot drop, he did make one rule: I had to climb back down on the same side we had come up on. We went up the second peak so I could get close to that classic old "Cyclone" sign, those beautiful red tin letters studded with lightbulbs. It felt like a pilgrimage. Back on the ground, I walked among the broken sunglasses that had been whipped from screaming faces.

"It's the ultimate," says Colleen Whyte, director of the American Coaster Enthusiasts of Metro New York and Connecticut. "I don't care what they build, taller is not better. Nothing can come close." She recommends

the second-to-last car: "It's rough, but not too rough." For the ride's seventieth anniversary, Whyte rode seventy times, from three to seven in the morning. "It just confirmed how I've always felt about it. The view from the hill early in the morning when the sun rose—it was the best thing that has ever happened to me."

Part of the ride's appeal to Whyte and other diehard Cyclone fans is feeling transported back in time to the glory days of "Sodom by the Sea." Seven years before the birth of the Cyclone, Coney Island boomed with the arrival of the BMT elevated and the subway. This was the last step in the democratization of Coney Island's mechanized amusement and fried-clam "Nickel Empire." Soon on an average Sunday afternoon there was literally no space on the sand to lay your towel.

Coney is where the world's first roller coaster was introduced in 1884. During the Depression, the Wildcat, Thunderbolt and Tornado all cut their prices, but the prescient Cyclone held firm, and now its watch has lasted more than seven decades. It has seen an eyeful— Steeplechase horses, soldiers on leave, Skeeball and penny arcades on the Bowery, Cary Grant on stilts, confetti six inches deep on the street during Mardi Gras. The Aquarium rose out of Dreamland's ashes, and the boardwalk has more than doubled in length. Nathan's Famous and the Cyclone have remained the same—and

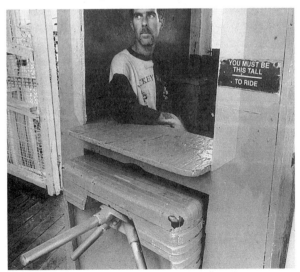

Abandon four dollars all ye who enter here.

the Cyclone is the only operational coaster left at Coney.

The 1970s were a pivotal time in the coaster's history. It was bought by the city in 1971 for a million dollars from Silvio Pinto and was almost turned over to the Aquarium but ended up being leased back to Pinto. In 1975, in need of repair, it was leased to Dewey and Jerome Albert, the father-and-son team of the Astroland amusement park on Surf Avenue. The Alberts resurrected the Cyclone, and to this day Astroland maintains and operates the ride. The Cyclone is, literally, irreplaceable since current New York City building codes prohibit the construction of a timber-supported coaster. Now on the National Register of Historic Places, it also has been declared a city, state and national landmark. It cannot be altered, so the Cyclone will never have a tight spiral added. But as Mendito says, "On a ride like that, you don't want to change nothing, because you can't improve it. The ride is perfect."

He's not the only one who thinks so. Coaster enthusiasts regularly rate it among the best in the world. Richard Rodriguez made the Guinness book by riding for four days straight. Colleen Whyte spoke of falling in love with the ride, but for some people that's not enough. They feel the need to declare their love on the Cyclone. Mendito estimates that there have been a dozen weddings in the last twenty-five years. Vows are exchanged on the platform. "When they say 'I do,' we lock 'em in and then they take the *big* plunge."

The Cyclone manages to be one of the oldest, safest and most thrilling coasters all at the same time. Of course, there are lots of people who won't even go near it. But the ride's fans know it has . . . a special power. Just ask Emilio Franco, a West Virginian who rode the Cyclone on a visit to Brooklyn in 1948. Franco had been rendered mute five years earlier while a private in the army. He screamed his way all through the drops and turns. On his way off the platform, he was suddenly able to speak again. This miracle was reported in the *New York Times*. Franco's words? "I feel sick."

Mara Faye Lethem, a documentary photographer and writer, has lived all her life in Boerum Hill.

On the Boardwalk

The great escape from crowded city streets

INTERVIEW WITH LEONARD GARMENT

Len Garment at ten, topped by two brothers.

There are many places in Brooklyn that had magical qualities to them when I was growing up. The most exciting was Coney Island. It was a place that represented escape—a place of "tomorrow." It was a place of sensuality. I remember going there at age ten, and it seemed to me a continuous dreamland. But what I really remember is the boardwalk—especially under the boardwalk, where it was all wet and shady, and full of intimations. It was a place of crowds and sun and water. I went there with my father and mother and my two brothers. It was the one time when our family was all together. We'd go to the Steeplechase and Luna Park and to Nathan's, of course. It was the happiest time for us.

Things were very difficult during the week for immigrant families like mine. We really struggled to make ends meet. My mother was from Poland and my father came from Poltava in Latvia—then part of Russia. I was born in East New York, at 370 Pennsylvania Avenue, near Atlantic Avenue in Brownsville. (It's no longer there. It was demapped, and is not a street anymore. So in my case, I really can't go home again.) We also lived in two or three locations on Eastern Parkway. Later I found out that mobility was common then because so many families could take advantage of a common deal: new tenants often got one month's free rent. So I remember living in a lot of places: Crown Street, Schenectedy Avenue, Fenimore Street near Ebbets Field.

All those second-generation Americans struggling . . . There were a lot of tortured and gifted people. There was also a lot of anger, with parents bringing up these rough kids and trying to make a good life for them. Families like ours had a hard time as outsiders trying to become insiders—and even struggled over whether to try to become insiders.

So for us those weekends at Coney were the high point of the summer—the high point of the year, really. The place provided a great sense of release. There was something dreamlike about it all—and the dream is sometimes more important than the reality.

Leonard Garment, born and raised in Brooklyn, was counsel to President Richard Nixon, U.S. representative to the Commission on Human Rights of the United Nations Economic and Social Council, and Counselor, U.S. Delegation to the United Nations. He is with the law firm of Verner, Liipfert, Bernhard, McPherson and Hand.

Courtesy of Leonard Garment

For the Coney Kids

On the darkest shore, a beacon…

BY DENIS HAMILL

Over the last quarter of a century, Rozella "Moms" Bradley probably steered more Coney Island kids away from Rikers Island and Potter's Field than all the combined fingers on the stingy hand of government. "The way I see it," says Moms, a thin, strong woman with an explosive smile and eyes as warm as a June day, "if you don't have time for children, you don't have time for life. And if you don't have time for life, why are you even here? All our problems start with the kids. So the solutions start with them, too. All kids ever ask for is a little attention, so you just have to find the time."

The Coney kids who have grown up in the public-housing projects amid the gunslingers of the crack wars and the pimps and prostitutes of Surf Avenue refer to her as "Moms" Bradley, because she dotes on them like a tireless den mother. Over the years, while working and raising her four kids on her own, she has voluntarily organized a 400-member boys and girls basketball league, double-Dutch tournaments, tutorial programs, arts and crafts classes, cheerleading squads, summer job programs, and chess, song and dance competitions. She holds an annual Fourth of July cookout, a back-to-school block party and a Mother's

Day parade to celebrate the people who hold together this part of the city. And in her spare time she holds a full-time job as a counselor at the nearby Boys and Girls Club.

"When I first moved up here from down south," she recalls, "I got a job in a nursing home on Nostrand Avenue, lived in Crown Heights, saved my money. Later, I went back down south, got back together with my husband, we had a couple more kids, then we broke up again. I came back to Brooklyn and in 1976 I moved into 2007 Surf Avenue, two years after the projects were built. I've been here since."

Her building was a nice place to live at first, she says, but crack changed everything in the 1980s. People began locking themselves in as soon as the sun went down. "The hallways were filled with drug pushers, junkies and prostitutes, so I started a tenants' association. To make sure the kids and old people could come and go safely." Tenants worked in shifts around the clock, checking identification and asking the destinations of strangers. The parents of any kid caught doing graffiti had to pay a $500 fine. If they couldn't pay, they had to scrub the walls of an entire floor of the building. Anyone caught tossing trash from a window or littering the hallways was also heavily fined or put on garbage detail. "It worked," Moms says. "Since we formed the tenants' association, we've never had to call the cops

Russell Christian

once. We have the safest building in Coney, and we do it for the kids. If they learn young that this is how you must behave where you live, they'll behave out there in the rest of the world."

A few summers ago, in a single magical season, I watched Moms transform a weed-strangled empty lot on the corner of Surf Avenue and West Twenty-First Street into a bountiful eden of sweet peas, collard greens, summer corn, squash, lettuce and tomatoes. All of it had been planted, nurtured and harvested by Moms' Coney kids and then distributed to the projects' poor and the local senior citizens, which they still do every year. "I thought the best way to show the kids an alternative to death was something that symbolized life," Moms says. "I'm from Georgia, where we see things grow from the good earth. Most of these kids never knew what a seed was. Then when they planted them, cultivated them, watered them and watched from their projects' windows as the vegetables sprung to life where the dead bodies used to lie in the morning light, they got excited—by life, instead of death."

After a column about this little garden appeared in the *New York Daily News,* the people of Publishers Clearinghouse presented Moms with a check for $10,000, to be spent as she saw fit. Instead of treating herself to a Hawaiian vacation, she spent it all on the kids—buying uniforms for the basketball teams, food for the cookouts, supplies for the arts and crafts workshops, sneakers for the kids who couldn't afford them.

On a recent August Saturday, Moms was found riding a horse at a block party she'd organized on West Twenty-Second Street where, in conjunction with a local Kiwanis Club and the Victor Fellowship Church, she had distributed 500 back-to-school packets of school supplies. A group of kids surrounded her, laughing hysterically at the sight of Moms on horseback.

When asked why she chooses to do what she does for the young people of Coney Island, she shrugs. "Someone has to," she says. "My own kids are doing great. One daughter is in the army reserves, another son is retired from the air force, one son works as a scenic designer at Paramount Studios in Hollywood and my youngest is managing a restaurant in Los Angeles. Never had any problems with my own kids—no drugs, no arrests. So I figure I was blessed. Maybe the Lord chose me to help other young people.

"Some of these kids have parents who are into drugs themselves," Moms continues. Most have no fathers. I watch them grow up hard. And many slip away on me. There was one prostitute, call her Ruby, who was working the street near the community garden, half-dressed, all doped up. When she saw me coming, she got so embarrassed. But I know when they have shame there's still some hope. So I stopped to talk to her as the men hooted from the car windows. I never mentioned what she was doing. I just asked how she was, how her two little kids were. As soon as I mentioned the kids, she started crying and said they took them away from her. She had a drug habit. I told her to come see me later. She did, and I helped her get into a rehab program. Then she got clean. Then she got a job. She stopped selling herself on the street. Last week, I was walking past the garden and here she came with her two kids, all three of them clean and well-dressed. She looked healthy, and she just smiled and said hello. She was proud. That's three lives salvaged, a whole family.

"Why do I work with young people? I guess I'm just a sucker for stories with happy endings, and although not many people hear about them, there are quite a few down here in Coney."

Denis Hamill is a columnist for the New York Daily News.

I look into the milk-white smile of the barker, that fanatical Arabian smile which came out of the Dreamland fire, and I step quietly into the open belly of the dragon." **Henry Miller**

Brooklyn's Big Day at the Beach

PHOTOGRAPHS BY RALPH GINZBURG

New Orleans has its Mardi Gras and Greenwich Village its campy Halloween Parade, but for sheer outrageous spectacle Coney Island's Mermaid Parade wins the brass ring. Staged on the last Saturday of June and led off by King Neptune and his queen, the parade ends up marching right to the breaking waves where a pageant breaks out. A Haitian voodoo band casts fruit upon the water, a gigantic thermometer gets poked into the surf and the mayor of Coney Island turns a huge key to "open" the Atlantic Ocean for a season of swimming.

"It's an anarchist parade!" says one regular participant. Nearly anything goes, as long as it has a nautical theme. Anyone can dress up, make up, sign up and step off. Recent King Neptunes have included ex-Talking Head David Byrne, Guardian Angel Curtis Sliwa and against-the-tide attorney Ron Kuby—flamboyant characters all. On homemade floats and antique cars, on foot or flippers, hundreds of mermaids, mermen, mer-kids, and mer-critters follow Neptune, riding, marching, flopping and dancing to the tunes of musical ensembles like the Sea Monkey Orchestra, Manhattan samba bands and the "Toes" Tiranoff tap dancers. There's also a judging of sorts—for Best Mermaid Costume, Best Marching Group and so on—and plenty of hooting and heckling from the sea-loving spectators.

Photojournalist Ralph Ginzburg was formerly publisher of Avant Garde *and* Eros *magazines.*

Everybody Loves a Parade

The Mermaid Parade is big and getting bigger: it now draws over a half-million spectators. But it's still an informal, homemade event. Anyone with a nautical costume can register and pay a modest entry fee to enter the parade either on foot or with a vehicle or float.

Over-the-Top Spectacle

A "can you top this?" character has emerged in recent years, with such entries as the mermaids from hell in red, the Siberian mermaids in fur, the biker-chick mermaids, mermaids on stilts and/or topless mermaids vying for crowd approval with, say, an all-blue mermaid clad only in MetroCards. Then there was the *Exxon Valdez* float, complete with a drunken captain...

"They asked me to be King Neptune. I got this long, flowing gray-and-white Shakespearean robe, and I carried a homemade trident and let my hair out. I looked like Father Time on acid." **Ron Kuby, maverick attorney**

Marriage, Cyclone Style

A roller coaster like the Cyclone would seem to have only one purpose—to frighten its passengers without actually harming them. But for some people, it has other functions and meanings. For some, it's a pop metaphor for the journey through life—"lots of ups and downs, some thrills, you don't really go any-where, and it's over much too soon." Accordingly, the Cyclone strikes some bold couples as the perfect place for a wedding.

Take Mike Lustig and Suzan Alparslan, he a musician and she a massage therapist. Both were quite fond of Coney Island and the Cyclone, and they had spent some courting time there among the amusements. They're just the most recent of the dozen or so couples who have in living memory tied the knot within the Cyclone's white wooden framework.

On an exceptionally warm, muggy evening in late spring, nattily attired family and friends of the bride and groom gathered on the platform of the boarding area. Mike and Suzan entered at the turnstile accompanied by Mendelssohn's "Wedding March" played gamely by a straw-hatted accordionist and a clarinetist. The happy couple took their places on the greased steel tracks, joined by Rabbi Ethan Greenberg (who had never before married anyone on a roller coaster). The bride looked radiant in a creamy silk gown; the groom perspired in his dark suit. Waiting directly uphill—poised like the future itself—sat the two-ton yellow cars of the Cyclone. On and about lounged the tattooed, piratical-looking crew of ride operators, raptly attentive to this special moment.

Over the traffic noise on Surf Avenue, and the music and rumbling from the adjacent amusement rides, Rabbi Greenberg read from notes that the bride and groom had written earlier about why it was that each wished to marry the other. Some of the reasons drew appreciative nods and wry laughter. The rabbi moved on to the familiar pronouncements. Then rings were exchanged, hands were held, and finally the declaration of "man and wife," and the kiss—several of them, actually—to thunderous applause and cheers.

There was a merrily confused rush to the seats in the Cyclone cars, with Mike and Suzan in the first seat, naturally. Family and friends—the more daring among them—filled in the other seats. The crew checked all the passengers, released the brakes, and off went the wedding party, up into the humid sunset. All of Coney Island was at their feet when they clattered to the crest at the big red "Cyclone" sign. Then the rush, the downs and ups and downs. Three rumbling, hurtling trips, with much screaming and arm-waving along the way. Like life itself. —*M.W.R.*

Russell Christian

Coney Island Lives

And it's as raucous as ever

BY DICK ZIGUN

Sure Coney has changed, but we still get 15 million people a year coming here. And usually a million on the Fourth of July. A lot of these people don't even know about Coney Island's past. They just come and have a terrific time without knowing the history. The beach is the big draw, and it's always been the draw. It's the biggest public beach on the eastern seaboard, and in recent years the water quality has really improved. It's clean and neat.

Most accounts of Coney Island stop at the 1950s. No one wants to talk about racism. It was a hard time here in the 1960s and '70s. Rioting started in the 1960s when Steeplechase refused to integrate its swimming pool. Then there was a lot of white flight from Coney, and it went from being a place for families to a place for teens and then gangs and danger. So there was a real decline in the 1970s. And by and large the landowners neglected the place because they thought they were going to get casino gambling here—they tried hard to get it—and there'd be a lot of new building. But that didn't happen.

I think things at Coney began to change with the beginning of the arts movement, with the onset of what I call "Honky-Tonk chic." In the 1980s, some of the landowners began to bring the rides back, to fix them up and get them going again. See, Coney was never just one amusement park. No one person controls it. It's a whole neighborhood zoned by the city for amusement. Actually, I'd say about thirty or so people own and run it. And this is a stable group. Some of the same families have been running rides and attractions for generations.

The first Mermaid Parade, in 1983, was the turnaround event for Coney. Richard Egan and something he called the Coney Island Hysterical Society got it going. The Sixtieth Precinct of the NYPD was also important. We went to them with the idea of a big parade, a Mermaid Parade. That was silly—everyone knows mermaids don't have feet, so how can they parade?—but the police liked the idea. They didn't want to do it on the Fourth of July since they already had their hands full on that date, so we decided on a parade to kick off the season at the beach. The first parade, there were probably more people in it than watching it. It draws half a million spectators and it's getting bigger every year.

There have been a lot of changes, but Coney Island is alive and well-maintained. There will probably be some additional development here—there's been a lot of talk about a baseball park. Whatever it is, it needs to be big and urban and colorful and gaudy. We've started having fireworks on the beach again, every week, every Friday during the summer season. And we're working on bringing an air show to Coney, featuring the Blue Angels from the U.S. Navy.

Yale graduate Dick Zigun is an artist, a sideshow operator and a spokesperson for Coney Island USA.

A hard day's work at the office

Kathy Willens/AP/Wide World

The Streets

Brooklyn has long been characterized by the range and diversity of its citizens—in national background, ethnicity, language, religious persuasion, color, occupation. It is, simply, the most diverse urban population in America. Still, there are commonalities, shared characteristics, that seem mysteriously and not quite definably to attach themselves to anyone and everyone who is born, raised or just chooses to live in Brooklyn.

Chief among those commonalities is in-your-face *attitude.* Toughness is certainly part of the attitude, but there's more. There is also street-smarts, resilience, skepticism, bluntness, a dash of wiseass humor, plus a ready willingness to confront almost anyone on any occasion. The attitude is not easy to deconstruct, but it is there as a kind of hard core, a tough structure within the slangy exchanges heard every day on the streets, in the subways, in the stores. And what the attitude provokes is *respect*.

Previous spread: The streets are where the action is—whatever your age and whatever the game.

Previous spread and this page: Martha Cooper/City Lore

City Sports

The pavement was our Garden

INTERVIEW WITH
JERRY
REINSDORF

On warm summer days, everybody hung out on the street. All the parents and children, the babies in their strollers. Just to catch whatever breeze there was. We'd mostly talk about the Dodgers and the movies. And sometimes we'd go stand in front of the movie theaters to feel the air-conditioning: when someone walked out the door, you'd get a whiff of it. Now everybody has air-condition- ing and they don't go outside. *That's* what destroyed the Brooklyn neighborhoods.

We had a million street games back then. We had one called box baseball, where we used the squares in the sidewalk as boxes. Two guys would face each other with four boxes in between them. One guy would be the pitcher, and the other the batter. The pitcher would throw the ball—not hard—into the box right in front of the batter. Then the batter had to hit the ball to the box right in front of the pitcher. If it bounced once, it counted as a single; twice, it was a double; and so on. You could play it on different levels. Box baseball was

The requirements: a piece of chalk, some friends and a quiet street.

Arthur Leipzig

played with a pink rubber ball made by Spalding in Brooklyn—everybody called it the spaldeen. Now, if you squeezed the spaldeen when you threw it into the batter's box, you could make it bounce in any of four directions. Otherwise, it would have been pretty easy for the batter to hit the ball wherever he wanted. I could make the ball come back toward me. Or I could make it speed up and go forward. I could make it go left or right. But I wasn't any better at it than anybody else. We all just put English on the ball.

There was another street game called smackball, where you smacked the ball right back in the pitcher's face. Punchball was also a favorite. We used a spaldeen for that one, too, but we played it on a field in the schoolyard. The field was laid out just like a baseball diamond, and you'd punch the ball with your fist and then run the bases.

We played stickball according to the Brooklyn rules. Up in the Bronx and in Manhattan they used to pitch the ball so it bounced before it reached the batter, but we pitched on the fly. Also, today you hear people talk about hitting the ball for two or three "sewers," but that isn't how we measured. It wasn't sewers, it was manhole covers out in the middle of the street. I remember there were a couple of guys who could hit it for a couple of manhole covers. Duke Snider, the Dodgers' center fielder, used to come out and play stickball with us. He wasn't much more than a kid himself—he was about nineteen or twenty years old. He couldn't get the hang of stickball, though. He just couldn't hit with that skinny little broomstick. He didn't have an apartment; he lived in a rooming house

between Albemarle Road and Beverly Road. He stayed there a couple of years and then moved to Bay Ridge when he got married.

We also played basketball. It was one of our schoolyard games, and we played either two-on-two or three-on-three. But there was no Brooklyn team. And sometimes we played baseball on the diamonds at the Parade Grounds. You didn't have to be in a league. If you had eighteen guys who wanted to play baseball, you could get a permit.

I was good enough at playing sports on the street, but I didn't play on any of my high school teams. We were all first- and second-generation Americans, and the emphasis on education was tremendous. My mother and father never went to college, and they wanted their kids to go. I was kind of a slacker. What I used to do was work out my schedule at Erasmus Hall High School so I could get home by one o'clock. The Dodger games started at one-twenty on the radio, and I'd listen to the game out on the street.

I loved going to Ebbets Field. When you first walked in, it was dark and dingy. You'd go up a ramp and turn to the right at the top of the ramp, and all of a sudden there was this bright sunlight and green grass. I always got goosebumps. When the Dodgers left for Los Angeles, I got very bitter. I didn't pay any attention to baseball again until years later in Chicago, when one of my kids was about eight years old and became a fan of the White Sox.

Jerry Reinsdorf now owns the Chicago White Sox and the Chicago Bulls.

 "For me the whole world was embraced in the confines of the Fourteenth Ward. If anything happened outside, it either didn't happen or it was unimportant." **Henry Miller**

A My Name Is Alice

Three Feet to Germany. Hit the Penny. Double Dutch. Running Bases.

BY GRACE LICHTENSTEIN

The names of my childhood games evoke the image of a dead-end street in Crown Heights opposite not one but two schoolyards, a paved playground of boundless creativity where I and my pals spent hours horsing around in the post–World War II years. Certain games were almost exclusively for girls. For "potsy" (the Brooklyn name for hopscotch), we would draw the rectangular hopscotch grid with chalk on the pavement, fling a bottle cap on a square and begin hopping. Jump rope—a swinger at each end, a lineup of girls ready to perform in the middle—was a favorite game during recess at P.S. 241; later, at John Marshall Junior High, we white girls looked on in awe at the remarkably complex, rhythmic double-rope maneuvers performed by the black girls.

"A my name" was the most popular among the many individual tests of spaldeen skills. While you bounced the ball, you turned your leg over at each accented word of the chant: "A my name is *Alice* and my husband's name is *Al*. We come from *Alabama* and we sell *apples*. B my name is *Betty*..." Miss a turn or lose the ball and the next girl had her chance. "A my name is *Alan*"? Never happened.

The majority of our games were played by both sexes. Our game of baseball resembled a kind of ping-pong with an imaginary net; we used our hands as paddles. Any two manhole covers in the middle of the street served as the bases in "running bases," where the runner would sprint like Jackie Robinson from third to home while a thrower stationed at each manhole tried to tag her out. Punchball and slapball were simply adaptations of stickball, without the stick. In "hit the penny," the coin was placed on a line in the sidewalk with the two contestants a box away from each other. If you could make the spaldeen not only hit the penny but flip it, you won extra points (and maybe even the penny).

Girls got game, too, and the sidewalks are their field of play—whether original or traditional.

Arthur Leipzig; inset: Martha Cooper/City Lore

No equipment was needed for "three feet to Germany," just a gutter, with the "it" girl in the center. Contestants lined up at one curb and paced off three big steps into the asphalt. Then it was a free-for-all—could you elude being tagged by "it" and make it to the opposite curb? If not, tough nuggies. You became "it."

The girls who were fanatic Dodger fans collected bubblegum cards with the same avidity as the boys. In playing "flipping cards" with the boys, we gambled our unwanted Solly Hemus or Don Mueller cards in hopes of winning someone's Snider, Hodges, Reese or Campanella. The skill and poise you showed in flexing a card between two fingers and flicking it toward a wall went a long way in gaining respect from boys. But dexterous flipping was not always enough to get an invitation to play softball. I managed to get some invitations—as long as I brought a ball.

Grace Lichtenstein is a former New York Times *reporter and bureau chief, a graduate of Brooklyn College, and a contributing writer to* Business Week *and* Wired News. *She is the author of six books on sports and music.*

THE SPALDEEN: Mostly Gone, but Certainly Not Forgotten

Had French novelist Marcel Proust grown up in Brooklyn during the Depression, he very likely would have written 1,500 pages of evocative prose on the squishy pink ball known as the spaldeen. Ask any New Yorker who came of age in the 1930s, '40s or '50s about these cheap hollow tennis ball cores and you're likely to get an outpouring of childhood nostalgia.

My grandfather, who fled Russia in 1904, landed in the Lower East Side. Mired in the most densely populated place on earth, his primary form of recreation was swiping apples from a pushcart and sprinting into the teeming streets. But my father grew up in relative prosperity in the East Flatbush section of Brooklyn. As a boy, he spent his free time on the street playing stickball, boxball and his favorite, stoopball—all with a spaldeen (also known as a "pinkie").

"No single ball was used for more games than the spaldeen," he said sixty years after his last stoopball game. "It was ubiquitous." When I asked him the details of the game, he seemed stunned. "Do you live in Brooklyn or Boise?" Sorry, Dad, I missed the stoopball craze.

The Spalding, which Brooklyn diction morphed into "spaldeen," was sold in virtually every candy store on every corner in the city. Willie Davis, a stickball star in Brooklyn before playing eighteen years in the major leagues, called it "the soul of the streets." Discontinued in 1978, the spaldeen made a comeback in 1999. In the 1950s the ball cost a quarter; today it's being manufactured in Taiwan and costs $2. While the spaldeen is used once more in organized stickball leagues, its venue is gone. Why? More television, more video games, more cars and fewer parents willing to turn their kids loose to play on city streets.

The spaldeen, however, continues to live large in the psyche of those who whiled away the long hours of youth out on the sidewalks, the stoops and the streets.
–Joe Glickman

Arthur Leipzig

Play's the Thing

The rules according to Karp

BY
GENIA
GOULD

Ivan Karp, art dealer and proprietor of the renowned OK Harris gallery in Soho, professes unfaltering affection for the borough where he grew up. And when visiting the old neighborhoods from Flatbush to Midwood, "the atmosphere of life in the streets of Brooklyn still permeates my spirit," he says. "I get emanations of my formative years.

"Games," Karp says, "were a constant from neighborhood to neighborhood, and vital to the life of every Brooklyn boy. There were at least fifty games, played on the street (because there were hardly any cars) and in empty dirt lots. They were woven right into the fabric of life," he says. "Games were critical for well-being and balance. And if you didn't have someone to play with, you played on your own. You played.

"A game that everybody played was called ring-a-levio," Karp says. "It didn't have many apparent rules; it had to do with running and capturing people. There was also a very vigorous and almost violent game called 'Johnny on the pony,' where one person—hopefully a very robust and energetic person—would lean against the wall and others would leap on top of his back until it was a tower of characters. Finally he would collapse." Karp reflects for a moment, then adds, "I don't remember anymore if I was ever the one on the bottom. I never professed to having the strength to support the large mass of Brooklyn humanity at that time."

Other neighborhood games called for more finesse: "There was a game called 'territory' that you played with your penknife. Every boy had a penknife. On the ground, you shaped out the circumference of the earth and divided it into various portions. Then you opened the blade and threw it into the ground. You would try,

Ivan Karp looks back on the games of his childhood.

according to your skills in throwing the knife, to achieve the largest portion of the earth. In another game, you flipped baseball cards in a certain way, and you had to match one card with another card face up. There were experts at that, and I learned I was excellent at it.

"We had endless games of war," Karp recalls, "where everyone had a toy gun. Some were wooden guns for

Courtesy of Ivan Karp

Precursors to the rollerblade: noisy steel wheels rolled on ball bearings, but nothing worked without that key.

which you cut out pieces of cardboard that were shot with a rubber band."

Although most games involved a minimum of equipment, roller skates were among the most important types of gear. "We would fashion scooters out of milk crates (they were heavy wooden boxes in those days). A crate would be mounted on a two-by-four length of wood, and roller-skate wheels would be attached to the bottom. You could skate that around the neighborhood and do all kinds of maneuvers with it. Roller skates were very important; every boy and girl had them, and the roller skate key was one of the most valuable appendages in your life.

"Marble games were myriad," Karp notes. "One of them was a gambling game. A boy would set up a little cheese box at the curb and put three holes in it with the numbers 5, 10 and 15 written above them. You would roll your marble from the center of the street toward the holes, and if it went in you would win the number of marbles indicated above the hole. But you can imagine how hard it was to get in there! So the person who had the stand won most of the marbles. He was like the casino operator."

Karp must have won plenty of those games: he still has his original collection of hundreds of marbles. "I can even remember some of the names I assigned to them," he says. "Little Bluey was one, and Big Brownie, and The Streaky One."

Writer Genia Gould once edited her own Williamsburg-based magazine called Breukelen.

NOW & THEN Scooters were created by attaching a pair of skate wheels to a two-by-four and a wooden box. Sleek successor skateboards are no less creative.

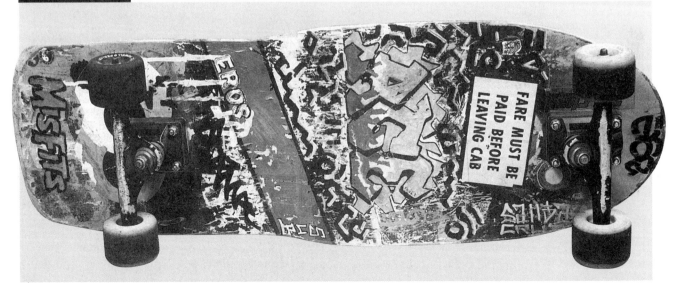

Martha Cooper/City Lore

Hoop Dreams

From street basketball to the pros…and back again

BY
ROGER
RUBIN

In big-time basketball, talent isn't always enough. James "Fly" Williams is the proof.

If talent were enough, Fly Williams would have been the greatest basketball player you've ever seen instead of the greatest player you've never seen. If talent had been enough, he would be a permanent icon of the city game instead of a vague and fading memory among fans of playground basketball in Brooklyn—where the competition is tough and some truly great players have honed their game.

Put Fly Williams on a basketball court in 1974, and he is a nineteen-year-old personification of Brooklyn viewed through the lens of basketball. There was creativity and expression, intelligence and motion, bravado and the physical gifts to back it up. He became a high school All-American and an NCAA record-holder for scoring in his college freshman season. But put him back on that same court fifteen years later and he is a living monument to dashed dreams. Fly Williams did not realize his potential. Instead he gave it away in a world of paranoia and narcotics and crime. Those who saw him in his prime got a treat. Those who didn't . . . well, this is the reason why old men tell stories.

In a city where people strive not to be merely part of the crowd, Fly Williams was a standout. Who else would come to a playground game wearing a white rabbit fur coat? Who else would leave his gold Rolls-Royce double-parked outside a game at Foster Park and, when asked by a police officer to move it, toss him the keys and reply, "You move it"? Who else would run with characters named Country James and Wow Diamond?

Out of a Brownsville project on Stone Avenue, Fly Williams became a source of borough pride before he was twenty. Droves turned out to see his games in the

Fly Williams: a shooting star from the streets of Brooklyn.

neighborhood and in school, and children graffitied walls with his name. Basketball was his obsession from an early age. In winter, he would go to the playground with a shovel and clear off part of the court, then practice his dribbling and shooting with his gloves on. "I remember it was thirty below one day when I saw Fly there," says Keith Williams, who went by the name of Wow Diamond. "We always told him he was crazy, but Fly always said, 'I'm going to get there.'"

UPI/Corbis

His talent was recognized as soon as he began playing ball at James Madison High School, where he became an All-City player and then an All-American. His senior year, this thin but sinewy 6'5" shooter averaged 28.2 points and 21 rebounds per game, and he was recognized by collegiate coaches as one of the nation's very best prospects. "He had as much talent as anybody I've seen on the high school level," says Bill Aberer, longtime coach at LaSalle Academy. "Here was a guy who was six-five and handled the ball like a guard. He had three-point range and then some. And he could jump out of the building."

Recruiting analyst Tom Konchalski, who has evaluated basketball players in New York for more than four decades, states: "Fly was an extraordinary talent, capable of getting the ball in the basket from almost anywhere on the court. Inside, outside, you name it." But even then, there were signs of the traits that would become Fly's obstacles. He was not a motivated student and could not academically qualify for a college scholarship at the end of that season. He had to be enrolled at a prep school in upstate New York for a year—which proved to be the finest year for the basketball program at Glen Springs Academy as Fly averaged 33.9 points and the team went 33-2.

Fly was recruited heavily by colleges, but ended up choosing little Austin Peay State University. And though it might seem that small-town Tennessee life would not satisfy a city boy from Brooklyn, Fly always shrugged it off with lines like "I just want to be in a place where I won't get lost."

In fact, to the rest of the country, Fly Williams seemed to really hit his stride in Tennessee. Word got around about the freshman who was averaging nearly 30 points and 20 rebounds a game. People wanted to see the kid who would tell his defenders how bad he was making them look while he was doing it. And Austin Peay became a very hot commodity, selling out road games on the way to its first berth ever in the NCAA's annual basketball tournament.

Fly once bragged that he told Moses Malone that he'd score 60 points on him in an All-Star game. "But I messed up," he said. "I scored 63."

It was in that first NCAA tournament that Williams began to reveal just how erratic a personality he was. In Peay's second game in the tournament, Fly and Coach Lake Kelly began to argue. Kelly ended up benching Williams, and the team lost to Kentucky.

Before Fly's sophomore season, the school heralded its star with labels on all its outgoing mail that read "Super Fly is coming." He was a phenomenon. That season, too, included a couple of disagreements with Kelly and a suspension by the coach. Fly again averaged close to 30 points per game, but he was done with college. The Fly was going pro.

The summer basketball scene in those days was wild. There were pro-am tournaments all along the East Coast, and groups of pros would play together as a team. Fly played with his posse from Brooklyn, which consisted of Williams, Lloyd Free, Ed Searcy, Mel Davis, Jocko Jackson and Reuben Collins, and they would often get the best of the pros, courtesy of Williams' performances. In the summer of '74, they were good enough to reach the title game of the D.C. pro league to face a team made up of players on the Washington Bullets. Fly's gang didn't win that one, but they won plenty of others.

Again there was controversy surrounding the Fly. In the championship game of one summer pro-am tournament in New York, Williams spent much of the first three-quarters of the game complaining to referees that he was being roughed up by the opposing team's defenders. By the fourth quarter, Fly had had enough. He walked off the court and did not even hang around to hear about the game's outcome.

Still, he did turn professional, and his first year as a real pro was splendid. He signed a contract with the St. Louis Spirit of the ABA. He averaged 9.4 points and was one of the league's most colorful personalities. That proved to be the apex for Fly as a professional. Things never got better after that. The ABA was going to merge with the NBA, and though Williams got looks from a number of teams, he caught on with none. Today he believes it was because the Fly was simply too big a headache for coaches to tolerate.

Coney Islander Stephon Marbury scores for the Nets.

The Big Time

A roster of Brooklyn playground and high school basketball players who did make it to the NBA with at least one of the teams in the league.

Billy Cunningham (Erasmus Hall HS),
  Philadelphia 76ers
Mike Dunleavy (Nazareth HS), Milwaukee Bucks
Lloyd Free (Canarsie HS), Detroit Pistons
Sidney Green (Thomas Jefferson HS),
  New York Knicks
Connie Hawkins (Boys HS), Phoenix Suns
Vinny Johnson (Roosevelt HS), Detroit Pistons
Albert King (Fort Hamilton HS), San Antonio Spurs
Bernard King (Fort Hamilton HS), Washington Bullets
Doug Moe (Erasmus Hall HS), played in the ABA;
  coached the Denver Nuggets
Stephon Marbury (Abraham Lincoln HS),
  New Jersey Nets
Chris Mullin (Xaverian HS), Indiana Pacers
John Salley (Canarsie HS), Detroit Pistons
Lenny Wilkens (Boys HS), Cleveland Cavaliers

"Why didn't I ever make it?" he wonders aloud. "Attitude. I needed a serious attitude adjustment. I had a short temper." He played a few seasons in leagues on the periphery of the NBA, but the fact that he was not getting his shot at the big time was wearing on him. He began to sound bitter. He insisted he was being blackballed, that people were out to see he never made it.

Eventually the opportunities dried up. When things didn't work out for Fly in the Continental Basketball Association and the Eastern League, it was off to play for teams in Europe. And when those chances ran out, it was back to Brooklyn and the streets he came from. But instead of Fly taking the streets, the streets took him. Fly got hooked on drugs and spent his days wandering the neighborhood and getting high. He hung out in doorways. As he says, he "was nowhere." At his physical worst, he was regularly freebasing cocaine, and his weight was down to 106 pounds.

Rock bottom came in February of 1987. After a pickup game in Starrett City, there was an argument about money. Fly was one of the combatants. An off-duty court officer wielding a shotgun was a friend of the other man. When the buckshot started flying, Fly sustained severe injuries. He lost a lung, part of his stomach, part of one kidney. And he ended up doing fourteen months in prison on robbery and weapons convictions, among others. He would later return to prison when he got two years for drug possession. In jail, Fly was a sort of celebrity. Prisoners asked him for his autograph.

That's not the end of the Fly Williams saga. He got out. He got straight. He is married with children. He occasionally plays ball in an over-forty league. And best yet, he is trying to help today's children learn from his mistakes. He often speaks to kids at youth centers and junior basketball clinics: "I'm trying to give something positive to kids," Williams says. "Tell them my story. Maybe they can learn from it."

Roger Rubin is a student of the "city game" and a sports-writer for the New York Daily News.

AP/Wide World

Survival of the Toughest

Do unto others, but do it first

INTERVIEW BY MICHAEL KAMBER

I've been in this area since day one, sixty-eight years ago. I was born on the corner of Navy and Prospect Streets, right across the street from the Navy Yard. Woke up with reveille and went to bed with taps. My father helped build the Big "A," the *Arizona* that went down at Pearl Harbor.

My grandparents came from Naples around 1860. My parents were born here. My father—first he worked at Wallabout Market. Then he worked for the sanitation department, made thirty-three dollars a week. I had five brothers and four sisters. My brother Peewee took care of Carmine. Carmine took care of me. I took care of Frankie. Frankie took care of Benny. And last my brother Ally came in, and we all took care of him. We took care of each other. I had hamburger, you had hamburger. I had steak, you had steak.

Back then we had respect. I used to be standing on the corner of Hudson Avenue and Prospect Street, and my grandmother would come out of the store with a bushel of groceries. God forbid if I didn't run over and take them from her. And when you seen the old-timers from the neighborhood, if you were smoking on the corner and the ladies passed by—you threw the cigarette away, you tipped your hat, you said, "Hello, Grandma."

We had a couple of rich families down the neighborhood, and they used to give my mother clothes. My mother couldn't afford to buy us all shoes, so I put on the shoes they gave us one day and went to school. This rich kid said in front of the class, "Hey, he's got my shoes on." I felt that big. Never again. I took those fuckin' shoes off. I decided to rob everything that ain't nailed down. Robbed shoes, socks, you name it, so nobody would say, "You got my shoes on."

When I was old enough, I went out and shined shoes on Sands Street for the sailors. And robbed 'em—whatever they had. They'd be drunk, their wallet hanging out of their pocket. I'd take two dollars, three dollars, buy my brother some shoes. One brother, he helped the other brother.

We used to rob the freight trains. That building there—that used to be Scripps pharmaceutical. We used to go in there and rob aspirins. On this corner, we had Mason Mints candies. We used to rob them, too. Robbed everything that wasn't nailed down.

Our gang—we were the Sands Street Boys. You had the Navy Street Boys, the Coney Island Boys, the Red Hook Stompers, the Gowanus Stompers, the South Brooklyn Tigers. We were the toughest gang in Brooklyn. We beat up marines and robbed them. The Navy Street Boys come down here one time with about thirty-five guys. Thirteen of us take them down to the tanks, and the Italian bookmakers are on the side, taking bets. Our bookmakers tell their bookmakers, "These kids down here, they fight sailors and marines. They'll knock their fuckin' brains out." We all came out with chair legs. They were fighting with their hands. Whack 'em across the top of the fuckin' nose, break their nose.

I got arrested twenty-seven times. My uncle went down the Eighty-Fourth Precinct and paid off every time. The last time I had six guns on me, and he had to pay $100 a gun to the lieutenant. That was a lot of money back then. They only booked me once out of all them arrests, but I got so hot I had to leave the neighborhood. So I joined the army.

After I came back from Korea, I found a nice girl. She was good. So I got married, and I said, "Let me change my ways." I took the city test, and I passed it. I worked as a gardener in Williamsburg, in one of the

Dockhand Genaro Filosa: tough enough to survive the Brooklyn waterfront.

city projects. Once I was on my lunch break, and we were playing knock rummy. One of the city housing cops comes in and throws the arm on me. And he pulls me out of the chair. So I says, "Take it easy, pal, you're hurting me." He won't let go, so I come down with my boot, and I break his toe. They rushed him to St. Catherine's Hospital. Couple hours later he comes back, he catches me in the room, and he says, "I wanna see you at five o'clock."

So I says, "No problem."

Michael Kamber

I was about twenty-eight years old. Had a legitimate job, I wanna be a nice guy, okay? I punch my card, we're going home from work, and he's waiting outside with his partner. His partner's got a uniform on. He had a gun on him. So I says to the guy, "If you're gonna start something, take the piece off." "Naw, don't worry," he says. "I ain't gonna do nothing with the gun." As he's talking I hit him, and he goes down. But he was drunk. I could smell it. So the first thing he did was go for the gun. As he went to the gun, I kicked his brains out. The superintendent came out and saw me kicking him 'cause he went for the piece. They stopped the fight. I had to go before the civil service commission. I had seventeen witnesses, but nobody showed up for me and I got fired.

Now I got no more job, and I got a baby. So I seen some people, went down to the pier. Nine years I worked down on the piers on Buttermilk Channel, at Van Brunt Street, right by the old Domino sugarhouse. I was about the only Italian down there. I worked with the Polacks from Greenpoint, we took coffee off the barges, loaded it into the warehouses. Had a small hook for the left and a big hook for the right. Grab the bags with the hooks and throw 'em up on the flats—stack 'em twenty-five high. Hundred-and-ten-pound bags, three or four thousand bags a day.

First day on the job, end of the day, I went home half-dead. And I was out for three days 'cause I couldn't move. My hands were all cramped up. They actually had to open my hands to get the hooks out of them. They had blisters on top of blisters on top of blisters. How we

BROOKLYN ON FILM

The Chase of the Century

Good guys in hot pursuit of the bad guys have become a staple of modern urban crime films, and the streets of Brooklyn are a favorite location both for crime films in general and chase films in particular.

One defining example of this genre is the 1971 film *The French Connection*, based on the real-life story of two detectives who in the early 1960s uncovered a multimillion-dollar smuggling ring between Marseilles and New York. In cat-and-mouse fashion, the pair of undercover cops (portrayed by Gene Hackman and Roy Scheider) track the heroin-importing criminals throughout eighty-six locations in New York City, including the Brooklyn neighborhoods of Bedford-Stuyvesant, Coney Island, Brooklyn Heights and Bensonhurst.

Bypassing the tidy look of backlot studio re-creations, the movie's atmosphere of urban conflict is enhanced by the gritty realism of its on-location filming. Andrew Sarris wrote in *The Village Voice* at the time of the film's release that he had never seen "a movie as capable of making me fall in love again with every last shred of rubbish and garbage that constitutes the New York experience."

The famous chase scene—one of the most suspenseful in the course of movie history—was filmed in Bensonhurst.

The French Connection, 1971

Detective "Popeye" Doyle (Hackman) races after one of the murderers, who has hijacked an elevated subway train and shot the operator. Pursuing the perpetrator in a car on the streets below, he careens wildly around innocent pedestrians and has hair-raising skirmishes with interfering surface transport.

This Brooklyn-based chase scene made an indelible impression upon the contemporary moviegoing audience and evidently upon the Academy. The film garnered five Oscars for best picture, best director (William Friedkin) and best actor (Hackman), as well as screenplay and editing awards.
—*Jon Gartenberg*

MOMA Film Stills Archive

cured them—we broke the blisters and put the axle grease from the hi-lo on there. And my hands, they were like rock after that. If I were to smack you, I woulda took your head right off your shoulders.

We had hard work. That's the way it was down there. You broke your ass. And it was nice—you could go swimming off the docks when it was warm. I was making maybe two hundred, two fifty a week—'cause we don't work every day. When the ships were in, we worked. When the ships was out, we didn't work. So then, if I came home with two hundred a week, I was lucky. But when you worked, you worked right around the clock to get the stuff unloaded and get the ship out of there. And that was it 'til the next day, the next week, whenever the next ship came in.

The clothes used to come in. Leather coats, leather jackets, from Italy. Shoes used to come in from Brazil, and they used to take a walk. They used to walk away. We all got a little bit of it, that's all. It wasn't much.

About 1971 we heard the pier was closing down. There was no more work. The containers ruined everything. A container ís like a big truck. They put cars in it, refrigerators in it. And they take a crane and put it right in the hold of the ship. If you have fifty or sixty containers on a ship, you don't need all these guys. Instead of twenty guys, you need six. So the piers closed down and the jobs went to Jersey.

I was in the union from the 1950s until 1984. They took care of the workers. Your wife was sick, you went to the union. Your kid was sick, you needed benefits, they gave them to you. Any problem you had, you went to the union, they settled it for you. If you had trouble with the boss, you went to the union and they took it to arbitration or whatever and settled it. That's why you paid dues. You need the union, without them, forget about it. And if you don't belong to the union, you do not work. You don't work on the docks, or you don't work in the Navy Yard.

They give you thirty days to join once you start work. If you don't join in thirty days, they put you out. It's a union shop. I went to the Navy Yard and joined the Maritime Union. I was there ten, eleven years. You paid dues by the month, they took it right out of your pay—eight,

nine dollars a month, that's all. Wasn't big money. The union is necessary—without a union the bosses'll kill you down there. They don't give a shit. "It ain't safe down there," guys say. But the bosses don't give a damn: "You don't wanna go down? We'll send somebody else down." To get killed.

Yeah, we had shape-ups. You checked in at the hiring hall in the morning, and if they needed you, they put you to work. If they didn't need you, they told you to come back the next day. They go in there and say, "We need twenty guys," boom, boom, boom, boom. Whether the guy's experienced or not, they put him on the ship. They make him a sweep-up man. Or they say, "We need ten pipe fitters." They take ten pipe fitters out of the union hall and put 'em on the ship. That's what a shape-up is. You had guys that went down to the union hall year after year. They just wanted to be shape guys—they didn't want to work steady. They worked two, three days a week.

This neighborhood where we lived, they destroyed it, tore it down to build the projects. They drove us all out. Before they knocked it down, this was all two-family houses. This wasn't no slum. The people were poor, but you could eat off the floor. We made sure of that 'cause we used to rob the Kirkman's soap factory. You washed your dishes with it, you washed your clothes with it, you washed your head with it. Best soap in the world, and one bar would last you two years. It looked like a brick. What we used to do with it, we'd put it in a sock and hit you in the head with it. Just exactly like a brick.

Any regrets for the heads I broke? No, 'cause I got my head broke, too. Got my jaw broke, too, and my arm. When we got picked up by the cops, we got the shit kicked out of us. We didn't holler that the cop hit us. We knew we done wrong. If we didn't do wrong today, we done wrong yesterday. We didn't get picked up yesterday, so we got picked up today for yesterday.

You do unto others, but you do it first. That's the Good Book. And don't get caught.

Michael Kamber is a photographer and writer. He is compiling an oral history of DUMBO, the Navy Yard and Williamsburg.

OF MEN & BIRDS

Tales from the Coney Island Pigeon Exchange

TEXT & PHOTOGRAPHS
BY MARA FAYE LETHEM

After my first visit to the Coney Island Pigeon Exchange, I knew I would never look at a pigeon the same way. Like all New Yorkers, I'd always known a pigeon when I saw one. I even knew it was illegal to feed the hardy "street rats." But I found that pigeon raising can easily become a full-time job, with feeding, inoculations and coop maintenance. Plus breeding and racing…

The Pigeon Exchange is mostly a pet-food store with birds downstairs, but it's also a social club upstairs for a group of maybe twenty men whose bond is their love of pigeons. It's not a passion that everyone can feel: "I would tell you a lie if I was to say we just saw a pigeon and liked it," one guy told me. "Most of us flyers grew up around our fathers' flocks and got into it that way." There aren't many young flyers, or women. Raising pigeons is so much work that it is often done in partnership. "It's a big job," the men agreed. "It takes discipline. We are not raising poultry."

Fancy pigeons aren't as smart as homing pigeons, or "homers," and the pleasures of raising them are simpler. Let the pigeons out in the morning and evening, and they fly around and around the coop. You get them going with a long pole with a T-shirt tied to the end. And you can herd them into another flyer's flock, hoping that when they mix, some of his birds will come home with yours. That's called "catch and keep." You can charge a buck for each bird's return. That's as competitive as it gets.

Mara Faye Lethem is a Brooklyn photographer, writer and pigeon watcher.

"

Who doesn't
love this
life is crazy.
This is a
beautiful life."

Sal and Danny

Sal has flown pigeons for
fifty-seven years. He learned
it from his father. "Who
doesn't love this life is crazy.
This is a beautiful life," he
tells me one morning as we
watch the birds fly. Sal's
nickname is Sally Bird.

Danny Triola started flying
when he was twelve years
old with two pigeons in an
abandoned dumbwaiter. "I
don't want to say they saved
my life," he cautions, "but I
grew up in Coney Island, full
of riffraff…"

When Danny talks of
the value of pigeon flying,
of going up on his roof when
he's frustrated or aggravated,
it evokes the young Marlon
Brando of *On the Waterfront*.
Danny flies only one kind
of fancy—West of England
"Tumblers," named for their
somersaulting flight. The
West of Englanders have
"boots"—feathers on their
feet that give them a
somewhat comical gait. They
could not be confused with
street pigeons.

Breed the Better Bird

Ironically, it is the purebred homers that most resemble "street rats," but they are bigger, more muscular, with creamy blue colors. "They are not pets," I was reminded.

Breed the better bird and take home the trophy, experienced racers say. It's your strain plus your system, your handling, your training. The pigeons are bred on a schedule to be a certain age and already trained when the racing season begins. If you don't want your birds to mate, you can trick them by putting wooden eggs in the nest. Both sexes incubate eggs, but won't mate while incubating. Eventually you have to separate the hens and the cocks—they wise up after three weeks when the wooden eggs don't hatch.

Once the chicks reach maturity at two and a half months, the race training begins. At first the homers just hang out around the coop. Then you start taking them about ten miles away and letting them fly home. Gradually you increase the distances, fine-tuning the birds' internal compass. What drives that homing instinct? "Pigeons want safety. And mating—same thing what makes a guy come home."

> Pigeons want safety. And mating — same thing what makes a guy come home."

"When you win a race, the guys in the club shake your hand."

The Pigeon Races

The birds race at up to sixty miles per hour for five to six hundred miles. They may encounter hawks and falcons. Some farmers shoot at them. If they run into bad weather and have to land, there can be many casualties.

The Frank Viola Pigeon Racing Club, on Bay Fiftieth and Cropsey, governs the complex betting and is the place where Viola and others check clocks and calculate times. Because homing pigeons race to their own lofts, which are various distances from the release site, figuring out who won takes some math.

Each homer has a leg band for each race, and when he arrives at his coop, his owner quickly takes off the band and puts it into a special clock. The clocks are then taken to the club for tallying.

For the Frank Viola Futurity Race, the bands are $100 each. A proven race-winning pigeon can cost up to $10,000. But with the costs, even if you win the first-place prize money and a lot of bets, there's no way to make a profit. "When you win a race, the guys in the club shake your hand," one flyer explained. "But there are also guys that don't want to shake your hand."

Potluck in Red Hook

The kids who came to dinner

BY JERRY NACHMAN

When I was a kid and lived in the Red Hook housing projects at 452 Columbia Street, it never occurred to me that we were technically poor. We ate well, some kids had bikes, we played ball in Coffey Park, our parents played poker four nights a week, and in the summer we took the buses, trains and trolley cars to Coney Island and Brighton Beach.

One thing we did not have was air-conditioning.

In the 1950s it was a violation of Housing Authority policy for a project tenant to install a window air conditioner in an apartment—not that many residents could afford one. The theory then was that if you had enough money to buy an air conditioner, you had too much money to live in public housing. My father recalled that in the 1940s, when we arrived in the projects, having a telephone was prohibited for the same reason. I assume that by the time I came along, telephones had gone from the luxury to necessity category. My earliest memories include our telephone number: TRiangle 5-3333. Air conditioners are permitted today, of course. In recent years, as I would drive along the FDR Drive to the *Post*, I would note the window a/c boxes and the service trucks from Manhattan Cable parked outside, and be thankful that current residents of the projects no longer suffered under those old Dickensian rules.

My strongest recollection of life in the Red Hook Projects has nothing to do with crime—which is what most people now associate with them. It's a situation that would be unimaginable in most projects today. Because of the air-conditioner ban, the apartments were stifling hot in the summer. Remember the architecture: six-story buildings of steel, brick and concrete, with linoleum floors and thin paper window shades.

So, in a vertical South Brooklyn imitation of Levittown, tenants (I'm certain at their own expense) installed screen doors each summer. Plain old-fashioned wood-frame screen doors with a hook-and-eye "lock" on the inside, usually left unlatched. The thick metal regular doors stood open day and night, permitting what-

ever breeze there was to enter the apartments. Imagine today's city housing project tenants reducing their security to a door you could literally poke a hand through. It was noisy, of course. This was before the time of transistor radios—which changed everything—but there was much clucking about the loud parties.

These screen doors provided a special benefit to us kids. Late each afternoon, after playing baseball on the grass or "Johnny on the pony" in the courtyard, we

Russell Christian

would ride the elevators and roam the hallways, sniffing. And we would land in a bunch in whatever apartment was transmitting the most compelling aromas: Mrs. Sheehy's corned beef and cabbage on the stove. Franks and beans at the Schwartzes'. Arroz con pollo at the Sanchezes'. The Motisi family's spaghetti and meatballs, which would always mean sausages and chicken necks.

We were The Kids Who Came to Dinner. Of course, it was called *supper* in that world. Happened right around five o'clock. Sometimes there were two seatings, since all fathers didn't appreciate finding half a dozen strange kids at the table when they came home from work. But no one ever questioned who was there or why. Often a mother would burst in wondering why her kid was eating in someone else's house. The "host" mother would reassure her neighbor not to worry, her kid would probably be showing up in the other lady's apartment tomorrow afternoon.

My memories of those suppers do have a tinge of guilt: my mother, as I recall, was the lousiest cook in the building, so I spent a lot of evenings eating out.

Jerry Nachman, former columnist and editor in chief of the New York Post *and former news director of WCBS-TV, is now a writer in Los Angeles.*

NOW & THEN A number of Brooklyn thoroughfares remained unpaved until the twentieth century. Flatbush Avenue was once a mud-choked turnpike complete with toll booths.

The Joint Is Mobbed

"Leave the gun, take the cannolis."—The Godfather

BY JOE GILFORD
& DAVID SEIDEMAN

When you talk about organized crime in New York, it is really Brooklyn that has long figured most prominently as both territory and seat of power for most of the crime families in the five boroughs. Among the notable native Brooklynites of recent history: Lucky Luciano, Joe Colombo, Joe Bonanno, Vito Genovese, Crazy Joe Gallo, Sammy "the Bull" Gravano and John Gotti. It may be no coincidence that Brooklyn probably has more good Italian restaurants per square mile than any city in America. Not to say, of course, that these and other Italian restaurants in the borough are themselves mobbed up—only that the Men of Respect have never needed to go hungry here. When looking for a place to relax and enjoy the good food and drink, their choices are many and varied. Listed below are some of the favorites in neighborhoods traditionally dominated by certain families.*

Carroll Gardens

(Colombo/Gambino families)

Territory favored by both the Colombo and Gambino families, the latter having become the more powerful through the last forty years. Old man Carlo and his brothers held sway over the whole borough for fifty years. John Gotti is its most recent fallen—and possibly last—real leader. Though the other families held small

enclaves, they were always considered colonies of the ever-dominant Gambinos. Despite wholesale yuppification, some observers continue to regard this neighborhood as a *Goodfellas* theme park.

Casa Rosa (384 Court Street) has been owned and operated by the Illiano family for generations. Two brothers, Tony and Frank, inherited it. Tony took over while Frank, a former boxer, continued his own consulting for the Genovese faction. He's known as "Punchy." Try the house linguine.

Nino's (215 Union Street, just down the block from the Seventy-Sixth Precinct house) still boasts a parade of Ban-Lon for lunch. Don't worry, everyone's here to eat and maybe to listen to Sinatra on the juke. Just don't say names like Carmine Gallante or Roy DeMeo too loudly—some bad memories there. The Sicilian pizza is hearty.

Park Slope/Gowanus

(Colombo family)

At the foot of the slope is a piece of the waning Gowanus panhandle between Third and Union Streets and Nevins Street and Fourth Avenue. A holdover from the days when this little part of the "flats" between the inclines of Park Slope and Carroll Gardens was once the center of upper Brooklyn's mob activity, and several places here were favorites of the Colombos.

Jackie's Fifth Amendment (down Fifth Avenue at Seventh Street). Straight out of *Donnie Brasco*. Sure enough, it is named after the testimony of the most famous stool pigeon in history, Genovese underboss Joe Valachi. In 1961 he squealed good for the Kefauver commission. So Jackie felt a statement needed to be made.

---

*Our sources for the choices include a veteran NYPD detective and a prosecutor who has long kept tabs on the Brooklyn wiseguys; in fact, it's worth noting that some of New York's finest have held dinner parties at some of the same restaurants.

Left: George B. Brainerd, Brooklyn Museum of Art/ Brooklyn Public Library–Brooklyn Collection

This is a no-nonsense bar, and food is not really its reason for being here. Sure you can get a sandwich, or even send out for a pizza. But if you're just looking for a nice place to hold a meeting, try Jackie's.

Monte's (451 Carroll Street). Open here since 1906, and long a favorite spot for Joe Profaci's boys. Until its recent redesign, known as Monte's Venetian Room (a sly reference to the nearby Gowanus Canal?).

This nabe is where the early machinations of one of the last mob wars took shape: in the late '60s, racketeer Joey Gallo, and his brother Albert tried to wrest control from the then community-minded Joe Colombo. Old man Colombo had founded the Italian-American Anti-Defamation League in an attempt to dispel the myth that all Italians were mobsters. He was assassinated in—where else?—Columbus Circle on Columbus Day by shooters allegedly hired by Joe Gallo. Gallo, in his turn, bought it in Little Italy at the now-famous Umberto's Clam House. The hit was authorized by succeeding boss Carmine "the Snake" Persico. What distinguished this hit from all others was that Gallo's family was with him at the time—a big mob no-no. But at least Persico had the decency to do it in Manhattan and not back in the neighborhood.

Legend has it that Sinatra's "Rat Pack" held a post-Copacabana party at Monte's, featuring Sammy Davis, Jr., in an all-night, doors-locked sing-a-thon.

Monte's appetizers are not to be missed, especially the deep-fried mozzarella sandwiches and the breaded stuffed eggplant with marinara sauce.

Two Toms (255 Third Avenue). Old factories and shops surround this pocket-sized joint from the heyday of the Gowanus Canal as a Brooklyn industrial center. Its cofounders, both named Tom, started the place about forty years ago and promptly sold it to the present owners. No one remembers their last names. Always a friendly hangout. There's no menu; they tell you what you're going to eat. You'll like it—especially the antipasti, the raviolis, and the biggest and best pork chops in town.

Bay Ridge
(Gambino family)
Pastel's disco is now called Ecstasy, the Brown Derby is now called Gazebo, and Club Rio is gone. These three were the tonier hangouts. Generally, Bay Ridge has long been "international" territory, as everyone was there to drink, enjoy, dance, charm the ladies and possibly exchange blunt objects. But rough stuff was frowned upon in these establishments.

Latavola (9202 Fort Hamilton Parkway), noted in the autobiography of Salvatore (Sammy "the Bull") Gravano, the murderous underboss of the Gambino family who turned coat on John Gotti and lived to talk about it, as the place where he liked to take his wife out to dinner. To this day, the hairdos on a Friday or Saturday night are worth the trip. Gravano probably appreciated the utility of the mirrored walls . . . and the linguine-and-lobster, which is served with both red and white sauces.

Bensonhurst
(Colombo/Gambino families)
Still an unreconstructed Italian-American nabe, one that even Sammy "the Bull" Gravano described as "pretty tough," and he grew up there. So, earlier, did Joe Profaci and Joe Colombo. A tight-knit community that knew where the power was, and knew when to keep its mouth shut. Witnesses to almost any kind of action generally could be counted on to come down with "Bensonhurst amnesia," a common local affliction.

Joe's of Avenue U (287 Avenue U). The name probably says it all, but you need to go there for the riceball with sauce and ricotta. This is just the kind of quick diner that most wiseguys favor for a fast lunch or snack. Now operated by Russians, but this hasn't hurt the food or changed the clientele much, as Joe's has been a popular neighborhood spot for decades.

Villa Vivolo (8829 Twenty-Sixth Avenue). A miniature fairy-tale castle complete with drawbridge, plunked down right in the middle of the squat red-brick two-family homes of this quiet residential block. Famed for its austere interior and fine cuisine. This is where old man Gambino came for the linguine with garlic and oil. One can almost see the neighbors still peering through their blinds as he made his weekly pilgrimage.

Sheepshead Bay

(Gambino family)

The center of it all is Emmons Avenue, where the gentle bobbing of fishing boats brings a touch of coastal New England to Brooklyn. The street had fallen on hard times in the '60s and it looked like a long-shot comeback. But with the expansion of the incomparable Randazzo's and the reopening of the landmark Lundy's, the old festive atmosphere has returned to this bayside strip with new outdoor cafés and restaurants. On a nice summer night it was like being in Fellini's boyhood Rimini. With today's immigration patterns, however, you could be anywhere from the Crimea to Shanghai.

Randazzo's Clam Bar (2023 Emmons Avenue). It's been here, facing the waterfront, for half a century. The longevity probably can be traced to its reliability with its namesake clams—and oysters and shrimp. Try the fried calamari with their famous hot sauce. Old man Gambino loved Randazzo's and was a frequent patron of the live bar: after a hard day of racketeering, anybody's entitled to a cold beer and a little scungilli.

Canarsie/Mill Basin

(Lucchese/Bonanno families)

Here in the outlying extremities of the borough, the pace slows down a bit. The chance breeze from Rockaway Bay will cool any summer night. The lovely suburban streets have prefixes, e.g., Paerdegat Seventh Street, in tribute to the original landowners.

The Market Bar (Remsen & Foster Avenues). A mob landmark in what used to be the

bustling wholesale fruit and vegetable market. A guy named Blackie ran the market for Lucchese underboss Paul Varrio (played by Paul Sorvino in *Goodfellas*). Later, the Gambinos were able to muscle in. This is the site of one of the most famous gaffes in mob history: early in the tenuous partnership between the two families, hotheaded Varrio soldier Tommy Zumo, feeling a need to prove his continued loyalty to the Lucchese faction, went out of his way to jostle and then verbally abuse Carlo Gambino with words to the effect of "No one fucks with Paulie's crew!" It's been suggested Varrio was instructed to help Tommy attain a deeper understanding of mob protocol. Whatever enlightenment Varrio was able to provide is not known, as Tommy was never heard from again.

Joe Gilford and David Seideman are—each in his own way—writers and Brooklynites.

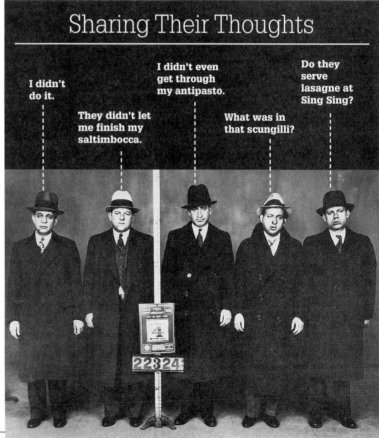

Sharing Their Thoughts

I didn't do it.

They didn't let me finish my saltimbocca.

I didn't even get through my antipasto.

What was in that scungilli?

Do they serve lasagne at Sing Sing?

NYC Municipal Archives

Godfathers?

Organized crime in America is, to a great extent, a Brooklyn phenomenon. In the early 1900s, there were water-front gangs and affiliations of criminals by ethnic or national groups. The first famous criminal organization arose in East New York (it came to be known as Murder Inc.), and the major mob bosses and predecessors of today's organized-crime families came from the Brooklyn streets. Among them: Joe Adonis, Carlo Gambino, Alphonse Capone, Vito Genovese, the Gallo brothers, Bugsy Siegel, and those whose official portraits appear here.

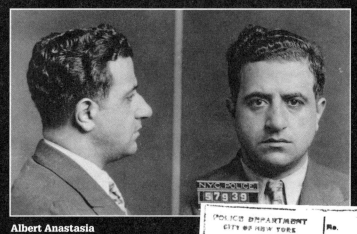

Albert Anastasia

POLICE DEPARTMENT
CITY OF NEW YORK　　　No.

Name Albert Amastasio
Alias
Residence 387 Clinton St Bklyn
Crime Vagrancy
Age 34--1936　Height 5 09
Weight 202　Build
Hair Brown　Eyes Brown
Color White　Comp. Dark
Born Italy
Occupation Oil Salesman
Date of Arrest
Officer
Remarks

　　27　　11
　　28　　01　　19
F. P. CLASS

POLICE DEPARTMENT
CITY OF NEW YORK　　　No.

B-72321
Name Chas. Lucania "Lucky"
Chas. Reed.
265 E. 10th St.
Fel. Assault
34-1931　Height 5'9 3/4
152　Build Med.
Blond　Eyes Brown
White　Comp Dark
N.Y.
Chauffeur
of Arrest 2-2-31
Phillips, M.O.P.

Lucky Luciano

72321

Meyer Lansky

POLICE DEPARTMENT
CITY OF NEW YORK　　No.

B.70258
Meyer Lansky
Residence 125 & 3rd St.
Homicide
26 (1928)　Height 5-4
136　Build
Dk Chest　Eyes Bl
W　Comp Sallow
Russia

Carmine Galante

66994

NYC Municipal Archives

One Tough Judge

On putting John Gotti away for good

BY DOROTHY WEISS

he 1991 trial of mobster John Gotti for murder and racketeering, held in the federal courthouse on Cadman Plaza, was a landmark event in recent Brooklyn history. It was the end of a long line of failed attempts to convict the most powerful don in organized crime. Often indicted for murder and other criminal activities, Gotti, alleged head of the Gambino family, had become known as "the Teflon don" because no charges would stick to him—until the '91 federal trial.

The key players—and the best witnesses to that epic trial—were U.S. Attorney John Gleeson, the prosecutor who tried the case (and who was then appointed to the bench in 1994), and Judge I. Leo Glasser, who presided over it. In 1999, Gleeson and Glasser were interviewed about the events from the start of the trial in January 1991 until June 1994, when Judge Glasser sentenced John Gotti to life in prison.

What kind of judge did it take to convict John Gotti?

Prosecutor Gleeson: In a case like this, everything depends on the judge. There was nothing more important to the defense lawyers and the prosecution than who

John Gotti, boss of the Gambino family, presides over the defense table at his 1991 racketeering trial.

UPI/Corbis

Prosecutor John Gleeson

would be the judge on the Gotti trial. We make arrests, we indict, we prosecute, but the outcome of a case depends on the judge. I'll never forget the day when Judge Glasser was selected to preside over the Gotti case. It was December 11, 1990, to be exact.

The selection of judges for cases in the federal system is totally random. The judges' names are literally pulled out of a drum. I didn't go to the assignment lottery that day. I waited by the phone. I was extremely anxious about the selection. I had been privy to the activities of the "Gambino Squad" at the FBI during the course of the investigation. They'd done months of stealth work leading up to the indictment for murder and racketeering of mob boss John Gotti, underboss Sammy "the Bull" Gravano and Frank LoCascio, consigliere to the Gambino organized crime family.

On the day of the judge selection, everyone on the Squad was in the room—prosecutors, FBI agents, defense lawyers. I was told that the feeling in the room was like an old-fashioned maternity ward . . . expectant fathers pacing, wondering, "What's it gonna be?" "What's it gonna be?"

When the call finally came from the assignment room, the disappointment was palpable. I could hear the groans. Judge I. Leo Glasser's name had been pulled. Judge Glasser doesn't have a reputation as a prosecutor's judge. He doesn't favor the government. He doesn't favor *anyone*. He's fiercely independent. He's stern in the courtroom. He'll chew you out if you're less than meticulous in discharging your constitutional obligations as a prosecutor and less than professional in following procedure.

Judge Glasser: I never heard the story about the groans from the prosecution.

Judge Glasser, you had no leaning toward the prosecution? Even though you had the chance to go down in history as the judge who de-coated "the Teflon don"?

Judge Glasser: No. I try to be fair. I call the shots as I see them.

What were the key decisions at the beginning of the trial?

Prosecutor Gleeson: The granting of the motion to disqualify Gotti's counsel, and the judge's decision to sequester the jury—the only jury ever to be sequestered in the Eastern district, as far as I know.

Why did you disqualify Gotti's lawyers?

Judge Glasser: The evidence—the video- and audiotapes that were presented to me—left no doubt that they were house counsel to the Gambino organized crime family. The frequency with which their names turned up on the audiotapes and their faces on the videotapes would have, in effect, made them unsworn witnesses at the trial. There is a common misapprehension that a defendant has an absolute right to the counsel of his choice without exception. But the integrity of the judicial process trumps the defendant's right to counsel of his choice.

Did either of you feel intimidated during the trial?

Judge Glasser: No.

Prosecutor Gleeson: No. There was an occasion when members of the Gambino family brought in a prizefighter, and he sat with them in the front row of the spectators' section. One juror sent a note to the judge saying that she was feeling intimidated by a man in the front row who was glaring at the jurors in a menacing way. He was immediately excluded by the judge from further attendance at the trial.

Did the Gotti people try any other shenanigans during the trial?

Prosecutor Gleeson: As a matter of fact, there was a stunt during jury selection. Flyers started appearing on the Long Island Railroad, and then all around town, with a drawing of a rat with the face of [chief government witness] Sammy Gravano. I had a fit. Of course, I thought the bad guys were behind it all, and I was afraid prospective jurors would be tainted. No one would claim responsibility. The defendants shrugged. The defense lawyers said they had nothing to do with it. I brought the flyers to Judge Glasser's attention.

A less experienced judge would have held a hearing. But Judge Glasser took care of the situation on the spot. Turning to Gotti, who was sitting at the defense table, he said, "You've been complaining that you're not getting a fair trial. I don't know who posted all these flyers around town. I'm not accusing you, but if you're really interested in getting a fair trial it might be a good idea to stop those flyers if you can stop them."

It was a great moment: Boss meets Boss.

How did Gotti respond?

Prosecutor Gleeson: The flyers mysteriously disappeared the following day.

Did the trial take a toll on you?

Judge Glasser: I don't know about a toll. I'd wake up in the morning, shave, look at myself in the mirror and say, "Try to preside over this trial as fairly and objectively as you can."

Prosecutor Gleeson: It was definitely tense in court.

Judge Glasser (nodding toward Gleeson): He took a lot of abuse.

Prosecutor Gleeson: So did you, Judge.

Judge Glasser: Yes, but I had the power of contempt.

Prosecutor Gleeson: There was some high school stuff. I'd walk by the defense table on my way to a bench conference with the judge, and Gotti would invariably make disparaging remarks.

How did that make you feel?

Prosecutor Gleeson: It got on my nerves. I told the judge what was going on. He said to Gotti, "If you continue the inappropriate remarks, you'll be observing the rest of your trial on a TV screen in a cell."

Judge Glasser, you've been described in the media as a strict and stern judge, a grouch and a curmudgeon. Also as sharp, wry and witty. During the Gotti trial, were there occasions for wit?

Judge Glasser: I suppose I had to use my wits one day during the trial when I received a note that some of the jurors, who'd been sequestered for weeks, were requesting conjugal visits.

How did you handle that?

Judge Glasser: I called the only other federal judge I knew who had sequestered a jury. I told him about my dilemma. He said, "What are you going to do, Judge?" I said, "I think I'll allow it." He said, "Good for you. I think that's what I would do."

There may be no non-mob person on earth who has spent as much time with real gangsters as the two of you. What are they really like?

Prosecutor Gleeson: Most people, including myself, tend to see the world in black and white, good guys versus bad guys. I remember seeing John, Sammy and Frank for the first time. I thought Sammy Gravano was the baddest-looking guy I'd ever seen. We had all heard that he was a killer. He had slit eyes. He looked evil. Then Sammy flipped [i.e., became a witness for the prosecution], and I spent a great deal of time with him. It was literally hundreds of hours. I got to know him well. I laughed with him. He was smart, engaging and funny.

Through Sammy, I discovered that in the majority of people the lines of good and bad blur. It's easier for me to see that now. These characters are more complex than myth makes them out to be.

Judge I. Leo Glasser

AP/Wide World

Judge Glasser, you observed Sammy Gravano during the course of many trials—the Gotti trial and the subsequent trials at which he testified. What kind of man is he?

Judge Glasser: To answer that question one must begin to understand the kind of man he was, and that requires an understanding of the structure of an organized crime family and the protocols by which it functions. Briefly, one becomes a member of such a family by being "made." Members are "made" by the boss of the family in consultation with his underboss and consigliere. Your father must be 100 percent Italian; you must be willing to murder and, not unusually, must have demonstrated your ability to "do a piece of work," meaning murder in the argot of the mob, on behalf of the family. Indeed, in a conversation between Gotti and Frank LoCascio in the apartment above the Ravenite Club, a Manhattan storefront at 247 Mulberry Street that was the secret meeting place of the Gambino organization, Gotti was heard to say, "I want this guy to do more than killing."

In addition to pledging absolute loyalty to the boss and to the family, you must take the oath of *omerta*, or the oath of silence. The ceremony prescribed for the taking of that oath is burning the picture of a saint in the palm of the hand of the member being "made," who swears "I should burn like that saint if I violate that oath." Among the many rules "made" members have to obey is the rule that forbids cooperation with law enforcement, or, in the vernacular of the mob, becoming a "rat."

As a "made" member—indeed, as the underboss of the Gambino organized crime family—that was the life Gravano was sworn and bred to lead. When he made the difficult decision to cooperate he, in effect, made the seemingly impossible decision to become a different person and to live by a completely different set of values from those that ordered his life until then. He was surely aware that by violating his oath of *omerta*, the rest of his life was at risk of assassination by a gunman who, by killing him, would achieve instant status with the Mafia.

The jury obviously found Gravano a credible witness, and found him sincere when he said he was attempting to put the life of organized crime behind him. Investigators who have spent countless hours with him have come to believe that as well.

Do you believe that?

Prosecutor Gleeson: Gravano was the best witness of all time. There are forty-seven guys in jail because of Sammy.

Judge Glasser, you sentenced Gravano to five years in prison for nineteen murders. Four of the five years had already been served in detention. You were widely criticized for your leniency.

Judge Glasser: Yes. I took a beating for that. The saddest thing for me about the trial was the media's failure to publish the sentencing memorandum. I spent many hours preparing it. I thought it important to attempt to educate the community about the pernicious and costly impact the mob has upon it. In this city, organized crime has a virtual stranglehold on the construction industry. A yard of concrete could hardly be laid in this town without paying tribute to the mob. Trucks transporting building materials, clothing and other goods were taxed by the mob through its control of unions. The influence of the mob has been masked to a large extent by the media, which romanticizes it by printing images of smiling gangsters in thousand-dollar suits clambering in and out of limos and fashionable watering holes.

Portrayals of mob bosses as "godfathers" and neighborhood benefactors have raised them to folk-hero proportions. I thought it important to convey to the public that the Mafia exists for the sole reason of generating money for its members through crime—hijacking, gambling, extortion, loan-sharking, bribery, corruption and control of labor unions, drug dealing and murder.

The glamorizing of the mob and the destructive influence of that distorted view was brought home to me one day when I was in chambers in the midst of the Gotti trial. The phone rang and the operator asked whether I would accept a collect call. I asked what the call was about and a female voice on the line said, "It's about John

Gotti." I accepted the call. The voice then said, "I want to know what's happening to John Gotti." I asked, "What is your interest in him?" "He's my idol—I write to him and he even wrote back" was the reply. I asked what her name was and she told me. I asked where she was calling from and she said from a state in the South. I then asked, "How old are you?"—and the answer was "I'm fifteen." I wondered how many fifteen-year-old children across the country were seduced to idolize the likes of John Gotti.

Prosecutor Gleeson: If Gravano's sentence had been harsh, the guys on the street who kill people would have been popping corks. There was an important calibration to be made in the interest of encouraging cooperation. People who swooped in to criticize the sentence don't get it. There's a colossal disconnect over the demand for law enforcement, clean streets, ethics in government—and the disdain over friend betraying friend. Federal investigations use informants as a tool; this is how we take down criminals. Gravano is just a high-profile example. People like results, but they don't want to know about the job along the way—the business of fingerprints, voiceprints, informants and the like. No one wants to think about process. Judge Glasser's toughest decision was sentencing Gravano.

What is your response to the argument that Gravano's reward could encourage tainted testimony from other defendants looking for a light sentence?

Prosecutor Gleeson: A good lawyer can ferret out a liar and demonstrate lies to a jury.

Judge Glasser: I can't recall seeing any reference to Gravano that wasn't "rat," "snitch," "turncoat" or some other term of betrayal. I wonder whether there is a valid distinction to be drawn among informants. I'd assume that the informant who reported to a Nazi that his neighbor harbored a homosexual, Gypsy or Jew would deserve our contempt, and that the member of the World Trade Center bombing conspiracy who informed on the perpetrators would not. Gravano "ratted" on murderers.

Dorothy Weiss is a native of Brooklyn and a writer.

Why Sammy "the Bull" Flipped

Sammy Gravano began to feel betrayed by John Gotti and the rest of the mob. He had heard a snippet of one of the taped conversations in which Gotti was giving a diatribe about "Sammy making all the money." He knew John no longer trusted him. He must have been privy to conversations with Gotti like the one intercepted in the Mulberry Street apartment: "... every time we get a partner that don't agree with us, we kill him. You go to the boss and your boss kills him. He kills them. He okays it. Says it's all right, good...."

When it dawned on Sammy that Gotti didn't trust him, he said, "I knew the next step would be John giving the order to get rid of me. Once I realized that, I realized I'd have to kill him first. Then I thought if I kill John, I have to kill Frank. And if I kill Frank, I have to kill Tommy... and on and on... and I said, fugehdabboudit...."

AP/Wide World

Hot Summer Day

PHOTOGRAPH BY
EUGENE RICHARDS

"I was on my way home from a shoot at Gleason's Gym," recalls Richards, "and I passed these people all splashing and having a great time under the Manhattan Bridge. I knew there were some nice pictures there, but I felt it was such a private time that they'd tell me to go away. I got all the way to the subway and thought *I'm being stupid to pass this up.* So I walked back and asked, 'Would you mind my taking pictures?' By way of an answer, the little girl playfully threw a bucket of water on me. She got everything wet, but it was all in fun. They even offered me a seat. I realized it was my mistaken fantasy that city people weren't friendly. There were two daughters and a granddaughter. The grandmother is the one in the pool. Her husband ran a bodega within sight of the corner. I stayed there as long as I could. Finally I took the pictures, took off my shirt and got soaking wet myself. It turned out to be the opposite of a bad city day."

Eugene Richards is an award-winning photojournalist whose books include Americans We, The Knife and Gun Club *and* Cocaine True, Cocaine Blue.

Williamsburg Days

Being poor was good!

INTERVIEW WITH
MEL BROOKS

Okay now, I was born in Brooklyn at 515 Powell Street. I'm not sure exactly where Powell Street is, because I was very young when I was born and I couldn't even hold a pencil to write down my address.

My mother had four children. I was the baby, and when I was born my brother Lennie said he thought maybe a cat had snuck into the house. Because there were cat yells and screeches. But then he found out it was me and he was very disappointed, because he was dying to have a cat. He was eight years old at the time.

Sometimes people would ask me, years ago, "Where were you born?" And I'd say, "Williamsburg." And they'd say, "Virginia?" And I'd say, "Yes." Because I just wanted to be from Williamsburg, Virginia. I was young and foolish, and I thought it was somehow better. Now I know that the Brooklyn neighborhoods, especially Williamsburg, were possessed with *joie de vivre.*

We moved from Powell Street after my father died of tuberculosis, at thirty-four. I was about two years old then. His name was Maximilian Kaminsky. My son is named Maximilian Michael Brooks, after my father. My dad was a process server. My brother Lennie said it's too bad we don't have pictures or movies of our father serving these summonses, because he served summonses to some famous people, like actress Marilyn Miller, and he'd often get into the picture with them. He was known at the courthouse as "Process Server to the Stars." So you see, there was show business in my blood, even before I had blood.

My mother's name is Kate. Kate Kaminsky, but everyone called her Kitty. She was a redhead when I was a kid, and she was very good-natured. She was only in her early thirties, I think thirty-two, when my father died. And she had to raise these four boys. It wasn't easy, I'll tell you. My grandfather on my father's side lived in Bensonhurst, on Seventy-Sixth Street, and he helped her. He owned a herring business. He gave us money sometimes, or gobs of herring—which nobody wanted. But it was generous of him anyway. Lennie used to collect the herring, and when he'd leave Bensonhurst to go back to Williamsburg, he would have to sit in the motorman's cage, a little compartment in every car on the BMT that was more or less closed off. So the herring wouldn't, you know, fumigate the entire car.

I had a wonderful childhood. I often say everything was good up until nine and then it all went downhill. Up until nine, I didn't really have homework. I didn't have any responsibilities. We were really poor, but so was everybody else. And we always had enough to eat. Our poverty didn't really bother us, emotionally. There was always a gang of kids, and we were always playing one game or another. At Jewish holidays, we'd send hazelnuts spinning after walnuts, and if you hit the walnut, you got it, you owned it. We played all these wonderful games: we filled the tops of bottle caps with either orange peel or banana skin, to give them weight, and used them as checkers. We didn't have enough money to play pennies against the wall.

My mother took in work at home, and we'd help her. Her sister worked in the garment center, making bathing suits, and she'd bring back work for her sister—homework. She couldn't really leave us for too long because my brother Bernie and I were too little. So she went to work and had someone watch us for a few hours, until about noon or one o'clock, and then she'd come home with enormous bags of homework—bathing suit sashes that she turned inside out with a long metal rod.

One night she brought home some other work,

The Brooks brothers in arms (Mel at left). Below: Grandparents Abraham and Beth Rachel Kaminsky in Bensonhurst, 1936.

sewing rhinestones together with a little machine. They gave her bags and bags of rhinestones. Each one had a little metal star, and behind the metal star there was an eyelet. She'd put the gadget down on the star and the machine would grab it, and then she'd sew it together, through the eyelet, with other rhinestones. That way, she'd make a little sheet of rhinestones. It would take her all night. I have no idea when my mother slept; she was always working or cleaning or sewing rhinestones. I got out of bed one night and there was this huge mound of rhinestones, like a mountain, on the kitchen table. And they were gleaming under the light. I said, "Mom! Mom! You don't have to work anymore!" She said, "What?" And I said, "Look at all the diamonds there!" She laughed and said, "I wish they were. They're really glass, they're called rhinestones." I thought we'd struck it rich.

Anyway, she was a busy little woman. She couldn't have been more than five feet tall. I told a story on the Johnny Carson show once that my mother was so short she could run under a coffee table with a high hat on. They used to call me "Stretch" because I became five-seven—an enormous height for a Kaminsky, for a Brooklyn Jew.

Later, when I got in the army, I found out I was the shortest one there. My whole family was short. My uncle Joe was five feet. He drove a taxi and had to sit on a couple of phone books. When you saw a taxi coming down the street with no driver at the wheel—that was Joe.

It was a great victory two or three years later when both my brothers got part-time jobs and made enough money so that my mother's dream could be fulfilled. Her dream was to live in the front apartment so she could see what was going on in the street. We had been living in the back, where she had a view of the backyards, of the clotheslines and the cats. We were paying sixteen dollars a month. It wasn't exactly a railroad apartment. It was railroad up until the kitchen and then it fanned out to the kitchen and the living room. There was a bedroom for my mother and a bedroom for the four boys. There was one big bed for us, and we slept across the mattress. I loved it because I loved my brothers and I loved all the action, and I loved being warm. You know, being poor was *good*! It was a good thing for me.

So one of the front apartments came available, and my brothers ran down to the landlord and plunked down the extra, I don't know, two dollars, and we moved to the front, with the windows where you could look down at the street. That was great, and that's where my story begins. The ladies used to sit on the stoop, on pieces of cardboard, and read the newspapers. I thought they were old crones. They must have been about forty, but when you're five, you know, everybody seems old. So they were sitting there chatting one evening, and suddenly I had to pee. I looked around. My brother Bernie had locked the bathroom door. He was doing dooty and you know you couldn't interfere with that, that was big stuff. I couldn't use the sink because it was full of dishes that my mother hadn't finished, so I couldn't pee there. So here I was running around like a crazy little boy and . . . the window was open! And I couldn't help it. I went up to the window and just let go. A minute later I looked down and I saw all these Jewish ladies screaming and pointing, and shouting, "Looks like it came from your window, Kitty!" I was frightened and ran into the bedroom and pulled the covers over my head. Then I heard the door slam and the building shaking as my mother charged up the stairs like a mad rhino, up five stories chugchugchugchugchug! The front door burst open and she ran down to the kitchen. My brother Bernie had just walked out of the bathroom, and he said, "Hi, Mom." And all I heard was bam! biff! bang! crash! and Bernie's voice, "What did I do?" And Mom saying, "You know what you did! You dirty thing!" Bernie's gonna get a big shock when he reads this, 'cause I don't think I ever told him. To this day he's probably wondering why he was beat up that time.

Living in Williamsburg was good. We played cards in the backyard and on the stoop—with dirty old, very thick cards. We shuffled them one by one. Ofttimes, we'd walk over the Williamsburg Bridge to the Lower East Side and maybe buy a hot dog or a knish and a root beer. We saved up our pennies to do that. I learned to smoke on the bridge. My friend Eugene Cogan, who's a press agent now in Manhattan, was my best buddy. He was named Cohen then. We learned how to smoke together. "Sensa-tion" cigarettes was the brand, and we bought a pack of them and every night we'd go to the middle of the bridge so we wouldn't get caught. We'd smoke, throw the butts in the river, and be coughing and spitting but feeling very grown up. We must have been about thirteen. Eugene was a dangerous kid. If we were ever in the same class in school at P.S. 19, and if I caught his eye, we'd get hysterical. We couldn't help ourselves. We'd fall down, shaking helplessly with laughter, both of us. Then we'd get dragged into the principal's office—and we couldn't stop laughing *there*! We knew how dangerous *that* was, but we just couldn't stop. One time we snuck into the RKO Republic, and we were caught and taken down to the manager's office. And we started laughing *there*! I sobered up when the manager said, "You have your choice, I could call the police or give you a beating." At the same time I shouted "Beating," Eugene shouted "The police." He didn't want a beating, and I didn't want the cops, I didn't want anything on my record. The manager gave up. He said, "Just get out of here."

One time, when I was about ten years old, I stole a cap pistol from Woolworth's. I thought nobody had seen me, and I was almost out of the store when I felt this hand and the manager grabbed me. Without thinking, I turned the cap gun on him and said, "Lemme go or I'll blow your head off!" He was so surprised that he stepped back, and I ran around him and out the door.

We had some great days, and Eugene is still my friend. We went to junior high together. Then my family moved to Brighton Beach for a couple of years. It was right near the sea and I loved that, loved the smell of the ocean. I started high school at Abraham Lincoln. I went there for roughly a year, did well there. Then we went back to Williamsburg; I think my mother missed her mother and her friends. Then I went to Eastern District High School.

I was supposed to go to Brooklyn College, but it was wartime and the army accelerated us, so I could be part of the Army Reserve Specialized Training Program. I got my diploma from Eastern District High School, I was about seventeen years old, and the army sent me to college at Virginia Military Institute in Lexington, Virginia. So I got to Virginia after all. My only college alma mater is VMI, which is pretty wild for a little Jewish boy from Brooklyn. But I loved it. We army cadets were treated well, just like the "rats," which is what the freshmen at VMI were called. It was like the play that was written about VMI called *Brother Rat*—which later became a movie starring Ronald Reagan, Wayne Morris and Eddie Albert. It was a wonderful school: I learned to ride a horse. Learned to eat a cheeseburger. Learned to drink a Southern drink called "Dr Pepper," which became popular later. Learned to dance the waltz with beautiful Southern belles at Washington and Lee College, adjacent to VMI. They had a lot of dances called "cotillions." It was oh so different from living on the asphalt and cement all my life.

I just want to add this one thing: I must have been twelve or thirteen, and I was studying for a test in American history about the signers of the Declaration of Independence. I thought, "George Washington, maybe."

But after Washington, everything else was a blur. Or a Burr. Maybe Aaron Burr. There was nothing else I could put together. My eldest brother, Irving, who was working and going to Brooklyn College, said, "Lemme give you a tip. Where do you play punchball?" And I said, "On Rutledge." He said, "Well, there's a signer." Then he asked, "Where else?" And I said, "On Rodney." And he said, "There's another signer." And he kept asking me where I played and where I hung out. It seems that almost every street in Williamsburg is named for a signer of the Declaration of Independence! So all I had to do was remember the names of the streets, Jefferson, Franklin, Hooper, Hewes. So I got a hundred on the test. It pays to have grown up in Williamsburg.

Mel Brooks is responsible for The Producers, Blazing Saddles *and* Young Frankenstein.

SIGHTINGS In 1962, the year she won an Oscar for playing Annie Sullivan in *The Miracle Worker* and two years before she married Mel Brooks, Anne Bancroft dined out at Nathan's.

Brooklyn Snaps

BY HARVEY SHAPIRO

1.

Another gaudy spring in Brooklyn's Botanic
    Garden.
Under the heavy-laden cherry trees
the scattered families sit, so
many Japanese among them, I think
the trees bend low to catch the talk.

2.

The sky itself is a painterly blessing,
a pale wash of blue
with delicate white clouds.
So is the red brick of the low houses.

3.

Blessings on the traffic cop who says
"Move your vehicle, sir" to her double-
parked black brother. How the ancient
words ring out on the Brooklyn street.

4.

Watching the perps and the cops and the lawyers
    on Court Street enter the Supreme Court,
    State of New York.
Maybe the ugliest building in the borough,
massive concrete bunker with slits for windows,
uglier than the jail on Atlantic Avenue,
only a few blocks south.
Stalin would have loved it.
Still, the juries I've sat on there
have delivered justice. And the open square
leading to it catches the December sun
brilliantly in the morning,
gilding the green benches—if you have
the time and money to enjoy it.

Russell Christian

5.

A black queen
approaches my car
at the corner of Atlantic and Henry.
"I need $100,000
to help me pick up
the pieces of my life."
A shrug, moves off.

6.

A hot haze envelops the city.
Even the buildings seem worn out,
their windows sag. On a bench
in Fulton Ferry Park
an elderly gent sits, killing time.
Yesterday he was young and hopeful.
Tomorrow he might be dead.
In the meantime, he looks at the East River.

7.

All his life, he sat on a roof in Brooklyn
as on the deck of an ocean liner. He thinks,
though his voyage was brief, it was sweet.

8.

They lift the Chinese delivery boy
from his shattered bicycle.
The Vietnamese taxi driver
stands in the rain, sucking
on a cigarette. White cops
take it all down.

9.

A very trim green and white
Circle Line boat passing under
the Brooklyn Bridge. It's nice
to see the multitude on board
enjoying the sun and scenery.
Manhattan is my favorite island,
seen from this shore. These days
when I see it in sparkling sun
I think of the poems of Schuyler and O'Hara
as I used to think of Reznikoff and Crane.
Yesterday I saw a man land
a two-pound striper on the pier near
the bridge. A noble fish. But the fisherman,
speaking in an accent I couldn't place,
told me the Russians were killing all
the fish, big and small. They take
babies, he complained. I figured he meant
off Brighton Beach, not Vladivostok.
Dandelions and lilacs are out in Fulton Ferry Park.

Harvey Shapiro is the author of A Day's Portion,
The Light Holds, National Cold Storage Company,
New and Selected Poems, *and an editor at the*
New York Times Magazine.

Haitian Brooklyn

Novelist Edwidge Danticat comes of age

INTERVIEW
BY SU AVASTHI

lthough Danticat no longer lives in Brooklyn, the borough remains an important element in her fiction. Her observations here are based on an interview by Su Avasthi, a former New York Post *reporter.*

When I first moved from Haiti to the United States, my family lived in a six-story building on Flatbush Avenue—2101 Westbury Court—near the Parkside train station. For me, the sound of the D train rumbling over its tracks will always be representative of Brooklyn. It epitomizes my first impression of the city and that is what I recall most about Brooklyn—the trains going by. I moved here at age twelve, and when I first got to that building, right out of the airport, I thought I never would be able to sleep with the D train going by day and night. But soon I got used to it and after a while it became white noise. I was also awestruck by the large buildings. My parents moved into the building in Flatbush because a lot of their friends from church were living there. The building was owned by the Haitian pastor of our church, a Pentecostal church in East Flatbush called Evangelical Crusade of Fishers of Men. We were part of a very large community. The Haitian families outnumbered all the other families in the building.

On special holidays, everyone in the building would exchange plates of food. We did that on Thanksgiving and on January 1, our Independence Day, when everyone made Haitian pumpkin soup. We had parties after church, taking turns in different people's apartments. People baby-sat other people's children. It was like a small village. When we moved to our house in East Flatbush, a lot of the other families were moving on, too. Almost everyone had saved and bought a house by then. I went to school at Jackie Robinson Intermediate School 320 near Empire Boulevard, and all the girls in school would go roller-skating at the rink on Empire Boulevard. I remember being sad because my parents would not allow me to go, which might have been a good thing because I didn't know how to roller-skate and might have broken my neck trying.

Brooklyn seemed much bigger to me then. It seemed like the biggest metropolis in the world. My impressions of Brooklyn changed when I became a driver two years ago. I discovered the waterfront near Coney Island and a lot of other little neighborhoods I'd never seen before.

In 1981, Edwidge Danticat left Haiti to join her family in Flatbush, where a West Indian community was forming. As a child, Danticat absorbed the Haitian practice of storytelling, as well as a sense of oral history and tradition. Her talent was nurtured at Clara Barton High School in Flatbush, at Barnard College where she majored in French literature, and at Brown University, where she got her MFA in fiction. Her first novel, *Breath, Eyes, Memory,* was published in 1994 and gained a wide audience via Oprah Winfrey's book club. In 1995, *Krik? Krak!* Danticat's short-story collection about Haitians and Haitian immigrants, was a National Book Award finalist. Danticat was selected by *Granta* magazine as one of the Best Young American Novelists. Her latest novel is the highly acclaimed *The Farming of the Bones,* a haunting story about a Haitian maid and her lover caught in the political turbulence and violence in the Dominican Republic during the late 1930s. Danticat belongs to a long tradition of writers who came of age in Brooklyn and draw inspiration from the people who make there way here. Her fiction revolves around her experiences as a Haitian-American and gives voice to one of the most underrepresented cultures in American literature.

Stephen Chin

A small stretch of Haiti in the borough of Brooklyn. At right: Le Bistrot.

The campus at Kingsborough Community College, so close to the water, is one of Brooklyn's hidden treasures, I think. It's so close to the water, it was like another world to me when I finally went there a few years ago.

My favorite place in Brooklyn is Le Bistrot in East Flatbush. It is a Haitian restaurant, where all my brothers and I went for meals with our parents after our school graduations. One of the stories, "Caroline's Wedding," in my short-story collection *Krik? Krak!* is set in East Flatbush and mentions the restaurant and the number 8 bus.

I like Prospect Park and the drummers who play there every Sunday afternoon. And the shops on Pitkin Avenue—my three brothers always got their new suits there, right before Christmas, for the coming year. My whole family would go there and choose their suits with them. (My mother made my clothes when I was in my teens.) Another favorite place is the Brooklyn Botanic Garden. I always walked through there from the Clara Barton end near the museum to Prospect Avenue to catch the number 41 bus home. In the winter, my best friend in high school, Norma Autry, and I loved to walk in the fresh-fallen snow in the Botanic Garden. It was as if we had the whole place to ourselves. I also like the view of Manhattan from the Brooklyn Bridge during the day and the view of Brooklyn from the Williamsburg Bridge at night.

For me, the spirit of Brooklyn is captured in the wide variety of people living here, the different neighborhoods, Caribbean, Russian, Italian. On some level, Brooklyn is a microcosm. You can meet people from anywhere in the world here, from every corner of the globe. It's like a United Nations city.

Michael Kamber

Sammy's Kids

Doing what needs to be done

BY DENIS HAMILL

Y

ou gotta love Sammy. He's a little guy with a big heart who does the right thing for good kids in one of the toughest 'hoods in Brooklyn.

Back in 1995 I received a voice-mail message at the *Daily News* from a guy who said, "David, I mean, Denis Hamilton, okay, look, I got like 200 kids who want to play some ball and got no money. I need your help. Gimme a call, man. Oh yeah, my name is Sammy Jackson. I think I'm gonna call my organization East New York Kidspower. Whaddaya think?"

I loved Sammy Jackson's act right away. First he got my name wrong, which meant he was more interested in getting to my readers than to me. Also, he had called himself, didn't use a secretary and didn't send me a slick prospectus or offer to buy me lunch. I called him up and went out to visit him in East New York.

Back in the late 1980s when the city seemed doomed, with homicides reaching over 2,000 a year during the crack epidemic, I spent a lot of time looking at dead bodies in East New York. New Lots Avenue rattled day and night to the sound of machine-gun fire. And I'd seen kids thirteen and fourteen bopping down Pennsylvania Avenue with crack stems in one hand and Uzis in the other. Yellow crime-scene tape draped the neighborhood like a wicked bunting.

Now in the mid-nineties here was a local guy, a handyman with no formal organizational skills, absolutely no political connections, no knowledge of how to fill out a grant proposal, who wanted to put baseball bats into the hands of the kids who had survived that terrible decade in the city's history.

"I got no dough," said Jackson when I went to meet him. "No equipment. Just a handful of coaches and plenty of kids. I was hoping maybe you could do a little write-up in the *Daily News* and ask people to help out." Behind him was a collection of kids who were literally sitting on a fence, waiting to see which way fate would tip them. "I want to see these kids play sports again," Jackson said. "The only thing that kept me straight as a kid was sports. I'm tired of seeing these kids get taken away in hearses. I wanna see them steal second base instead of a car."

You gotta love a guy who sees the world the old-fashioned Brooklyn way—play fair with these kids or they'll go foul. I wrote the column, and the *Daily News* readers—who also like a genuine old-fashioned pitch—responded big time with money, equipment and volunteers. The kids played a splendid season on the baseball diamonds of Brooklyn, most of them playing organized sports for the first time in their lives, delirious with the idea of a hat and T-shirt and a baseball glove.

Sammy soon had 275 kids and cheerleading teams, Boy Scout and Girl Scout troops, and a basketball tournament in the works. He had his kids out "canning" (canvassing for donations on the street), doing car washes and holding fund-raisers in the neighborhood. He opened a headquarters, got letterhead stationery printed up and rented some business machines. Some of the local utilities and cable stations gave him money. When Christmas rolled around, he organized a toy drive, again appealing to the *Daily News* readers. Toy companies, banks, supermarkets and big-hearted citizens sent checks and toys, and candy and ice cream, and regular food.

A blond, blue-eyed woman named Ellen Peluso from Howard Beach—regarded by some as Klan Kountry

On a shoestring, Sammy Jackson has organized hundreds of East New York kids into sports teams.

© Kathy Willens, 2000

after an infamous racial stabbing—read about what Sammy Jackson was doing and volunteered her time. "Of course, there was that initial awkward moment when the local people wondered why this white woman was coming here to help organize a Christmas party for a bunch of black kids," Peluso remembers, adding that neighborhood people thought she was a detective getting out of an unmarked car. "But we got over that real quick because the kids were all that mattered here. Kids are the same everywhere no matter what color they are, and these kids were just dying to have a Christmas."

Together, Sammy Jackson and Ellen Peluso organized the biggest Christmas party anyone could ever remember in the neighborhood, with over 700 kids jamming Genesis House on Hinsdale Street to sit on Santa's lap and receive a toy and eat cake and ice cream. "It turned out to be the best Christmas of my life," Peluso says.

Sammy Jackson wasn't finished. He started com-puter classes, tutorials, after-school programs for the kids of East New York, while still not receiving a dime from the city, state or feds. He also started a football league and began taking high school seniors on bus tours of colleges in the American South, helping several of them secure scholarships.

Still, without formal funding, every year gets harder. "It's always about money," Jackson told me recently. "We've had a good run, but there is only so long before your volunteers take paying jobs to feed their families. I keep getting turned down by the city whenever I submit a proposal for a grant. We're in danger of losing our headquarters. But as long as there are kids who want to hit a ball, shoot a hoop, run for a long one, we'll make sure there's a place for them to do it."

In October 1996 the first trophy night was held for East New York Kidspower. Sammy Jackson invited me to the auditorium of P.S. 238 on Alabama Avenue to see his kids receive their trophies. He had told them that there would be no jeans, sneakers or hats allowed that night. "This is about kids who learned teamwork, discipline, competition, honesty and the rewards of hard work on the ballfield," Sammy said. "The same qualities they'll need in life. So I didn't want them showing up looking like gangstas. I wanted them to look respectable for their parents and families. But mostly I wanted them to take pride in themselves and each other."

That night these kids gave each other standing-O's as the names were announced and each kid walked to the stage to receive a shiny trophy. It was a long, long way from the dead bodies of the crack wars in East New York.

Then Sammy Jackson startled me by calling me up to the stage and giving me a plaque that I'll forever treasure. It was inscribed to David Hamilton.

You gotta love this guy!

Daily News *columnist Denis Hamill is a sucker for a happy ending.*

Storefront #1: *South Brooklyn, 1948.* **One in a series of neighborhood photographs by Ivan Karp.**

Ridden in Anger

Brooklyn's master of motorcycles

BY MICHAEL
W. ROBBINS

Motorcycles and tough guys. It's a common connection, and it's true that tattooed characters in Hun helmets astride hot-rodded Harleys blasting along the streets of Brooklyn are a commonplace sight and sound. But there's a surprising and little-known other connection: the finest private collection of vintage racing motorcycles in America rests right here in downtown Brooklyn, firmly in the grasp of a tough Brooklyn biker named Rob Iannucci.

Iannucci, onetime Peace Corps volunteer in Barbados, onetime federal prosecutor, more or less full-time attorney and full-time motorcycle aficionado, owns and operates a vintage road-racing enterprise called Team Obsolete, with its collection and headquarters in Brooklyn. It's here not because Brooklyn is a logical motorcycle venue like Daytona Beach, Florida. It's here—artfully located within earshot of a police precinct house—because Iannucci is a Brooklyn guy.

How Brooklyn is he? At lunch one afternoon in a venerable Carroll Gardens Italian restaurant, Iannucci took great pains to select his appetizers, pasta dish, entrée and dessert, and was settling in to enjoy the meal when he detected the sharp scent of freshly lighted cigarettes. The perpetrators were readily identified: four very hard-eyed fortyish males hunched over a table in a back corner. Anyone not just off a bus from Nebraska instantly would have recognized them as wiseguys. The real thing, not some Hollywood pretenders. Accordingly, most realistic mortals would have shrugged these guys off as a stroke of bad luck or

Perfectly preserved: Rob Iannucci's 1961 Matchless G50, an all-conquering road racer.

brought them discreetly to the notice of the manager and let him deal with the situation. Most realistic mortals would not have dreamed of confronting four of them directly.

But that's not Iannucci. Hesitating not at all, he pushed back from his antipasto, lumbered straightaway to the rear of the restaurant and leaned directly into the foursome's conversation. He pointed at the smoke, gestured around at the restaurant, pointed to the kitchen, made several palms-up appeals to reason, talking earnestly and directly all the while. The foursome reacted with initial surprise and palpable hostility that gave way to skepticism, then something like agreement and finally amusement. Heads nodded. Smiles broke out. Cigarettes were extinguished. There were handshakes. Handshakes! Returning to his table, Iannucci summoned the relieved and shaken manager, ordered up an excellent Tuscan super red and had it sent to the guys in the back. More smiles and waves all around.

A foolhardy egomaniac who takes incredible chances? Or a fearless streetwise guy? Let's just say that Rob Iannucci knows a thing or two about negotiating.

Gathered in Iannucci's deliberately anonymous razor-wired complex of buildings in downtown Brooklyn are somewhere between thirty and sixty of the most successful Grand Prix racing motorcycles of the modern era. Legendary machines, ridden in their prime by legendary riders at the world's legendary race circuits: Daytona, Monza, the Nürburgring, the Isle of Man. He's got the only surviving 1964 Honda Six still in running condition, once ridden by such champions as Mike Hailwood and Jim Redman. The thundering BSA Rocket 3 on which Dick "Bugsy" Mann stunned all opposition at Daytona in 1971. The fire-engine red MV Agusta, ridden to glory by thirteen-time world champion Giacomo Agostini. The 1969 Benelli Four, raced by greats Kel Carruthers and Renzo Pasolini. Plus numerous other MV Agustas, Triumphs, Ducatis, Harley-Davidson XRs, Manx Nortons, Matchless G50s, BSAs and AJS 7Rs. It is one man's own "Art of the Motorcycle" show.

The sunlit moments of cheering and champagne have passed, the riders are dead or retired now, and the electric tension of those world-class competitions of the 1960s and '70s has faded to memory. But the machines . . . the fire-breathing bikes themselves have faded not at all. Restored to peak condition, they sit in rows of gleaming paint and polished aluminum, colorful and fit. Many of them are parked in one room or another (Iannucci declines to state exactly how many he owns or what they could possibly be worth, though it's got to be in the millions of dollars). Some are up on stands, but they are not simply being restored by Iannucci and his co-obsessives for static display as *objets* in a gallery. They are being race-prepared: these Grand Prix machines, some of them now as old as their owner, not only still run—they still *race*. Not, of course, in today's Grand Prix events. With the racing team he

owns and operates Iannucci takes them all over the United States and Europe to race in vintage road-racing events, believing as he does that a racing motorcycle is only fully itself, fully realized, when—as he likes to say—"it's being ridden in anger"—that is, ridden in serious competition.

Anger is something that Iannucci himself appears to have no shortage of. Legal action is not just what he does to pay the bills (his motorcycle team, restoration shop and collection lose money, he says), it's part of his way of life. He was a founder of the American Association of Historic Racing Motorcycles, the largest vintage-racing organization in the country, but his running feud with the management over rules and rights culminated in court action. He acquired the bulk of the MV Agusta stable of Grand Prix racers from the home factory in Italy, but kept them only after a yearlong legal wrangle with his onetime partner in the deal.

No longer a motorcycle racer himself (though he rides a Matchless G50 or a Norton Commando on the streets of Brooklyn), Iannucci has for many years fielded an array of racing bikes ridden by friends, associates, and some living-legend retired champion racers at some of the great racing circuits in the United States and Europe—in what amounts to a traveling road show of rare and priceless machines. He knows the risks to his collection, but feels fervently that his is a stewardship of immortal machines that were simply born to run.

"These are the products of people's passion about racing," Iannuci says. "They are about guys in a motorcycle company—like Matchless or Benelli or Honda—building the fastest bikes they could build at the time, regardless of the money." That makes them very special, and Iannucci has never lost the enthusiasm he felt—back in Barbados and well before his career-setting stint at Brooklyn Law School—when he first discovered the enchantments of purebred racing machines.

Michael W. Robbins, a writer and former editor of Audubon *and* Oceans *magazines, also knows a thing or two about old motorcycles.*

Hair Story

Flat hair? What's that?

BY
GENIA
GOULD

Is there a Brooklyn look? Yes, there is, and hair is surely the key element. But whatever the look is *exactly,* it's a little like what Justice Potter Stewart once said about obscenity: it's hard to define, but you know it when you see it. To see the Brooklyn look, to seek a definition, I visited some of the 2,500 or so hair salons, beauty parlors and barbershops in the classic borough neighborhoods of Bay Ridge and Gravesend.

"Flat hair, what's that?" asks Janet, a twenty-something original Brooklynite and top hair stylist at the New York Hair Factory in Bay Ridge. "Everything here is about *body*, you know? Flat just doesn't work for hair. I personally love big hair—the bigger, the wilder, the better."

But is it purely a matter of big hair?

"Another big thing now is the short, spiky look, out of control and, like, not symmetric," says Janet. "But I still enjoy doing the big do's. You see all these girls that go out at night? They want big hair. In the past it used to be *really* big hair and some people still like that, but—*plus ça change, plus c'est la même chose.* As much as styles change, it's always pretty much the same thing. People do different things but, like, they continue to want body—to have fullness in their hair."

Like so many hair operations, this is a unisex place. What about the guys' look? "For the guys," Janet says, "the fade is the thing. Guys come in religiously every week to have their hair buzzed. It's always done with clippers, and the clipper numbers tell the story: number one gets you very tight to the skull; number four is longer. Guys want a tapered fade or a high-top fade like Kid 'n' Play, or they want a design. Or a name. We do anything they want us to."

Under an overpass off the Belt Parkway lurks a salon with a sign that says RAIDED X in dramatic neon. (What is it about hair stylists and catchy-cute shop names? There is more word play in the Yellow Pages under "beauty parlor" than in the collected poetry of Ogden Nash.) The windows display numerous head shots of women's hairdos. It turns out the place is located on Avenue X (get it?) in Gravesend.

"I've had my hair done and now I'm hanging out," says Phyllis Delmonico Sweeney, a petite, striking, middle-aged redhead with nails as red as her coif. She and a friend are sitting at a small table toward the back near the register and a telephone that rings without letup. Her friend is drinking coffee and eating an egg sandwich from a nest of aluminum foil. Even though they are just customers, they are the ones who greet me.

It's the middle of the afternoon, and Phyllis has been at the salon since 9:30 this morning. She gets her hair done at Raided X every week. Sometimes twice a week. "They just did the color Thursday and I decided I

Russell Christian

wanted to cut it today," she explains. "I also want to darken the red a drop and change the style. You know, you just get tired of some things. They're really good here. Every one of them knows how to do my hair."

The salon is crowded with customers and four stylists are at work, each stationed in front of a large mirror: two are shampooing, one is creating an elaborate braid, while another is briskly pulling a woman's hair through a plastic cap for highlighting. On the radio, WKTU is pumping out what sounds like '80s disco at the highest volume and cigarette smoke fills the room, giving it the air of a brightly lit, high-spirited saloon without the hard drinks.

"Did you ever go to a beauty parlor where you had to put on full makeup just to go there?" asks Phyllis. "There are plenty of those, but this is not one of them. You could come here in your pajamas and they'd take care of you. It's a happening place and we just laugh all the time."

About her own hair, she says, "I can't wear my hair flat—the so-called 'natural' look. I physically just can't do it. I'm five feet tall and I like height. That's how it started for me. Denise, the owner, works miracles. She also has the old-timers, women in their seventies. They still come in for those old-style perms."

Flat, it seems, is totally out for all ages in Brooklyn.

Genia Gould is a Brooklyn resident, writer and observer of native Brooklyn styles.

Storefront #2: *Barbershop on Columbia Street, 1948.* As a young photographer, Ivan Karp had a good eye for window art.

A Cinematic Dream of Brooklyn

Wolfe was wrong: You <u>can</u> go home again...

BY
KENNETH
TURAN

I often go back to Brooklyn, where I was born and raised, but only when I dream. I have never actually returned, as an adult, to the blocks where I grew up. Growing up in Brooklyn was an intense, particular experience that influenced who I am, and what I became, in ways more pervasive than I could ever imagine. But that doesn't mean I want to live it all over again.

In my dream, it's always the same. I've just gotten off the IRT at the Sutter Avenue stop, and I'm taking the shortest way home: East Ninety-Eighth Street followed by Portal Street, two bleak and utilitarian blocks. And though I saved time that way, the trip had its own wages of fear. The first half is dark and unsettling in the deep pervasive gloom of the ominous elevated tracks that shadow it. There's always a subway accompanying me, its noise, fury and proximity more terrifying in the dream than I allowed it to be in person. Then the train is gone, but though I'm walking in full sun on Portal Street, I'm more frightened. For this stretch of vacant lots and silent garages is deserted, and without people to appeal to; aloneness always meant danger, vulnerability, fear.

Finally I reach my block of Union Street, such an isolated cul-de-sac that cars rarely disturbed our solitude. At the top of the block, two six-story apartment buildings, 1920 and 1933 Union Street, face each other as proud and defiant as the twin fortresses of a medieval town. I lived in 1920, this street was home, and though it had dangers of its own, none had the power to surprise me. The dream is over.

Everything in Brooklyn comes down to your neighborhood and your block. Mine was a peculiar corner of the borough, in the ill-defined border country where Brownsville, Crown Heights and East Flatbush meet. It was the setting for *The Amboy Dukes*, a novel about street-gang life. The book was a revelation when I read it a generation after Irving Shulman wrote it in 1947, but my neighborhood was not so dangerous when I came along. It has since gotten worse and, I am told, better again.

People from outside often think that growing up in Brooklyn, an integral part of the great metropolis that is New York, is cosmopolitan in ways it is not. The rich

A pinnacle of glamour: Loew's movie palace in 1930.

Brian Merlis Collection

A film critic in the making —author Kenneth Turan.

textures of the entire borough, let alone Manhattan, are unknown and unavailable to a solitary child. Instead you cling to your block, to the few streets your parents let you explore, as tenaciously as your will allows. Union Street was so isolated and off by itself, so uncompromising in its lack of attraction for disruptive automobiles, that all the games of my childhood and teenage years took place right there. Lincoln Terrace Park, as vast as Montana in my imagination, was scant blocks away, but its organized sports and designated fields seemed alien and anti-Brooklyn to me and my friends, something suited to the *Father Knows Best* world of tidy lawns and single-family homes that never got closer to us than the TV.

The games started on the sidewalk for the very young, from flipping baseball cards to the mysterious "skelly," played with bottle caps on an intricate diagram drawn with chalk on a square of concrete. The ball games were endless in their variety, but the ones the older kids played with lively pink spaldeens took place exclusively on the street. Punchball and stickball were pastimes of the summer and spring, and they functioned as surrogates for the kind of real baseball the Dodgers played at Ebbets Field, which everybody listened to on the radio.

In the fall and winter, as with the professionals, thoughts turned to football. Given our concrete field, it had to be two-hand touch, and there were other wrinkles distinctly our own. "Cut in front of the '56 Chevy," the quarterback might say, and if you executed it deftly, no defender could stop you. If you didn't, your next assignment would be exile: "And you, you go long."

Involving as all this was, observed from the living room window of the three-room apartment (kitchen and bedroom were the other two) I shared with my parents and my older sister, I could see the beckoning larger world of the neighborhood outside my street. Every toe I tentatively put in that fast-moving stream sent out ripples that widened my circle of experience and led to the next step farther out.

The first step was the most basic—toward food. Though it was across the enormous width of East New York Avenue, I could see from our window the little grocery store where we shopped, its brine-soaked wooden pickle barrel looking as old as the Diaspora, its full-color posters enticing us to vote for the beer-sponsored Miss Rheingold—as close to glamour as the neighborhood managed. But the grocery was only an outpost; the main event was Sutter Avenue, just a few blocks away. When I spent time in France, decades later, I realized how European plain old Sutter Avenue was. It was, just like Paris' celebrated Rue Daguerre, a vibrant shopping street, with individual merchants for all the major food groups. There was a separate store for meat, for fish, for bread. Here was the store for farmer cheese, here the one for candy and cigars. Most serious were the chicken pluckers, barely willing to take time off from the demanding work of pulling feathers to part with a carcass, even for ready money. Most raucous were the fruit and vegetable men, their wares displayed on large bins, their loud voices importuning, always in Yiddish, "Women, women, women, do we have peaches for you. Just give a look, just a look." Who knew flirtation could be so everyday?

After food, it was religion that drew me farther from the world of my block. Not that I had a choice; my father was a fierce observer of old-country Orthodox Judaism, and not going to Saturday services at his *shul*, a large synagogue on the far side of that most elegant of boulevards, Eastern Parkway, was not even to be imagined. As with Sutter Avenue, I needed distance in time and space to understand my father's *shul*. I see it now as a swirling tapestry out of Isaac Bashevis Singer and Roman Vishniac's Poland, a Yiddish-language fantasia somehow reincarnated in Brooklyn. The rabbi haranguing us with biblical injunctions, old men blowing their noses in prayer shawls and arguing about points of law and imagined personal slights. Finally there was

Courtesy of Kenneth Turan

the cacophonous post-service *kiddush,* shots of Cutty Sark downed neat and followed by crumbling egg cookies heavily laden with sugar.

Not surprisingly, religion's grip on me gradually weakened, and as I pushed farther afield in my neighborhood, I discovered the comparatively cosmopolitan world of Pitkin Avenue, to me a boulevard of dreams. Pitkin Avenue bustled, glittered, even shone. It was on Pitkin Avenue that all the serious clothiers had their stores, and all the serious window-shoppers went to look on Saturday afternoon. Pitkin had restaurants, even nonkosher ones like the Chinese place where my sister and I occasionally snuck off to mock the Commandments and, not incidentally, horrify our parents in the bargain. Best of all, Pitkin Avenue had the Loew's Pitkin, one of Brooklyn's celebrated movie palaces. This ornate pleasure dome was such a draw that every Saturday evening Sally Glassman, by acclamation the best-dressed older woman on the block (could she have been as old as forty, I wonder now),

would get seriously decked out, leaving word with us kids to tell her husband "I'll be in my regular seat at the Loew's." Even Miss Rheingold had a hard time matching that for glamour.

Almost my last memory of Brooklyn before I left for good—first for college (after attending P.S. 189 and then Wingate High School) and later for life in America— was an errand for my father. He was a floor layer who worked on the endless subdivisions of Long Island. He'd left his saws to be sharpened far outside the neighborhood, and I was dispatched by bus to pick them up. In my memory, at least, I rode that bus to the sharpener's for what seemed like hours. Willa Cather awed by the wheat fields of Nebraska had nothing on me as I sat astonished at the energetic vastness of the borough that was my home. All this time on the bus, and still in Brooklyn. Could any one place be this vast? And if it could, what did that mean for the rest of the world?

Kenneth Turan is a film critic for the Los Angeles Times.

Boulevard of dreams: Pitkin Avenue, the busiest commercial strip in Brownsville.

Brooklyn Historical Society

Growing Up Poor

The lessons of the schoolyard

INTERVIEW
WITH
HOWARD
SCHULTZ

I grew up in Brooklyn, in Canarsie, in the federally subsidized Bayview Projects. I moved there in 1956, when I was three years old. Prior to that, we were living in the East New York section of Brooklyn.

The projects were in many ways a wonderful place to grow up, despite the stigma that the outside world attached to the blue-collar workers or the lower-middle-class people living there. And the great equalizer of the projects for a young kid was the schoolyard—which was where I spent 90 percent of my time. That's where the boys were separated from the men, if you know what I mean. You had to be a good athlete to get chosen to play, and you had to be tough just to stay in the game. It was so diverse, in terms of black, white, Hispanic, Jewish, Italian, African-American and Puerto Rican. You learned to get along with people, and you also learned to defend yourself at a young age. You got in fights, sure, and had kids waiting on the corner for your milk money—all those kinds of things. But despite all that, it was an incredible place.

My most vivid memory as a kid was walking through the projects and the streets during the summer nights and seeing people on their porches or hanging out their apartment windows. I could hear the echoing of the radio and the baseball games. Primarily it was the Yankees. I would walk through the streets and pick up the radio play-by-play

from one house to the next, or one building to the next.

My love for baseball today is deeply rooted in what Brooklyn was about. The Dodgers had just left, which broke my father's heart. After they moved to Los Angeles, he would never allow the word "Dodger" to be spoken or a radio or television to play a Dodger game. Then we became die-hard Yankee fans. People defined their existence then by which team they rooted for. That doesn't exist anymore. You were not a baseball fan, you were either a Yankee fan or a Dodger fan. And of course there were the great debates on every street corner over Willie Mays and Mickey Mantle. For me, it was Mantle. I had number seven and everything about Mickey Mantle all over everything I wore.

As I got older, I was very proud of telling people I was from Brooklyn, but in high school I dated a girl who lived in Long Island. I remember her father's response when I told him I was from Brooklyn. And from Canarsie. It wasn't positive.

When people today hear "Brooklyn," they may have no idea what it means. To me, it's positive. I think Brooklyn taught us toughness and survival. We were proud of where we came from, but nobody wanted to stay in Brooklyn—we wanted to get out to improve our standing in life. I think we recognized that we were part of a class of people who in many ways were striving for the American dream. Certainly that was true in my case. Once I got older, I wanted to use that as a competitive advantage because

Russell Christian

it gave me passion, incredible desire. The toughness that I have as a person today came from the schoolyard. I know that. At the same time, my sensitivity around different cultures also came from that experience. People teach diversity in schools today, but we lived it.

One of the things that I remember vividly in the last few years is taking my kids back to Brooklyn, when they were thirteen and ten, and showing them where I lived and hearing them say in awe, "You really lived here?" It was very, very different from the way they're growing up in Seattle. I wanted them to experience and see Brooklyn firsthand, because they've heard me talk about it their whole lives.

I showed them Canarsie High School, where I played football. The school didn't have enough money then for its own field, so we practiced in a rocky public park— Canarsie Park—about a mile away on Seaview Avenue. Today the school has a football field.

I got out of Brooklyn because I was lucky enough to go to college—Northern Michigan University—for football. Then I got hurt and never played, but I stayed there anyway. That experience was something I needed. My parents encouraged me to get out and experience life and try to make something of myself. My father had a series of blue-collar jobs and was kind of a bitter man because the American dream that he chased after the war—he was in the South Pacific—never came true. He was not a valued worker as a blue-collar worker, and as a result I have tried to build the kind of company that my father never got a chance to work for.

Howard Schultz is CEO of Starbucks Coffee Company.

Storefront #3: *South Brooklyn, 1948.* Ivan Karp's unadorned precursor of New York City's "cow parade."

Pulpits
& Stages

If Chicago was the city of the big shoulders, Brooklyn is the borough of the big mouth. Brooklynites simply *will* be heard, whether from a floodlit stage, a church pulpit, a political soapbox or a truck stuck in traffic. It's the venue where sounding off—musically, religiously, politically or comically—is not only expected but respected.

In music, there's no Brooklyn sound akin to the famous genres of New Orleans, Liverpool or Seattle. But masters of every musical style from ragtime (Eubie Blake) to rap (Jay Z), from bebop (Max Roach) to dub (Bill Laswell) have sprung up from Brooklyn roots. The roster of jazz greats, for instance, who lived or worked in the borough reads like a Who's Who of twentieth-century music. And Brooklyn is one of the best places in America to hear Grammy-winning gospel music, whether traditional or contemporary.

The other guys are the joke.

Speaking out, whether for a vote, an issue or a laugh, is a Brooklyn tradition. Brooklyn sent the first Communist Party member to the New York City Council, and it's now the base for the Reverend Al Sharpton, who can be counted on for a political comment anytime. As for the laughs, it's a rare American comic who was *not* born in the borough.

**Previous spread: Ecstatic fans, bored cops
at a Paramount performance in 1957.**

Previous spread: New York Daily News

Presidents & Kings

They came, they saw, they did a little politicking

BY
GLENN
THRUSH

In the summer of 1776, during the Battle of Long Island, president-to-be George Washington established a protocol that commanders in chief have followed on most of their visits to Brooklyn over the subsequent two centuries: gather a crowd, make a big impression, then leave as quickly as possible.

One out of every seven Americans may be able to trace his or her origins back to Brooklyn, but none of the forty-three men to serve as president came from Kings County. And few have stayed very long when they've dropped by.

Washington did pay a return visit as president, conducting an inspection of his troops. And Abraham Lin-coln made an appearance to see Henry Ward Beecher in the Brooklyn Heights pulpit of Plymouth Church in 1860, just before making the antislavery speech at Cooper Union that led to his presidential nomination. Curiously, the two losers of the 1872 presidential race—Democrat Horace Greeley, founder and editor of the *New York Tribune*, and George Francis Train, an iconoclastic industrialist and all-around eccentric who made his name in the railroad business, are interred at Green-Wood Cemetery. (That year's winner, General Ulysses S. Grant, is entombed in uptown Manhattan.)

As the twentieth century progressed, Brooklyn grew into the largest and most reliable Democratic county in America, drawing the party's big shots whenever they needed a friendly crowd or a million or so votes to

President Franklin Roosevelt—here in 1940—loved to visit Brooklyn.

Bettmann/Corbis

throw them over the top. Today, Republican excursions into a borough where Democrats enjoy a four-to-one advantage have assumed an accidental, larky and occasionally suicidal quality, but things were much different a hundred years ago. Republican Teddy Roosevelt, the only president born in New York City, made two trips to Brooklyn while in office, but they must have stirred painful memories of an earlier tragedy: within a few hours on Valentine's Day, 1884, TR's mother died of

ries of the borough. Like his presidential cousin Theodore, Franklin Delano Roosevelt first made his political name as assistant secretary of the navy, and like Teddy he used the job as a bully pulpit for his national political aspirations. On June 19, 1915, FDR was on the podium at the Brooklyn Navy Yard for the launching of a state-of-the-art dreadnought christened by his boss, Secretary of the Navy Josephus Daniels, as a ship "torpedoes cannot sink." FDR, speaking in front of the

Flanked by Ted Kennedy and Muhammad Ali, President Carter spoke at the Concord Baptist Church in 1980.

typhoid and his twenty-two-year-old wife, soon after delivering her namesake, Alice Roosevelt, succumbed to a kidney ailment. Their twin rosewood coffins were laid side by side at the family plot in Green-Wood Cemetery on February 16. Roosevelt, then a boyish state assemblyman, stood over them in a daze, so devastated by the loss that it is said he never spoke of his wife again—even to the daughter who bore her name. "The light," he wrote in his diary at the time, "has gone out of my life."

Another Roosevelt would have far happier memo-

national press for one of the first times in his career, proclaimed the ship "a tangible mass of well-wrought metal that today has been floated on the waters of the East River." Daniels may have been right about the torpedoes but not, unfortunately, about the sinking: the ship was the ill-fated USS *Arizona*, which would be destroyed at Pearl Harbor twenty-six years later.

As president, FDR always enjoyed Brooklyn's ecstatic crowds and nearly unconditional love. During his first three campaigns—1932, 1936 and 1940—he made boisterous appearances at the traditional Friday Before

AP/Wide World

Election Day rallies at the Brooklyn Academy of Music. "A campaign," he told the 1936 gathering, "would not be a campaign without a trip over here to the Academy." His last speech at BAM came during his toughest political fight, a race against moderate Republican Wendell Willkie. At the time, FDR was beset on all sides by former supporters who pilloried him for seeking a third term and accused him of having an autocratic stranglehold on the White House. Among his critics was heavy-

candidate accusing the national Republican party of being in lockstep with the international Communist conspiracy. Citing a Vote-for-Willkie advertisement that ran in *The Daily Worker*, a straight-faced FDR thundered to the delighted BAM crowd: "There is something very ominous in this combination which has been forming within the Republican party between the extreme reactionary and the extreme radical elements in this country." Their applause was so loud and sus-

President Clinton met with African-American leaders for breakfast at Junior's.

weight champion Joe Louis, who campaigned for Willkie in Brooklyn's black neighborhoods and drew crowds of 15,000 on the day of the speech.

The president roared back. Three heavyweights, ex-champs Jack Dempsey, Max Baer and Jim Braddock, were enlisted to join him at BAM. And as his campaign train rolled toward Brooklyn, he stunned his speechwriters by handing them thirteen pages of uncharacteristic vitriol aimed at the GOP. By the third draft, the speech had turned into something extraordinary—perhaps the only instance of a Democratic

tained that a beaming FDR held his watch up to the crowd to show them that valuable national radio time was ticking away.

Instead of making an appearance at the Academy before his fourth victory, Roosevelt chose to campaign from the seat of his touring car at Ebbets Field in late October 1944. The pallid, war-weary president was clearly in no physical shape even to be out of bed—but he braved a bone-chilling downpour mainly to counter claims that he was too feeble to serve a fourth term. FDR aide Bill Hassett recalled a soggy but inspiring scene:

Tom Callan

"Undismayed, the president threw aside his Navy cape and, standing bareheaded in the storm, captured the enthusiasm of the crowd by declaring that this was his first visit to Ebbets Field although he had often rooted for the Brooklyn Dodgers."

Seven months later, the president was dead. Ironically, FDR's predecessor, Iowa native Herbert Hoover, was a lifelong Dodger fan and a regular in the box seats whenever he was in town. Moreover, Hoover enjoyed a friendly relationship with Dodgers owner Walter O'Malley that lasted after O'Malley shipped the Dodgers out to Los Angeles in 1957. It seems that two of the least popular figures of twentieth-century Brooklyn were fast friends.

Woodrow Wilson stopped by the Brooklyn Navy Yard to honor U.S. Marine casualties in 1914.

In 1948, Harry Truman renewed the BAM tradition to cap off his desperate whistle-stop campaign against "unbeatable" challenger Tom Dewey, the governor of New York. The turnout on October 29 was a forecast of haughty Dewey's impending doom. Truman began his tour with a torchlight motorcade through Williamsburg and Bedford-Stuyvesant, with hundreds of thousands of hoarse-throated Democrats howling "Give 'Em Hell Harry" along the way. By the time he had pried the crowd aside to mount BAM's podium at 9:17, the hall was jammed with 4,000 people who treated him to a fifteen-minute ovation. Outside it was complete mayhem: 1,800 cops tried to keep the 16,000 well-wishers at bay. Even the most jaded warhorses of the county Democratic machine recalled the scene for what it was—the last grand political spectacle the borough would witness in the twentieth century.

If Brooklynites were wild about Democrat Harry, they didn't much like Republican Ike. Eisenhower's trip to Ebbets Field for the 1956 World Series was met with polite ballpark applause, a mere 200 gawkers at La Guardia Airport and a deflating *Times* headline:

"President Cheered at Ball Game, But Few Line Route To and From Park." The president had received a warmer, if somewhat befuddled reception during an east coast campaign swing two years earlier, when he toured the Farragut Houses, the public housing project across from the Navy Yard. About a thousand curious residents hung out the windows, and the apartment of one tenant, Leonia Maxwell, was selected for a presidential tour on a half-hour's notice. She loved the attention, but complained she wasn't given enough time to rescrub her already immaculate floors. "If I knew the President of the United States was coming," she told the *Times,* "I would have rubbed extra hard."

By 1960 Brooklyn's predictably pro-Democrat voting patterns had made it hostile territory for the GOP, and it would be sixteen years before another Republican president would pay a visit while in office.

Lyndon Johnson carried Brooklyn by a landslide in 1964, but he paid only two visits. One was a quick stopover at Floyd Bennett Field on Columbus Day in 1966; the other was a stealthy mission to Brooklyn a few months earlier. In March 1966, Stella Celler, the wife of Brooklyn congressman Manny Celler, one of LBJ's close friends from their days in the House (and author of an autobiography called *You Never Leave Brooklyn*), died after a long battle with heart disease. Without telling reporters where they were headed, LBJ loaded *Air Force One* with members of Brooklyn's congressional delegation, Lady Bird and a handful of luminaries including FBI chief J. Edgar Hoover and headed north to Kennedy Airport. The reason for the secrecy was never fully revealed, but at the time LBJ's staff had begun taking pains to shroud the president's flight plans, possibly due to threats that Cuban agents were planning to ram *Air Force One* in midair. Whatever his reasons, Johnson

Library of Congress

made it clear that the trip was intended as a strictly personal gesture to his close friend.

When a crowd of schoolchildren started chanting "Viva Johnson" in front of Beth Elohim in Park Slope, they were hushed by the NYPD. LBJ made no speech; he simply sat in the sixth row, a few seats from Bobby Kennedy, and grimly listened to the eulogy. When it was finished, he leaned over for a long, whispered conversation with the grieving Celler, walked back to his limo and was back in Washington by midafternoon.

Richard Nixon's recollections of Brooklyn were more personal than political. In November of 1960 Nixon rallied the 3,500 Republicans who jammed into the St. George Hotel in Brooklyn Heights, but lit out fifteen minutes after his speech ended—much to the disappointment of the faithful, some of whom had waited up all night for his early morning arrival. Then, in late 1963, a few weeks after the Kennedy assassination, he revisited Brooklyn during an attempt to establish a lucrative white-shoe New York law practice. Nixon's longtime friend Leonard Garment, a Democrat who would later serve as his counsel during Watergate, invited many of the borough's most prominent lawyers and judges to a get-to-know-Dick cocktail party at his Heights brownstone. To Garment's surprise, Nixon scarfed meatballs-on-toothpicks and moved effortlessly among life-long liberals who were eager to hear tales about Khrushchev, De Gaulle and Checkers the dog. At 7:30, when it came time to leave, Nixon hitched a ride back to Manhattan with a young lawyer, Jerry Leitner, and his pregnant wife. Nixon, relaxed after enjoying a few highballs, requested a quick look at the Promenade before the trio plunged into the evening traffic on the Brooklyn Bridge. At mid-span, the car sputtered, lurched and stopped cold. Leitner jumped out and tried to flag help, his gaze darting anxiously between a pregnant wife and an impatient president-to-be. Finally, Nixon opened his door and lifted a commanding arm. "Sixteen cars stopped," Garment recalled years later. "I knew he was destined to be president because everybody, even in Brooklyn, immediately knew who he was. That ski-slope nose of his stopped the traffic dead."

During his presidency, Nixon was politician enough to know he should keep out of enemy territory. Feckless Gerald Ford wasn't and didn't. Less than six months after he declined to bail New York City out of its financial crisis (earning him the famous *Daily News* headline "Ford to City: Drop Dead"), the president stumbled into Brooklyn on a misguided campaign jaunt. His briefing papers warned him that "Local officials, who are heavily Democratic, believe the Federal Government is insensitive to [their] financial problems." The trip, ill-conceived as it turned out to be, was intended to energize conservative Jewish voters. But Ford's campaign team did so little advance work that the visit turned into a bizarre hazing ritual. There were virtually no pro-Ford crowds, and the two pool reporters who rode with him witnessed only two placards reading, somewhat mysteriously, "Stop Pay Toilets" and "Toilet Liberation." The chief was booed during a brief speech at the Yeshiva of Flatbush and heckled during a street-corner speech in Borough Park. They even egged his limo, yellowing a Secret Service agent's dark suit. Ford's day brightened only in Bay Ridge, where Republicans handed him a two-year-old girl named Heidi Rudjord for a hug. She cried.

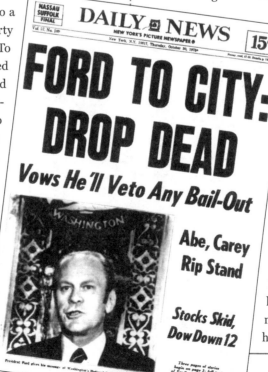

New York Daily News/AP Photo

Harry Truman: Live and In Color in Brooklyn

By David McCullough

The one and only time I saw Harry Truman with my own eyes was in Brooklyn on an evening in 1956. I was all of twenty-three years old and had just started my first job in New York, as a trainee for *Sports Illustrated*. My wife and I, with our infant daughter, had moved to a small walk-up apartment in Brooklyn Heights and were both happily star-struck with the excitement of our new lives.

On the evening in question I was coming home from work about six o'clock or so, and just outside my subway stop at the old St. George Hotel on Clark Street was a small cluster of people, maybe a dozen at most. Governor Harriman, I was told, was coming to the hotel for a political dinner. It was an election year, and politics were much in the air.

Having never seen a real-life governor before, I decided to wait, and it wasn't long before the big car pulled up to the curb where we stood. The back door opened and Averell Harriman emerged, looking appropriately tall and elegant. But then immediately after him, and to the astonishment of everyone, out stepped former president Harry Truman.

The response of the little crowd was immediate delight, and I remember him beaming with what was obviously genuine pleasure. I remember also that he did not seem in the least a "little man," as so often portrayed.

But what stands out most of all in memory, what seemed most amazing by far, is that he was in *color*—which was startling in that day of black-and-white television and black-and-white newspaper photographs. Moreover, his color was vivid, ruddy. He seemed to glow with good health, and his eyes, much magnified by his thick glasses, were a bright blue.

It was all over in an instant. He disappeared into the hotel, and I continued on home. As a story it isn't much, but the impression has never faded. It was there on Clark Street, I think, that I saw and understood in a way I never had until then that presidents are human beings.

David McCullough is the author of Truman, The Great Bridge, Brooklyn and How It Got That Way, Mornings on Horseback *and* The Path Between the Seas.

Since then, presidential visits have been increasingly rare and unmemorable. Jimmy Carter visited just long enough to give a speech. Ronald Reagan and George Bush came not at all. And when President Clinton came to Kings County in April 1997, he appeared only briefly for a Democratic fund-raiser held in the Palm Garden of the Brooklyn Botanical Garden. There were no torchlight parades, no speeches, no spontaneous displays of public affection. In fact, there was no public at all. To get to see the president in Brooklyn on that day, you had to donate $10,000.

Glenn Thrush, a native of Sheepshead Bay, is a longtime observer of Kings County politics.

Russell Christian

Flatbush Girl

The making of a radical

BY SUSAN
BROWNMILLER

Brooklyn brought the world to my door and showed me the portal, but all I wanted was a boyfriend. Dateless and self-conscious, I slunk to the movies on Saturday nights with my mother and father. Let others sing the praises of the Loew's Paramount, its majestic staircase and Technicolor dreams. Our family's destination was the Kent, a run-down art house on Coney Island Avenue where the weekly attraction usually had subtitles and was always in black and white. In that musty sanctuary a few blocks from our three-room apartment on Nineteenth and H, I imbibed the wondrous foreign films of the great post-war renaissance. Surely some Hollywood movies must have infiltrated my youth, but *Miracle in Milan, Open City, Kind Hearts and Coronets* and *The Lavender Hill Mob*—all shown at the Kent—are what I remember.

Weekdays my father worked in the garment center, and my mother took part-time jobs as a bookkeeper or secretary to flesh out the family coffers. If a neighbor asked any nosy questions, I was instructed to chirp, "My mother takes the train into the city to go shopping." The deception probably didn't fool anyone.

I, too, was a daily commuter, on the Ocean Avenue trolley before it became a bus. I rode it for a nickel to Avenue L and walked to Bedford, where P.S. 193 hosted a pilot program for children whose IQs had

tested high on the Stanford-Binet. This experiment drew thirty boys and girls from all over Flatbush. We got supervised trips to the Brooklyn Museum on Eastern Parkway and to the main public library on Grand Army Plaza. One term we studied Spanish, and another term the boys took homemaking and the girls took shop. I thought that was dandy. After school I skated or biked to Wingate Field, which had a circular track and some concrete handball courts. Handball with a pink spaldeen at Wingate was my sport of choice, although

On the track at Wingate Field in the 1940s: Brownmiller (right) sidesteps the competition.

Courtesy of Susan Brownmiller

punchball in the P.S. 193 schoolyard ran a close second.

My parents decided I should have some grounding in my Jewish heritage, so twice a week I mumbled through Hebrew lessons at the East Midwood Jewish Center on Ocean and K, where Rabbi Harry Halpern was the presiding force. The volunteer teachers were ardent young Zionists who dreamed of resettling in Israel. Catching their fervor, I developed a passion to reclaim the Negev and work the land. I remained a devout Zionist for a couple of years, until I discovered the theater.

Our family made solemn excursions on the Brighton Line to Saturday matinees on Broadway and ballet at City Center, but downtown Brooklyn, where the seats were cheaper, was a second mecca for the performing arts. Occasionally my mother would splurge on a season's subscription to the Academy of Music, where I was dutifully exposed to the mime of Ruth Draper, the Katherine Dunham Dance Troupe and the piano recitals of Katherine Bacon. I believe there was more than a touch of latent feminism in my mother's choices. We parted company when it came to the piano, however.

My father didn't know or care about Ebbets Field—some things a girl has to find on her own—but he introduced me to the Subway Circuit, the urban equivalent of summer stock where Brooklynites saw famous plays that had worn out their welcome on Broadway. At Brandt's Flatbush, on Flatbush and Church, I saw *The Madwoman of Chaillot* with Estelle Winwood, one of my favorite plays to this day, and *Private Lives* with a raspy-voiced Tallulah Bankhead, who shocked my tender adolescent sensibilities by camping outrageously for her admiring fans.

When Henry Wallace ran for president in 1948 in his doomed campaign, my mother demurred but my father and I ventured out to an American Labor Party rally at Erasmus Hall High School a few nights before the election. Wallace was late because he was barnstorming the entire borough that day—we Brooklynites were used to waiting—and when he arrived he looked so exhausted that I thought he was going to keel over and faint. But the warm-up attractions had been a revelation. For the first time in my life I heard a folksinger with a guitar. In another memorable first I saw a woman (a *woman*! in a big hat!) deliver a fiery political speech at a microphone, to wild applause. Her subject, rent control and tenants' rights, is still dear to my heart.

Some older kids came over as we left the rally and said I should join the Young Progressives of America. They took down my name and address and asked if I'd help them get out the vote. A postcard with my Election Day assignment arrived in the mail a few days later. I read the message with the sinking feeling that I wasn't up to the task. "To Win with Wallace," they were counting on me to report to a polling place in another part of Brooklyn at six A.M. Didn't they know I was thirteen years old?

My father ended up voting for Harry Truman, as did most of the nation's liberals who had flirted with the idea of Wallace that season. I didn't sneak out of the house at six A.M. to help at the polls, but I did go to some of those YPA meetings. It turned out the Midwood branch met above a store on Avenue J, our neighborhood thoroughfare for meat and grocery shopping. To be perfectly honest, the Young Progressives were a little advanced for me. Not politically, but sexually. After the meetings they'd turn out the lights, crank up the Victrola and get down to real business. Slow dancing. I date my interest in radical politics from that time.

Susan Brownmiller, author of In Our Time: Memoir of a Revolution, *runs both a snappy Web site and a regular poker game.*

 I tramped the streets of Williamsburg, Crown Heights, and Bedford-Stuyvesant, telling people my story. I didn't have the money for a conventional campaign; I had to make up for it with hard work." **Shirley Chisholm**

Lifting the *Giglio*

Penance and respect on the North Side

BY GENIA
GOULD

al lives and breathes the *giglio*," said his wife, Roseanne, referring to the festival of Our Lady of Mt. Carmel and St. Paulinus. "I always planned on retiring out west or in Florida, but I can't take my husband away from the church."

"I'll never leave," said Sal, a retired sanitation police officer, investigator for AT&T and lifelong resident of the parish. "We did our confirmations here, our communions. We married here. My mother-in-law and my mother and father were buried here." Salvatore Miranda himself, now seventy, would miss playing trumpet in the Sunday Mass folk group, teaching music at the church, his friends and family, and above all the *giglio* festival, which takes place every year in the Italian and Polish neighborhood where the North Side of Williamsburg meets Greenpoint.

Considered the most colorful neighborhood-church feast in all of New York City, the twelve nights of reveling, sausage stands and zeppoli, carnival games and Ferris wheels draw many thousands in late June and early July to Mt. Carmel Square at North Eighth and Ninth and Havemeyer Street. The main attraction, though, is the lifting and carrying of a four-ton aluminum-and-wood tower on two consecutive Sundays. Seventy-two feet high, the tower consists of an elaborately fashioned papier-mâché sculpture representing a gigantic lily, or *giglio*. A sculpture of Paulinus, the saint for whom the feast is celebrated, sits on the pinnacle of the tower. The base of the structure is large enough to accommodate a band. The entire tower—band and all—is ceremonially lifted into the air on the shoulders of at least a hundred men. A second large sculpture, a boat, is

Each year, the seventy-two-foot-high *giglio* is marched through the streets of Williamsburg.

Tom Callan

A hundred strong men shoulder not only the four-ton tower but a band of musicians performing on its base.

lifted by another hundred men. The effigies are usually moved twenty to thirty feet at a time, forward and back along the street.

The ritual lifting of these enormous sculptures, also known as "the dancing of the tower," is a grueling—even painful—test of strength, endurance and coordination. "There's about two hundred pounds on each man's shoulder," said veteran lifter Jimmy Dell. "They might lift thirty times a day, and then again the following Sunday. It's an act of respect. It's a penance." The older men are part-time lifters and might lift one of the sculptures just a couple of times during the day.

The Beginning

The legend of the *giglio* arose with St. Paulinus, who was bishop of the seaport town of Nola in Italy. When children of the town were kidnapped by Turks, Paulinus gave himself up to free the children. After his ransom was negotiated, he was returned to Nola on a boat. "The story is that the townspeople came down the side of the mountain carrying lilies in their hands. It looked like one giant lily coming to greet him," explained the monsignor of the Lady of Mt. Carmel Church. "They did it because of the great act of love that he had given the people. In the festival, the boat meeting the *giglio* is the high point of the day, and it symbolizes the return of Paulinus and being greeted by the lilies of Nola."

A *capo* directs the men doing the lifting. He holds a stick and has a repertoire of commands for moving right, left, up, down, forward and backward. One false move could be disastrous. "The *capo* is the number one guy of the day," said Sal, whose father was a founder of the festival and *capo* for twenty years. "He creates the show. Every *capo* does his own routine, whether it's a song that he has the band play or how he directs the lifters to move. There was a guy who invented a cha-cha step under the *giglio*." Over the years, the rules of participation have become more democratic: "You used to have to wait for the old guy to die. But we decided to let more people have the experience, so since 1976 the *capo* changes every two years."

Lifting the *giglio* is also a neighborhood rite of passage for the sons who are introduced to the ritual in childhood. "It's in their blood. They look forward to participating as their fathers, brothers, uncles, grandfathers and great-grandfathers have," said Sal. "We have all kinds of people who want to try it. They come back every year to get that feeling on their body of carrying the *giglio*. To me it's like carrying your mother. You're proud of your mother, so that's *our lady*. You treat your mother with respect, and that's what the whole thing is about: respect and religion, and honoring the saints."

"It's your pledge to the saint," said Jimmy Dell. "And sometimes the fellows, for fun, would go to the first lifters and ask them, 'How you doin'?' And slap them on the shoulder and, you know, make them suffer a little more." The exercise leaves the lifter with what Sal called "a big eggplant." "The guys who do it year after year have a permanent lump in their shoulder. It creates a wound, but that's the suffering you have to do."

"It's a thrill, that feeling when you command the group to lift," said Sal. "But the biggest thrill was when my son and I lifted together, and we were a father-son team. Since then there's only been one other father-and-son team to do the lifts." And when he saw his grandson lifting the giglio? "He's showing respect," Sal said proudly.

Genia Gould, a writer and editor, once started and ran her own weekly Brooklyn newspaper.

Tom Callan (both)

ONLY IN BROOKLYN

Ten thousand Muslims from Brooklyn observe Eid al-Adha, or the feast of the sacrifice, on the sands of Coney Island in the shadow of the defunct parachute jump.

Passionate Company

A public school for dance

BY ELIOT FELD

I don't know how I knew, I just knew that I wanted to dance. I may have gone to the ballet once or twice in my life, but I just knew I wanted to be a dancer. Finally, when I was in the sixth grade, my mother took me to the School of American Ballet, which was in Manhattan on Madison Avenue.

This was around 1953 or '54. There were only two or three boys in the whole children's department in the School of American Ballet, the premier ballet school at the time in this country. So when I auditioned, it wasn't really a question of talent, it was a question of genitals. They said, "Boy," and "Scholarship," and "Come." That was it. It was not an issue of talent, believe me. That didn't mean I wasn't talented, but you didn't need talent. You needed the right package, and I had the right package.

Nobody else in my family wanted to be a dancer. But I loved to dance, and I took to the study because that was the way to become a dancer. It was very, very difficult, because ballet is extraordinarily rigorous.

I was a closet dancer. I played punchball and stickball—I was a two-sewer player at stickball. I loved doing that, and I danced on the side. I remember playing punchball in the schoolyard until I absolutely had to catch the subway to go to my ballet class. But I used to carry a little black attaché case, so the other kids thought I was a stockbroker or something. Certainly none of them knew I was going to ballet classes. Back in the 1950s, that was not a thing that one announced.

That was the beginning of Feld's own career as a dancer. Years later, he took the step that would help to launch many other careers in dance.

I started Ballet Tech about twenty-two years ago: I saw a group of third, fourth and fifth graders on the subway taking a field trip—so thrilled to be going somewhere, so animated. I had been a choreographer for many years at the time, and it occurred to me right then that there were hundreds of thousands of children in the New York City public schools, almost none of whom had an opportunity to discover if they had a talent or a passion for dance. Clearly, out of these hundreds of thousands of children, there were talented people who would never be dancers. To their detriment, because they would not have found something that they had a gift and passion for. And to the detriment of dance and ballet in particular, because a whole resource would have been ignored. So I thought, "My God, there is this incredible untapped resource." And that was really the beginning of the school.

Since that time, we've auditioned just under half a million children in 450 schools. We audition 35,000 children a year, in Brooklyn and three other boroughs. We call the schools and say we have this program—they know us by now, after twenty-two years. We visit 225 schools in one year to audition third and fourth graders, and then the next year we do the other 225. You don't get out of fourth grade without us getting a look at you.

The audition takes place either in the auditorium or in the gymnasium. All of the children come, boys and girls. A lot come just to get out of class. We give them a set of very rudimentary exercises to see if they are flexible, and to see their proportions: Are they big boned or small boned? Are their heads enormous? (You don't want someone with a giant head because they could topple over.) Do they have good coordination in the sense that they can emulate what's demonstrated? Because that's the great tool of learning how to dance. Are they athletic? Can they run and jump? You look for children with some

Eliot Feld (at left) became a professional dancer while still a schoolboy. Then he returned the favor by founding a special ballet school for New York City public school children.

of the physical attributes that would enable them—if they develop a passion for dancing—to become dancers.

We call back those who we think have potential and put them into leotards so we can see their bodies more clearly. The selection is made, but we don't tell the children then. They get a card later, saying, "If you would like to, you have been invited to participate. Congratulations." And that's how it starts.

Why am I doing this? I love the tradition of ballet dancing. It is a thing of such consummate beauty, and such extraordinary rigor, but it is European in its heritage and we need to find some continuing useful American hybrid. As our culture changes, as our demographics change, as we continually redefine ourselves as

a nation of people—as a democracy and as a society— the mutations that make this form animated must take place or else ballet dancing will become a kind of dusty, antediluvian, irrelevant relic. It will be a souvenir and not a breathing, living, vital gritty thing. So there are these two somewhat conflicting imperatives, the beauty of the tradition *and* what it feels like to be alive now.

It's also about what it felt like to be alive when I was growing up. I wasn't born in Leningrad, I was born in Brooklyn, and my musical impulses included some classical music, but I was brought up on Dion and the Belmonts, and Frankie Lymon and the Teenagers, and the Cadillacs, and the Shirelles. And then Elvis Presley, and the Who and Cream and the Rolling Stones and the Beatles and Nirvana.

Lois Greenfield (top); Jim Varriale

When I had the idea to teach children ballet dancing, I thought we would be teaching them everything. And we are teaching them a lot, but they're also reminding me of me growing up. Because they don't have a nineteenth-century European iconography, either: they

Student Dancer

Among the next generation of American dancers groomed by Eliot Feld is a Brooklyn boy named Jabin Waterman. A recent graduate of the New York Public School for Dance, he was recruited as a fourth grader at P.S. 93 in Bedford-Stuyvesant.

"Four people from the Feld Ballet came to our school and invited third and fourth graders to an audition," Waterman recalls. "They picked a few of us and gave us notes for our parents. My mother was all excited, but I didn't know what I was getting into."

Waterman admits he didn't like the dance classes right away; he found them too rigorous and demanding. The school day was 8:35 to 1:45, then it was dance classes and rehearsals from 2:00 to 7:00. "The rehearsals were a lot of work," he says. "Mr. Feld is hard to work for."

His younger brother and sisters used to make fun of him, but "once they saw me perform, they liked it." The performing was rewarding for him as well. Waterman danced in productions at the Joyce Theater in *The Nutcracker* and in *Papillon*. "I was in two company dances and four of the kids' dances," he said. "I was really nervous every time. But I really like performing, and I liked the laughter and the applause." —*M.W.R.*

don't want to be swan queens, they don't want to be Giselles. They have a different image of themselves. These are late-twentieth-century urban Americans, of all different colors, of all backgrounds.

Ballet Tech has a public school, so when you enter the sixth grade, if you really have demonstrated an interest and a passion in dancing, you have your academics right here on the seventh floor. It's a public school for grades six through twelve, officially called the New York Public School for Dance. Generally we will have between ten and twenty-five children as they enter the sixth grade.

And this only costs $1.6 million a year. That's all! I think it really is great. These kids, whether they become dancers or not, are the future of our country. They are going to inherit this place. And with this kind of program, you have a possibility of making this a better place, of leaving a trace of yourself, culturally. You will have passed on something that can be sustained. You will not have left the kids bereft of a past, bereft of opportunity, bereft of self. So I like what we're doing. I like it a lot.

My whole company—Ballet Tech—now is composed of graduates from this school. It became very important that the students in the school had a proprietary interest in the company. Before I could make that change, I essentially had a white company and a minority school, since the New York City public school system is about 90 percent minority. So our school reflects the makeup of the school system. Our company did not reflect the makeup of the school system, because generally it was white middle-class people who had the opportunities and the kind of cultural background to study ballet dancing at a young enough age that permits them to be dancers. It just seemed to me that I needed to make the universe a little bit more consonant. To give the young people who were coming up the sense of "Oh yes, this is ours, we belong here."

Eliot Feld, choreographer and president of Ballet Tech, danced in West Side Story *at age sixteen and went on to win international acclaim.*

The 1990 production of *O Vertigo Danse* helped to put BAM as well as Brooklyn on the map of the performing arts.

BAM!

Bringing the art world to Brooklyn

In 1999, on retiring from his post as president and executive producer of the Brooklyn Academy of Music, Harvey Lichtenstein listed the pluses and minuses of nurturing a world cultural institution in Brooklyn:

INTERVIEW WITH HARVEY LICHTENSTEIN

One of the big minuses is that the cultural and financial life of New York City has generally gravitated to Manhattan. BAM was founded in 1861 when Brooklyn was an independent city, and it became a major institution in that city (Caruso, Toscanini and Isadora Duncan performed there). But then, in the 1930s, '40s and '50s, there was a real question about whether the institution would survive.

Still, I wanted to try and give it a shot. So when I came here, I thought, What do I do to make a mark? How can I attract attention to BAM? How do I grow an audience? I decided to stick with things that I knew about and to go for new activity—things that were needed. There was a need then in New York for a *big* theater for dance.

The first thing I booked into BAM—actually even before I arrived on the premises—was Sarah Caldwell's production of Alban Berg's *Lulu*. Her company was doing *Lulu, Tosca* and Verdi's *Falstaff,* and we put on all three, but *Lulu* got the attention and drew the biggest crowd. Leonard Bernstein came over to see it, and we were on our way. We got the Living Theatre in here in 1968 and also the Chelsea Theater Center. They took space in the building, the 400-seat theater on the fifth floor, and for the next ten years they did four or five pro-

Just one of Harvey Lichtenstein's transformations: once a ballroom, now the incandescent and popular BAM café.

The Rebirth of BAM

One of the best things that ever happened to Brooklyn occurred in 1967 when a little-known ex-dancer and arts administrator named Harvey Lichtenstein made a big career decision: to leave his job at City Center and accept the post of president and executive producer of the Brooklyn Academy of Music. The fact that Lichtenstein grew up in the shadow of the BAM building on Lafayette Avenue, and went to high school around the corner at Brooklyn Tech, had little to do with his decision. It was his zest for a challenge that tipped the balance in BAM's—and Brooklyn's—favor.

And it *was* a major challenge. "Why go there?" Lichtenstein was asked by his then-employer and mentor, Morton Baum. "Nothing can be done

there. BAM is a dying institution."

That was *then.* In the thirty-two years that Lichtenstein ran it, BAM not only escaped death but grew and prospered and burgeoned into what is arguably the liveliest, most innovative and influential perform-ing arts center in America—if not the world. Its Next Wave festival is an annual series of highly original and innovative performances of dance, opera, theater and orchestral music that is now considered the American benchmark of the avant-garde. BAM has put Brooklyn on the world map of the performing arts. For evidence, one has only to examine the lineup for any one of the Next Wave schedules for the past fifteen years. Along the way, Lichtenstein has showcased the

work of Robert Wilson, Steve Reich, Peter Sellars, Philip Glass, Laurie Anderson, Merce Cunningham, Bill T. Jones, Mark Morris, Twyla Tharp, Pina Bausch, Ingmar Bergman and Peter Brook, among many others.

Other major steps have been taken: BAM renovated its own theatrical spaces, took over and renovated the nearby Majestic Theater (it's been renamed the Harvey Theater), an enormous old movie house that was redone as the venue for Peter Brook and the Royal Shakespeare Company's 1971 production of *A Midsummer Night's Dream.* BAM also opened a four-screen art and first-run movie facil-ity—the BAM Rose Cinema—and a café for conversation and live music. —*M.W.R.*

ductions a year here. Then, in 1971, we booked Peter Brook's *A Midsummer Night's Dream*. It was a matter of a negative turning into a positive: we did anything that wasn't being done in New York City.

The really positive thing about BAM's being in Brooklyn was that it gave us the strength and incentive to try things, to do experimental things. Unlike the established institutions in Manhattan, we were not bound by a traditional and conservative board and a conservative audience. We didn't have a lot of blue-haired ladies being shocked. We had a board that understood there were a lot of questions about the viability of BAM, so they were prepared to give me a lot of rope.

We had to manufacture an audience *here*. And to do that, we couldn't do the conventional things. Those were being done at big places in Manhattan, so why would anyone come to Brooklyn to see them? We had to take a lot of risks, and that was a good thing. It wasn't really a matter of drawing an audience of Brooklyn people;

For thirty years the driving force behind the renaissance of the Brooklyn Academy of Music, Lichtenstein delivered such innovative performances as Bill T. Jones' *Last Supper at Uncle Tom's Cabin* **and campaigned to renovate the great Opera House interior.**

it was a matter of pulling an audience of adventurous theatergoers from all over. Enough to fill a large theater. And it did take a long time to build an audience. I started here in 1967, and the place didn't really come together until about 1980. That's thirteen years. It was hard, it was discouraging. Merce Cunningham was here with a wonderful program and drew just 400 people in a 2,000-seat theater.

For a while, the artists themselves resisted. "Why work here?" they'd ask. Some didn't like the place, and some even thought it was a music school of some kind that put on occasional performances. Now that's all changed, and artists elsewhere in the United States and Europe *want* to perform here.

The media took notice, though, and generally felt that what we were doing was important. And we began to get support from the National Endowment for the Arts and also from the foundations—Rockefeller and Ford. It all really coalesced with the start of the Next Wave Series in 1981.

Once in the 1970s when Martha Graham was to do a performance here, I overheard one New York critic say, "I'll wait until she brings it to London." In other words, he thought it was easier to travel to London than to Brooklyn. And I suppose there are still some provincial people in Manhattan who won't cross the East River. But for us, for BAM, the prejudices have been overcome.

Harvey Lichtenstein was born in Brooklyn, attended Brooklyn Technical High School and graduated from Brooklyn College.

All About the Brooklyn Music School

A community school of the performing arts, the Brooklyn Music School stands—literally—in the shadow of BAM on St. Felix Street. It's not a world-famous venue for avant-garde playwrights and choreographers, but a local institution that offers music and dance instruction, as they say, "without regard to income, age, previous experience or professional aspirations," all for an affordable tuition.

The school was founded in 1912, and its four-story building contains classrooms, rehearsal rooms, dance studios and a professional-quality 266-seat theater in which recitals and performances are held. There's great variety in the instruction by some thirty professional musicians and dancers: children can take classes in movement and instrumental music, plus ballet, tap and modern/jazz dance. They can then participate in choruses and in chamber or jazz ensembles that perform in their theater. Over the years, a number of children who got their introduction to sight reading and music theory have gone on to grown-up careers as performers and composers. Older students can take instruction on all orchestral instruments, piano and organ, plus voice, composition and theory. There's even an opera workshop in the summer. And every Christmas season the school stages a Brooklyn version of *The Nutcracker* that would make Tchaikovsky proud. —*Patricia Curtis*

Ensemble work is an integral part of the children's ballet training at the Brooklyn Music School.

Courtesy of Robin Osborne

Defining Olga

The woman who floated the idea of waterfront chamber music

BY MARGARET A. DALY

Barge 1. Any large flat-bottomed boat for carrying heavy freight on rivers, harbors, canals. 2. Boat purchased by Olga Bloom in 1970s for $10,000 to house chamber music series. 3. Rehearsal space for five guys preparing to perform Schubert's *Trout Quintet in A Major*. 4. Platform from which to take in striking views of lower Manhattan, the Statue of Liberty, the great bridges and the entire expanse of New York Harbor.

Bargemusic 1. Incorporated arts organization established in 1977 by Olga Bloom. 2. Fifty-two-week series of chamber music concerts presenting primarily classical pieces for trios, quartets, quintets and piano; includes annual performance of complete Brandenburg concertos. 3. Transcendental setting to present the music Olga Bloom loves while providing musicians a place to perform at above-scale pay. 4. Founded in reaction to growing regimentation of entertainment.

Bloom, Olga 1. Eighty-year-old former Broadway pit musician. 2. Widow of Tobias Bloom, violinist in NBC Symphony Orchestra conducted by Arturo Toscanini. 3. Founder of Bargemusic. 4. Grandmother-like person with gray hair cut in ready-to-go pageboy; often seen dressed in skirt, sweatshirt, stockings and sneakers.

Chamber music 1. Music for performance by a small group, usually with one player to a part (as in a string quartet) and intended usually for small audiences. 2. Type of music played Thursday nights and Sunday afternoons on a renovated barge docked near the Brooklyn Bridge.

IN CONSIDERING OLGA BLOOM, IT IS DIFFICULT TO SEPARATE her from Brooklyn, Bargemusic, chamber music or the barge itself. If Olga were a person less stubborn and tenacious, the entire concept of live musical performances on a barge might never have been pursued. And it seems certain that it could only have happened in Brooklyn. At Fulton Ferry Landing, Olga created a musical presence and then got the city's blessing.

It started as a lark in the mid-1970s, when Olga was complaining that society had become too homogenized: nine-to-five jobs; processed, flavorless food; banks that were all the same; supermarkets, clothes; even personal opinion shaped by huge newspaper conglomerates. "It was all regimented for economic gain," says Olga, who wanted a way out.

A family member put her onto an advertisement for a *barge*, of all things, and she bought it for $800. She anchored it at a makeshift slip behind the Statue of Liberty and occasionally picnicked on board with her husband or gathered with friends to jam to Bach and

Russell Christian

Schubert. The barge was all wood and not seaworthy. "It couldn't even be moved," Olga recalls. She abandoned that first barge for a newer, more expensive one—there were plenty of them available at the time. "It was spongy," says Olga, pushing her finger into the air and pulling it back as if it had just sunk deep into the hull of her barge. That barge gave her the idea to present music and led her to purchase—at the cost of $10,000—the barge now moored near the Brooklyn Bridge.

The next years seemed to take Olga away from music in her effort to build something that would bring more people closer to music. She was more Bob Vila than Itzhak Perlman: "I worked like a Communist in those days," she says emphatically. "The people on the waterfront took me in. They watched out for me and gave me advice. Someone turned me on to Witte Marine. It's a barge salvage place in Staten Island, right on the waterfront. There were lots of barking dogs yelping at me, and the yard sloped down to a marsh. I had no business being there, really," Olga continues, telling the story like a barfly looking for free drinks. "I went to the yard about once a week and loaded up my Volkswagen van. It rode about four inches off the ground."

Olga was then in her sixties, an age when her contemporaries were poring over brochures deciding whether to retire to Palm Beach or Palm Springs, but she enjoyed every minute. "It was the adventure of my life; I leapt from one barge to another, picking out what I needed."

On her first trip to the yard, a gruff old guy had poked his head out the doorway and demanded to know what she wanted. It wasn't long before the two were fast friends. His son-in-law now sits on the Bargemusic board of directors. In doing the repairs, Olga explains proudly, "We never used a ruler." She points to the crosshatch pattern of the cherry paneling on the interior walls of the performance space. "We lined up the panels, which we got off of old Staten Island ferries, to fit into the steel frame. It was like putting a puzzle together. That big oak table—now a concession stand—was a sliding door on another barge."

Every aspect of getting Bargemusic under way was something of an adventure. Olga did not want to book the Juilliard String Quartet or Kronos or other established chamber ensembles. That would have been easy. "What I wanted was an environment that contributed to the creative spirit," she says. Established groups were part of the regimentation she was avoiding. So, as talented musicians in the area come available or travel through the city, they are booked. Often the musicians onstage are playing together for the first time after three or even fewer rehearsals. "That's as it should be," says Olga. "They may not be able to give a piece the precision that comes from a group that plays together over and over, but they bring a freshness and enthusiasm that I think is heard in the music and makes it more exciting."

In reality, many of the musicians are part of a stable that regularly plays the barge. When her longtime artistic director, Ik-Hwan Bae, became too busy with conducting obligations, Olga formed the Resident Artistic Committee. It's a group of seven players who have worked the barge for years and now program and book the fifty-two weeks of concerts. "I'm a firm believer in nepotism, too. I tell the musicians on the committee, I trust your taste, and your wives, your husbands, girlfriends, friends and family." By way of example, violinist Paul Neubauer is married to Kerry McDermott, who is a sister of Anne-Marie McDermott. All three perform at Bargemusic.

The musicians' approach follows Olga's. Music is rigorously rehearsed, the programs are innovative, but the musicians take advantage of the close quarters to reach out and include the audience. Paul Neubauer explained a modern and difficult Schnittke piece to the audience: "If it sounds wrong, it's right."

That's one way to ease the audience into the music, and sometimes it's a challenge for the audience to get settled. A stiff wind or a ship passing along the East River can leave the music lovers clutching their seats and rolling their eyes. That fact and the barge's breezy waterfront location may be what separate this concert crowd from others. At Lincoln Center or Carnegie Hall events, people promenade about the concert hall flashing furs and jewelry. The barge audience is out simply to hear music performed at close range. Lots of hats are worn: straw hats, golf hats, baseball caps, sequined caps, wide brim and short.

It takes Olga's personality and wisdom to fuse it all together—the music, the place, the musicians and the audience. After nearly twenty-five years at the barge's helm, Olga is as enthusiastic as a child. In the midst of an interview, she answers the telephone. She knows the caller and announces, "Tomasini is coming to see me on Monday from the *Times*." She exudes genuine excitement at the prospect of attention from the *Times* even years after receiving regular mention.

Olga's good humor, which has kept Bargemusic afloat in the face of many temptations to take the whole project too seriously, also brings her closer to the musicians. Recently at a rehearsal, one musician raced to the refrigerator to pour a glass of water for another musician who was coughing. "That choking is going to kill him," he told Olga. "I happen to know," Olga replied, "he's not that easy to kill."

Perhaps her greatest resource is her ability still to be a lone artist. Every morning, Olga arrives at the barge at about 7:30 A.M., takes a look at the East River, watches the cormorants dive toward the water, and uncases her violin to play scales and then a favorite work of Bach.

Margaret A. Daly is a veteran journalist who writes about music, food, politics and neighborhoods—often in the borough of Brooklyn.

BROOKLYN ON FILM

An Act of Courage in Flatbush

If the Brooklyn Bridge stands as the borough's most beloved icon, then the Brooklyn Dodgers certainly have endured as the borough's most outstanding live-action phenomenon and Jackie Robinson stands tall as the team's most memorable player.

The Jackie Robinson Story (1950, directed by Alfred E. Green) stars the legendary hero playing himself. The film recounts his years growing up, going to college, excelling at sports and playing in the all-black baseball league. It then follows the process of his being groomed by Branch Rickey to play first in the minor leagues and ultimately as first baseman for the Brooklyn Dodgers.

This film effectively portrays how racial prejudice impedes equal opportunity. In a low-key style and in poignant fashion, it highlights the ongoing discrimination suffered by Robinson, whether refused service in a restaurant, shunned by some of his teammates or being booed on the field by sports fans. Robinson counters this racism by playing his absolute best and by conducting himself in the most upstanding fashion, even in the face of relentless provocation.

Ken Burns' famed televised series *Baseball* (1994), in stylistic contrast to *The Jackie Robinson Story*, employs the techniques of on-camera interviews, dramatic voice-over narration, and period newsreel clips. In telling fashion, the filmmakers focus in on Opening Day at Ebbets Field, when Robinson took the field as an active player on the Dodgers team (April 15, 1947) and how this action epitomized in one transcendent moment America's

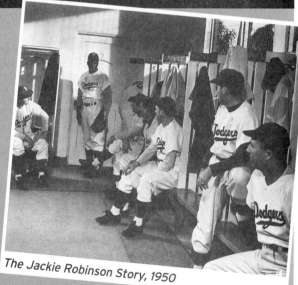

The Jackie Robinson Story, 1950

capacity for greatness. At the end of this passage, they use the dramatic conceit of a Passover service taking place the same night in the Borough Park neighborhood of Brooklyn in order to suggest the common bond of diverse ethnic and racial groups in uniting to overcome prejudice. *—Jon Gartenberg*

MOMA Film Stills Archive

Big Beat at the Paramount

When Brooklyn was the home of rock and roll

BY BILLY
ALTMAN

If you were a teenager in the mid-1950s and lived anywhere in the Greater New York area, you know where you were—or wished you were—every Easter or Labor Day weekend and Christmas vacation during that era. *Brooklyn* was the place to be. The corner of Flatbush and DeKalb Avenues, to be exact, because that was the site of the Brooklyn Paramount Theatre, the epicenter of live rock and roll. That was where WINS disc jockey Alan Freed hosted his "Big Beat" shows featuring a who's who of rock from Little Anthony and the Imperials to Little Richard.

These mythic Brooklyn concerts were nonstop extravaganzas whose cross-section of performers from all over the map (both geographic and stylistic) helped define the 1950s musical and cultural revolution known as "rock and roll"—the term that Freed himself had a large hand in popularizing.

In January 1955, just a few months after his debut on the WINS airwaves, Freed presented his first New York "Rock 'n' Roll Jubilee Ball" at Manhattan's St. Nicholas Arena—a sporting venue hitherto known for its boxing cards. With such rhythm-and-blues stars as the Drifters, Fats Domino, Big Joe Turner, Ruth Brown, the Clovers and the Harptones, his show was a sellout. Moreover, while all the performers were black, the audience was half white—irrefutable proof of the growing interracial appeal of the music and its lusty, hepcat-vibed subculture. That appeal had already provoked dread and loathing in mainstream America, which saw rock and roll as part of everything that was threatening—from juvenile delinquency to Communist plots.

So it wasn't surprising that when Freed sought to upgrade from a sporting arena, the Paramount Theatre chain, with whom he was negotiating, was too nervous to let him book their Times Square house. Instead, Freed wound up at the strategically "safer" 4,400-seat Brooklyn Paramount, where his April 1955 "Rock 'n' Roll Easter Jubilee" began a series of shows that, for the remainder of the '50s, made Brooklyn the epicenter of live rock and roll.

Presented revue-style, the big Freed shows were all-day affairs with at least four separate performances over a period of twelve to fourteen hours, and theoretically one admission price was good for the entire day. There were usually ten or so featured live musical acts, each performing no more than two or three songs. Even the headliners rarely appeared for more than ten minutes. And to thin out the crowds some utterly forgettable Hollywood B movies, mostly Westerns, were shown between sets. The customary response was a hysterical barrage of groans, catcalls and talking-back-to-the-screen commentary for *The Americano*, with Glenn Ford as a Texas cowboy in Brazil, or *Raw Edge*, with Rory Calhoun and Yvonne De Carlo amidst greedy land barons in frontier Oregon.

Waiting out the awful movies, though, had its rewards. The stage soon exploded with the appearance of the stars of early rock and roll: duckwalking Chuck Berry and guitar-slinging Bo Diddley; the mascara'd Little Richard and the ominous Jerry Lee Lewis; bespectacled Buddy Holly and the dreamy Everly Brothers; coffin-dwelling Screamin' Jay Hawkins and sex kitten Jo Ann Campbell. Plus there was a stream of the doo-wopping vocal groups that were so much a part of the fabric of New York street-cornered life in rock's golden age. Appearances by local heroes such as Manhattan's Frankie Lymon and the Teenagers, the Bronx's Chantels, Queens' Cleftones, Staten Island's Elegants

Dancing in the aisles at the Brooklyn Paramount was a common sight during Alan Freed's raucous "Rock 'n' Roll" revues.

and—of course—Brooklyn's own Little Anthony and the Imperials standing shoulder to shoulder alongside such national stars as the Platters, the Flamingos and the Moonglows helped underscore the communal we're-all-in-this-together spirit that was at the heart of rock and roll in its formative years.

The shows were a raucous—and perhaps a bit too threatening—success when the fates, and the feds, began to conspire against Alan Freed and rock and roll.

New York Daily News (top); Brooklyn Historical Society

In 1957, Freed's prime-time television show *The Big Beat* was canceled by the ABC network after just a few weeks on the air when Frankie Lymon was viewed dancing with a white girl, setting off a wave of protest in the South. A disturbance at a Freed-promoted show at the Boston Arena in May 1958 made national headlines—as did a growing congressional investigation into the pay-for-play radio/TV practice called "payola." Even though Freed was then the top-rated DJ in New York, WINS, fearing the stain of a scandal, fired Freed from its station. Then the ever-jittery Paramount chain canceled his upcoming Labor Day rock-and-roll extravaganza. Freed promptly hooked up with Ed Fabian, owner of the Brooklyn Fox, and it was there, just blocks away from the Paramount, that Freed presented several more big shows. The last one was a Christmas '59 affair starring Jackie Wilson, the Skyliners and Brooklyn's own "Sleep Walk"–ing instrumental duo, Santo and Johnny.

It was the payola scandal that drove Freed off the New York airwaves, and clear out of Brooklyn, in the spring of 1960. (He died a broken man in California in 1965.) But Freed's demise was not the end of Brooklyn as a rock-and-roll concert capital. Murray "the K" Kaufman, another legendary New York disc jockey—who'd assumed Freed's evening time slot on WINS—followed another Freed lead by promoting his own rock-and-roll shows at the Brooklyn Fox. Kaufman's shtick was as thick as the schmaltz at the Borscht Belt hotels where he'd cut his showbiz teeth putting on shows in the late 1950s, and he became, in Freed's wake, New York's hottest radio personality. By that time, America had reached an uneasy, détente-like truce with rock and roll, and in the early '60s Kaufman showcased the latest trendsetters at the Fox, from clean-cut California surfers Jan and Dean to soul-stirring Motown artists such as Smokey Robinson and the Miracles to "uptown r-'n'-b" girl groups such as the Shirelles (the Passaic, New Jersey, quartet whose breakthrough hit "Will You Love Me Tomorrow?" was penned by Brooklynite composer Carole King) and Washington Heights' Ronettes, whose sultry sashaying earned them extra status as the official "Murray 'the K' Dancing Girls."

In 1964, Kaufman succeeded in glomming on to the Beatles ahead of the competition (the Ronettes, who'd met them in England, introduced him), and his heavily self-promoted association with the Fab Four—he began calling himself "the Fifth Beatle"—gave him access to numerous British Invasion rock groups whom he then booked for his shows at the Fox. Brooklyn thus became a kind of musical Ellis Island for young performers such as the Zombies, who made their American debut at the Fox in December of '64. They almost *ended* their careers right then, too, when, in a scene straight out of *A Hard Day's Night,* several members of the band innocently ventured onto the street between shows to get some air and nearly got trampled by hordes of hormone-charged teenage girls. They were saved by New York's finest, who in fine NYPD fashion told them they'd have to fend for themselves the next time they stuck their mop-topped little heads outside the theater. Neither the Zombies nor any other English group dared face Flatbush Avenue again without a security force.

By 1967, as the civil rights movement, the Vietnam War, drugs, feminism and black power helped turn rock and roll into rock (or, as Kaufman dubbed it, "attitude music"), Brooklyn's big-beat palaces had all but gone dark for the multi-starred shows that Freed had introduced just a short decade-plus before. That March, Kaufman held his last old-style shindig, "Music in the Fifth Dimension," at the RKO in Manhattan. Jettisoned by WINS when the station went to an all-news format and disillusioned by the growing formulaic approach in AM radio, Kaufman joined other disgruntled broadcasters as the first rock DJs on WOR-FM. No more "Swingin' Soirees" for Murray the K, and no more Big Beat jubilees for the Paramount or Fox theaters. The times were indeed a-changin'—though they would never be forgotten by two vital generations of Brooklyn rock and rollers.

B.J. "Billy" Altman is a music journalist, critic and historian whose work has appeared in magazines such as The New Yorker, Esquire *and* People. *He is the author of* Laughter's Gentle Soul: The Life of Robert Benchley.

Midnight in "Moscow"

The Brighton Hustle is not a dance

BY GLENN
THRUSH

The small, mirrored lobby of the National Restaurant in Brighton Beach is crammed with very well-dressed middle-aged Russians, the air thick with their nasal chatter and their Chanel No. 19. When the double doors to the huge main hall burst open, the talk stops and the perfumed air is blown away by the overpowering aroma of smoked sable.

The sign in the lobby says the maximum occupancy is 240, and on this Saturday night the crowd seems to be barely within the limits of the law—even with a third of the tables still empty. Most of the diners are seated at long communal tables arranged in a huge L-shape that could easily accommodate 500 people. The stage and dance floor are in a shallow sunken pit, along with a dozen more of the long tables covered with sequined handbags, Absolut bottles and platters heaped with fish. A baby's-breath tangle of white Christmas lights runs along the ceiling. "No Smoking" signs are posted every ten feet or so—considerably farther apart than the smokers themselves. To the Russian émigrés who make up most of the crowd, the big hall must seem like the gilded ballroom of a Black Sea cruise ship.

"You came on a good night," proclaims the waiter, a young swarthy guy named Artom. "The floor show begins at ten-thirty."

There are scores of nightclubs, restaurants, "caffes" and hang-abouts on the ten-block stretch of Brighton Beach Avenue commonly known as Little Odessa. And many more are springing up on the boardwalk and on the adjacent residential side streets, with a typical Russian disregard for such stodgy formalities as New York City's zoning laws. Some of these nightspots are hipper than National, and some offer better food or more up-to-date decor. But National is a place with a history, and in Brighton, a neighborhood where whole blocks are transformed in a year's time, there is something solid and reassuring about the three-story stucco-and-concrete edifice that rises above the D and F trains' elevated tracks.

"I don't know how long it's been here," says Roman Gershgorin, a poet and publisher who emigrated from Moscow to Brooklyn in the late 1989. "It's always been here, as far as I know." Every weekend, Gershgorin, a former screenwriter for Soviet TV, sells all twenty-nine of

Russell Christian

his self-published books from his chosen spot next to the second-floor coat check. He says he makes a living off them—enough to live in upscale Manhattan Beach. His elegant little books are a curious hybrid of erudite translations of Aristophanes and French poets, his own quirky fiction, and pornography. A slim white volume he titled *Eroticheskiye* is a collection of 137 sonnets, illuminated with dozens of wonderfully vivid pen-and-ink drawings of the author *in flagrante* with one, two or three sexual partners. Although his body type changes from drawing to drawing, Gershgorin is identifiable by his balding pate and black goatee. Opening another book, he points to a faceplate photograph of a demure Russian lady wearing a dignified smile and a Brezhnev-era blouse buttoned up to her chin. "This is my wife," he says.

Gershgorin's entrepreneurial zeal is nothing compared to that of two little old men who run the nearby coat check. Their wares include a dozen varieties of toy guns, statuettes of naked dancers with a cigarette lighter hidden in their breasts, cheap battery-powered dogs and good European cigarettes. When an American customer buys a pack of Dunhill Menthols (retail: $5) with a ten spot, one of the men pockets the remaining $5 without so much as a "*Spasibo*" for the involuntary tip. "Have a nice night" is all he says.

For most of the night, the stage is occupied by a five-piece club band that cycles through an un-kitschy set of Yiddish-tinged Russian dance tunes, slow-dance ballads and "Hotel California"—its five-minute guitar coda lovingly replicated from the record, note for note. But at ten-thirty on the dot the band disappears and is replaced by a set of dancers: three men and five women. The crowd bunches up at the railings, leaving their bowls of Stroganoff to harden behind them.

The principal performer is a stunning young man with a two-foot platinum mane flowing under a fedora. He is a dead ringer for the ballet dancer Alexander Godunov. The first song is "Zoot Suit Riot," and between spins he pantomimes machine-gunning the crowd. The women dancers twirl and kick, but it soon becomes apparent that all their jazz-dance moves, even the dirtiest derriere grinds, are performed with a certain balletic formality. During the cancan finale, with all dancers clad in white feather plumes, *Swan Lake* keeps threatening to break out.

The show is more spectacle than sex, but the same cannot be said of the crowd. Sometime during "Zoot Suit," three single women in their late twenties sweep into the hall: a blonde, a brunette and a redhead. The headwaiter, a tough-looking guy with a Mafiya razor cut who was distractible to begin with, ditches his duties completely when he sees them. He brings them a bottle of champagne, which they sip indifferently as he hovers. Then comes a box of wrapped chocolates, followed by a platter of strawberries, watermelon and pineapple. Finally, he pulls up a chair and begins running a stray hand down the small of the redhead's back.

The place is filled with beautiful women in all heights and widths, all united by an evident disdain for loose-fitting attire. But when the redhead rises from the table and shakes off her shawl and the waiter's paw, the men at the neighboring tables are simply dumbstruck. The forlorn waiter watches her walk away, but only for an instant. He begins chatting up the brunette.

By the end of the night, the waiter is back on the job, helping the customers settle up their $200 tabs. Roman Gershgorin is still at his post, soberly answering questions from tipsy patrons as they retrieve their furs and leather trench coats.

Glenn Thrush writes for numerous publications in the New York area and is actually a native of Brighton Beach.

It's dark on Atlantic Avenue and all the bars around the Long Island Railroad station are bright and noisy. We go from bar to bar looking for Dad." **Frank McCourt**

Bass Revival

Brooklyn lays claim to dub

BY S.H. FERNANDO, JR.

A renaissance of dub music —the Jamaican-born studio specialty—has been brewing in Brooklyn in recent years. It started in a massive loft-like warehouse in the Greenpoint section, home of Greenpoint Studio, a unique laboratory of sound where producer and bassist Bill Laswell has worked with and mixed the music of every genre of creative player. Behind the gray, graffiti-scrawled door, the musings of Pharaoh Sanders' saxophone have mingled with tabla master Zakir Hussein's rollicking percussion, the legendary Public Enemy producers "the Bomb Squad" have detonated their block-rocking beats, and master tapes by Bob Marley and Miles Davis have been respectfully remixed by Laswell. In Greenpoint Studio, Laswell has brought together hip-hop heavyweights George Clinton, John Zorn and the Jungle Brothers. The Last Poets have staged poetry slams (spoken-word events), and all manner of musicians from every corner of the world have come to lend their talents to the endless sonic permutations and combinations that Laswell has created during a twenty-year career. After producing Herbie Hancock's Grammy-winning *Rock It* in 1983, Laswell could have continued on his trajectory of mainstream success, but he chose instead to continue his exploration of world music, "underground" music and the more obscure genres like dub.

In Williamsburg, a few blocks away from the studio, Laswell found allies among the dub fanatics of the fervently underground WordSound label. In turn, the WordSound team was equally inspired by the futuristic dub that Laswell was producing for the Axiom label distributed by former Island Records mogul Chris Blackwell. Laswell began working with WordSound and with homegrown Brooklyn dub talent and in the mid-'90s was pushing a stateside dub revival. Their output included the best-selling Crooklyn Dub series *Certified Dope*, Volumes 1–3. And even before "dub" became a buzzword in the music industry, the WordSound team had proposed the idea of a dub summit to Laswell and to legendary Jamaican reggae drummer Style Scott of

Dub almost died out in Jamaica before it erupted in Brooklyn studios.

Courtesy of S.H.Fernando, Jr.

The Origin of Dub

In Kingston, Jamaica, in the late 1960s, a young studio engineer by the name of Osbourne Ruddock was cutting instrumental versions of some popular songs on his then-state-of-the-art, four-track mixing console when he stumbled upon an interesting discovery. He found that by working the faders he could accentuate certain sounds like the bass or the drums. And then, using his custom-made echo box, he could make a snare-drum hit or keyboard riff rise above the rest of the mix and fade away, thus creating radically different versions of the same song. The next time Ruddock, who ran a mobile sound system and worked as a DJ under the moniker of King Tubby, played acetates (or "dub plates") of his mixes at a dance, the crowd went wild—especially when Tubby's master of ceremonies, a man by the name of U-Roy, also started "toasting" or ad-libbing rhyming phrases over the spacey-sounding instrumentals.

Tubby had thus started a new musical craze called "dub," which developed hand-in-hand with the phenomenon of toasting, the Jamaican precursor to modern-day rap. Dub was entirely a studio art that made such innovative record producers as Coxsone Dodd and Augustus Pablo artists in their own right, and dub *ruled* Jamaica throughout the '70s. But then, as vocalists became the dominant stars of the music business, studio-bound dub was all but forgotten outside the Jamaican enclaves of England, where it had become very popular—until its stateside revival in Brooklyn. —*S.H.F., Jr.*

Dub Syndicate and the Roots Radix band, who have backed virtually every reggae performer of note—live and on album—for the last twenty years.

Laswell and Scott agreed to put together a summit session, but it almost didn't happen. On a cold, rainy Saturday in December, Laswell and engineer Bob Musso arrived at the Greenpoint Studio at noon to begin preparations for the session. Style Scott was supposed to show at two P.M., but five hours later he was still absent. Finally, just as everyone's last hopes were slipping away, Scott strutted in with a Kool-Aid smile. Shrugging off the rain, he proceeded directly to the drum kit and, after exchang-

ing a few laughs with Laswell, began to put his drums to the test. From the start, his hits were hard and precise, almost stinging the ears with their power. And when Laswell started plucking the strings of his black Gibson bass (which was connected to several effects pedals to enhance its low-end capabilities), it took only moments for the duo to lock into a deep groove that was the essence of reggae and dub. Musso quietly hit "record" on the massive Studer tape machine, and a reel of two-inch tape began to capture their session.

Without rehearsal, and with hardly a pause, the jam-down continued through groove after groove of what Jamaicans call "crucial riddim"—original drum and bass in a dub style. Scott effortlessly kept time like a Swiss clockmaker as he made his high hat do things that no rhythm machine could ever do. Laswell, all the while, sounded like he'd been schooled to play bass on the streets of Kingston. Within just a few hours of meeting, they created the raw material for *Dub Meltdown*.

But as dub is always achieved "in the mix," these raw tracks were given the final treatment by Laswell and "The Eye" from WordSound. This time, during a swelter-ing week in July, the two convened in Laswell's studio to subject those master tapes to all the studio wizardry at their fingertips. They tweaked knobs and flicked switches, mixing in all manner of sound effects. They cut and spliced tape, running it backward or slowly, to create the disorienting spatial effects for which dub is known. In short, they made a classic dub album for the '90s, released as *Bill Laswell Meets Style Scott Inna Dub Meltdown*. The album's reverberations (and sales) have been felt in Europe, Canada and Japan as well as America, regenerating the magical appeal of this almost-lost Jamaican artform.

So while Seattle is associated with grunge, Brooklyn lays its claim to dub—not as a retro musical form, but as a futuristic manifesto on the infinite potential of sound. Some thirty years after King Tubby first defined it in Jamaica, dub has taken on new life in Brooklyn.

S.H. Fernando, Jr., is a musical producer and a con-tributing writer for Notorious *magazine. He is writing a book on Sri Lankan cuisine.*

NOW & THEN

Band music enjoyed great popularity in Brooklyn. In 1909, John Philip Sousa penned this march to celebrate the famous resort at Manhattan Beach.

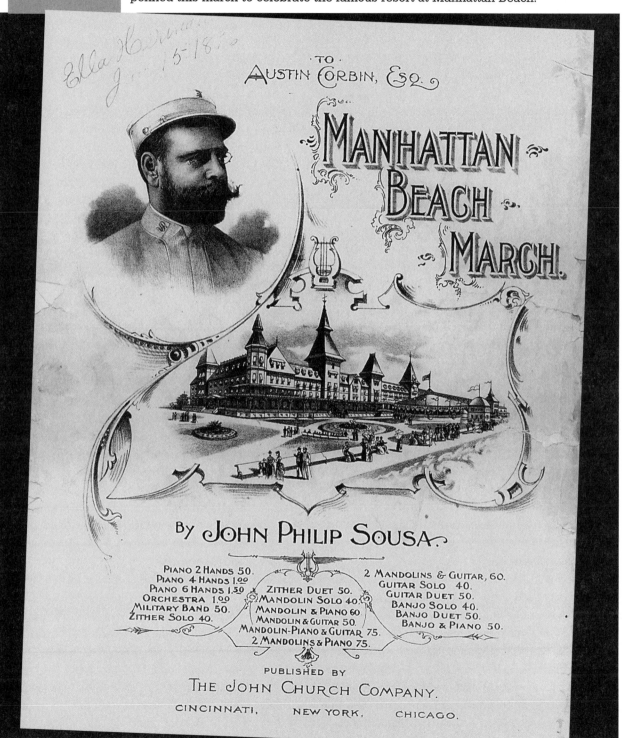

Kingsborough Historical Society

The King in Kings County

Elvis ships out from the Army Terminal

BY MARC
KIRKEBY

To announce the end of the world, will they hold a news conference? We may laugh at the thought. But a world did come to an end on September 22, 1958, when Private Elvis Presley boarded his troopship for Germany— as good a date as any to mark, if not the death of rock and roll, then at least the close of its wonderful first chapter. And they did hold a news conference. It was right here in Brooklyn on the day the King set foot in Kings County.

The troop train, en route from Fort Hood, Texas, had crawled up through the Jersey commuter dawn that Monday, the first day of autumn. By the time it passed under the Hudson, under Manhattan and up into the light again in the Sunnyside yards, the train was a couple of hours late and just beginning the long, lazy arc that would take it from central Queens down through Brownsville, the Brooklyn Terminal Market and East Flatbush, along the railroad cut just below Brooklyn College and on to Borough Park, Sunset Park and its destination—the Brooklyn Army Terminal on Second Avenue near Fifty-Eighth Street.

Elvis was twenty-three years old, just a month past the death of his mother, to whom he had been utterly attached. On his lap, we're told, was a copy of *Poems That Touch the Heart*, a sentimental anthology someone had given him; the poem he remembered later was called "Should You Go First," about the death of a loved one. We imagine him looking out the window at Brooklyn homes and neighborhoods, glancing down at his book, thinking his thoughts. But not for long: it seemed that every one of the 350 other soldiers on the train wanted to meet Elvis, and he didn't mind. "I don't like to sit alone too much and think," he would say that morning.

Rock and roll, like the newly Dodger-free Brooklyn, had seen happier years than 1958. That week's *Billboard* singles chart had plenty of *American Bandstand*–style teen pop, but only two of thirty records (neither of them by Elvis) could really be called rock and roll. *Billboard*'s news stories included a wishful piece about older pop artists like Perez Prado and Doris Day making a comeback, and a piece about the potential impact of the hula-hoop craze on teen record sales ("Plastic Hoops Put Music Fraternity in Vinyl Tizzy"). In Brooklyn, the Joseph J. Jones hi-fi stores were demonstrating just-arrived stereo equipment, but stereo was for grown-ups; the 45-rpm singles that kids bought would remain monaural for almost two more decades.

The train arrived at what Elvis biographer Peter Guralnick has called "a scene worthy of P.T. Barnum [or] Cecil B. DeMille": more than a hundred reporters, cameramen, broadcast crews; army brass; representatives of Elvis' record company, music publishing company, management and mobile entourage. (But no fans: the kids, perhaps another hundred of them, were kept far away, beyond the gates, out where the Terminal grounds met the sullen neighborhood, the heart of *Last Exit to Brooklyn* turf.)

The King kept them waiting for another hour while the 382nd Army Band, under the direction of Chief Warrant Officer John R. Charlesworth, played "All Shook Up," "Hound Dog" and "Tutti Frutti." "I felt we should make it a Presley field day," Charlesworth said. "Any man who takes care of his mother and father the way he does, I admire."

Finally Elvis emerged and the questions began. His favorite songs, he said, were "Padre" by Toni Arden (!) and

Elvis in uniform, boarding the *General Randall* in 1958.

Bettmann/Corbis

"You'll Never Walk Alone." He had bought the Domenico Modugno single of "Volare" right away, but doubted he himself "could cut the mustard" singing in Italian. What about Jerry Lee Lewis' (third) marriage to his fourteen-year-old (second) cousin? "If he really loves her, I guess it's all right." For himself, though, "It's helped my career not to be married." Nobody asked him about Brooklyn.

Mostly he fielded snide variations on the same question he'd been answering for years: What'll you do if (read "when") rock and roll (read "this garbage") dies out? "I'll starve to death," he quipped, then went on, in a more serious vein, to talk about pursuing his career in movies (just what his manager, "Colonel" Tom Parker, had in mind in any case). Four years after starting the upheaval that would transform American popular culture, Elvis remained the kindly, earnest, unaffected kid he had been when he was driving a truck in Tupelo.

It went on for an hour. He posed for pictures, with a borrowed duffel bag, on the gangplank of the USS *General Randall.* He gave a stagy hug and kiss to WAC specialist Mary Davies of Albany, who had been chosen for this honor. Musical theater buffs will recognize this tableau as the germ of the 1960s musical *Bye Bye Birdie,* the Charles Strouse–Lee Adams–Michael Stewart hit whose happy ending has Dick Van Dyke giving up his successful career as "Conrad Birdie's" favorite songwriter to become, yes, an English teacher.

He gave out some glossies, signed some autographs, and was gone. For all the media frenzy, the next day's New York papers gave out a collective yawn. "Elvis's Latest Rock 'n Roll is Ocean's," read the *Herald-Tribune* headline. The *Daily News* ran a back-cover photo of Elvis, with trademark lip-curl, on the gangplank, captioned, "Does he look happy?" The *Times* buried a little item on page 29, amid some leftover brides and a traffic tie-up on the Hutch. The *Post* ignored it, but ran an Elvis photo in Earl Wilson's column to illustrate an item about comic Dick Shawn's act at the Latin Quarter, featuring such boffo yocks as "On TV, they've toned [Elvis] down to an orgy."

Elvis, of course, did not fade away. RCA Victor released *Elvis Sails,* an extended-play album of nothing but the Brooklyn press conference, which sold 100,000 copies. The record company also continued to dole out stockpiled singles by Elvis, which kept him on the charts until he mustered out of the service in 1960. And throughout the ensuing decade Elvis continued to record the occasional rock-and-roll tune, as if to prove he still could.

But Peter Guralnick puts it plainly in the *Rolling Stone Illustrated History of Rock & Roll,* noting that by the time Elvis entered the army in 1958 he was what Sun Records owner Sam Phillips had said he would become: "a genuine pop singer. A pop singer of real talent, catholic taste, negligent ease, and magnificent aplomb, but a pop singer nonetheless."

And rock and roll? Call it coincidence or call it fate, but as the *General Randall* passed through the Verrazano Narrows that September afternoon, the bell was already tolling. Jerry Lee Lewis, owing to the aforementioned nuptials, was banned from the airwaves. Little Richard, after freaking out on tour in Australia, had enrolled in Bible college. Carl Perkins still had not recovered from a car crash two years earlier. In less than half a year, Buddy Holly, Ritchie Valens and "Big Bopper" J.P. Richardson would be dead in a plane crash. A year after that, a London taxi accident would kill Eddie Cochran and injure Gene Vincent. Then, in short order, Alan Freed and Chuck Berry would both find themselves under indictment, Freed for paying off disc jockeys and Berry for a trumped-up morals charge. Berry went to jail; Freed never worked again and died broke in 1965.

Elvis' ship has sailed, leaving no monument of any kind. But if you stand for a moment at the old Port of Embarkation in Sunset Park, some sort of Afro-hillbilly-youth music will surely waft by, maybe even something he would recognize. And that may be the most fitting monument of all.

Marc Kirkeby, a Brooklyn native and resident, is Sony Music's vice president for archives development. His written work has appeared in The New Yorker, Rolling Stone, *the* New York Times *and* The Village Voice.

Pips

Brooklyn's comedy boot camp

BY JOE GILFORD

A walk down Emmons Avenue along Sheepshead Bay on a sultry evening is like a stroll through the lobby of the United Nations. No fewer than a dozen languages are heard on a normal weekend night here. You could easily imagine yourself at any international crossroads—Casablanca, Marseilles, Athens. Within earshot there's Chinese, Russian, Italian, Greek, Spanish, Syrian, the lilt of Jamaican patois, all with undertones of various regional dialects of Brooklynese.

Carried along on this multinational breeze, you step into Pips Comedy Club with a sense of avid anticipation and mystery. What on earth is a comedy club doing here in Sheepshead Bay at the very edge of Brooklyn—a place where fishing boats still take anglers away on day trips? Let's just answer that this outpost is here to keep the franchise alive, to make sure that the nation's fun-

The Funniest Borough

It has been observed that Brooklynites (or Brooklyneers, as some of us prefer to be called) somehow possess a better sense of humor, maybe a more developed ear for jokes and a sharper instinct for comedy than "normal" folks—those from Manhattan and other parts of the Midwest. It may be impossible to account for this geographic—or ethnographic—trait. However, one does not need a Ph.D. in anthropology to see that we, of the Second Borough (it was the second logical step for the first settlers), are equipped with a Seventh Sense, or perhaps a fourth eye—an intuitive sense of things funny that's unlike the senses of other mortals.

nier citizens still have a place to work their trade; to hold open the gate to those who have bravely chosen the noble and indispensable profession of making the rest of us lighten up—maybe even laugh.

Pips appears to pride itself on its downscale ambience. Simple Masonite paneling along the walls boldly reflects local decorating standards, although the obligatory bare brick wall—à la The Improv—backs the performing area. Tables surround a wide, shallow platform stage, and comics compete for audience attention with neon and mirrored signs promoting beer and spirits. About twenty-five tables are squeezed into a split-level area leading up to a good-size bar. In short, there is nothing pretentious about Pips. If you don't like the comedy routines—get a burger and a beer. And if you don't like the vittles—you might as well get lost.

The international flavor of Emmons Avenue carries through the doors of Pips. Many comics complain that their best laughs don't fall so much on deaf ears as on

Russell Christian

uncomprehending ones. Performers are easily lured by stage-side couples who smile engagingly as if understanding every nuance of the routine, but when spoken to directly—"Hiya folks, where ya from?"—respond only with a "Nay" or "Vus?" After a particularly tough show, one comedian shook his head in despair and remarked, "They didn't understand a fuckin' word I said." To which one of his colleagues replied, "Oh no, they understood every *fuckin'* word—just not every fuckin' *word*."

But these barriers are not insurmountable. The languages of pantomime, impressions and general silliness are still universal, as is the oddly international language of American profanity. Curse words, like the language of love, are understood and can cause a titter no matter what one's origins or culture. And as more than a few comedy veterans have remarked, if their A-material *bombs* at Pips, it's sure to *kill* at better venues. Pips is the trial by fire, the gamut, the comedians' hazing ritual since 1965, and the oldest still-cookin' comedy club in the United States. Bill Cosby, Robert Klein, Andrew Dice Clay, George Carlin and many others either began their stand-up careers here or performed here during their formative years to revisit and refresh at Brooklyn's comedy boot camp. The unspoken motto of the place seems to be: If you can play Pips, you can play *anywhere*.

Recently, an Italian-American comic who developed his act at Pips and is now one of the regulars passed along his firsthand observations of the onstage experience here: "Pips is a great club because it's got culture; a lively place with some atmosphere. But that's a double-edged sword. And don't get me wrong, I love Brooklyn. But there's something strange about the crowds here. Believe it or not, it's very rare to get a great comedy crowd at Pips. Like I'm onstage at Pips, and I'm doing stuff that always hits, but they just kind of sit there. I don't know why. I start laying into the Russian people, maybe they just don't get it, or it's the language, or the brand of humor or what the hell I'm talking about in general—I don't know! It's a tough club. And for someone like me, it shouldn't be. Like if I do something in Staten Island, it's like—boom!—these are my people. And Brooklyn should be the same way. I do better at some little town in the middle of nowhere than I do at Pips. But I don't take it personally.

"I kind of appreciate a *good* heckler. Even before I did stand-up comedy, I used to go to shows at Pips and would be kind of a heckler myself. 'Cause it was always in me to do stand-up and this was all part of wanting to do it. I was at Pips one night and this girl comic onstage was just dying. So I seized the opportunity and said something, and that gave her fuel. We were going back and forth—and the crowd was just blowing up.

"Pips has gotten branded as a very hard-hitting club. Unless you get a great night, and you get all the stars aligned in the sky, your great act is probably not going to kill there the way it normally does—unless you get a little down and dirty. Pips crowds have come to expect anything from dirty language to abusing people. It's a very in-your-face kind of club. Like they say: 'Wednesday is open-mike night. Call in advance if you want to throw yourself to the lions.'"

Joe Gilford is a Brooklyneer cook, writer, raconteur and scion of the venerable Brooklyn-comic Gilford family.

> I loved everything about the jazz culture—practicing, listening, searching for the perfect reed, walking the Brooklyn streets with musician friends singing the recorded jazz solos we knew by heart. Most of all, of course, I loved playing jazz." **Leonard Garment**

Jazz Scene in Fort Greene

Was there a Brooklyn sound?

BY LARRY
BLUMENFELD

Once in late 1999, trumpeter Terence Blanchard was wrapping up a recording session for an album. I was interviewing him as he packed instruments away in the dressing room of a recording studio on Manhattan's West Side. Bassist Dave Holland poked his head in, nodding as if in strong assent. "That was fun," said Holland, a guest star with Blanchard's fine working quintet. "It reminded me of old times with Steve."

He was referring to the 1980s, when Holland would drive from his home in upstate New York to Brooklyn to hook up with Steve Coleman and his cohorts. Holland, by then an established leader and veteran of the '70s Manhattan loft scene, had just recovered from heart problems; with his energy renewed and the loft scene fading, he began looking elsewhere for musical adventure. There was, in fact, some intense and liberating jazz activity happening in and around Fort Greene, much of it catalyzed by Coleman.

By the late 1980s, Blanchard was dividing his time between recording for Columbia Records and composing scores for Spike Lee, whose burgeoning film company was just a short walk from Blanchard's apartment.

Knowing where Holland's reminiscences were based, I asked, "A Brooklyn thing?"

"A music thing," Blanchard shot back.

Holland laughed. "A time in our lives."

If this exchange between Blanchard and Holland were occurring in one of Spike Lee's films, we'd get a fade about now and the next scene would open some fifteen years earlier in a Fort Greene bubbling with creative ferment—*Entertainment Weekly* would later dub the area "Black Bloomsbury." The camera would trail Coleman, a young alto saxophonist with a Charlie Parker fixation, some advanced ideas about rhythm and key changes, and a real knack for organizing musicians around concepts.

Having honed his chops in Chicago, Coleman moved to New York in 1979, living for a short while in a Manhattan YMCA, though more and more he found himself drawn across the East River bridges to Brooklyn. Complaints began at the Y: he was practicing his horn too much, disturbing others. He tried playing on the roof, but the people in nearby buildings wouldn't have it. Coleman didn't like Manhattan's vibe anyway. It was restrictive.

Steve Coleman was at the center of the Brooklyn jazz revival.

Robin Holland

"So I moved to Prospect Place because a trumpeter I knew had an extra room," Coleman explains. "Then I found a place in Bed-Stuy." He began to feel more at home. "Brooklyn reminded me of Chicago. Brooklyn and Harlem were the two places that reminded me of the South Side of Chicago. But Brooklyn more so because it was more neighborhood-oriented.

"For one thing, you could relax. It was very hard to relax in Manhattan. And another thing—and this is crucial for musicians, though it may not sound like a big deal—you could make noise. A big deal with musicians is to be in a place where you can play without worrying. And I'll tell you, traditionally, in black neighborhoods it's easy to practice. When you go into white neighborhoods, expensive neighborhoods, people are not used to people making noise."

The "noise" that Coleman and his cohorts—soon to be labeled by the press "the M-BASE crowd" (after Coleman's concept of "Macro-Basic Array of Structured Extemporization")—was fascinating and original. And it's important to understand the context in which this sound emerged. Like New York City in general, Brooklyn has hosted its share of jazz figures: from Flip Phillips to Max Roach, Randy Weston, Cecil Taylor, Betty Carter and many others; a major swath of the music's history stretches through the borough. Jazz, which had all but been pronounced dead in the 1970s, was suddenly coming back into vogue in the '80s: record companies had begun releasing and promoting more jazz, and the press was writing about it again.

A young trumpeter that Coleman recalled seeing at an audition for the Thad Jones-Mel Lewis Orchestra—the one who Jones said "wasn't ready yet" (but who Jones and everyone else knew would soon be heard from)—Wynton Marsalis, was already on his way. Marsalis would soon be seen as the poster boy for a pride of "young lions," players heralded as the ones who'd return jazz to its traditional values and its rightful place in American cultural life. They were articulate about jazz's history, and they played everything from swing and bebop.

Wynton and his brother, saxophonist Branford, hailing from an intensely musical family in New Orleans, soon turned up in Brooklyn and moved in right down the street from Coleman. If the Marsalis brothers had a view across the East River, Branford might have been able to see the landscape that would soon open for him: a burgeoning recording career, a stint with pop star Sting, a gig as bandleader for Jay Leno's *Tonight* show. And perhaps Wynton could see where he'd soon be ensconced as jazz's most recognizable figure and musical director of the jazz program at Lincoln Center.

Although Steve Coleman played some with Branford and shared his love of jazz's fundamentals (he studied Charlie Parker, for instance, as if his life depended on it), his roar was of a spirit different from that of the Marsalises' "young lions." Coleman had made some key contacts in New York: drummer and composer Doug Hammond and saxophonist Jimmy Cozier. He also worked with a number of other young musicians who found it easier to breathe in Brooklyn, a growing coterie

Pianist Geri Allen: one of the early participants in Coleman's M-BASE collective.

Robin Holland

The House That Betty Built

All jazz musicians are students. The good ones end up being educators, too. Only a few leave legacies so profound that they touch generations to come. Drummer Art Blakey was such a presence. Musicians who passed through his band spoke of it as a university; they talked about how Blakey molded them on and off the bandstand. Singer Betty Carter was another. Watching her perform through the years, I could see how Carter commanded her bands with equal measures of love, authority and body English. Invariably, there were young musicians in her band, players Carter tapped because, as she used to say, "they had the energy, the enthusiasm that I need."

But there was more to it. One night not long before her passing in 1998, I caught up with her between sets at the Blue Note. She was not satisfied with what she saw as the status quo in jazz. She could not forgive the record labels for not caring about "audience development" (she enunciated those words as if they were lyrics), for packaging but not nurturing young artists. She was relentless. And for the most part, she was right.

Although much of the training that Carter herself undertook occurred on the bandstand or on the road, it could all be traced to her five-story brownstone in the Fort Greene section of Brooklyn. Her place, at 117 St. Felix Place, was the main campus of the institute of higher education in jazz that was Betty Carter. There she'd rehearse her bands and offer wisdom, practical advice, even sanctuary to musicians who showed enough promise and sufficient mettle. When a Brooklyn-based nonprofit organization, 651 Arts, teamed up with the singer in 1992, they created Jazz Ahead!, a program to gather young, talented musicians from across the country to work with their peers under Carter's careful tutelage. As with any operation Carter ran, there were some strict rules, the first of which was that each musician had to bring an original composition. Jazz Ahead! was a simple idea that bridged the gap between the worlds of instruction and gigs. And it worked. Launched through a residency with 651 in 1993, the first Jazz Ahead! involved some thirty-five musicians ranging in age from seventeen to twenty-eight from seven

Betty Carter herself, "live" in Prospect Park.

states. After a week of preparation, Carter performed with her charges at the (then) Majestic Theater in Fort Greene. The demand for tickets compelled them to add a matinee performance. The next year Carter expanded the program, bringing it to stages in Harlem and Atlanta. By 1997, the Kennedy Center had approached her to create a version of the program for Washington, D.C.

Some of Jazz Ahead!'s participants—pianists Jacky Terrasson and Cyrus Chestnut, and drummers Gregory Hutchinson and Brian Blade, for instance—have gone on to make substantial names for themselves. Others, like young trumpeter Pevin Everett, reaped more personal rewards. "Betty taught me a lot more than how to play," Everett said at a memorial service for Carter in 1999. "She taught me how to be a man."

Carter's initiative lives on in Fort Greene, through "The Music Never Stops," a 651 Arts program that's currently led by pianist Geri Allen, drummer Jack DeJohnette, singer Abbey Lincoln and saxophonist Mark Shim. Together, the four represent several generations of jazz lineage. More importantly, they embody the enabling kick that was Carter's method and the reach of her influence to yet another crop of talented aspirants. They continue to work on the house that Betty built. –*Larry Blumenfeld*

Enid Farber

of players who filtered in. There was trumpeter Graham Haynes, the son of legendary drummer Roy Haynes. There was Marvin "Smitty" Smith from Illinois. There were the Eubanks brothers—guitarist Kevin and trombonist Robin—from Philadelphia. There was pianist Geri Allen from Detroit. There was singer Cassandra Wilson, who'd moved north from Jackson, Mississippi. And there was saxophonist Greg Osby, from St. Louis, who was quick to absorb Coleman's compositional strategies. For these younger players, Holland's presence was a shot in the arm. "I'd introduce him around," Coleman says, "and we'd just play. We were surprised that someone with such a powerful reputation would come to the 'hood."

"As far as I'm concerned," Holland told Coleman's crew, "you guys are trying to push the envelope and do something." It was a musical workshop in part about exploration, in part a response to a growing conservatism among young players. Mostly, it was about a community of players looking for solutions to the problem of creating jazz that sounded progressive—music of its time.

Coleman began playing in Holland's band and gigged at clubs around New York, including the Blue Cornet in

Saxophonist Greg Osby played with Coleman in the 1980s.

Brooklyn (perhaps best known for an October 1969 incident in which a gangster's bullet grazed Miles Davis). But the real action was going on largely out of view. "A whole lot of stuff was happening in people's houses," Coleman recalls. "People did play in clubs, but there was more development in music going on privately." Brooklyn was not as commercial as it is now. And the end of the Manhattan loft scene had kind of taken the air out of things there for collaborative work: "I remember doing a gig with Cassandra Wilson and Dave Holland in a loft in Brooklyn," Coleman says. "I don't even think it had a name. People would find out by word of mouth. No advertising in *The Village Voice* or anywhere."

As Wilson remembers it, "the situation in Brooklyn was a way to get away from the jazz status quo, something that was being enforced diligently in those days."

In 1988, the Brooklyn Academy of Music tapped Coleman to mount "M-BASE Jams at BAM." The show was a success, widely and well reviewed. Yet there was one small catch. "One critic called our music 'the Brooklyn sound,' " Coleman remembers. "And the thing is that people can sometimes be kind of fierce about where they come from. Geri Allen said, 'What about Detroit?' Cassandra Wilson said, 'I'm a Southerner, not a Brooklynite.' They were telling me, 'We don't like this.' "

Wilson has since moved to Harlem and achieved the kind of broad-based success most jazz singers only dream about. Allen crossed the river to New Jersey, becoming a standard-bearing pianist whose music knows few categories. Greg Osby no longer lives in the borough, but he's extended the vocabulary he and Coleman worked on in Brooklyn to become a forceful leader in his own right and a mainstay of the Blue Note Records roster. Coleman resettled in Allentown, Pennsylvania, and he's continued his musical quest, largely through travel to Cuba, India and other countries. Holland is still playing strong, lately leading yet another fine quintet of young players.

"But for a while there," Coleman says, "Brooklyn was where things were at."

Larry Blumenfeld covers jazz from his Park Slope home.

Robin Holland

On Any Sunday

Reverend Timothy Wright and the gospel sound

BY CAROL
COOPER

raveling on Sunday morning out Atlantic Avenue toward the intersection of Utica and Pacific Street can be a revelation if the day is sunny and the weather is sweet. You're moving deep into Bedford-Stuyvesant, and under the bright glow of a low-hanging sky that extends to the blue horizon, the inner city looks like a multicultural suburb: the flags of Jamaica, Haiti and Honduras announce the cuisines of various restaurants, and a three-story Islamic school and library towers above the family-business storefronts. The wide streets are nearly deserted, and the only human sounds are those that emerge from the churches on nearly every other corner. One source of especially powerful singing: the Grace Tabernacle Christian Center Church of God in Christ.

There has been an active black church at 1745 Pacific Street since 1938, and since 1991 this large store-front has been the location of Grace Tabernacle, under the leadership of Reverend Timothy Wright, one of American contemporary gospel music's most dynamic personalities.

Brooklyn-born, Reverend Wright grew up living over a tiny church on Fulton Street—St. John's Fire Baptized Church—where his father was assistant pastor. It was also where, when he was just eleven years old, Pastor Myrtle Feemster Grayer anointed Wright's calling to the musical ministry. "At St. John's we

used to have all-night 'Tarry' services," the fifty-two-year-old Wright recalls, referring to the times when worshipers vowed to stay as late as possible, praying to accomplish some specific spiritual goal. "My mother and grandmother would stay all night, and they'd make me and my sister go. This particular night, at about three o'clock in the morning, Pastor Myrtle had somebody wake me up and she anointed me and prayed for my hands. And I started playing piano that very night. It was a miracle. They had never seen anything like it in their lives."

Wright was obsessed with music from that moment on. "My father used to work for Larson's Baking Company on Henry Street in South Brooklyn," says Wright. "He'd wake me when he left at five in the morning, and

From this humble church emerged one of the great gospel sounds.

I would go downstairs into the church and practice piano for two and a half to three hours until it was time to go to school. Then I'd come home in the afternoon and go right back downstairs and practice until eight or nine at night. I was totally consumed by it."

Michael Kamber

Hearing the Gospel

Brooklyn's African-American heritage stretches back to the borough's earliest days, and its churches have traditionally played a major role in the community. Their choirs are justly famous: some have toured Europe; others have appeared on Broadway. Below is a selection of churches throughout the borough that offer gospel music. Call to check for information on services.

Washington Temple
   Church of God in Christ
1372 Bedford Avenue
789-7545

Institutional Church
   of God in Christ
170 Adelphi Street
625-9175

Lafayette Avenue
   Presbyterian Church
102 Lafayette Avenue
625-7515

Brooklyn Tabernacle
290 Flatbush Avenue
783-0942

First Church of God
   in Christ
221 Kingston Avenue
774-0960

House of the Lord
(Rev. Herbert Daughtry)
415 Atlantic Avenue
596-1991

Greater Bibleway Temple
261 Rochester Avenue
774-0401

New Life Tabernacle
1476 Bedford Avenue
636-4938

Pilgrim Church
Gates Avenue &
   Broadway
452-5180

Pilgrim Church of
   Brownsville
572 Rockaway Avenue
485-1098

International
   Revival Temple
2260 Pacific Street
346-8839

Love Fellowship
   Tabernacle
(Hezekiah Walker)
464 Liberty Avenue
235-2266

He learned to play trombone as well as piano and organ, rehearsing the popular black hymns of the 1950s and early '60s as performed by Mahalia Jackson, the Caravans and his "idol," Reverend James Cleveland. He also began composing his own material, putting poems and music together under the influence of these "golden era" gospel stars.

By age fifteen, Wright was playing full services at St. John's and rehearsing both young adult and children's choirs. It was common practice in the 1960s for musicians to migrate among various locations and offer to do guest stints for other pastors as the spirit moved them, and Wright was no exception to this process. By sixteen, he'd begun sitting in on the live Sunday night radio broadcasts of the Radio Choir from the Institutional Church of God in Christ on Adelphi Street in Fort Greene. He'd play slide trombone with them and hang around picking up organ skills from the Radio Choir's principal musicians, Alfred and Jason White. After a short stint in the army, he returned to Brooklyn in 1968 and picked up his musical ministry right where he'd left off.

In gospel music, the cusp of the 1970s was an exciting time. Wright began his affiliation with the Washington Temple Church of God in Christ (C.O.G.I.C.) at 1372 Bedford Avenue. Through the 1970s and '80s he served as minister of music at Washington Temple, where he—along with a fifteen-year-old Reverend Al Sharpton—worked with the choirs and congregation under the guidance of the legendary Bishop F.D. Washington himself. Andre Crouch, Edwin Hawkins, the Clark Sisters and many other major gospel innovators all emerged from Washington Temple during those years. Wright vividly remembers the controversy within the church when musical ministers like himself had to choose between following the then-radical new pop-soul inflected rhythms of breakthrough hits like "Oh Happy Day" and adhering to the edicts of the church. In fact, soon after "Oh Happy Day" debuted on pop radio, church choirs around the country were forbidden to sing it.

Once he began recording himself and was secure in his position at Washington Temple, Wright became keenly aware of shifting gospel trends as he presented his choirs and new compositions at yearly C.O.G.I.C. convocations and Reverend Cleveland's national Gospel Workshops. Over the past thirty years he has been asked to work with choirs across the nation and around the globe, stamping some of his own distinctive, Brooklyn-based sound on choirs around the world. Even a few secular artists, including Carly Simon, Lenny Kravitz and Patti LaBelle, have either recorded Wright's compositions or worked with his choir. Four of his five sons are also musicians, and they now accompany Pastor Wright's sermons on drums, guitar, organ, piano and percussion both at Grace Tabernacle and when Wright is on the road.

Wright has recorded more than eighteen critically acclaimed gospel albums, several in collaboration with other leading choir directors. A student of the "golden era" choirs of the 1960s, he is also partial to many newer area choirs, including the ensembles directed by Bishop Nathaniel Townsend, Jr., Bishop Eric Figueroa, Reverend Albert Jamison from Pleasant Grove Baptist on Fulton and Howard, and nineteen-year-old prodigy Leon Lacy from Far Rockaway.

In 1993 Reverend Wright organized the New York Fellowship Mass Choir by calling together pastors and choir directors of leading New York–area ministries in his office on Pacific Street. This powerful aggregation of talent was videotaped and recorded at Brooklyn's Pilgrim Renaissance Convention Center. Hezekiah Walker, Donnie McClurkin, Eric McDaniels, Albert Jamison and Jay Nixon all came to Pilgrim along with key members of their respective choirs. A second live recording of the Mass Choir is being contemplated at Brooklyn's landmark Washington Temple.

Carol Cooper is a music critic and writer.

NOW & THEN   Long before the arrival of doo-wop and rap, ensemble singing was big in Brooklyn. This quartet of volunteer firemen appealed to audiences in the 1920s.

Scenes

On a streetcorner, in a bar, on a bench, on the beach or in a bistro, Brooklyn is a get-together kind of place. It's not the exact location that matters, it's the talk, and it takes only two Brooklynites together to make a scene. "Everybody, it seems, is here," notes observant author and sometime resident Ian Frazier. "At Grand Army Plaza, I have seen traffic tie-ups caused by Haitians and others rallying in support of President Aristide, and by St. Patrick's Day parades, and by Jews of the Lubavitcher sect celebrating the birthday of their Grand Rebbe with a slow procession of ninety-three motor homes—one for each year of his life. Local taxis have bumper stickers that say 'Allah is Great.'" Whatever the venue or the occasion, appreciating the talk, the food, the art, the people-watching or simply the diverse and colorful urban pageantry is a major element of daily life in Brooklyn.

372 Fulton Street
Brooklyn, New York 11201
718-875-5181
Brooklyn's Famous
Landmark Restaurant
Gage & Tollner

**Previous spread:
Williamsburg has emerged
as a congenial place for
artists—and for making art.**

Previous spread: Ted Hardin

The Williamsburg Scene

Artists in residence

BY
ANN LANDI

Fred Tomaselli's introduction to Williamsburg was a trial by Dobermans. The young artist arrived in New York from Los Angeles in October of 1985. His gallery had folded, he'd just lost his job and his girlfriend, and he was ready to start a new life on the funky bohemian frontiers of Manhattan's East Village. But, recalls Tomaselli, still wild-eyed and amiably boyish at forty-three, that neighborhood was peaking fast: a headline in *The Village Voice* that same week declared "The East Village Is Dead." Rents were on the rise as gentrification moved in and the art crowd moved on.

Where were the artists going? *Brooklyn.*

"Check out the Williamsburg area," friends from L.A. told him. A couple of weeks later he scoured the waterfront, looking for an affordable place to live and work. A sign on the door next to a motorcycle repair shop advertised an apartment for rent, "Inquire next door." There was no answer at the door to the left of the sign, so Tomaselli entered the cycle shop. When no one appeared, he yelled out, "Anybody know anything about the sign?"

"The next thing I knew," he says, "I heard this chomping noise. I looked down, and there was this Doberman pinscher totally consuming my leg." Tomaselli jumped on the counter. The dog was on a short leash and, once it discovered its limits, began to bark ferociously. Within seconds, another Doberman charged out of a back room. This one, too, hit the end of its chain.

With both dogs snarling and choking on their leads, Tomaselli crouched on the counter out of harm's way, wondering what to do next. The noises drew the attention of patrons in a diner across the street, one of whom happened to be the shop's owner. He bounded to the rescue, still with mayonnaise and ketchup all over his face,

It wouldn't be a real art scene without the street cafés.

Ted Hardin

screaming and yelling at his dogs. Later he explained that his premises were often a mark for local junkies and prostitutes, so the Dobermans were his protection. But since Tomaselli was about the sixth innocent casualty of their enthusiasm, he'd had enough. "'That's it, that's it,'" he recalls the owner swearing. "'I gotta gun. Let's go in the back and I'll let you shoot 'em.'" Tomaselli declined the executioner's role.

Despite the scrappy welcome, Tomaselli today lives with his wife, a graphic designer, and baby in a house they own in East Williamsburg. He works in a spacious

Galleries in Williamsburg

Art Moving, 166 N. Twelfth Street
Bench Dogs, 60 Broadway
Brooklyn Art Gallery, 283 N. Sixth Street
Driggs Art Gallery, 908 Driggs Avenue
Everything is Everything, 245 S. Third Street
eyewash, 143 N. Seventh Street
Flipside, 84 Withers Street
Holland Tunnel, 61 S. Third Street
MWMWM, 65 Hope Street
Momenta, 72 Berry Street
N3 Project Space, 85 N. Third Street
Pierogi 2000, 167 N. Ninth Street
Rock It Studios, 60 Broadway
Roebling Hall, 65 Roebling Street
Studio, 84 S. First Street
Velocity Gallery, 281 N. Seventh Street

Annie Herron in her pioneering, influential Test-Site Gallery

studio in North Williamsburg, and his huge and dazzling assemblages—made from pills, leaves, dead insects, and photos culled from catalogs and magazines—are now shown internationally. "We got respectable," Tomaselli notes with a grin. Indeed, his work has been installed at the Philip Morris/Whitney gallery, and one of his paintings recently graced the cover of *Art in America.* He's just one of many artists who have settled in the area, part of an influx that began in the late 1970s and shows no signs of tapering off. Williamsburg started to become a *scene* in the early '90s with the opening of L Cafe, an artists' hangout on Bedford Avenue. "At this point," says Tomaselli, "all of Williamsburg is lousy with artists."

Like SoHo thirty years ago, Williamsburg attracts because of its relatively cheap rents (which are, of course, now on the rise) and large spaces. The area along the East River from the Navy Yard to Greenpoint is a mix of old factory and warehouse buildings and two- and three-story houses. The subways offer easy access to Manhattan's gallery districts; the L train in particular is a kind of artist's express, taking just minutes to go from Bedford Avenue to the East Village. The area itself has its own share of emerging galleries—storefront spaces for showing art. If once the art-world movers and shakers thought twice about venturing far from their traditional precincts, Williamsburg, with its concentration of notable talent, is now a must-stop on the itinerary.

Much as an exodus of painters in the nineteenth century to the woods around Paris led to the Barbizon School and a crowd of gritty realists in turn-of-the-century Manhattan gave rise to the Ashcan School, one might expect that a high concentration of artists in Brooklyn could produce a "Williamsburg School." Tomaselli says that will never happen. Everyone with an interest in art reads the same magazines and attends the same art fairs on two hemispheres. Collectors and museums acquire from an international pool of talent. "The art world is global now," he says.

Artists have brought something of an activist consciousness to a traditional blue-collar neighborhood that in the past has been passive in the face of governmental

Ted Hardin

indifference and big-business abuses. In part because of its mixed residential and industrial character, Williamsburg is extremely polluted. Some paint companies, now shut down, left behind a legacy of heavy metals in the groundwater; just two blocks from Tomaselli's studio, on North Sixth Street, is Radiac, a medical waste processing and storage facility. Neighborhoods made up of older Catholics, Italians and Poles have traditionally been targeted "when authorities and corporations want to do something bad," Tomaselli says. "But a coalition has developed among bohemians and local ethnics, and there's very vocal opposition to making this neighborhood more toxic than it already is." That coalition has succeeded in barring a major waste incinerator and a garbage transport station, which would have meant a few hundred trucks a day hauling in "tons and tons" of garbage.

Apart from reasonable rents, a community of like-minded friends, cafés and superb local stores—like Joe's Busy Corner, where they smoke the mozzarella right on the street—Tomaselli values the benevolent small-town character of the neighborhood. "People really watch out for each other," he says. When his father was visiting from California to see his new grandchild, he got lost while taking a walk one day: "All the row houses can look alike, and he forgot which was ours." A neighbor noticed his confusion and came outside to inquire if he needed help. The senior Tomaselli explained his predicament. "Oh, them," said the neighbor, "they've got the new baby," and directed him to the right house.

"My dad got really turned on," says Tomaselli. "Where he's originally from, in Italy, there was a very old-world, connected way of living, and he lost all that when he came to the States. He couldn't believe I knew the butcher, the dry cleaner, the guys in the pizzeria. Now he thinks Williamsburg is the greatest place in the world."

Ann Landi, a writer and editor, has covered the national art scene (and many other scenes) for major magazines.

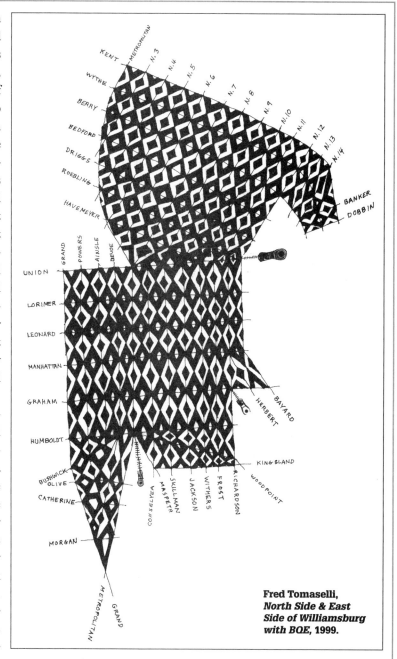

**Fred Tomaselli,
North Side & East
Side of Williamsburg
with BQE, 1999.**

Collection of Susan Swenson and Joe Amrhein

Red Hook's Last, Best Bar

There's no place like Sunny's home

BY MICHAEL
KAMBER

O n a warm Friday night, the cobblestone streets of Red Hook are dark, nearly deserted and very, very quiet. A family sits in lawn chairs by an open hydrant on Van Brunt Street as a silver Lincoln Town Car glides past two kids riding bikes near the shuttered factories and scattered, tar-papered houses. The car moves nearly to the water's edge before turning onto Conover Street and stopping at a small red-brick storefront. A trendy-looking young couple emerges from the car and steps across to the storefront's wooden door. Others appear: a couple in thrift-shop fashions, a trio aboard mountain bikes flanked by trotting dogs, and from a dented red pickup truck, a guy with tattoos and black hair in a semi-pompadour. Then two beefy types carrying guitar cases.

Above the door, an unlit sign declares, "BAR." In the two windows are large dusty ship models, plus another sign: "Red Hook Yacht and Kayak Club"—though it appears unlikely that anything but barges have tied up recently along this stretch of New York harbor front.

Forget the sign in the window. This is Sunny's bar.

Time was, scores of bars served the waterfront in Red Hook. Sunny's is the only one left standing. And it's only open on Friday nights.

Sunny's grandparents opened a candy store on this site upon their arrival from Italy in 1915. In 1934, they turned it into a bar and grill, catering to the tens of thousands of merchant marines and longshoremen working along the Red Hook waterfront. Sunny was born in that year, christened Antonio Rafael Balzano, and he remembers vividly how active and noisy and crowded this neighborhood was in the 1940s: "During World War II, the whistle sounded at noon and all us kids had to run inside. The huge gates over at the shipyard would slowly swing open and thousands of men would sprint down the street, fighting to get into the bars along here—they only had half an hour to eat lunch. Pushcarts were parked up and down the street; people even sold soda and plates of food out their apartment windows."

The lots adjacent to his bar are now largely empty and weedy. But in those days, "within a few hundred yards of here, ten thousand men worked day and night. During the war, we couldn't sleep. We would just lie there and listen to the torches popping and the banging from the welders. Even breathing was difficult: clouds of spent acetylene, diesel exhaust and coal dust wafted into the bedrooms."

Now, on this warm Friday night, Sunny's friends and patrons are the only ones moving on Conover Street. Inside the narrow and crowded room, Sunny stands behind the long mahogany bar, a cigarette dangling from his lips, looking vaguely angelic in the light of a Pabst Blue Ribbon lamp. He leans forward to hug and kiss each newcomer, his face relaxing into a smile at once joyful and sad, and sincere. Around him, as always, is a circle of people basking in his radiance. Over in a corner, the musicians set up their equipment and start to tune up. On the wall nearby hang a Vargas pinup, a huge abstract canvas (one of Sunny's own paintings), a semaphore flag, Budweiser and Pabst lamps, an American flag, some leftover Christmas lights, local art-show announcements and an old pair of boxing gloves with the stuffing falling out. In framed faded photos over the bar, men stand proudly next to fishing boats, all long gone from Red Hook. The older decorations are layered with dust.

Sunny at home in his members-only, Friday-nights-only bar in Red Hook.

Michael Kamber

The first singer of the night brings his weathered face to the microphone; a piece of twine substitutes for a guitar strap. He picks some chords and launches into an old Merle Haggard song, a steel-guitarist joining in behind him. He sounds and even looks a bit like the "Okie from Muskogee" he's singing about, but he turns out to be Tony Rossi, a sixty-one-year-old truck driver from Bensonhurst. "I started listening to country music on the radio when I was six or seven," he says. "Dan Larkin was the big country DJ then. I fell in love with country, and when I went in the service, I learned to play from the Southern boys." By the time he launches into "I Walk the Line," the bar and tables are crowded. The bartenders hand each newcomer a small scrap of cardboard and then serve up whatever is asked for, mostly bottled beer and shots. Drinkers keep their own tabs and pay whatever they want at the end of the night. The bar has no liquor license—the donation policy keeps everything legal and the honor system works flawlessly. If someone is broke or forgets, Sunny will find an envelope of cash under his door in the middle of the week.

Some nights the crowd is predominently young and hip, but completely lacking in the *attitude* found in most big-city bars. It's reminiscent of a college-town art bar: people strike up conversations with whoever sits or stands next to them. There's a lot of laughter and some singing along with the musicians. Many customers bring their dogs in. A woman embraces an old friend at the bar, while down at floor level their dogs sniff each other, tails wagging.

Izzy Hornstein and her daughter Chelsea, a SUNY film student, are among those at the bar. They moved to Red Hook fifteen years ago, and Izzy is emphatic: "This is the best bar in Brooklyn. It has a friendly atmosphere and it's an old-time bar. There's no airs here. You just hang out and be who you are." Barry O'Meara, sitting nearby, agrees, adding that Sunny's reminds him of the bars in his native Ireland. "Back home, the bar isn't just a place to drink, it's the center of the community. Grandma and the kids are there, you go to meet your neighbors. This place is just like that. And it's because of Sunny. He's like a shaman. If you don't come in here as a friend, you definitely leave as a friend."

Ironically, Sunny's father had groomed him to take over the bar, but he resisted. "I told my father, 'I don't want to do what you did all your life.' It sounds cruel but he understood what I meant. He worked fourteen hours a day and supported seven kids with this bar, but he gave me his blessing and signed my enlistment papers. I joined the air force and left Red Hook. I was seventeen years old. I didn't come back for thirty-five years." The air force was his ticket out of Red Hook, but his interests lay elsewhere: "Even when I was kid, I was fascinated by art. There was no art in Red Hook, so I'd go to the church and stare at the murals for hours."

After the Korean War, Sunny made his way back to New York and was one of the first to settle in SoHo ("$75 a month for a loft I could ride my motorcycle in"), where he became an artist, protested the Vietnam war and started a family. But by the late sixties, he says, "a lot of us were confused, we'd gotten caught up on the decadence of New York." In 1970 he left for India and spent ten years as the follower of a spiritual leader he declines to name. "Let's just say he's famous, or rather, infamous. I brought a lot of students to him, but eventually he started to separate his followers from their families, and he was taking in huge amounts of money. I knew several multimillionaires that literally surrendered all their wealth to him. So I began to have doubts and I wrote an open letter criticizing him."

In 1980 Sunny returned to the States, one step ahead of the cult leader's vengeful bodyguards, and eventually came back home to Red Hook to nurse his dying father. "When I came back," he says, "I helped my uncle run the place. The shipyards were gone by then—he was clearing about fifty dollars a day and I got twenty-five. I knew all the artists in the neighborhood and thought maybe they'd like a place to hang out. My uncle resisted, so I told him I wanted to have a private party one night. He said okay. I invited all the artists down, and the next day I went to my uncle and handed him the eight hundred dollars we took in."

With the eventual passing of his father and uncle, Sunny took over the place, using it during the week as his painting studio and making the Friday-night-only openings a regular event. He also moved back into his uncle's house around the corner, where he'd been born. "I was delivered by a midwife in the upstairs bedroom. Now I sleep at night in the room I was born in. Many people come back to Red Hook to find an empty lot where they grew up. I'm lucky—I've come full circle."

Michael Kamber is a professional photographer and writer who lives in another part of Brooklyn.

Joe Durso, Handball Wizard

The greatest athlete in the history of Brooklyn?

BY JOE GLICKMAN

To make the game competitive, Joe Durso, perhaps the greatest handball player who ever lived, was using only his left hand against an opponent allowed to use both. They split the first two games. During the pivotal third game, Durso decided his opponent was too angry and unworthy of all the attention he'd drawn to the match. During a pause in the action, the 6'1", 185-pound Durso ran up on the boardwalk overlooking the courts, dropped his shorts, mooned his opponent and walked away from the deadlock. "He wanted to win so badly," he said, laughing. "And I took it away."

Most people who have ever heard of Joe Durso know this handsome handball legend as a foulmouthed egomaniac, part Howard Stern, part Muhammad Ali—a man so scornful and profane that even Lenny Bruce might blush at some of the verbal daggers he hurls at the brawny goombahs who dare spar with him on the cement courts on Surf Avenue in Coney Island. Durso's on-court shtick is half-improv, half-rehearsed, often vicious, always irreverent, but never boring. "Whether you love me or hate me, I'm like a car crash," he says, "compelling to watch."

True, Durso, a forty-four-year-old elementary school teacher turned assistant district attorney in the Brooklyn office, has spent his life angry—very angry. His parents, who never married, handed him off when he was a year old to his paternal grandmother, a kind but uneducated Italian woman. As a youth he spent a lot of time reading voraciously, all the while dealing with the deprivations of life in the Coney Island Projects. Says Durso: "Every-

A moment of beauty: Joe Durso strives to make art even as he makes points on the handball court.

thing I did, I did on my own. The fact that I graduated from law school is insane. The guys I grew up with did so much drugs they can't even spell their names."

Were this nine-time national one-wall handball champion just another cocky jock talking trash in the playground, this story might be the tale of a colorful character—big game, big mouth—who has dominated the quirky world of his sport like few others. (*Sports Illustrated* recently cited him as one of the fifty best New York athletes of the twentieth century.) But the

Courtesy of Joseph Durso

story is more complex. It is the saga of a gifted, fiercely determined kid who spent twenty years becoming the unchallenged master of his game, the game that defined manhood in the rich, bubbling cauldron that is Coney Island. The poignancy of Durso is that once he got to the top of the heap, once he controlled his anger and refined his rap, he looked around and saw how much bigger the world actually was—and that no one was watching him. "I had a lot to offer besides my physical talent," he says, "but because I didn't exist on TV, the world lost me." Citing three of his heroes, Muhammad Ali, Bruce Lee and Bobby Fischer (another Brooklyn legend), he says, "I was special, too. I still am. I really am. My story is a tragedy. It really is."

On a sunny Saturday in September, I went to Surf Avenue to check out his game. He was tanned and shirtless, his slicked-back dark hair speckled with gray, and he had the long limbs and lithe, muscular body of a light-heavyweight boxer struggling to make weight. His sly smile featured a prominent gap between his top front teeth. When I told him I was writing a profile of him,

he pulled me aside and unleashed a torrent of words that seemed to have been pent up for years. While "fuck" is a staple in his vocabulary (it serves as rhythmic pause, verb and exclamation mark), his rapid-fire speech is peppered with references to classic literature, art and cultural icons. If his anger is apparent, so is his intelligence and ability to command attention. "I tower over the game like the Colossus of Rhodes," he said. Or "I'm like Jackson Pollock submerged in my own creation." Or "Like Plato's shadow world, when I play I try to create a moment of complete beauty." Imagine Spalding Gray, Ice-T, with a bit of De Niro's *Raging Bull* tossed in, and you've got Durso in action.

The scene around the Sea Breeze courts is vintage Coney. Tanned Jewish men, some of whom have been hanging out at the courts for forty years, schmooze in the salt air, betting on the action and carrying on a running dialogue with each other and the players. "We're not spectators," says Morris Levinsky, the eighty-three-year-old grizzled park historian. "We're kibitzers." The players—characters with nicknames like Steve the Judo Man, Louie Shoes and Red Face Benjy—are straight from central casting. Here, Russians, Puerto Ricans, blacks, Italians and Jews coexist while trying to bash each other into oblivion on the courts.

In the first game, Durso, playing lefty, teamed with a stocky fellow with a serpent tattoo to play a two-on-one match against a short, rock-hard park regular named Billy. "Should this be considered child abuse?" Durso asked after winning the first point. But the gritty, grunting Billy, who chased down nearly every ball, even diving on the concrete like a man returning a grenade, was the man of the hour. Stiff from the long workweek without exercise, Durso was nimble but a tad slow and more fallible than I expected. "You're not catching me on a

Courtesy of Joseph Durso

good day," he repeated after an errant shot. After he'd fallen hopelessly behind, a mop-top surfer dude smoking a joint shouted: "Where's the cape now, Joe? You look very mortal." Durso ignored the taunts, cast a glance at his tormentor and put away the next shot with the finality of a man killing a fly. "Don't hit it to me," he shouted. "Hit it to me and you lose!"

Handball is a simple game with an endless variety of options and angles available to the participants, who smack a tiny rubber ball against a wall with their bare hands. It's a game of violence and finesse—two combatants vying for a small piece of real estate—more like a hybrid of boxing and squash than tennis. It is, says Durso, highly addicting. Archaeologists theorize that handball was around for thousands of years before it surfaced in tenth-century Ireland as a game called "fives." In fact, given that it's pictured in Egyptian hieroglyphics, it could be the world's oldest game. Brooklyn handball originated in Brighton Beach in the early 1900s when locals passed time by battering a ball against the breakwaters at low tide. Over the decades, the timeless bounce and whack and attendant wisecracking has become as much a part of the Coney Island scene as Nathan's or the Cyclone.

While Durso looked less than stellar in that first game (remember, he was using only one hand), when he faced off later with a young stud named Robert Sostre, the national paddleball champion, you could see why he ruled the one-wall handball world for so long. His serve exploded off the wall low and wide, nearly pulling Sostre off the court. His ability to attack off a defensive shot, his anticipation and sharply angled shots, revealed a master craftsman at work. In a world that rewards close-to-the-ground types, this rangy shotmaker brought size, speed and power as well as a wheelbarrow of chutzpah to the caged courts. And just for the record: not once during that match did Durso say anything more inflammatory than "Nice shot."

Two days later, I drove to Bay Ridge for our interview. Just back from work, Durso—looking very much the well-tailored attorney—ushered me into his modest one-bedroom apartment. It was more like a gallery than a bachelor pad. One wall was filled with framed photos celebrating the human form—nudes by Robert Mapplethorpe, Michelangelo's *David,* a shirtless, pensive David Bowie, and other mysterious, sublime images of muscular men and women. The other side of the room was dominated by copies of marble busts and paintings from the Renaissance period, his favorite. "I've fused the classic nudes of antiquity with modern erotic images," he said. "But the perfection of the human form unites the two."

In between were action photographs of a younger, shaggy-haired Durso, lean, fierce and focused, belting the crap out of a small blue ball, along with neatly aligned head shots of movie stars like Clark Gable, Laurence Olivier and Dennis Hopper. Not to mention a dandy collection of sugar bowls.

Durso sees his artistic sensibility as a mixture of Ayn Rand's philosophy (a man's noblest effort should be reflected in his work), the Homeric concept of heroism, Michelangelo's obsession with physical perfection, Ali's transcendence and courage, Bruce Lee's guts, Howard Stern's humor, Gable's masculinity and Bowie's innovation. Along with his long-simmering anger, it informs his attitudes and actions on the handball court. "For whatever reason, my way of contributing to the pantheon of human achievement was through the handball. I wanted to step in there with Da Vinci and Ali and Rand. And I was great," he said. "I was. I really was."

At his best, he was less interested in winning than in winning in a certain way. He tried to create volleys that were beautiful. Between mouthfuls of takeout Chinese food and red wine, Durso said, "I could move my opponent around the court wherever I wanted to. It was like choreographing a dance within the game. I was trying to create a living art form using my opponent." In essence, Durso was trying to make himself "a living David or Mapplethorpe photograph"—which tied in with the Randian concept of human achievement. In his own poetically tortured Brooklynese, Durso considers himself "a painter on a planet of blind people."

What strikes Durso as capricious and unjust is that he achieved true greatness in a sport that functionally ceases to exist beyond the narrow strip of pavement he ruled. "The world didn't value what I did," he says. "The anger fueled me. It gave me strength. I was angry that I had to work, that I had to do things that took me away from handball. Did John McEnroe ever have to work as a mailman?"

After years of practicing and striving and then finally reaching the pinnacle of a sport that demands so much—and that he loved above all else—all he has to show for it is a closet full of trophies and the grudging admiration of the locals who watched him dominate the competition.

"I'm a gifted athlete with no money who's stuck in a toilet bowl," he says. "Time kind of marched me by and I'm fucking cranky. I was cranky when I was younger because I was trying to become supergreat. Then I was cranky when I was supergreat because no one was paying attention. Now I'm cranky because I'm getting older and I'm not what I once was. People should see that and understand. I'm not a bully. I'm not a bad person. I'm providing these guys with quality entertainment. I'm interesting to watch. Why can't they appreciate that?"

Joe Glickman is a magazine writer, world traveler and competitive long-distance kayaker.

BROOKLYN ON FILM

What Makes a Neighborhood?

Metropolitan Avenue, an independent film made in 1985, addresses the issue of community and the question of what brings—and holds—a community together. The answers found by director Christine Noschese in the Greenpoint neighborhood where she grew up include the surprisingly strong legacy of the borough's major league baseball team, which left Brooklyn for Los Angeles well over a generation before. But the sense persists there in Greenpoint that the Dodgers were a presence, a force, an idea and a very human team, loyalty to which transcended every other difference of age, ethnicity, color, gender and politics.

It is a legacy to be conjured with, and Noschese goes on in *Metropolitan Avenue* to explore the long-standing conflicts between the Polish/Slovak, Italian and black communities that have long existed side by side in this area. We learn that in the 1950s this was an ethnically and racially divided neighborhood that was buffeted hard by large changes in the greater city. In the ensuing decades there were cancellations of regular bus routes, the closing down of many factories that had employed residents and cutbacks in community services.

But the residents of this neighborhood consider themselves part of a community, and they are able to find common ground and strength as they learn to stand up and be counted, whether fighting against eviction or organizing to oppose the closing of a local police precinct or to build a center for senior citizens. In the process of these personal transformations, a group of local women overcomes mistrust of one another in order to fight city hall and to revive their community. Despite their obvious differences in ethnicity, race and cultural traditions, they come to realize

Metropolitan Avenue, 1985

how profoundly similar they are in their common aspirations for safe neighborhoods, decent housing and affordable social services.

What they discover is, in a sense, the true bedrock legacy of all those years of allegiance to the Dodgers. Just as Jackie Robinson pioneered in integrating his team, so do these Greenpoint neighbors work together to fight injustice and sustain their community. –*Jon Gartenberg*

MOMA Film Stills Archive

My Night with Norman Mailer

The shelter, the salon and the Great American Novel

BY ANNE KOSTICK

I t was a dark and stormy night. I'd set out the ingredients for dinner and placed fresh sheets, blankets and pillows on his bed. Now there was nothing to do but wait for Norman to arrive.

When the doorbell rang at the stroke of seven, I ran to answer it. I could hardly wait to give him his orders. After all, when famous people volunteer to spend the night helping out at their neighborhood homeless shelter, the least we can do is make sure they know the rules, and that was my job as Tuesday night coordinator. Norman had been invited to do his part as a citizen of Brooklyn Heights, and he had accepted. The venue was a brownstone synagogue, ground floor. It promised to be a classic event: New York Street Fighter meets New York Street Residents.

He walked in at seven, limping more than a bit on his bad leg. Behind him was a tall, handsome young man whom he introduced as his son. I'd fantasized about instructing Norman in the fine points of making up twelve beds so that the city-issued sheets actually fit the city-issued folding cots. But as I launched into my weekly spiel, Norman gestured toward his son. Junior would make the beds.

On he went into the main room, where our ten guests were eagerly waiting. The men who spent four nights a week here were the crème de la crème of the down-and-out. In order to qualify for a private shelter, they had to be not too drunk, not too contagious and not too crazy—in other words, just like us. But of course, they weren't really like us. We had jobs, homes, bills to pay—they had little more than the contents of their pockets and, sometimes, a plastic bag of clothes. A few were Vietnam vets; others were just born unlucky.

Wherever these men had begun their lives, they'd since experienced the Brooklyn we like to keep on the far side of a triple-locked door. And now they were about to share a meal with the American writer best known for celebrating gritty detail—why, one of them had probably panhandled a buck from him at the corner of Clinton and Montague Streets! They were pleased to see him, and had saved the prime seat at the dinner table for him (with a good view of the TV), which he graciously accepted.

Now came the part I'd been waiting for. What would they talk about? If you imagined they discussed Norman's books, you'd be partly right. Three of the men had read *The Naked and the Dead,* more of them at least knew of *The Executioner's Song,* and they had questions aplenty. They were a little shy at first, but pretty soon it was sounding like a creative writing seminar at Columbia.

Russell Christian

Norman Mailer's Brooklyn

Of the many writers who have lived, worked, loved and otherwise made their presence felt in Brooklyn, few have been as prolific or as prominent as Norman Mailer. Author of a long line of remarkable and popular works from *The Naked and the Dead* (1947) to *The Gospel According to the Son* (1997), Mailer was actually born in Long Branch, New Jersey, but at age four moved with his family to Brooklyn and went on to Boys High School, where he developed an interest in both aeronautics and writing. After graduating from Harvard and a watershed stint in the U.S. Army infantry in the Philippines, he moved back to Brooklyn to write.

At one time in the mid-1940s, Mailer lived in the same Brooklyn Heights apartment building as Arthur Miller, at 102 Pierrepont Street. Later, he wrote in a studio in the same Fulton Street building with artist David Levine and Russian spy Colonel Rudolph Abel. For many years, he's lived in a large brownstone at 142 Columbia Heights, where he writes in an oddly nautical loft on the top floor (dividing his time between the Heights and Provincetown, Massachusetts).

In addition to publishing ten novels and nearly twenty sizable works of nonfiction (for which he's won both a Pulitzer and National Book Award twice), Mailer has also found time for such other activities as cofounding *The Village Voice*, producing and acting in films, running for mayor of New York and feuding with other writers and artists. Over recent years, Mailer sightings in the Heights have been frequent.

I was so busy eavesdropping, I forgot to see how the younger Mailer was coming along with the beds. But after a while this asphalt-jungle literary salon seemed to tire everyone out. Or, like college students, the men had simply run out of prepared questions. Norman had been pleasant throughout (maybe a bit flattered? or was I imagining it?) but now the TV was flicked on and the main topic of the evening began—basketball!

Here was a subject all those present could attack, dissect, deconstruct and parse with equal pretension to expertise. Norman may have been polite before, but now he was truly engaged. So was everyone else at the table. In polyglot New York, basketball is the universal language. It doesn't matter if you sleep in a brownstone overlooking the Promenade or in a chair at the Bond Street Drop-In Center—basketball is the great leveler.

Young Mailer, bless him, cleared the table and washed the dishes (he'd finished making the beds), and I had a good time giving him the lecture about late arrivals, wake-up calls (5:30 A.M.) and locked doors. Norman and the guys continued to talk game until it was time for me to go.

I never spend the night. I prepare, lecture, listen, and have my brief encounters with guests and volunteers both famous and obscure. Then I go home and thank my lucky stars I have a home. That night, snuggled into my quilt, I wondered, "Is Norman *really* sleeping over?" It was hard to imagine The Great Writer of Columbia Heights trying to catch some z's in the midst of the incessant snoring, hacking and periodic wafts of unpleasant odors that characterized shelter nights. Maybe a limo was picking him up right that minute, and Junior was on duty all by himself.

On the other hand, what stories! An evening at the shelter has got to be a gold mine for a novelist. Every man at the table has a tale to tell, and believe me, they all want to tell. After more than a decade, the perennial victims of New York's "housing crisis" constitute a separate minority group—a voting bloc, practically. If they ever got off basketball, this core group of men could provide grist for the next Great American Novel! Think Dreiser! Dos Passos! Sherwood Anderson!

But not Mailer. Either basketball ruled until bedtime, or the limo swept him away, or everyone was too awed, respectful and polite to share stories. By the time the next Tuesday came around, I was too busy with the current volunteers and the latest crisis to ask the men about their night with Norman. Too bad. I've been watching for a Mailer novel that made use of what must've been a Significant Experience, especially for a Great American Novelist.

Nothing so far.

Anne Kostick is a writer, editor, community volunteer and resident of Windsor Terrace.

An Inner-City Inn

Putting the bed in Bed-Stuy

BY MONIQUE
GREENWOOD

Rolling hills. A small lake. Rocking chairs on the porch of a stately historic house. Plus great coffee and breakfast breads in the morning. That's what everyone pictures when you say "inn" or "bed-and-breakfast." Okay, but what if you're talking about a bed-and-breakfast that is not located in a rural county of rolling hills and sparkling lakes, but is instead in the center of Brooklyn? In Bedford-Stuyvesant, to be exact.

Akwaaba Mansion Bed and Breakfast lacks the hills and lakes, but it does have the rocking chairs, and the expansive porch, and the high-ceilinged parlor with antique sofas. There's even a coal-burning stove in the kitchen, flanked by framed food ads and packages featuring such 1950s black "spokespersons" as Aunt Jemima—the place has a sense of humor.

Still, the question lingers: Why would anyone open a bed-and-breakfast in *Bedford-Stuyvesant*? We ask, Why not? We had noticed that as big as Brooklyn was, there were at the time no hotels downtown, and only motels near JFK. In other words, no good place for

Innkeepers extraordinaire: Monique Greenwood and husband Glenn Pogue in front of their 1845 Bed-Stuy mansion.

Mara Faye Lethem

family and friends to stay. Most folks thought an inn in the middle of Brooklyn was a contradiction in terms. Bedford-Stuyvesant has long been portrayed as the kind of place where even the most ruthless gang member wouldn't want to travel, but the reality is something else. The fact is, this Brooklyn neighborhood is mostly a residential community, composed largely of upstanding, responsible citizens who take visible pride in their beautiful historic homes and their tree-lined streets.

In its earliest days, Bedford-Stuyvesant was a perfect setting for a "country" inn. Its history dates back to the

The mansion is nearly all original: well preserved and painstakingly restored, with thematic guestrooms.

mid-1600s, and like the rest of Kings County at that time it was essentially agricultural. Interestingly enough, though, there was, long ago, a major intersection at Bedford Avenue that linked the Brooklyn ferry with the settlements of Jamaica, Flatbush and Newton. The presence of travelers along this part of Long Island encouraged some early commercial developments, including an inn. In 1668, a gentleman named Thomas Lambertse was authorized to operate an inn "for the accommodation of strangers with diet and lodging and horse meals" at this crossroads.

Kings County boomed in the nineteenth century, and by 1855 the population in what is now Bedford-Stuyvesant began to increase as real estate developers touted the neighborhood as the ideal location for "genteel suburban residences." It was about that time that the Italianate villa, which we now call Akwaaba Mansion, was built. Its original owners were beer barons who constructed the eighteen-room dwelling as their private residence. Filing papers with a city agency like the Buildings Department wasn't required back then, so we've learned what we know of the mansion's history from the third owners of the home, Irish immigrants who apparently purchased it in the early 1920s from the children of the original owners.

One of the descendants of that third family read a *New York Times* article about the opening of our inn and telephoned. She could hardly contain her excitement. When she saw the picture of the big yellow house in the paper, then read the address, she dug through old family documents and found some mail that listed our very same address. Several months after her call, she and about sixty other members of her family held a reunion at the Mansion.

My husband and I purchased the house from the fourth family and the first black owners, the Lilleys, with the idea of making it into a B & B. Mr. and Mrs. Lilley, along with their eight young-adult, working children, had pooled their money to buy the house as their family home in the mid-1940s. In those years, about a quarter of Bed-Stuy's residents were black, and indeed the majority of the blacks in Brooklyn probably lived here. Brooklyn experienced the phenomenon of blacks migrating from the South to the North during and after World War I. But up until the forties, most blacks in Bed-Stuy lived along a narrow axis that centered on Atlantic Avenue and Fulton Street, both considered less desirable locations due to the noisy presence of the Long Island Railroad on Atlantic and the elevated railway on Fulton. The "el," built in the 1880s, brought the area within reasonable commuting time of downtown Brooklyn and Manhattan. With blacks moving beyond this stretch and into the more residential

Courtesy of Akwaaba

blocks, there was white resistance, then white flight, leading to Bedford-Stuyvesant's becoming the black neighborhood it is today.

When we moved into the mansion in 1995, ready to set up an inn, we were convinced that people of all backgrounds would be enriched and inspired by a community—and a place—that bears witness to the heritage of African-American people. We named our inn Akwaaba because it means "welcome" in the language of the Akan people of Ghana, West Africa.

The eighteen-room Victorian-era villa retains much of its original detail, now painstakingly restored: intricate white marble fireplaces in just about every room, six different complex patterns of parquet wood floors throughout, original gaslight fixtures, extremely high ceilings with either ornate molding or decorative tin, and impeccable tilework around mantels and on bathroom walls—even a fancy cast-iron radiator in the dining room that doubles as a food warmer.

To make it a truly welcoming place that lives up to its name, we incorporated African and African-American artifacts and details into the original Victorian structure. Twelve-foot doors hand-carved in Nigeria to depict a market scene frame the huge bay window in the ballroom. And each of the four guest rooms is designed to capture a different slice of African-American life. The Black Memorabilia Suite evokes memories of visiting Grandma's house down south: with country antiques, lots of black collectibles like handmade rag dolls and one-of-a-kind quilts. The Ashante Suite transports guests to Africa with boldly printed African textiles and an "art" wall that showcases African figurines and artifacts. The Regal Retreat Suite is elegantly appointed in rich fabrics and massive Victorian furniture. And the Jumping the Broom Suite is a romantic oasis for honeymooners—its name comes from the African-American slave tradition of jumping over a broom to sanction a marriage and to symbolize the sweeping away of all bad and evil; a print of a couple jumping over a broom hangs above the white marble fireplace, together with an actual antique broom.

Since opening, Akwaaba Mansion has been home to countless guests, about half of them visiting in Brooklyn

Courtesy of Akwaaba

An Akwaaba Valentine

One evening when we dined at Akwaaba, there was live music. At one point the singer took the microphone and went from table to table, inviting patrons to participate. "Now, I see you trying to hide," she said to a couple in the corner. One man who sang had an extraordinary voice, and afterward she said, "Let's hear a big round of applause for brother Kyle," and we all obliged. Inevitably, she reached our table. She named some songs we had never heard of, and then she mentioned "Blue Moon."

"Oh, 'Blue Moon,' of course," I said.

"Well, then," she said. "We're about to hear from—what's your name?"

"Patrick," I said nervously.

"My name's Patricia. Canya stand it? Let's hear from brother Patrick."

I stood and sang one verse of "Blue Moon," then sat down to undeserved applause. Patricia observed, "I don't see why we need Valentine's Day. Why just one day to love one another?" That summed up the mood at Akwaaba.—*Patrick Robbins*

from places as far away as Paris, Barbados and Montreal. The other half live in the metropolitan area and come for a getaway or to celebrate a special occasion. And it is clear from the guests' comments that Akwaaba has become a special place for many: "Your place is filled with our history," wrote Brenda from Montreal. "I came to Brooklyn for my aunt's funeral, and I laid my head down with a great sense of comfort." And how, one guest asked, "did we find this Southern type of ease by traveling north from Washington, D.C.? Unpretentious elegance and comfort, the sense of being around relations, sitting under an old chestnut tree in a secluded garden in Brooklyn." Another, after staying in the Ashante Suite, noted: "Powerful memories of my ancestors were evoked with a strength and clarity not often felt."

Akwaaba co-owner Monique Greenwood is editor in chief of Essence *magazine.*

SIGHTINGS Two Williamsburg institutions: Betty Smith, celebrated author of the wildly popular *A Tree Grows in Brooklyn*, shares a toast with restaurant proprietor Carl Luger.

The Real Cow Palace

Some things never change

BY STEPHEN BYERS

Eating at Peter Luger's is a way of remembering my old man. He would always stay at the St. Regis Hotel when he came to New York, but it became something of a ritual for his first dinner to be in Brooklyn—at Luger's. My old man was a hearty eater at a time when steak was king. And Peter Luger's served up man-size porterhouse that no less a gourmand than Alfred Hitchcock (the old man's favorite director and a man not given to hyperbole) had proclaimed "the best in the universe." Moreover, James Cagney (his favorite actor) had been a habitué of this long-running Williamsburg establishment. According to Wolfgang (Dad's favorite waiter), Cagney had done some of his best acting in Luger's men's room—feigning drunkenness to avoid signing autographs for guys with the temerity to approach him at the urinal.

Peter Luger, the restaurant's namesake and founder (in 1887), enjoyed a huge reputation for offering the highest-quality porterhouse and for the brusque, Runyonesque attitude of his bar and wait staff. In fact, he and his restaurant became such revered fixtures in the history of the city that upon his death in 1941 the *New York Herald Tribune* saluted him on its editorial page, proclaiming that his passing marked "the end of an era." They couldn't have been more wrong.

Some Brooklyn citizens of a certain age believe, of course, that the grand old borough lost its allure after the Dodgers sold them out, Coney Island foundered and gentrification began to dilute stoop life. Change does that to some people—nothing is ever as good as it used to be. But Peter Luger's today flies smack in the face of that sentiment. It has been the high church of carnivorous delight for over a century and shows no sign of relinquishing that mantle. Not as long as the Forman family, who bought it from Luger's children fifty years ago, still runs the place.

Under their stewardship, Peter Luger's has succeeded on a scale that would have been unimaginable to its founder. They have over 50,000 house accounts (no credit cards are accepted but their own) and set out ten tons of nonpareil porterhouse per week. Even their biggest competitors concede the superiority of the Peter Luger product: Allen Stillman, general partner in New York's Post House and Smith & Wollensky Steak House, admits, "Peter Luger serves the best aged steaks in the world."

I don't exactly remember the waiter from the one occasion when I joined my old man at Luger's—that's lost in the mists of time—but I think now it must have been Wolfgang. I do recall that he wedged an upside-down saucer beneath one end of the meat platter to pool the juices and proclaimed the technique "German engineering." He laughed hysterically, as though it were the first time he'd used the routine. Later he slopped our table with soapy water and wiped it dry, saying, "There's your fresh table-

Left: Brian Merlis Collection; this page: Russell Christian

cloth." It was kind of lame, but it seemed appropriate at the time, given the sort of Teutonic beer-hall feel of the place. An ancient regulator clock loomed over the gouged-up bar and the peg-doweled oak floors and the high, smoke-darkened wainscoting topped by a shelf full of hammered brass trays and kitschy-looking beer steins. But ah, that meat! The old man swore it came from the pastures of heaven.

In fact, the secrets of Peter Luger's ethereal porter-house begin with the Forman family's dogged pursuit of the finest short loin. This would be the beef quarter from which porterhouse—the choice meat between the tenderloin and the sirloin—is cut. The family matriarch, Marsha Forman, was trained by a federal meat grader, and she trained her daughters, Marilyn and Amy, how to identify perfection. Almost daily, Marilyn, Amy Rubenstein and her daughter Jody Storch descend on Manhattan's wholesale meat district demanding the ultimate short loin from purveyors like Pacific Seh Hotel Supply. I envision the three women prowling freezing meat lockers like Rocky Balboa, whacking short loin carcasses—in their case, with an ink-tipped steel "hitter" to brand their choices. The meat is then butchered and dry-aged in-house at between 34 and 36 degrees for six weeks. But starting with the finest raw materials takes you only so far. The same painstaking perfectionism extends to the grilling and final preparation. Six Garland salamander grills are set to the maximum heat their 45,000 Btu's can produce. Each porterhouse, an inch and three-quarters thick, is topflame broiled for four minutes under the watchful eye of grill chef Amet Bajrami, who rides herd on five to six grillers working seventy-five steaks at a time and releases nothing but sizzling perfection to his waiters.

So on a sweltering summer day, I made the pilgrimage to Luger's to tempt fate by eating mountains of meltingly scrumptious porterhouse and regale my wife with martini-soaked reminiscences of my old man.

At the corner of Broadway and Driggs Avenue, Peter Luger Steak House occupies a wan, nondescript brick building in a funky, rough-and-tumble neighborhood. A quick peek inside revealed that nothing much had changed in the forty years since food critic James Beard

anointed Luger's with the coveted four stars. The place has recently slipped a star or two because, I suspect, food critics at the *Times* rate decor and service more prominently than James Beard did back in the 1960s.

I was amazed to hear Wolfgang was still on staff after all these years. He was delighted to wait on us, but admitted he had no recollection of my old man or me. That was a blow, but my wife begged me to let it go. I looked into my martini as we tucked into what I vaguely judged to be Dad's favorite table. My wife thought Wolfgang resembled a cross between Robert Loggia and Harvey Keitel, as he explained we'd chosen John Gotti's usual table—before he was shipped off to solitary in Marion, Illinois. Then a sweet thing happened. As Wolfgang slathered soapy water on the table and wiped it dry, he smiled and pronounced his shopworn joke: "There's a fresh tablecloth for you." Later, after the beeper on his belt alerted him that our steak was ready, he appeared with a gigantic platter of meat steeped in melted butter and beef juices. Then he carefully placed an upside-down saucer beneath one end of the platter to pool the sauce, the routine he described as "German engineering." We locked eyes and he smiled, as though he understood the connection this made for me.

My wife scowled at the three pounds of sliced porterhouse between us. To her it looked like a cardiac surgeon's dream; to me it represented a happy confluence of memories. She didn't seem totally convinced by my "remembering Pop" rationale for this dinner: "Make a habit of this," she warned, "and your rosiest future will be a triple bypass attention-getter followed by a quick death if you don't get the message."

So I've come kicking and screaming to the age where I must watch what I eat. To remain the apple of my wife's eye, I'm expected to search menus for fish and chicken and simple little pasta concoctions. But not tonight. Tonight I'm remembering the old man. I may have declared that, for me, steak is no longer king; but for tonight, if the king is dead, long live the king.

Stephen Byers is a writer and editor-at-large of National Geographic Adventure *magazine.*

Wholly Lights in Dyker Heights

You got a problem with Christmas?

BY
MARGARET
A. DALY

Light is precious in the winter months, when evening slinks in before the afternoon has fully retired. So the tiny holiday lights that illuminate trees and houses fire a gloom-dispelling glow within all who glimpse them. But in some Brooklyn neighborhoods like Dyker Heights, it's less a warm holiday glow than a Vegas blast of brilliance.

The practice of taking holiday decorations to excess —of rocketing completely over the (house) top with lights and figures and music—is turning into a Brooklyn tradition. How did it start? Where? Nobody really knows. But over on Flatlands Avenue in Canarsie one house that is so covered with lights that it looks like an all-night mini mall. A row of brownstones on First Place in Carroll Gardens doesn't stop at Christmas decor: their yards are sprinkled with hearts for Valentine's Day, plastic eggs and bunnies for Easter and shamrocks for St. Patrick's Day. Can tiny union workers for Labor Day be far behind?

The biggest and best domestic show of Christmas lights occurs in Dyker Heights at the home of Al

A merry excess to all! In some neighborhoods, competition among homeowners intensifies every year.

Melissa Brown, "Christmas in Dyker Heights," 1998

Polizzotto. "I get a glow on when this goes up," says Al, who each December decks his family's two-story house at 1145 Eighty-Fourth Street with 20,000 white lights and giant toy-soldier figures that march in time with the recorded carols he broadcasts from loudspeakers. "It's probably an ego trip." *Probably?*

Thirteen years ago, Polizzotto was diagnosed with non-Hodgkin's lymphoma and given just four months to live. When the four months passed and Al continued to live, he wanted to celebrate his good fortune with the biggest display of Christmas cheer ever seen in Dyker Heights.

Big is important to Polizzotto, who is a lawyer with his own firm nearby. When he bought his house years ago, it was unremarkable in a neighborhood of mostly red-brick, two-family duplexes with plain white trim. The uniformity of each block is interrupted only by a handful of small single-family houses. Al bought his house and then tore it down. In its place, he built a massive, two-story white house with Greek columns that frame a small window with the letter "P" standing alone like a family crest at the top. The house is too big for the lot, and when you add two twenty-seven-foot-tall toy soldiers on each column, plus eight six-foot toy soldiers dancing in the front yard, plus two more toy soldiers riding high on 3,000-pound white horses flanking a sixteen-foot Santa Claus, the total effect is pure excess: Christmas out of control. It's not about aesthetics, it's about over-the-top joy. No miracle on 34th Street could outshine Al Polizzotto's Christmas display, and each year it gets bigger. In fact, it probably outdraws some of the more renowned New York holiday displays: some 250,000 onlookers pass by during December.

Polizzotto hires a live Santa, too, and in 1998 began handing out presents—he buys some 25,000 dolls, trucks, tanks and games every year—to all the children who pass by. He used to hire a cadre of elves and a Mrs. Claus, but "stopped doing that because the elves were kids, and they stopped showing up on time. You can't tell a child, 'Hang on, the elf will be here, but he's dropping off his girlfriend first.'"

The whole routine is not simply a gift to the public. Al gets his own turn at fun. Though the giant Santa has a prerecorded thirty-minute greeting, Al, peeking out from behind the living room drapes (shades of the Wizard of Oz), can control the sound. "If a friend is coming by with their little ones, I'll call out their names," he says, grinning and shaking his head. "The kids'll go completely berserk.

"I get Muslims. I get a busload of Hasidic Jews every year. You know why? Because their kids love it, so they love it. One year I had a busload of senior citizens come by. I mean *really* senior citizens." They were too frail to get off the bus—one was only able to be there on an ambulance-type cot. Al went out to the bus with a sack full of presents. "I told them, 'None of you are as old as your mind says.' I gave fire trucks to the men and dolls to the ladies. Some of them cried. It was exhilarating."

As it gets closer to Christmas, the neighborhood streets become clogged with people who crawl by in cars loaded with laughing, screaming kids. Traffic officers from the Sixty-Eighth Precinct are on hand to blow whistles and wave their hands in the air to move the traffic along and make sure that the river of pedestrians stays on the sidewalks. It's more mayhem than merry.

And for Polizzotto's neighbors it's not all comfort and joy. The crowds make it virtually impossible for them to pull into or out of their driveways. And they'd better like Christmas carols, because the songs blast out of loudspeakers that are part of the display. When some residents complained to their local politicians, Al

Like many Americans, I fear living in a nowhere, in a place that is noplace; in Brooklyn, that doesn't trouble me at all." **Ian Frazier**

took them on. "You don't like the music, I'll turn it up," he told them. "You don't like the lights, I'll put up more. You don't like all the people, I'll invite more."

The attitude seems more confrontational than Claus, but Al says, "I don't notice any opposition anymore. It just faded away." However, he did take out a conciliatory advertisement in the local weekly, *The Home Reporter*, touting the joy and peace of the season.

It may have been the ad or Al himself that made the opposition disappear. Or it may be the "can't lick 'em, join 'em" syndrome. Other Dyker Heights residents began to get in the act. Al's neighbor Lucy Spata has all along featured a Santa's Workshop diorama in her front window, and about sixty angels light up the rest of the property on one side of her brick duplex. A block away, Mike Caso has erected thirty statuettes representing the cast of characters in the 1970 version of *A Christmas Carol* with Albert Finney. Around the block, another yard is crowded with Christmas in Toyland figures.

"My house is known throughout the world," says Al. "I've been on TV in Japan. All I have to say anywhere in the world is 'toy soldier' and people say 'Dyker Heights.' I think I give joy to a lot of people."

Margaret A. Daly is a veteran journalist who often writes about food, music, politics and neighborhoods— often in Brooklyn.

The Very First Children's Museum

A kids' paradise in the heart of Crown Heights, the Brooklyn Children's Museum is hopping with activity. Kids carom down the long, sloping central artery—a water wheel and an indoor river sheltered inside a huge recycled sewer pipe, lined with concentric rings of rainbow neon. They spill noisily into the exhibit areas that flow off the tunnel like tributaries. And they don't just look at static museum exhibits. Jump ropes, chalk and chessboards stand ready; interactive video displays respond to an eager touch; cozy nooks invite great story-telling or absorption in a favorite book. The kids can participate in the Pizza Garden, a project in which they grow tomatoes, garlic, onion, basil and peppers. Some join an after-school computer club.

Founded in 1899, this exuberant institution was the first museum in the world dedicated exclusively to youngsters. "The Children's Museum idea is Brooklyn's gift to the world," said museum director Anna Billings Gallup in 1926. Over the decades it drew on the Depression-era talents of WPA artists and craftsmen, and it built on post-World War II interest in science and technology. The museum has been moved and expanded several times, to its present location, where it now stands surrounded by once-elegant homes, brick row houses and a neighborhood playground. Overlapping, parallel, concurrent lives and cultures are the truth of the street and the norm of the museum. Firmly integrated into the community, the museum sponsors shofar-blowing workshops and Carib dance parties, family flamenco evenings and Chinese theater workshops.

Above all, the BCM offers curious children access to science professionals and mentors, and to a peer group to grow with. Teens are actively recruited for internships and paid employment, an important feature for those who can't afford to work for nothing.

The influence of the museum is reflected in the people whose lives it touches. Jonathan Ross, an eleven-year-old fifth grader, spends summers as a BCM volunteer-in-training. Flashing a hundred-watt smile, Jonathan says simply, "It's fun here." And Ronald Griffiths, a BCM alumnus and former staffer who is now a senior instructor at the Bronx Zoo, says

he grew up roaming the museum's exhibits. He credits the decades he spent there with giving him the foundation for his own dedication to educating children. *–Helen Zelon and Patricia Curtis*

Courtesy of Brooklyn Children's Museum

Flatbush Spectacle

Behind the scenes at a West Indian Day parade

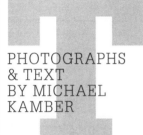

PHOTOGRAPHS
& TEXT
BY MICHAEL
KAMBER

he West Indian Day Parade, an annual Labor Day extravaganza along Eastern Parkway in Brooklyn, has become the largest, liveliest, most colorful, best-attended—and definitely loudest—parade in all five boroughs. Rooted in centuries-old pre-Lenten celebrations in the Caribbean, and a Labor Day tradition in Brooklyn for over three decades, it grows more spirited with each passing year. For the many thousands who put it together and participate as masqueraders, marchers, musicians, dancers and DJs, it has also grown from a day's event to an entire summer season of preparation, from a one-time celebration to a way of life.

But a *carnaval* this intricate does not simply grow like a tree or happen like a sunny day. Here's how, in the final frenetic days before Labor Day, the parade comes together.

Flatbush Avenue, Thursday, September 2, 1 A.M. at the Savage Camp:

"Right now we're in a war zone," Martin Heywood declares as he hurriedly cuts gold pieces of vinyl into a long diamond shape. Though it's well after midnight, Brooklyn's West Indian Day Parade is just days away and a chaotic mix of men and a few women crowds its headquarters, a tiny rented storefront on Flatbush Avenue—"the Bush." All of them are sewing, cutting and gluing costumes for the members of their parade ensemble, the Savage Camp, which is just one of the thirty-five or so highly competitive ensembles that regularly participate in the parade.

Labor Day on Eastern Parkway: the West Indian Day Parade is the city's biggest and most colorful event.

Most of the costumes will be worn by members of the mas camps—groups of masqueraders vying for the coveted People's Choice award.

On the sidewalk outside, huge speakers blast soca (soul plus calypso) music, and the smell of jerk chicken wafts from a fifty-five-gallon steel drum converted into a grill. A young man in an army vest is gently gluing flowers onto the costume of one of "Cleopatra's Maidens." Each camp does its costumes in accord with a chosen theme, and this year theirs is Cleopatra. Earlier there was concern that all the women would want to be Cleopatra. "You can't have Cleopatra without Cleopatra's Maidens and Cleopatra's Guards," Heywood explained. "If too many want to be Cleopatra, we'll have to close her out."

Fortunately this didn't happen, and so, though Savage is one of the smallest of the many entrant groups of

masqueraders, or "mas camps" (a term that goes back to the nineteenth century in Trinidad), they still have a chance at the Parade's "People's Choice" award, which they've won three years running. But very early on this morning, there are *dozens* of costumes still to be made. Risers for the DJ and two dozen loudspeakers (each nearly four feet high) still must be built; the forty-foot truck that will carry them, along with a 100,000-watt generator, still has to be rented. There's work to do.

Competition among the camps over music and costumes and dances is just as intense in Brooklyn as it is in Trinidad. Mel Simon, the Savage Camp's designer, explains that the costume sketches now lining the walls of his seasonal rented storefront (immediately after the parade, it will turn into a jerk chicken/roti joint) can't be put up too early in the season; spies posing as would-be masqueraders have been known to wander in and steal design ideas. One veteran masquerader remembers that, as recently as 1990, "If you were a member of one camp, you couldn't be caught snooping around another camp." What would happen? "Let's just say it could be bad for your health."

Parkside Avenue, Friday, September 3, 9 P.M. at the Parkside Pan Yard:

Every community in Trinidad has a "pan yard," usually an open-air site where the local "pan men," or steel drummers, gather to rehearse. Brooklyn has Parkside Avenue in Prospect Lefferts Gardens, and you hear the

Technicians assemble truck-size rolling stereos to create the big sound that is a hallmark of the festivities.

block before you see it: the normally silent street of empty lots and one-story parking garages and auto-body shops is alive with the sounds of several *hundred* steel drums, all being tapped and pounded furiously by band members trying to learn their parts at the last minute. Different parts from different compositions by different bands fill the air with a beautiful cacophony that only the pans can make. Hundreds of onlookers mill about the sidewalk, offering advice, eating roti purchased from vendors, or just enjoying the sounds and the scene. A welder's sparks fly through the night air as he works on a "rack," a large steel frame on wheels for drums; the drummers stand inside it as it's moved by "pushers" along the parade route.

Originally made from empty shipping barrels, the Caribbean steel drums can be counted among the few musical instruments that have been created in the twentieth century. Today pans are handmade, cost between $500 and $4,000, and come in soprano, tenor and bass sizes. Only in the last thirty-five years have pan makers developed a system that allows sharps and flats to be played. This development has meant an increase in musical flexibility and subtlety, and Trinidadians like Boogsie Sharp have achieved world renown as composers and session artists, playing alongside such jazz musicians as Wynton Marsalis and Max Roach. Boogsie is the composer for the Pan Rebels; he moves patiently from group to group, teaching them their parts by tapping out phrases as the drummers try to follow along.

Anthony Trebuse, captain of the Pan Rebels, points out some newcomers to his group. "Those three just flew in today to play with us," she says. The three turn out to be Trinidadians now hailing from Arizona, Texas and Washington, D.C., and Trebuse reports that increasingly females are becoming "pan men" as well.

Leandra Baptiste, the ten-year-old New Millennium Junior Queen of the Sesame Flyers, a popular mas camp, looks miserable as her mother dresses her in an extravagant white costume with feathered headpiece. Why? "I don't like being the queen. My mother (a 1977 'Queen of the Carnival' from Grenada) makes me do it. I like playing the pans."

Farther down Parkside, Rita Abood, Queen of the Metro Camp, sits in the back of one of the huge auto-body shops that serve as base camp, putting finishing touches on her costume. Each camp usually has a junior and senior king and queen who wear extravagant one-of-a-kind costumes called "characters." These outfits typically take weeks or even months to make. Rita is excited about being the Metro queen and claims she won't sleep the night before judging, but admits to having been the queen for fifteen years already and plans to be the queen "'til I walking with cane."

Rita has previously won first place in parades in Brooklyn, Antigua and Toronto as well as in Trinidad, where "the mas is plenty bigger"; her first prize there last year included $11,000 US. She has an inside track in

The Roots of the Parade

Brooklyn's West Indian Day Parade started in Harlem in the 1930s, but as New York's Caribbean community grew to over half a million people (especially after changes in U.S. immigration law in 1964) and most of them settled in Brooklyn, the parade moved with them. In 1967 the parade was transplanted to Eastern Parkway—which runs through the center of Crown Heights, home to many of New York's West Indians—and has for years been staged by the West Indian Day Carnival Association, Inc., or WIDCA. What may seem like a chaotic mélange of raucous music, dancing bodies and wildly fanciful costumes is actually a highly structured event with generations-old roots in the small villages of the Caribbean, and Trinidad in particular. Nearly all Caribbean nations, as well as Panama and Brazil, have some version of pre-Lenten carnaval, the festival upon which Brooklyn's parade is an outgrowth. But immigrants from Trinidad and Tobago dominate this one—easily the largest and best-known of these festivals in the United States. Though far outnumbered in Brooklyn by Guyanese and Jamaicans, "Trinis" started and still run most of the camps like Savage Camp.

On Parade Day, though, the emphasis overall is on being West Indian rather than narrowly nationalistic. So Jamaican revelers, floats and bands, waving their black, green and gold flag, will be followed by the blue and gold pendants flown by Bajun (from Barbados) marchers, followed by Haitian bands and dancers sporting the red and blue colors of their country.

The festival started in the nineteenth century as a slave procession to mark the beginning of Lent, according to Earnest Brown, an expert on carnaval who teaches at Williams College. Music and costumes were added over the years as the carnival metamorphosed into the world-famous event it has become. The early organizers of New York's version of the West Indian carnaval followed the general pattern of celebrations in Trinidad but after World War II shifted the event to Labor Day, mostly because New York City weather is better in September than in March.

In Trinidad today, each village or neighborhood still sets up its own "masqueraders camp," with a king and queen, dozens or even hundreds of masqueraders, a steel band and sometimes a DJ—all to prepare for the big carnaval parade. Beginning several months before carnival, members of the communities usually meet in the camps after work each day to make costumes, rehearse the band, and plan and assemble fanciful floats. Then on Carnival morning they go "on the road," that is, on parade, to dance, play music and compete for the prizes that bring a camp bragging rights—and, in some cases, a fair amount in cash prizes. And that pattern of long preparation for a one-day parade is followed in Brooklyn.
—M.K.

"I don't like being the queen," says Leandra Baptiste. "I like playing the pans."

Below: Pan men perform on handmade drums costing between $400 and $2,000.

these competitions: her husband, Pankey, is her costume maker. He made his first costume for her in 1983. With it, she won first place, and he has been in heavy demand ever since. Today he travels the United States and Caribbean year-round, making $3,000 costumes for a waiting list of kings and queens to be. Rita beams with pride as she takes a visitor behind a huge tarp in the corner of the garage to show off her costume: it's almost more a structure than a garment, sixteen feet high, weighing thirty-five pounds and containing 2,000 electric-blue feathers. Other than that, it's nigh indescribable. Speaking of Labor Day, she says, "I pray for the day to come. I so love it."

Flatbush Avenue, Sunday, September 5, 11 P.M., at Hawks International:

"Too many decibels?" Richard the DJ shakes his head and ponders the question. But it is the most absurd thing he's ever heard. He points to a 125,000-watt generator the size

of a Volkswagen on the back of the eighteen-wheeler. "There's no way you can get too many decibels," he says. Speaking of other DJs with names like Rude Boy Dexter and King Chow, he explains, "They'll pull up next to you on the parade road and try to blast you out." With his $50,000 sound system, Richard will never let this happen and that is why Hawks International, the largest of the camps, is paying him twelve grand for one day's work. They want to be sure *their* sound is the biggest; they want to be sure the parade watchers feel the bass vibrate in their chest as the truck rolls by, even from forty feet away.

So Richard's crew is unloading thirty-six massive speakers they've trucked in from Boston, stacking them twenty feet high on the back of a semi-trailer that will become one rolling wall of sound as it inches along Eastern Parkway. Richard will be perched on top at the mixing board like Captain Kirk at the controls of the *Enterprise.* "We play all the carnivals," he says. "Toronto, D.C., Miami, even Texas has one now—every year you got to keep putting out more and more sound to keep up with the other guys."

Frank Nasin stands on Flatbush and shakes his head

in wonder at the speakers towering above him. He started teaching Richard to DJ when he was just an eleven-year-old kid on the streets of Boston. "When I started DJ-ing in Trinidad in the 1950s," Frank says, "I'd load two speakers and a reel-to-reel tape deck in the back seat of my car and go to parties to play." Frank emigrated to Boston in the 1970s and started working small parties and weddings there, using old 78 records of calypso standards and mixing in disco and soul for the more Americanized crowds. He's retired now, and Richard has taken over the DJ business, just as Soca has exploded on the scene and replaced calypso as the parade's soundtrack. "With the new generation, you can't play very much calypso, they don't want it," Frank explains. He looks at the truck and shakes his head again as he watches the workmen lash another speaker into place. "Oh man, I started out with reel-to-reel and now they're mixing with CDs."

Eastern Parkway, Sunday, September 5, midnight:

The evening before the parade, there's a costume competition and a band competition, both staged behind the Brooklyn Museum of Art. Called the Dimanche Gras Finale, or sometimes Panorama, these events draw thousands of fans to hear the dozen or so reggae, steel-drum and soca bands.

After midnight another event, Jouvert (pronounced Joo-vay) unfolds, usually on Flatbush or Nostrand Avenue or Empire Boulevard. Jouvert is a chaotic, traffic-stopping prelude to the more organized parade proper. It is a big, rambling, all-night street party, featuring pan players from the various camps, a lot of drinking, and revelers sometimes inflicting impromptu "costumes" on each other with splashed paint and baby powder.

Then, on Labor Day morning, masqueraders, bands and speaker-laden flatbed trucks assemble at several points along Eastern Parkway and the parade finally gets under way. For the rest of the day, the entire vast spectacle inches slowly and very loudly along Eastern Parkway amid some two million spectators to end at Grand Army Plaza.

Flatbush Avenue, Monday, September 6, Labor Day, 9 P.M.:

The parade ended a few hours ago and only the street cleaners roam Eastern Parkway now, but on Flatbush Avenue a group of young girls, refusing to go home, sit on the curb still in costume, headpieces on the ground beside them. They look exhausted as they watch the crews dismantle the floats and speaker trucks that had been completed only the night before. Except for the whine of the crews' electric screw guns, the street is quiet for the first time in weeks and smells faintly of beer and urine.

Across the avenue at the Savage Camp, the store-front is a wreck—bolts of cloth and rolls of Mylar are piled haphazardly atop sewing machines and loud-speaker cases.

Camp members generally pay $70 to $150 for their own costumes, and some of the costs are covered by the sponsors whose logos hang from long banners festooned on the floats and on the camp storefronts. Heywood, the Savage president, was proud of his Keyspan Energy sponsor, but had laughed a few days earlier when asked if his camp broke even financially for its efforts.

"Every year we lose money on this," he explained, running down the costs of DJs, truck and storefront rentals, costume materials, and insurance. He'd worked at the Savage Camp six or more hours each night throughout the summer—after completing his shift at his day job. He even took his annual vacation during the two weeks before Labor Day so he could work at the camp round the clock.

The obvious question is "Why go to all this trouble for just one day?" Mel Simon, Heywood's good friend and the Savage Camp designer, seemed at first puzzled by the question. But then, bent over a sewing machine, eyes bloodshot and face covered with stubble, Simon said: "We did this in Trinidad all the time. This is our roots. This is our heritage."

Michael Kamber is an insomniac pan fan, writer and professional photographer.

Brooklyn's Grand Old Restaurant

Gage & Tollner exerts a timeless spell

BY L.J.
DAVIS

I once tried—not just thought about, but actually *tried*—to buy Gage & Tollner. I did it for love. It was the 1980s, when everybody had too much money, and I was flush. I came to my senses when a friend pointed out that I would very soon become *unflush* on the grounds that I knew as much about running a restaurant as I did about building an intergalactic warp drive. Eventually, Joe Chirico, who was already well versed in the Brooklyn restaurant business, bought the place instead, and I am glad.

Nobody goes to Gage & Tollner primarily for the food. You go to Gage's (as many regulars call it) for the *experience,* the way you go to heaven for the climate and to hell for the company. You go there to see and feel the past continued palpably into the present. You go there for the unaltered tables, for the gaslight, for the antediluvian waiters, and to see yourself reflected in nineteenth-century mirrors. This legendary eatery has often been remembered in the same breath with Rector's, Delmonico's, Ebbets Field, Steeplechase Park, the Hippodrome, the Navy Yard—all institutions that once defined a certain kind of New York, one that I

GAGE & TOLLNER,   Oyster and Chop House —   372 Fulton St. — Brooklyn, N. Y.

Brian Merlis Collection

would give much to visit again. But today, only Gage & Tollner survives.

Charles M. Gage opened his restaurant in 1879 and was joined by Eugene Tollner the following year. It has been at 372 Fulton Street since 1892, and in appearance and feel it has not changed substantially in the past century. For years, much has been made of the nine splendid brass gas chandeliers, still lighted early every evening and handy in a blackout, but in 1892 they were not a big deal. The chandeliers are also fitted with electric lights, and in 1892 *those* were the big deal. In advertisements that bordered on the hysterical, according to the sedate standards of the day, Messrs. Gage and Tollner announced that their eating establishment was the first in the city to be illuminated by Mr. Edison's incandescent bulbs. (Because the founders did not completely trust the wild-eyed Edison and his harebrained schemes, the gas lights were installed as a backup system. And for years, in the basement, as a belt to supplement these suspenders, there was a gigantic storage battery. Gage and Tollner were not men to rush blindly into the dark uncertain future.)

When the founding owners sold the restaurant in 1911, Eugene Tollner clearly felt that something important had gone out of his life. He returned as an employee and served as the official greeter, a post he occupied until past his eightieth year. The Dewey family, which had previously distinguished itself by introducing viniculture to the Finger Lakes, acquired the place in 1919, and on that date—inside this restaurant, anyway—time seemed to stop.

There is no need to dwell on Gage's sad twilight later in the twentieth century, or to rehearse the reasons for its decline. It was a sign of the institution's desperation that the owners briefly considered selling out to the Roy Rogers chain—or that I actually tried to buy it. Instead, suffice it to say that the unusually civic-minded Independent Savings Bank of Brooklyn approached neighborhood restaurateur Joe Chirico. A native of Calabria, Chirico got his American start in pizza and fast food, and rose in the approved fashion to become proprietor of the splendid little Marco Polo restaurant in Carroll Gardens.

CLASSIC HITS

From Gage & Tollner's "Classic" Menu:

APPETIZERS

Pan Roast Oysters, simmered in sherry cream, buttery croutons

Oysters Diamond Jim Brady, baked with tomato & crème fraîche

Soft Clambellies, egg & breaded, broiled or seasoned fried, tartar sauce

Crabcake, black bean & corn vinaigrette

Crabmeat Virginia, jumbo lump meat, spinach & potato galette, broiled

ENTREES

Soft Clambellies, broiled or seasoned fried on grilled vegetables, roasted potatoes

Pan Roast Oysters, simmered in sherry cream, vegetables & roasted potatoes

Fried Oysters, breaded & served on top of mushroom fennel ragout, roasted potatoes

Maryland Crabcakes, Vegetable slaw, black-bean and corn vinaigrette

Fried Shrimp, Spinach, rice, homemade tartar sauce

Shrimp Creole, Rice, spicy tomato pepper sauce

Shrimp Newburg, Sherry cream sauce with peas, pearl onions & carrots, rice

Lobster Newburg, Sherry cream sauce with peas, pearl onions & carrots, rice

He jumped in where a man of lesser self-confidence might have paused and dithered. "It was Gage & Tollner," he says. "It was part of America. I had to save it."

In 1995, Gage's was still coasting on its memories and on the fact that its menu had so long persisted

The Talk at Gage & Tollner

One summer, recently, Swiss diplomats and representatives of major, long-lived Swiss banks, seeking a hideaway far from the prying eyes of a hostile press, took their negotiations with a committee from the World Jewish Council to one of Gage's marble-and-brass fitted upper rooms.

"We weren't getting much of anywhere in Judge Korman's courtroom, and he felt a change of venue might advance the cause. Gage & Tollner is virtually around the corner from his chambers," says Elan Steinberg, executive director of the World Jewish Council and a member of the negotiating team. He was referring to Judge Korman of the Second Circuit, U.S. Court of Appeals. "There were, all told, between a dozen and twenty of us. It was a stifling-hot night in August and the air-conditioning didn't work. Some very formal people who had probably never in their lives removed their jackets in public had to take them off. Some of our people were kosher, and they had to settle for green salads." With its abundant offerings of clams lobster, shrimp, crab and oysters, Gage's menu is a festival of *traif*.

"There were some tense moments," Steinberg continues. "But by one o'clock in the morning we had the outlines of an agreement. We knew pretty much where we were going, and that's pretty much where we ended up." The Swiss negotiators finally agreed to admit that, yes, they were still sitting on the bank accounts of depositors who had died in the Holocaust.

It's unlikely that any conversations held in a restaurant in the twentieth century were more rewarding than the one held in that upstairs room at gaslit Gage & Tollner on a sweltering August evening.–*L.J.D.*

unchanged that it had become an anachronism. You could get a Yorkshire buck at Gage's, and not many contemporary restaurants could make that claim. The clambellies remained reliably delicious—Calvin Trillin once wrote that if he were taking Mao Tse-tung out to dinner, he would feed him Gage's clam bellies. The crabmeat Dewey was not named for the owning family; it was named for *Admiral* Dewey, the hero of the 1898 Battle of Manila Bay, and the red and yellow peppers therein symbolized the fallen flag of Spain. Steaks and chops were quickly grilled over anthracite coal, or so was the proud boast. (On taking over, Chirico took one look at the anthracite grill, realized that it hadn't worked in years and promptly threw it out.) Most of the seafood in the seemingly encyclopedic menu was bathed either in a simple béchamel or in ketchup (anything named "Chicago" had ketchup in it). It was good food—I used to dote on the potatoes hash-browned in cream—and there was a *lot* of it. It stuck to the ribs. It did not toy with the palate. At Gage's, surrounded by the furnishings of the past, you ate the past.

Until recently, it was also possible to believe that you were being attended by members of the original African-American serving staff. The waiters (there were no servers from the distaff side until the 1970s) wore service marks on their sleeves. A bar meant five years, a star ten, an eagle twenty-five. I have had my dinner brought to table by a two-eagle waiter.

The original Thonet bentwood chairs are gone now, but the mahogany tables are the same ones that graced the premises on opening day, the original lincrusta (the poor man's leather of its day) still adorns the walls, the old oyster bar brought from the restaurant's original location up the street is still in the same old place under its painted frieze, and the hundred-foot-long room with its arched, mahogany-framed mirrors still looks evocative of the dining car on a robber baron's private train.

So Gage's is alive and well, and again looking like its old self. Chirico cleaned the lincrusta, polished the mirrors, tore down the acoustic tiles to reveal the old curved ceiling, installed a drinks bar and spent a haystack of money. And the oldest restaurant in the city has again become a landmark (officially designated) and a place of importance. And, in all honesty, in all likelihood, none of this would have happened had I succeeded in buying Gage & Tollner.

L.J. Davis is a veteran writer who has lived in Boerum Hill since before it was known as Boerum Hill—when it was still called North Gowanus.

Satmar Life

A hidden world in Williamsburg

BY MICHAEL
KAMBER

On Kent Avenue, across the street from the Brooklyn Navy Yard, a double-wide trailer sags on cinder blocks, rickety steps leading to a door that's slowly delaminating. The structure seems barely habitable, but a sign on the roof identifies it as the Hall Street Kosher Cafe. Inside, a half-dozen Hasidim sit at worn Formica tables, reading Yiddish newspapers, talking on cell phones and eating from paper plates.

At the far end of the trailer, a group of Hasidim in black wool coats crowds around a glass case of fish, blintzes and matzo balls. A woman's voice calls out from behind the men: "What can I get for you?—what do you mean is it fresh?—of course it's fresh, it's all fresh. Try the gefilte fish today, it's delicious—a little horseradish with that?"

Another voice, this one male and heavily accented: "He would have asked you already for horseradish, he never eats horseradish."

"Well, maybe today he changes his mind."

"Why should he change his mind?"

The voices belong to Schlomo and Rachel, the husband-and-wife team that runs the Hall Street Kosher Cafe. The decor is probably the most down to earth in Brooklyn; the food is among the best. When the crowd disperses, a man goes up to the counter. "My mother-in-law is sick," he says. "We've been trying to get her on Medicaid. Do you know who can help?" Rachel and Schlomo immediately reel off a list of charitable agencies and addresses, discussing the merits of each one.

This is not an uncommon exchange in this neighborhood. In fact, there are dozens of charitable Jewish agencies active here, some providing assistance from the community, others helping residents to get government assistance. The Satmar neighborhood of Williamsburg is one of the poorest in the city, and it relies heavily on welfare and other government programs.

Stanley Rosenfeld, director of the local WIC (Women, Infants and Children) office, explains: "The Torah says, 'Be fruitful and multiply,' and birth control is not allowed. So the average family size here is eight to ten children.

In crowded Williamsburg, Satmar families average eight to ten children.

Michael Kamber

Twelve or even fourteen children is not unusual. Williamsburg has one of the highest birthrates in the nation. Most of the wives stay home, and for the men—even if they are working and making thirty or thirty-five thousand dollars a year, which is a lot in this community—it's not easy to support a family of ten or more on that."

After we've been talking a few minutes, Rosenfeld says, "Come with me," and steps into a back room full of filing cabinets. He opens the cabinet nearest the door and pulls out the first file. "This is the first case we opened in 1980, when this office was created. It was a young pregnant mother. She was twenty-two years old. You see this?" He turns to the last page of the file and points to an entry. "Her case is still open—she just had another child in May. It was her fifteenth."

In his café, Schlomo reflects on the matter of children. "We believe in old-fashioned, traditional education. Separate boys from girls. With that, you avoid a lot of problems—drugs, suicides, sex, shootings in the schools, children bringing in guns. You have all that on TV today. The parents try to have switches on the TV—this the children should see, this they shouldn't see—but sooner or later the children find all the buttons. So, you don't bring the TV or the radio into the home. Some Jewish schools, religious schools, they used to be more liberal. They started with the TV. With time, they came to the conclusion: just take

The Satmar hasidim created their own community after following Rabbi Joel Teitelbaum to Williamsburg in 1946.

Michael Kamber

it away. They tell the parents, We're not going to take any children if they have TV.

"Basic Jewish law, children have to have education through eighth grade," Schlomo continues. "Girls get more—maybe a high school degree. They don't have to learn Torah. Law says boys have to learn Torah. Boys in Williamsburg don't have high school degrees, so that eliminates them from some jobs. They're not going to find such a good job like other people. We're a little bit eliminating ourselves.

"Between eighteen and twenty, kids marry. A matchmaker finds boys and girls for each other. My philosophy is, when God created the world, a boy met a girl, so fifty percent of marriage is done. For twenty-five percent, we have to help them. We teach the children that life is not easy. You have to suffer. If you're married, then children are coming, especially with no birth control. So you're not finished with one child, and all of a sudden the woman sees herself pregnant with another child. Then you need money to support them, and you're not making enough money. So you pray a little bit, you hope a little bit, and you push this day so the next day is easier.

"Do I feel it's a good life? I feel it's a great life. We're happy in this community. The parents learn from their parents, the children learn from their parents, and the grandchildren learn from their parents."

John Talmadge, community liaison for city council member Ken Fisher, knows the Satmar people well: "I agree their high birthrate contributes to their poverty, but the bigger problems are jobs and housing. There are just no jobs for most of these folks. There's no higher education, and no such thing as a Satmar doctor, lawyer or accountant. About a third of the men are employed as teachers in the yeshivas, but the rest have low-paying factory jobs or are unemployed. They can't get jobs in retail because they can't work on Shabbat, and they have to take the whole month of October off for the holidays.

"As for housing, I can't tell you how many one-bedroom apartments I've been to where there are thirteen or fourteen kids. One of the saddest cases, the woman was eight months pregnant, but the house was so filled with cots she couldn't find a place to sit down. We finally did a fund-raiser and found a place for the family upstate. Another housing problem is that the Satmars have to live in proximity to a rabbi's house. One family can't say, 'We'll go live in Brooklyn Heights or Park Slope,' even if they could find affordable apartments there. Several hundred would have to move together to get a rabbi to come. Then they would have to have a synagogue, schools and kosher stores."

Local politicians know that the Satmars are a force to consider, that they will endorse any candidate they think is going to bring jobs or housing to the community. "The first time Ken ran for a city council seat in 1991, it was a very crowded race," says Talmadge. "But Ken had the endorsement of the Satmars. Their voting habit is to go to the polls between seven and nine o'clock at night. Ken's campaign team was sure he had lost. He was running eighth, no one was voting for him. All of a sudden, at seven o'clock, the lines started forming—the black hats had come out to the three polling sites in Williamsburg. The next thing you know, Ken had won the election."

How did the Satmar community get started in Brooklyn? One community spokesperson, Albert Friedman, explains: "Satmar is a city in what used to be Transylvania, a province in Romania. The rabbi there, Rabbi Teitelbaum, immigrated to Brooklyn in 1946, and his flock followed him and kept the name Satmar. Teitelbaum set up a whole infrastructure here, kosher stores, synagogues, schools. And because so many rabbis had been lost, he became a father figure."

Strict adherence to the Torah governs Satmar life. It dictates even the beards on the men in their black coats and wide-brimmed hats. "We're not allowed to use a razor blade on our faces," Friedman explains. "Some orthodox Jews cut their beards with an electric machine because it's not a blade. But we go one step further and don't cut our beards by any means.

"For every day that passes, we're one step closer to the redemption, when the Messiah comes," says Friedman.

Michael Kamber is a professional photographer, writer and community observer.

Rings of Passion

At Gleason's Gym on Front Street, the sweet science lives

BY PHIL BERGER

I first started coming to Gleason's in '78," says fight promoter Aaron Braunstein. "I had this crazy idea of becoming a fighter. I was already a successful businessman, and walking through those doors was culture shock. It was noisy as hell, everybody jumping around. Then, *bing!* this bell rings, and everybody stops and sits—like they're sitting shivah. Sixty seconds later, the bell *bings* again and everybody's up and at it again. Bap! bap! bap! working on the heavy bag. On the speed bag. Shadowboxing. They do three minutes on and one minute off. I found it fascinating." Braunstein's fascination with the fight game led to his becoming one of the many to-be-disappointed managers of an, ah, *eccentric* heavyweight named Mitch "Blood" Green, whose major claim to fame rests on his having brawled for neither prize nor money with a Brooklynite boxer named Mike Tyson at two o'clock in the morning on a street in Harlem.

Blood Green and Mike Tyson—and titleholders Riddick Bowe, Junior Jones, Kevin Kelley, Arturo Gatti and Mark Breland—all share the common bond of working out not on a post-midnight street corner, but in the legendary Brooklyn gym that intrigued Braunstein and a long queue of other boxing aficionados: Gleason's.

"I like the whole smell of the gym, the atmosphere," Braunstein says. "There's a comradeship if you're accepted. And there's nothing like it. It's closer than family. You go there, you see up-and-comers, you see bums, wiseguys. It's the only place I feel relaxed, like I'm home."

That now-famous atmosphere of Gleason's Gym is the creation of a man whose name is actually not Gleason, but Bruce Silverglade, and who was never a boxer but was once a credit manager for Sears, Roebuck, of all places. In his life "off the clock," Silverglade, now in his fifties, got involved with amateur boxing, which was something of a family tradition. His father, Edward, had been manager of the U.S. Olympic boxing teams in 1980 and 1984, and when Bruce confessed to feeling dead-ended at Sears, Roebuck, the old man got his son into the amateur boxing scene.

"I became a judge and a referee," says Silverglade. "But I found I didn't like that end of it. See, I'd transport the young fighters around, buy them lunches. I'd end up becoming their friend. So then I found it too difficult to have to judge these kids. I had too much of an emotional attachment to them. So I got into the administrative end of the sport, and eventually I became president of amateur boxing in New York City. Then, on the national level, that led to becoming the chairman for the Junior Olympic development program for boxers eight to fifteen."

Silverglade loved the sport but had never dreamed of operating a boxing gym, let alone a legend like Gleason's. Then, in 1985, he decided he'd had it with his day job. "I knew," he says, "it was never going to be Sears, Silverglade and Company. So I took an early retirement and then, hearing that Ira Becker, the owner of Gleason's, was looking for a partner, I used my profit-sharing to buy into the gym."

At the time, the gym was located on West Thirtieth Street in Manhattan, a few blocks from Madison Square Garden. Originally, it had been named for its progenitor in the 1930s, a fighter who anglicized his name from Peter Robert Galiardi to Bobby Gleason. The Thirtieth Street location was a bandbox space, with two rings against one wall and heavy bags and speed bags in the dimly lit back area. The constituency at that time included fighters like Gerry Cooney,

Gleason's Gym is a heavyweight kind of place with fighters on their way up and on their way down.

Roberto Duran, Vito Antuofermo, Saoul Mamby, Hector Camacho and Livingstone Bramble.

Gleason's was a favorite hangout of civilians—many from the nearby garment center—who would pay a dollar to get in and then stand around and watch, say, Emile Griffith banter with several of the boxers he trained or Roberto Duran skip rope in the corner. Because of the look of the place, a lot of movies and television commercials were filmed there. It also got to be a gathering place for media types. And heaven forbid if a newcomer tried to slip by the door without paying. Robert Mladinich, a New York City detective who moonlights as a writer for boxing publications, recalls: "An old gym rat stood sentry at the door, collecting a dollar from every visitor. Armed

with my first press card from the now-defunct *Worldwide Boxing Digest*, I muttered 'Press' as I breezed past him. 'Press your fuckin' pants,' he snorted. 'It's still a dollar to get in.'"

By the time Silverglade bought into Gleason's in 1985, the space at the New York site was proving insufficient to handle the number of fighters walking through the gym's door. So in January 1987, Gleason's moved to 75 Front Street in Brooklyn—a huge 20,000-square-foot loft space with 600 lockers. This latest locale of Gleason's is situated in the shadows of the Brooklyn Bridge, not far from the Navy Yard and the Jehovah's Witness international headquarters, and quite within earshot of the Brooklyn-Queens Expressway.

Robin Holland

Gleason's promptly became, and remains, a Brooklyn fixture, with Silverglade taking over as sole owner after his partner Becker died in 1994. On any day, the gym echoes with activity, its four rings occupied by fighters sparring and shadowboxing, its heavy bags being pounded, its five speed bags and four double-end bags resounding, and a mirrored wall reflecting the images of the motley lot—from no-names to champions—who work out there.

A sign painted by artist LeRoy Neiman hangs on one wall, quoting Virgil: "Now let whoever has courage and a strong and collected spirit in his breast come forward, lace on the gloves and put up his hands." Some things about boxing never change, but some things do: Gleason's on Front Street is a well-lighted place that today boasts 750 dues-paying members, including 200 professional boxers and 150 amateurs. There are, in this number, some 100 women and 300 businessmen. The recent popularity of the boxing workout has even brought a degree of chic to gyms, generating some resentment among purists toward the women and the white-collar presence. "There are two ways to look at it," Silverglade says. "Boxing purists will tell you that this is no longer a boxing facility. But, as a businessman, I don't look at it that way. It's a natural growth and probably a salvation of the sport. The white-collar boxers are saving the gym."

Why a white-collar presence? Why *women*? "The conditioning that a boxer gets is fantastic. Many other people now realize that it's available to them. One woman reads and hears that other women are doing it and says, 'Hey, that's for me.' We've had actresses, models, a police officer, businesswomen and writers. Even the choreographer Twyla Tharp trained at Gleason's. The way I see it, a woman's forty-five dollars monthly dues is just the same as a man's."

As in all boxing gyms, the real champions train side by side with a lot of wanna-be's and never-will-be's. Gleason's has accommodated its share of pugs with lopsided losing records, including a sixty-five-year-old gent who sued the New York State Boxing Commission to be allowed to fight. Although the old boy no longer graces the gym—he lost his lawsuit—the gym retains its diversity.

"We have Israelis and Arabs, Wall Street guys with more money than God and kids from the projects with nothing, cops and prosecutors as well as ex-cons," says Silverglade. "But in the gym there's total camaraderie. No one looks down on anybody else. They talk to each other and help each other. It's a really great feeling to be in the midst of that."

As often as the poor youths who see boxing as an escape route up and out of poverty come to Gleason's, so also come the schemers and dreamers who want to be part of the sport—but not as boxers. "I see many successful businessmen—Wall Street guys, doctors, attorneys—who get into boxing as partners or managers, and right away they forget all their business acumen," says Silverglade. "They get taken over the coals by boxers who know how to con them out of money. I talk for hours with these guys about the pitfalls, but they shrug me off—pay no mind to what I tell them. What happens is that they become emotionally attached to the fighter. But managing a boxer is like having another dependent. It's difficult. Within a year, most of them are fed up with the sport." Still, boxing—and a gym like Gleason's—continues to exert a powerful pull on many. Says would-be manager Braunstein: "There's hugging, loving, hating—all the passions. That's the essence of boxing—all the great passions."

Silverglade, nonetheless, takes pleasure in being the boss of his own sweat house: "It's a great life. I get to meet a lot of exciting people. Like Bill Richardson, when he was U.S. ambassador to the United Nations, or Mayor Rudy Giuliani, who've both stopped by to watch the fighters. Richardson was especially interesting. He walked around talking to the young fighters in five different languages."

Phil Berger was boxing editor of the New York Times *and the author of several books on the sport, including* Blood Season: Mike Tyson and the World of Boxing. *He wrote the screenplay for* Price of Glory, *starring Jimmy Smits (yet another Brooklyn guy).*

The Smith Street Turnaround

Smith Street, for years a moribund commercial strip no more distinguished than its name, has undergone the fastest transformation in the history of urban renewal without the use of a single bulldozer. Or a dollar of public money.

From the mouth of the Gowanus Canal to Fulton Mall, Smith Street was a forgettable sequence of secondhand stores, pizza parlors, repair shops and car-service offices. But its vacant storefronts and its proximity to increasingly affluent Cobble Hill, Carroll Gardens and Boerum Hill appealed to a restless chef named Alan Harding. Weary of the cutthroat restaurant scene in Manhattan, Harding wanted to open his own bistro. The trouble was, he had only $10,000 ("My mom gave it to me"). So he sought really cheap commercial property. At 255 Smith Street, he found an ex-pizza joint that had a floor, ceiling, walls and an exhaust plus two apricot trees and a fig tree out back. He signed a fifteen-year lease and hooked up with a partner, an experienced restaurateur from Bay Ridge. "Someone gave us chairs," Harding recalls. "And we pulled the banquettes from a Dumpster." They opened in December 1997, offering "classic French bistro fare." There was a two-hour line out front on the first night, says Harding, "and we've been really busy ever since." They named their restaurant Patois.

They got great press and great word of mouth. A lot of chefs lived nearby, and they noticed the long lines. Soon, other restaurants

The bistro that turned Smith Street into "restaurant row."

sprang up on Smith Street—seven in just over a year. Surprised, Harding and his partner bought a defunct Chinese takeout near Patois: "It was a defensive move. If we didn't grab it, one of our competitors would." Their second place, Uncle Pho's, features French/Vietnamese cuisine. Other entrepreneurs quickly moved in to open coffee shops, boutiques and antique shops. Commercial rents soared to over $3,000 per month. "The funky charm of the neighborhood brought us in," Harding says sardonically. "And we ruined it."—*MWR*

Michael Kamber

The Breakfast Club

A Brooklyn Heights Salon

BY SU
AVASTHI

"We call ourselves the Breakfast Club," says David Levine, long-time illustrator for the *New York Review of Books*, referring to the loosely defined group that has convened nearly every morning for the past ten years in Teresa's Polish restaurant on Montague Street for blintzes, coffee and conversation. It's a casual ad hoc gathering of some fifteen to twenty artists, photographers, writers and other opinionated individuals.

"It's not an official club," Levine hastens to add. "There are no membership dues and we haven't taken a loyalty oath. We just get together to waste most of the day talking about this or that. We tell each other about art exhibitions we've been to or books that we've read or heard about. We talk about politics and give our points of view on the arts."

Teresa's is a clean, well-lighted place, and on weekday mornings most of the varnished wood tables remain empty and a calm, unpretentious, unhurried atmosphere prevails. The waitresses use those quiet hours to joke around and catch up with one another in their native Polish language. There's not much for them to do but keep

refilling the coffee cups of the Breakfast Club regulars and maybe eavesdrop on the wisecracks and stories.

On a typical morning, the conversation among what Levine describes as "the liberals, lefties, righties and people of different religious backgrounds" ranges from local political/cultural uproars like the one set off by the controversial "Sensation" exhibit at the Brooklyn Art Museum, to the negative fallout from the soaring stock market, to the latest literary classic to be distorted into a big-budget Hollywood movie.

"This group isn't afraid of tumult," says Len Gelstein, a Brooklyn Heights photographer who shoots street scenes around the world. "It's not a place for the weak or faint of heart. If you want to tell a joke at that table, you have to suffer the insults of everyone who has a tongue in his mouth." Regardless of the heated discussions, however, the topics on the table don't revolve solely around the day's headlines and hot-button political issues. Talk often turns to matters more personal as members exchange family anecdotes, freely give out advice and offer encouragement about each other's creative efforts. Occasionally, a chess game breaks out.

"Kindred spirits," Gelstein says. "These are open, tolerant people who've been places and who've had many lives. Collectively, we have a lot of stories and experiences to share with each other." Gelstein became a regular several years ago after the death of his first wife. "It's our support group.

Russell Christian

We each get nourishment from a very accomplished group of people who are also warm and open and generous."

The Breakfast Club came into being shortly after Teresa (yes, there really is a Teresa) first opened the doors in 1989. Its unofficial founder, the late poet Norman Rosten, began to go there daily and struck up conversations with what turned out to be equally outspoken and creative patrons. Others noticed and joined in, and before long coffee at Teresa's became a regular part of the daily routine for many self-employed bohemians from the Heights and beyond who, as Gelstein put it, wanted to have "water-cooler conversations without having to put on a suit. It's 'Cheers' for the aging artistic set."

Though the club regulars frequently joke about wearing out their welcome, that's not a real danger. "They are wonderful people," says owner Teresa Brzowzowska. "Lively, with great humor. They're educated and well-informed, and it's nice to have them here." She notes that their daily routine has given her a sense that her relatively new restaurant had become a Montague Street fixture. "Our place is not very flashy or shiny. It's homey, so they make us feel like we are welcome in the neighborhood."

In return for being provided a congenial meeting place, several artists have contributed their work, which Teresa proudly displays throughout her restaurant. One of Levine's instantly recognizable caricatures hangs on one wall, next to a poem penned by Norman Rosten. Three of Gelstein's photographs adorn the opposite wall, next to a drawing of Ebbets Field by well-known children's book author Richard Rosenblum.

Some regulars even use the restaurant as a mail pick-up and drop-off site for packages. "For a number of us, the Breakfast Club creates the sense of a little village within the big city," says Levine. "Brooklyn Heights has always had the feeling of being a little town, and the club helps to maintain that even as it's growing."

A former beat reporter for the New York Post, *Su Avasthi appreciates a vigorous exchange of views.*

Brooklyn's Poet Laureate

During his eighty-one years, Norman Rosten wrote four novels, published seven volumes of poetry and wrote plays that were performed in venues like the Metropolitan Opera. But Rosten, Brooklyn's first poet laureate, will always be remembered as Marilyn Monroe's best friend, who once dropped to his hands and knees to spoon-feed scotch to Marilyn's dog.

In 1955, Rosten met Monroe through his friend Arthur Miller, who was married to the actress at the time. Over the next seven years, he became Monroe's most trusted confidant, a friend she called at the depths of depression and loneliness. She also became a devotee of his poems, particularly the verses he wrote for his newborn daughter, Patricia. "It touched me very much," she wrote in a letter to him. "I used to think that if I ever had a child I would have wanted only a son—but after reading *Songs for Patricia*, I know I would have loved a little girl as much."

Around that time, when Rosten and his wife were Monroe's houseguests, the actress left him a poem of her own—along with a note telling him to eat the "homemade strawberry shortcake" in her fridge. "Here goes," she wrote.

"Good Nite; Sleep; and Sweet Repose;
Where ever you lay your head—;
I hope you find your nose—"

Rosten's other great love, of course, was the borough of Brooklyn, which shared Monroe's unpredictability, restlessness and mystery. Although he was born in Manhattan and grew up on his father's farm in upstate New York, Rosten attended Brooklyn College and moved into Brooklyn Heights, joining a writers' colony that included Miller, Norman Mailer and Marianne Moore. His best-known novel, *Under the Boardwalk* (1991), chronicles a boy's childhood in Coney Island. In 1961, the year before Monroe's death, he adapted Miller's *A View from the Bridge*—also set in Brooklyn—into a screenplay for director Sidney Lumet.

In 1979, over bagels and coffee, borough president Howard Golden asked Rosten to be Brooklyn's first poet laureate. He took the job, even though it came with no salary, no secretary and no parking space. For the next sixteen years, he used the post as a bully pulpit for poetry and his unique view of the borough's importance in the literary life of America.

"Brooklyn seems to be compounded of some sort of reality, although myths often overpower it," he wrote in the *New York Times* a few years before his death. "There are areas of poverty (genteel and otherwise), crime and other urban horrors. But there are also gestures of humanity, pockets of physical beauty and a spirit to confound the despair of the streets." *—Glenn Thrush*

The Look

Brooklyn has a certain distinct look to it: Old, some might say. And *dark*. It looks that way because while Brooklyn was settled in the seventeenth century and is changing fast in the twenty-first century, most of it was built during the nineteenth and early twentieth centuries. So it reflects the styles and materials—low-rise with a lot of red brick and brown stone—popular in those decades. It had room to spread out, so it didn't need to grow *up*.

Brooklyn harbors the supreme engineering feat of the nineteenth century—the Roeblings' Great Bridge—but the commercial fabric of the borough is made up of the shops and warehouses and manufactures of a successful port city, most of it designed by anonymous builders. It is also a low-rise residential city that grew outward along the lines of roads, trolleys, railroads and subways. It took shape before the automobile, so its highways and expressways are late overlays.

Brooklyn took its appearance from a combination of individual enterprise, chance and civic planning. Those three elements explain its bricks and mortar, as well as its great green spaces.

Previous spread: By the twentieth century, once-rural Brooklyn had a big-city look.

This page and previous spread: Brooklyn Historical Society

Public Places, Public Spaces

The stones of Brooklyn

BY MATTHEW POSTAL

"City of Homes and Churches." Walt Whitman's oft-repeated image of Brooklyn has for almost two centuries defined the borough as a place of evenings and weekends, a place where residents return at night. And while there is certainly an element of truth in the description, Brooklyn's architectural landscape—the look of the place—is much more varied, shaped not only by private needs but also by public initiative.

From its incorporation as an independent city in 1834 to the consolidation of Greater New York in 1898, Brooklyn was anything but a drowsy suburb. Explosive growth is what the young city experienced during the second half of the nineteenth century as its population jumped from 16,000 to more than a million residents. The private sector supplied much of the housing, and places of worship were built by various religious groups, but public needs were met by Brooklyn's city government, which assumed oversight of major projects from the mapping of streets to the construction of parks, schools, museums and libraries.

From atop Fort Greene Park (Olmsted & Vaux, 1867), a commanding view of city and harbor.

Ted Hardin

Grand Army Plaza took shape before Brooklyn's reservoir (upper left) was replaced by the library and Museum of Art.

A healthy rivalry with neighboring Manhattan spurred the development of Brooklyn's public realm. In 1835 a commission was authorized by the State of New York "to lay out streets, avenues, and squares in the city." The plan that resulted, like Manhattan's gridiron of 1811, envisioned a rectangular street system punctuated by eleven public squares. The first of these, not surprisingly, was proposed for Brooklyn Heights, a community of considerable wealth and influence located near the East River. But Walt Whitman used his position as editor of the *Brooklyn Eagle* to oppose the scheme, arguing that this location ignored those who needed it most—citizens who were "not so wealthy nor so well situated." In the end, that populist sentiment prevailed and a sloping thirty-three-acre park site was chosen not far from Whitman's home near the Brooklyn Navy Yard in what is now called Fort Greene. Built atop the final resting place of 11,500 Revolutionary War dead, the new park

was popular with neighborhood residents, who enjoyed panoramic views across Brooklyn's growing downtown and toward rival Manhattan.

Whereas Fort Greene Park served just one neighborhood, Prospect Park—for which the city began acquiring land in 1860—had more complex intentions. Inspired by Manhattan's Central Park, which began construction in 1857, Prospect Park was Brooklyn's most ambitious and costly project to date. It was located near the borough's geographic center and was planned with the idea that it would encourage real estate development in the surrounding area. Initially, most visitors approached the park from the west, ascending along Flatbush Avenue into Grand Army Plaza, an oval flanked by sound-deadening berms, through the Meadowport or Endale Arch and onto the Long Meadow. Designed by Frederick Law Olmsted and Calvert Vaux (creators of Central Park), the park was envisioned as a

Brooklyn Historical Society

public environment where urban dwellers could escape the increasingly congested city to wander through grand and intimate landscapes that had important *lessons* to convey. The designers maintained that nature's "tranquilizing and poetic character" would have a civilizing effect on park visitors, promoting democratic values through social intercourse and observation.

Completed by the mid-1870s, Prospect Park was designed in the English style for long walks and carriage rides. Over a mile in length, the Long Meadow is Prospect Park's most extensive and memorable open space, extending from Grand Army Plaza to Fifteenth Street. Strollers can walk through or alongside a gently undulating lawn, intersecting with a sequence of natural and man-made forests, lakes and waterfalls. Such scenic paths became a signature feature in Olmsted and Vaux's subsequent work. Tree-lined paths known as "park ways" were proposed as linkages to developing

neighborhoods, and while a Parisian-style boulevard connecting Prospect with Central Park was never realized, two lengthy thoroughfares—Eastern and Ocean Parkways—were completed during the 1870s. Both have central roadways, side roads for slower local traffic and a public mall on either side for pedestrians —street arrangements that accommodated a variety of users. Even today, other multipurpose paths thread through the borough, such as the elevated footpath across Brooklyn Bridge, the Coney Island boardwalk, the cantilevered esplanade flanking Brooklyn Heights

Right: Prospect Park in a more formal period.

Below: A springtime view of the Botanic Garden's Cherry Esplanade.

Michael Kamber; inset: Brooklyn Historical Society

and the Shore Parkway Path along the Narrows.

New roads not only provided access to Prospect Park, but also encouraged the development of residential districts along their routes. Population growth placed increased demands on public services, including police and fire protection as well as education. Many fine civic structures resulted, including firehouses, police stations and, most notably, public schools. These buildings, many of them still in use today, are among the borough's chief architectural glories, especially the work of James W. Naughton, who designed all public

tower. Several years later, a separate and grander facility for boys was constructed on Marcy Avenue. Memorable for its remarkable size and striking corner towers, Naughton's Romanesque Boys High School stands out as one of Brooklyn's finest buildings.

Brooklyn's first free library was built as part of Pratt Institute in Clinton Hill in 1887. This and similar facilities were immensely popular (in the late nineteenth century, support for free public library systems was widespread), and in 1892 the Brooklyn Public Library was established as a department of the city government. Its first branch was housed in an old public school building in Bedford-Stuyvesant. Twenty more branches would be constructed over the next two decades, financed mostly by industrialist Andrew Carnegie, who paid for so many public libraries nationwide. From Carroll Gardens to Crown Heights, these neighborhood libraries (many of which received landmark status in recent years) are handsome to

Boys High (left) and Girls High: two of architect James W. Naughton's nineteen schools.

schools in Brooklyn between 1879 and 1898. Born in Ireland and trained at the University of Wisconsin and Cooper Union, Naughton was an architect and bureaucrat of unusual skill. Of particular note are two structures that rise proudly above the ordered rows of brick and brownstone townhouses in Bedford-Stuyvesant— Girls High School and Boys High School. Established as the Central Grammar School in 1878, Girls High School relocated here in 1885. It is notable as one of the earliest public high schools in New York City and for the manner in which Naughton successfully combined neo-Gothic and French Second Empire features, including a central entry pavilion that rises to a prominent bell

look at and pleasant to use. Designed by such leading Brooklyn architects as Raymond Almirall, William Tubby and Richard A. Walker, most have Beaux-Arts–style brick and limestone elevations and cozy interiors with fireplaces where "story hours" took place.

At the turn of the century, Brooklyn's ambitions grew. Prospect Park's once-bucolic entry, Grand Army Plaza, was transformed during the 1890s by patriotic structures, including the colossal victory arch commemorating the Civil War designed by John Duncan, as well as numerous bronze statues and a pair of Tempietto-like pavilions offering shelter to passengers awaiting trolleys. Three major public institutions were constructed in the

Brooklyn Historical Society (left); Brooklyn Public Library-Brooklyn Collection vicinity on sites originally set aside for the park: the Brooklyn Museum, the Brooklyn Botanic Garden and Brooklyn's Central Library. First proposed in 1888, the main library is best understood as a victim of the city's absorption into Greater New York. Ground was broken in 1911 for a grandly scaled Beaux-Arts scheme designed by Raymond Almirall and intended to rival the recently completed New York Public Library on Fifth Avenue. Support for the vast plan, however, was difficult to sustain. A succession of New York City mayors, from John Purroy Mitchell to Jimmy Walker, failed to maintain adequate funding, and by 1929 the Flatbush Avenue wing stood vacant but one-third complete.

The unfinished library was an embarrassment to the borough. Clearly, a new strategy was required. In 1935 architects Alfred Morton Githens and Francis Keally were hired to draft a new and less costly design for the library—one that would utilize the existing wing's steel frame and still be in keeping with current architectural taste. Opened six years later, the building featured a processional sequence of spaces that begins on a raised terrace overlooking Grand Army Plaza and the

The Brooklyn Public Library, an Art Deco masterpiece, was finally completed in 1941 after years of neglect.

park, extends through a concave, fifty-foot-high limestone entry decorated with gilt relief and culminates in a light-filled circulation hall. This atrium, rising nearly four stories and clad in oak panels and glass brick, is unlike any other interior in New York City. Synthesizing Art Deco and Scandinavian modern elements, it was described by the architectural critic Lewis Mumford in

Michael Kamber; inset: Museum of the City of New York

1940 as one of the "top" new libraries in the nation. In recent years, it has undergone a well-deserved restoration—an acknowledgment of its beauty and the important role it continues to play.

Following World War II, fewer public buildings were constructed in Brooklyn. While the school and library systems continued to expand, most plans tended to be modest or went unfulfilled as public officials were distracted by the suburban exodus, rising crime rates and, perhaps, the sour taste left by the long struggle for a central library.

But concern for Brooklyn's public realm has begun to revive. Cultural institutions, such as BAM and the Brooklyn Museum, have undertaken major building campaigns. Notable architects such as Arata Isozaki,

James Polshek and Hugh Hardy have participated and the initial results are promising. Of particular interest is the glorified decay of BAM's Majestic Theater on Fulton Street and the museum's lush and elegant Cantor Auditorium. Even an East River/Brooklyn Bridge park is finally being seriously considered. To be located on unused piers below Brooklyn Heights, the eagerly awaited (and much debated) riverfront park revives the idea that Whitman successfully opposed more than a century ago. With most Brooklyn neighborhoods now served by parks, schools, libraries and museums, perhaps its time has come.

Matthew A. Postal is an architectural historian who specializes in nineteenth- and twentieth-century buildings.

The Wildest Place in Prospect Park

Once upon a time there was a small municipal zoo in Prospect Park built in a neat semicircle of red brick buildings that were decorated with animal bas-reliefs and murals by WPA artists depicting scenes from *The Jungle Book,* Rudyard Kipling's famous collection of stories for children. The zoo was in every sense an old-fashioned menagerie: as many different exotic creatures as possible, including such large animals as elephants and bears, were crammed into cages or small enclosures behind moats to be gazed upon by the curious public. But in 1980 the Wildlife Conservation Society (in partnership with the City of New York) took over the Prospect Park Zoo and set about transforming it into a modern facility with a fresh emphasis on education of children.

Reopened in 1993, the zoo now exhibits small animals in appropriately naturalistic habitats, with many accompanying informative

signs and graphics. The red brick buildings remain, but their interiors have been renovated; there's a Nature Walk with animals alongside in spacious, woodsy outdoor enclosures; there's a small barn inhabited by domestic animals; there's a pool with sleek sea lions gliding through the water or lounging noisily on the rocks. Beautifully landscaped and well maintained, the twelve-acre zoo is now a fitting match for the Botanic Garden across the street.

And it has become quite popular: almost every weekday, yellow school buses pull up on Flatbush Avenue to release dozens, sometimes hundreds, of children and their teachers from Brooklyn public schools for a morning of fun and learning. Weekends, families arrive, and throughout the summer the zoo is alive with day

campers. They can admire the antics of the Hamadryas baboons, laugh at the meerkats, observe the docile, solemn capybaras—the world's largest rodents. Along the Nature Walk, they might spot a wallaby hopping through the grass, and out in the barn they can hand-feed the eager goats or the obese and blasé cow. The most popular program? An annual sleepover for children aged six to eleven (with adult), at which all can rise early and watch the animals at the hour when they're most active. *–Patricia Curtis*

Ted Hardin

Of Time and the Tower

Brooklyn's one-building skyline

BY JOE FODOR

Thousands of people keep track of the time by the huge clock, twenty-seven feet in diameter, at the top of the Williamsburgh Savings Bank. Once the largest four-sided clock in the world, it is still the borough's grand timepiece. The minute hands weigh 523 pounds each; the hour hands weigh 249 pounds. The clock faces are powered by individual Telechron motors, and when the clock was first put up, small lamps next to the twelve lights circling each face would give a three-second burst of illumination, followed by two seconds of darkness. When all twelve lamps had fired, exactly a minute had passed, giving Brooklynites a clock accurate to the second, controlled by telegraph from the national "time seat" in Arlington, Virginia.

Today the clock isn't nearly so accurate, and the sweep-second feature has been out of commission for decades. The four motors are reset daily and the clocks are closely monitored: if one of them is just a few minutes behind, people deluge the bank with calls until it is reset.

Construction on the building at 1 Hanson Place started in 1927, and the bank branch opened on April 1, 1929 (not an auspicious year to open a bank), back when Williamsburgh Savings, with $223 million, was the largest bank in the state of New York. The 512-foot-tall skyscraper was then, and is still, the tallest building on Long Island.

The powerful bank that spawned the building with the huge clock is no more, having been gobbled up by Manhattan Savings Bank in 1990. Republic National Bank took over in 1992 and in 1999 was in turn sold for

Built in 1929, the 512-foot Williamsburgh Savings Bank Tower is still the tallest building on all of Long Island.

Tony Velez

$10.3 billion to HSBC Group, a London-based mega-multinational financial company. Many are concerned that its new owners will shut down the branch that operates on the first floor. And that would be a shame, since the main lobby is one of the most impressive indoor spaces in all of Brooklyn. The floors, counters and wainscot are made from Rosatta d'Or marble, and the walls are cut from "simon-pure" French limestone. Inch-thick glass tables for customers have withstood seventy years of heavy use; the iron-and-brass grillwork around the tellers' cages is decorated with tasteful female nudes and heroic male figures.

The ceiling mosaics, by the Brooklyn-based Ravenna Mosaics, Inc., are executed in Cosmeto glass from Germany and depict various constellations and astrological signs. On the west wall, there's a huge map of Brooklyn and Manhattan, including the names of the five Dutch towns: Breuckelen, New Utrecht, Boswyck, Amersfoort and Midwout, topped by an American flag and the date 1928. Henry Hudson's *Half Moon*, which first sailed up the river that bears his name in 1609, is depicted bobbing in the waves just off Coney Island. The designer of this elegant mural, John von Wicht (1888–1970), was an émigré from Germany who settled in Brooklyn Heights in the 1920s. He worked as a ship's pilot in New York Harbor during World War II and would later go on to a thriving career as an abstract expressionist painter, splashing his canvases with thick globs of pigment. His *Half-Moon* mural is not as free-spirited as his later work but is remarkably adventurous for bank art.

According to promotional material put out by the Williamsburgh Savings Bank in 1929, the "atmosphere of the bank quarters is as inviting as that of a friendly home. A welcome seems to greet one at every turn. . . . The influence of the medieval architectural masterpieces of Europe may be seen in the bank's construction, and it may be truly recorded as a cathedral dedicated to the furtherance of thrift and prosperity among the people."

The cornerstone and base of the building are of polished rainbow granite from Minnesota. Bricklayers fitted more than three million bricks in place to complete the structure, which is built over a steel framework weighing 7,100 tons. The entire thirty-three-story building weighs 68,616 tons when empty.

The observation deck on the twenty-sixth floor is a spectacular and all-but-unknown feature, as it has been closed to the public since the 1980s. Building manager Tom Fitzgerald will sometimes allow people to visit it—

Got the Time?

The Williamsburgh Savings Bank Tower can be seen—and its clocks checked—from anywhere in the borough. Photographer Mara Lethem has been shooting it from every angle. Her favorite views are shown here.

From Atlantic and Fifth Avenues.

From the backyards of Boerum Hill.

From the Long Island Railroad.

but only after eliciting a promise that they will not use the occasion to jump. During the American Bicentennial, fifteen fiberglass plaques were affixed to the railings of the deck depicting a short history of the Battle of Long Island and pointing out the geographic landmarks that show where the fighting occurred on August 27, 1776. So if you can talk your way up there, you can study the plaques and then look out at the built-over terrain to see where General Washington was and where the British were.

One of the first major tenants in the building was *The Tablet*, the weekly newspaper of the Catholic Diocese of Brooklyn and Queens. Nationally renowned as an especially conservative Catholic publication for many years, *The Tablet* moved out a few years ago when the rents started to go up and is now published in a church-owned building on Hicks Street in Brooklyn Heights. Green-Wood Cemetery, the fashionable Victorian necropolis in Sunset Park, still has its main offices in the building.

Even though it has long dominated and defined the Brooklyn skyline and looks to be the epitome of stability, financial and architectural, the building actually stands on a questionable foundation. Unlike Manhattan, where all the skyscrapers are built on solid-rock foundations, this part of Brooklyn, around Hanson Place, sits on an underground hill of sand and is known to be somewhat unstable. On April 17, 1917, St. Felix Street, one block to the east, collapsed. The Brighton Beach subway tunnel was being built sixty-two feet beneath the street, and the timbering system holding the sides of the trench had failed. The seventy-year-old Hanson Place Methodist Church slid four inches to the east, and actor Clair Dockery, who was walking to work at the time, disappeared into a fifty-foot hole. (His remains were disinterred two weeks later.)

In 1927 the old Methodist church was torn down to make way for the building of the Williamsburgh Savings Bank Tower, but the earth underneath it was so unstable that the building engineers classified it as "approaching quicksand." To compensate, the building is anchored by four large concrete "feet" deep within the foundation of the buildings. Sixty-foot steel grillages, secured on top of the feet, have held the building securely in place ever

The Orthodontic Tower

This is not just a bank building—it's a temple of dentistry. There are some thirty dentists, periodontists, orthodontists, oral and maxillofacial surgeons and endodontists practicing in the building, along with a handful of physicians and one company that makes prosthetic limbs.

"There used to be forty to fifty dentists in the building," remembers Martin Handler. "We had dentists everywhere, on every floor. We also had doctors, chiropractors, ophthalmologists—you name it. It was a sort of medical arts building."

The tower is in a prime location for medicos. Located at the corner of Hanson Place and Ashland Avenue, it's only a few steps away from the Atlantic Avenue terminal of the Long Island Railroad and a major subway hub, making it easily accessible for commuters. "In the past few years, however, the dentists have been moving out," says Handler. He puts the blame on Republic Bank, which drove up rents and tried to force old tenants out of the building. "They once tried to evict me so they could put a restaurant on the top floor. But then, I guess, they realized how small a space it really is." Handler retired a few years ago after turning his practice over to Dr. Ian Lerner, who has a lease on the space until the year 2004.

Patients of the dentists and doctors often bring binoculars, cameras and out-of-town guests to the offices to marvel at the view, which easily encompasses the entire borough of Brooklyn, as well as lower Manhattan, Governors Island, Staten Island, a sweep of the nearby Atlantic Ocean and a good chunk of New Jersey. —*J.F.*

since. Still, should a major earthquake strike Brooklyn (as a few have over the centuries) the sandy ground beneath the building could liquefy and turn into a sandy soup. If this happens, the building will most likely not fall over, but might tilt at a strange angle. And thus Brooklyn would have a new landmark: the Leaning Tower of Savings.

Joe Fodor has been senior editor of Brooklyn Bridge *magazine since its founding in 1995. Formerly, he was an editor of* The (Dan) Quayle Quarterly.

Mara Faye Lethem

Brooklyn's memorial
to the Union Army
was dedicated in 1892.

TO THE DEFENDERS OF THE UNION 1861 1865

White/Monkmeyer

Grand Army Memorial

The arch is a triumph

BY HENRY HOPE REED

Of New York City's three arches—the Washington Arch in Washington Square, the Manhattan Arch of the Manhattan Bridge and Brooklyn's Soldiers and Sailors Monument—the Brooklyn arch takes first honors. In fact, after the Arc de Triomphe in Paris, this memorial to the Union dead is the greatest triumphal arch of modern times.

The Civil War is commemorated handsomely in Brooklyn. A monument erected by New York City in Green-Wood Cemetery honors the 148,000 New York soldiers who served on the Union side. There is an eagle-topped column to the Jewish dead in Cypress Hills National Cemetery, and an equestrian General Grant by sculptor William Ordway Partridge presides over Bedford Avenue near Huntington Avenue. Like the arch, these and other monuments underscore Greater New York's contribution to the Union cause.

A proper monument to the Union fallen was first proposed in the early 1880s by Brooklyn mayor Seth Low. Sculptor John Quincy Adams Ward submitted a design, but it proved too large and too costly. A competition was then held and won by John H. Duncan, the architect of Grant's Tomb and the Council Chamber of New York City Hall. The site chosen, the entrance to Prospect Park on Flatbush Avenue, was given the name Grand Army Plaza to honor the Grand Army of the Republic, the veterans' organization of the Union Army. General William Tecumseh Sherman laid the cornerstone in 1889, and on the occasion of the great Columbian Celebration on Columbus Day, 1892, it was dedicated.

Judging from his winning design for Grant's Tomb, where he even had an ancient chariot with horses at the top of its dome, Duncan was quite obviously an architect who thought in terms of the presence of the human figure. That is as it should be—a triumphal arch is nothing but a stand for sculpture—and the Soldiers and Sailors Monument did not have long to wait. By 1898, the sculpture was in place. On the west pier (left) is the army group; on the east (right) is the navy. The army bristles with some twenty soldiers spurred on by Bellona, the Roman goddess of war. An officer raises his sword above the gun and cannon. All is movement and organized rage. Bellona is also present in the navy group on

Putting the finishing touches on America Triumphant, one of sculptor John H. Duncan's figures atop the arch.

Glen Nison/Brooklyn Public Library-Brooklyn Collection

the east. Here, men and officers await an attack. One man, falling, would appear to be a soldier since he wears a shako (a military hat with a stiff high crown); often mistaken as a combatant in foreign uniform, a solecism on the part of the sculptor, he is actually a marine in the Corps uniform of the Civil War. One unusual distinction of the navy group is the presence of an African-American among the seamen.

At the top of the arch is what appears to be a four-horse chariot but is actually a quadriga, a two-horse chariot with, on either side, horses led by winged figures. In the chariot is America Triumphant with a sword in one hand and, in the other, an eagle-topped pilum with banner and wreath.

The work is realistic, even to the point where the officer of the army group is a self-portrait of the sculptor, Frederick MacMonnies. There is no question about the accuracy of the uniforms, down to that of the lone marine in the navy group. Yet the handling of the figures, their placement and grouping, reveals an artist who balanced his realism with the lessons of the traditional. This is also true of the figure of America, the winged figures and the horses at the top of the arch. There is a flourish, an élan, that brings life to this wonderful subject. To see it to good advantage it is best to go to the park side of the Plaza.

With his work on this arch, MacMonnies (a native of Brooklyn) takes his place among our great sculptors. An interesting fact is that MacMonnies worked in Paris and lived in the American colony at Giverny, a village in Normandy. A student of Falguière, who had an atelier at the École des Beaux-Arts, MacMonnies found it easy enough to remain in Paris, where his sculpture was executed. Like so many American artists who studied and worked in Paris, he appreciated the abundant studios, the presence of competent assistants, foundries and—not least—annual exhibitions.

So captivating is MacMonnies' work that the beholder may fail to note the work of other sculptors. The most notable is Philip Martiny. The winged figures of the arch spandrels are his. He was one of the outstanding artists of his era, and his work is found in several places in New York City, such as the two cherubs above the entrance to 597 Fifth Avenue, the two female figures at the entrance to the Peninsula Hotel at Fifth Avenue and Fifty-Fifth Street, and the doughboy as flag-bearer in Abingdon Square in Greenwich Village. His finest work is in Washington, D.C., where he carved the many cherubs of the stair railings in the Jefferson Building of the Library of Congress.

On the piers inside the arch are bronze reliefs of Generals Lee and Grant on horseback, executed by William R. O'Donovan after designs by Thomas Eakins. At different places on the piers are army and navy symbols carved in discs by Maurice G. Power, who may well have done the Ionic capitals of the extensions beneath the army and navy groups.

Surprisingly, the person responsible for inviting MacMonnies and Martiny to embellish Duncan's plain, if noble arch was a businessman named Frank Squier. He was active in paper manufacturing (his firm was the Perkins-Goodwin Company) and served as park commissioner of the City of Brooklyn from 1894 to 1896. During his brief tenure, he also doubled the extent of Brooklyn's parks by buying, among other properties, Forest Park (now in Queens) and Dyker Beach Park. Such was the spirit of the age that a little-known businessman was, in some measure, responsible for the nation's greatest triumphal arch.

Commissioner Squier extended his patronage beyond the sculptors to the architect Stanford White. Both MacMonnies and Martiny had worked with the firm of McKim, Mead & White at the great World's Columbian Exposition of 1893 in Chicago. Martiny had executed the sculpture for the firm's Agricultural Building, and MacMonnies had done such a splendid fountain of many figures for the Court of Honor that it was known simply as the MacMonnies Fountain. At Squier's behest, White designed a formal entrance to Prospect Park consisting of four Doric columns topped by MacMonnies-designed eagles and, at the Flatbush Avenue and Prospect Park West ends, small, round shelters with columns.

Squier's embellishments at Grand Army Plaza did not occur without opposition. One of Prospect Park's principal designers, Calvert Vaux, strongly objected to Stanford White's improvements. In this he was supported by his former partner, Frederick Law Olmsted, who not only objected to the park's new formal entrance but disliked the whole classical movement that had overcome American architecture starting in the 1880s. Privately, he denounced the new fashion. "We have an organized enemy before us," he wrote to a friend. "They are mostly cultivated gentlemen to be dealt with courteously. But they are doctrinaires and fanatics and essentially cokneys [*sic*]." The degree to which he disliked the classical taste of the era is seen in another incident: Olmsted, in charge of the planning of the Chicago exposition of 1893, was horrified to see his plan filled with classical buildings and sculpture. In fact, although he was slated to be a guest of honor at the celebratory banquet, such was his antipathy to what had been built in Chicago that he refused to attend.

Just as biographers of Olmsted have declined to explore this extraordinary aspect of the last years of his long career, so has the Soldiers and Sailors Monument been shunted aside in histories of American art. In a recent encyclopedia devoted to New York City, there is no entry for "arch" or "triumphal arch" and no acknowledgment that the city has three triumphal arches or that the Soldiers and Sailors Monument in Brooklyn is of world standard. Nor will readers who care to learn something about John H. Duncan find mention of the architect in any of the standard biographical dictionaries.

Henry Hope Reed is an architectural historian, author of The Golden City *and coauthor of* The Library of Congress.

NOW & THEN Getting safely around Grand Army Plaza was a concern even in the 1920s, but no data exist on mishaps caused by drivers squinting at the latest accident figures.

Late Bloomer

Lady of the Flowers

BY HELEN
ZELON

"Good morning, Your Highness," a groundsman says in greeting as he bows from the waist. Lithe and elegant in a bright silk suit and a strand of milk-white pearls, Elizabeth Scholtz drops a perfect curtsy and salutes him back.

Scholtz holds the formal title of director emeritus and the informal designation of resident grande dame of the Brooklyn Botanic Garden. The royalist ritual reflects not only the affection with which she is held but also her own passion for the BBG, its work and the people who make it thrive.

Now in her seventies, Scholtz began her professional life not in horticulture but in medicine. Despite her college degree in botany, she worked as a hematology technician—and cultivated not plants but a lively social life as a young white woman in her native apartheid-era South Africa. Seeking adventure, she traveled to the United States and while working here happened to meet a man named George Avery, the distinguished director of the Brooklyn Botanic Garden.

Director emeritus Elizabeth Scholtz has cultivated the Brooklyn community as well as the Botanic Garden itself.

© Kathy Willens, 2000

It was an encounter that would change her life. Months later, after her visa had expired and she was again living in South Africa, she received in the afternoon mail a letter from Avery offering her employment in the BBG's Education Department. "What I'd lacked in life at that time was a challenge," Scholtz recalls. "I had always hoped for something related to botany, and here it was, ten thousand miles from home." She packed her bags and moved to Brooklyn.

Scholtz arrived in 1960 and never left. "I've been with the Garden precisely half my life," she says. But the adjustment to Brooklyn didn't come easily. "The first children's course I taught was American wildflowers—imagine me, teaching that to Americans!" All winter, I pored over my books and wept. Frances Minor, the director of education, tried to encourage her, advising that cultivated plants are the same the world over. "It's not true!" Scholz says. "A marigold, yes, but I'd never *seen* an oxydendron before. The trees and shrubs were all different. Within the first month I was so discouraged, I nearly went back home. I didn't know whether I could succeed."

George Avery, however, was adamant. "He knew how to get blood from a stone," Scholtz recalls with affection. "Avery kept challenging me with all kinds of new things." His method was to shower his staff with recognition, to coax them into new responsibilities. "That was such a good idea of yours," he would say when a program or class he had initiated was carried to its successful completion on Betty Scholtz' shoulders.

Over time, Scholtz replaced Frances Minor in the Education Department, which expanded beyond children's programs to add many adult education offerings, including a demanding Garden Guide curriculum modeled on the Metropolitan Museum's docent training program. She cultivated those volunteers the way her horticulturists nurtured flowers and was rewarded with a generation of fiercely intelligent advocates who have introduced countless schoolchildren and tour groups to the BBG.

After more than a decade at the helm of the Education Department, Scholtz succeeded Avery as BBG director. During her tenure, she broadened the mission of the Garden to include community outreach programs such

How the Garden Grows

Founded in 1910 on a wasteland and smoldering garbage dump, the Brooklyn Botanic Garden was fortunate to have a farsighted director, Charles Stuart Gager, who established some of the major crowd-pleasers, such as the Japanese Hill-and-Pond garden, a miniaturized landscape surrounding a serene pond with shrines, lanterns and waterfalls, and the famous Cranford rose garden with its 1,200 varieties, both exotic and familiar. But Gager also set the direction for the Garden's emphasis on horticulture, research and education, and today the BBG is highly respected for its innovation in these fields. One of his projects was theworld's first children's gardening program, ongoing from 1914 and attended yearly by some 400 children who plant and tend their own flowers and vegetables.

The BBG encompasses 52 acres and more than 12,000 species of plants, including trees and shrubs, from all over the world. Besides the cherry trees and roses, favorites among visitors include the Fragrance Garden (designed with the blind in mind but sniffed with obvious pleasure by everybody), the Rhododendron Garden, the Magnolia Plaza and the Shakespeare Garden, which features plants of Elizabethan times.

The collection of dwarf potted trees in the Bonsai Museum is the oldest and largest in the country. The Steinhardt Conservatory, opened in 1988, holds an extensive indoor collection in three realistic environments: the Tropical Pavilion, which re-creates a rain forest with flora from the Amazon, Africa and Asia; the Warm Temperate Pavilion with plants from central China, the Mediterranean, Australasia, southern Africa and the United States; and the Desert Pavilion with spectacular plants from arid regions. The Herb Garden is enjoying a New Age popularity that reflects people's current interest in the medicinal and culinary uses of the 300-odd varieties of these ancient plants.

The BBG also offers dozens of classes for adults and children, trips and tours, fairs, festivals and special events such as the popular annual plant sale. But even when such attractions are going on, the vast lawns, gardens and allées ensure that the Botanical Garden is still the most peaceful place in Brooklyn. –*Patricia Curtis*

as workshops and courses on street gardens, urban composting, container gardening and the like, encouraging Brooklynites to help make their borough bloom.

Riding out deep funding cuts during New York's fiscal crisis in the 1970s meant adopting aggressive fund-raising practices. "I was never any good at that," Scholtz admits, adding that Avery was openly against fund-raising: "In his view, you didn't ask for money. You made it possible for people to give." Still, attracting high-profile donors was essential to the life of the Garden, and Scholtz credits Donald Moore, its first president, who "set a goal to raise $25 million, did so in a decade, and then retired, at quite an early age" after setting the current fiscal course.

Among the 60,000 children who visit the Garden for classes and workshops each year are dozens every day who like to teeter along the edge of the reflecting pools that lie just outside the Education Building. In the dark rectangular pools, water lilies and sacred lotus flowers hide schools of goldfish—good news for the sly gray heron

fishing for his supper. The young shoots of water lilies also provide tender fodder for the BBG's resident ducks. Every spring, just in time for the hatchlings, tiny wooden boardwalks are set in place, leading down from poolside; if the stub-winged, cheeping baby ducks are afraid to jump the distance between curb and water, they can use the little bridges to follow their parents into the pool.

Although she retired as director in 1987 with plans to return to her South African homeland, Scholtz's work at the Garden continues well into the eighth decade of her life. She leads tours of the world's finest botanical gardens with BBG members and has made trips to Morocco, New Zealand and the Azores, as well as twelve to Japan, all with ardent fans in tow.

"They still need me here. Why should I go back to South Africa?" she asks in earnest. "The Brooklyn Botanic Garden has become my life, and happily so."

Helen Zelon is a Brooklyn-based writer whose work has appeared in many magazines.

A Delivery from Hallowed Ground

One fine day in 1960, a groundsman at the Brooklyn Botanic Garden was standing out on Washington Street, on the east side of the Garden, when he saw an approaching truck filled with what to groundsmen is pure gold: topsoil—beautiful topsoil—a whole truckload of it. And then the wide-eyed groundsman noticed that the truck was followed by another, and another. All of them filled with gold.

He ran out and flagged down the driver of the first truck. "Where are you going with that?" he asked.

"To the dump," answered the driver. "It's from Ebbets Field. They got no use for it now." The Dodger's old home was being demolished to make room for a housing project.

"Buddy, would you wait a minute?" cried the groundsman. "We could use that dirt here."

The good-natured truck driver asked the other drivers to hold up while a quick phone call was placed to the director's office. The answer was "yes," and the small convoy of dump trucks bearing the soil from Ebbets was diverted to the Botanic Garden. To nourish the cherry trees, to be exact.

So today, if you're walking in spring along the Cherry Esplanade beneath the trees laden with glorious pink blossoms, you might just hear, very faintly, the crack of a bat and a chorus of cheering. And you could be treading the very sod from which Pee Wee Reese once snatched a hot grounder . . . —*Patricia Curtis*

Bury My Bats

Late baseball greats in Green-Wood

BY JEFFREY RICHMAN

Brooklyn's verdant Green-Wood Cemetery is the final resting place for a who's who of Brooklyn, of New York and, in fact, of the entire United States. Tombstones both showy and modest bear the names of political, artistic and industrial greats. But Green-Wood is linked to Brooklyn in another important way. Three men who played seminal roles in the early years of baseball are buried there: baseball's first professional player and first national star, Jim Creighton; "Father of Baseball" Henry Chadwick; and Charles Ebbets, who gave his name to Ebbets Field, the beloved home of Brooklyn's team, the Dodgers.

Brooklyn in the late 1850s was America's hotbed of baseball. As the *Brooklyn Daily Eagle* observed, "Nowhere has the National game of Baseball taken a firmer hold than in Brooklyn, and nowhere are there better ball players." When twenty-four East Coast teams formed a baseball federation in 1857, nine of those teams were from Brooklyn. Even a Brooklyn writer by the name of Walt Whitman was swept up in the enthusiasm for this new game: "I see great things in baseball; it's our game, the American game."

The First Real Pitcher

When seventeen-year-old Jim Creighton made his baseball debut in 1858 with the Brooklyn Niagaras, no one could have known that he would soon become America's first true baseball star. The game was then in its infancy, and its rules barred pitchers from snapping their wrists when delivering a pitch to the plate. A pitcher was supposed to make it *easy* for the batter to hit his pitches. But

Creighton ignored that rule and soon developed his "wrist throw," a low underhand delivery in which he snapped his wrist to throw his "speedballs," according to one observer, "as swift as [if] sent from a cannon," while also putting a spin on the ball. And he mixed in a few of his "dew drops," slow pitches that kept hitters offstride and made hitting against him even more difficult. Some conservatives criticized this aggressive style of pitching as illegal and

Bats and a scorecard decorate Creighton's monument.

Michael Kamber

The monuments of Green-Wood's forested rolling hills sit on the highest point in Brooklyn.

unsportsmanlike. Nevertheless, none could argue with Creighton's success as he won game after game.

A bidding war broke out for Creighton's services, with the top Brooklyn teams making their best offers. He signed with the Excelsiors in 1860, in so doing probably becoming the first professional baseball player, and led that team on baseball's first big barnstorming tour. As the Excelsiors played their way across upstate New York, Canada, Pennsylvania, Delaware and Maryland, opposing pitchers began to copy his delivery. Baseball clubs formed in the tour's wake were often called "the Creightons" in his honor.

The innovative pitcher was also a great hitter; he is said to have gone through an entire season without making an out. But it was his hitting that actually killed him. On October 14, 1862, Creighton batted against the Unions of Morrisania. As he swung, he heard an unusual sound and thought his belt had snapped. After circling the bases with a home run, he collapsed; his mighty swing had ruptured his bladder. Four days later baseball's first star, only twenty-one years old, died at his father's home at 307 Henry Street.

The Rulemaker

No man did more to popularize baseball than Henry Chadwick. A British-born newspaperman, Chadwick immigrated to America as a youth and made Brooklyn his home. He was convinced that the relatively quick pace of baseball was just right for Americans: "What they do, they want to do in a hurry." He persuaded the *New York Times* and other dailies that baseball was news fit to print and became the country's first baseball

Creighton's gravestone inscription is framed by a diamond.

editor, working at the *New York Clipper* and then the *Brooklyn Eagle* for the next half-century.

Chadwick created the baseball scoring system that is still in use today, assigning numbers to each of the positions in the field. He also introduced the newspaper box score and coined many of baseball's most enduring phrases, including "single," "base hit," "base on balls," "fungo," "whitewash," "double play," "error," "goose egg" and—perhaps most important to Brooklyn—"chin music."

In 1860, Chadwick wrote the first book on baseball. He then went on to edit and publish baseball guides and yearbooks, chair the Rules Committee of the National Association of Base Ball Players and supervise a game held at the beginning of every season at Brooklyn's Capitoline Grounds during which rules changes were demonstrated.

Chadwick's baseball obsession proved fatal. Though suffering from a fever, he attended opening day of the 1908 baseball season at the Polo Grounds. Pneumonia soon set in, and on April 20 Chadwick lay mortally ill. He roused himself just long enough to ask which team had won the game that day between his beloved Brooklyn team and the hated New York Giants. Told that the Giants had triumphed, Chadwick expressed his regrets and lapsed into an unconsciousness from which he never emerged.

Green-Wood's monument to "the Father of Baseball," as Chadwick was dubbed by President Theodore Roosevelt, was paid for by contributions made to a committee chaired by that other great Brooklyn baseball man, Charles Ebbets. The monument cost a bargain $600 (equal to about $10,000 today), and its dedication, originally scheduled for the first anniversary of Chadwick's death, was, in the parlance of baseball, rained out.

The Father of the Dodgers

Charley Ebbets pursued many careers as a young man, working as a draftsman on building projects and as a publisher and politician. He peddled his own novels door to door. In 1883, he took a job as bookkeeper, clerk, ticket salesman and scorecard hawker with a new Brooklyn baseball club. He even cleaned the grand-

The name says it all: Charles Ebbets' resting place.

stand. Ebbets was soon promoted to business manager of the team, and his real involvement with baseball began. He was now responsible for players' contracts, payroll and the logistics of road trips. He accumulated stock in the ball club, became its secretary and was appointed its president in 1898. Ebbets named his team the Brooklyn Superbas, then later changed its name to the Brooklyn Dodgers, in honor of the informal and popular sport of trolley dodging.

Charley Ebbets' dream was to build a modern ballpark way out in the countryside of Brooklyn, a two-tiered structure that would seat first 18,000 fans, then 32,000—to be called Ebbets Field. Friends tried to talk Ebbets out of his dream, but he had a ready reply for them: "Mark my words," he said, "someday Ebbets Field will be in the heart of Brooklyn, and thousands of fans will come to see the team play baseball. Someday, the Brooklyn club will be so famous that Ebbets Field will be too small to handle the crowds!"

Ebbets Field opened in 1913, and by the time Charley Ebbets died in 1925 the Dodgers and their home were Brooklyn institutions. But some three decades later, in 1957, Ebbets Field was abandoned by the Dodgers when they deserted Brooklyn for Los Angeles. It was torn down in 1960.

Jeffrey Richman is the author of Brooklyn's Green-Wood Cemetery *and an attorney with the Legal Aid Society in New York City.*

Michael Kamber

Little Green Gatekeepers

Green-Wood is where thousands of souls rest in peace, but it is also the place that some forty or fifty very noisy and very much alive residents call home. Flitting among the elaborate spires of the cemetery's famous Gothic gates is a flock of bright green parakeets.

Parakeets are certainly not native to Brooklyn, and many visitors—attracted by the incessant squawking—look up in wonder at these exotic oddballs. About thirty years ago, the story goes, a crate of birds on its way from South America to pet stores in the United States broke open as it was being off-loaded at Kennedy. No fools, the crate's liberated occupants took wing. Some flew west across Jamaica Bay and dispersed in the borough of Brooklyn, and at least one pair found the upthrust spires of Green-Wood's gates a suitable nesting place. They, their friends, their offspring and other relations have been living there ever since. For a few years, the growing colony migrated south in the fall and returned in the spring. But now they stay all year.

"They displaced the pigeons who usually nested there, and simply took over," says cemetery superintendent Ken Taylor. "They're cleaner than pigeons, but they make an awful racket sometimes." A few years ago, Taylor found one of the parakeets lying on the ground with a broken wing, took it home and nursed it. "It wasn't a good guest—it made a lot of noise. So we were glad when its wing finally healed," he says. "I brought it back to Green-Wood, of course, and immediately it

flew back up into the gate with the others."

Taylor says these are monk parakeets, a larger and altogether different species from the little bright-colored pet birds that we call "parakeets" but that are actually budgerigars, or "budgies." As to the name "monk parakeet," a spokesperson at Brooklyn's World Class Aquarium, a pet store that specializes in birds as well, said they're also called "Quaker parakeets." Why Quaker? "Because they look like little monks." Go figure.

—*Patricia Curtis*

Michael Kamber

Trapped in Green-Wood!

When they lock the gates, you want to be on the side of the living

BY ANNE KOSTICK

The sign at Green-Wood Cemetery says the gates will be locked at 4:00 P.M. It turns out they really *mean* 4:00, not 4:10 or even 4:01. Green-Wood does not kid around about endings. So when you arrive a little late from your walk-around and discover that the gates are indeed locked, here are some things you can do to stave off that rising sense of panic:

■ Stop, drop and roll on the grass.

■ Admire the truly beautiful scenery, the mature trees of widely varied species, the rolling hills with the great views, the formidable memorial sculpture, the mausoleums that remind you of little playhouses.

■ Reflect on the deeper significance of being *locked* inside a cemetery: Man, it's like, you know?

■ Consider that Green-Wood Cemetery is, at 150 years, one of the oldest and most remarkable troves of Victoriana remaining in Brooklyn, or all of New York, or even the whole country for that matter. In fact, on Memorial Day, 1999, Green-Wood Cemetery had its first-ever "live" concert, featuring compositions by some of its permanent residents—Leonard Bernstein!—and performed by the Goldman Memorial Band . . . what you might call "underground music" (the cemetery is not without a sense of humor).

■ Appreciate that, at 478 acres, Green-Wood Cemetery is the second-largest green area in the entire borough of Brooklyn (only Prospect Park is larger), and if you wander off now for further sightseeing, you're almost certain to miss the guard.

■ Think about the fact that tens of thousands of people sojourn within Green-Wood's sturdy fences every year; another 600,000 (approximately) stay overnight, all the time. The main gate, a landmark Gothic Revival extravaganza of carved sandstone designed by architect Richard Upjohn and dating to 1863, is located on Fifth Avenue at Twenty-Fifth Street. (Upjohn's sandstone, a.k.a. "brownstone," kicked off the popularity of the building material that still symbolizes large parts of residential Brooklyn.)

■ Take comfort in the sign that also says that if you wait—oh so patiently—by the gate, the guard will eventually come around and let you out.

■ Notice that other people are also confined on the wrong side of the fence and that one of them is a clergyman, so maybe you'll get out a bit sooner than you otherwise would have. On the other hand, another one is your (former?) best friend who is now so mad at you for saying, "Oh, we've got lots of time" that she looks to be hoping you'll never leave the cemetery!

Russell Christian

■ Make a mental list of all the famous people buried in the cemetery, such as Elias Howe, Samuel F.B. Morse, Peter Cooper, Boss Tweed, George Catlin, Eastman Johnson, Horace Greeley (in the end, he did not go west), F.A.O. Schwarz, both Currier & Ives, Lola Montez, Louis Comfort Tiffany, the Brooks brothers, Duncan Phyfe and Crazy Joey Gallo.

■ Make another list of your favorite tombs and memorials, such as the weeping angel near the corner of MacDonald Avenue and Fort Hamilton Parkway, Pierrepont's little church, Garrison's Moorish tomb and the cozy Egyptian mastaba over by Twentieth Street.

■ Remind yourself that it's the middle of summer and unlikely to get dark and scary anytime soon... *certainly* not before that guard comes around (which has got to be any minute now) to let you out.

■ Accept that there is no telephone, no water fountain and no restroom on the premises and that only twenty feet and a huge wrought-iron and razor-wire fence separate you from the freedom of the street.

■ Try not to call out to passing cars on the other side of the fence, *"Help! Help! I'm locked inside Green-Wood Cemetery and the guard will never come to let me out!"* Don't bother trying to climb the fence (see above).

■ Ponder the idea that if you have to spend some unplanned leisure time somewhere, you could do worse than loiter within the borders of one of the first non-sectarian Victorian final resting places in the whole country, with practically the whole history of Brooklyn at and/or beneath your feet.

■ Thank the guard profusely after he finally shows up, unlocks the gate and sets you free, even though he did so to the accompaniment of great sighs heaved and eyes rolled. And assume that with thousands of visitors daily, he's probably unlocked this gate for the tardy many, many times and is only trying to reinforce for your benefit Green-Wood Cemetery's 4:00 P.M. curfew.

Anne Kostick is a writer, editor and resident of Windsor Terrace who arrived in Brooklyn in 1976 just in time to see the Bicentennial Tall Ships sail into the harbor.

Who's Who in Green-Wood

Where are the famous and infamous of yesteryear? For many of them, Brooklyn is their final resting-place. Herewith, a guide-map to the glitterati of Green-Wood. (Note: Locations of graves are approximate; for exact locations, check the guide furnished by the cemetery.)

1. Frank Morgan, 1949: actor; played the wizard in *The Wizard of Oz.*

2. Susan McKinney-Steward, 1918: first black female doctor in New York State.

3. Jean Michel Basquiat, 1988: popular young painter and guitarist.

4. Lola Montez (b. Eliza Gilbert), 1861: dancer, international vamp.

5. Martha B. and Alice H. Roosevelt, 1884: the mother and the wife of Theodore Roosevelt; died on the same day.

6. Eastman Johnson, 1906: influential genre painter and portraitist.

7. James M. Ives, 1895: lithographer; half of famous nineteenth-century printmaking duo.

8. James Creighton, 1862: Brooklyn Excelsior, baseball pro, inventive pitcher.

9. Henry Chadwick, 1908: sportswriter; baseball's pioneer rulemaker.

10. Elmer A. Sperry, 1930: engineer, industrialist; invented gyroscope.

11. Charles Ebbets, 1925: manager, owner of Brooklyn Dodgers; builder of stadium.

12. Leonard Bernstein, 1990: composer, conductor, arranger, author, teacher.

13. William Marcy Tweed, 1878: famously corrupt political boss; ran Tammany Hall machine.

14. Samuel F.B. Morse, 1872: prominent painter, inventor of the telegraph and Morse code.

15. Nathaniel Currier, 1888: lithographer; other half of printmaking duo.

16. Joey Gallo, 1972: hit man for Gambinos.

17. Brooks brothers (Daniel, John, Elisha, Edward), early 1900s: clothiers; purveyors of button-down shirts and other preppy essentials.

18. Asher B. Durand, 1886: landscape painter of the Hudson River School.

19. Pierre Lorillard, 1901: tobacco mogul, socialite; inventor of the tuxedo.

20. George C. Tilyou, 1914: Coney Island showman; Steeplechase founder.

21. John T. Underwood, 1937: industrialist; marketed the first practical typewriter.

22. Albert Anastasia, 1957: mob boss; founder of Murder Inc.

23. Frederick Augustus Otto Schwarz, 1911: founder of world-famous toy store.

24. Henry Ward Beecher, 1887: Plymouth Church pastor and abolitionist.

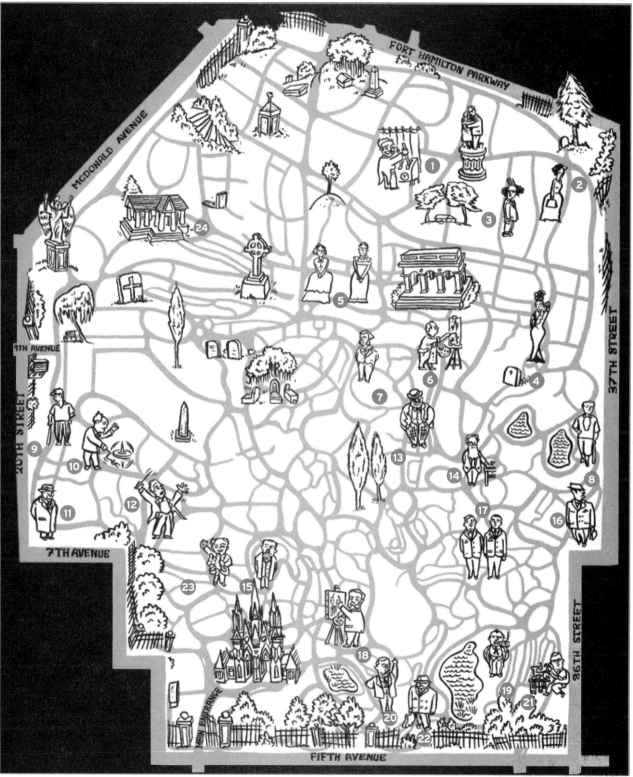

Russell Christian

The Lost Airmen of Floyd Bennett Field

Does HARP stand for Hopeful Aircraft Restoration Projects?

BY STEPHAN WILKINSON

Floyd Bennett Field was New York's first city airport. The canny politico Fiorello La Guardia, as mayor, gave the old airfield on Jamaica Bay its only brush with commercial notoriety. "I bought a ticket to New York, not New Jersey," La Guardia announced as his flight from Chicago taxied to a stop at an airport gate in Newark, New Jersey. "Says so right here. Take me to New York." Abashed, American Airlines fired up its DC-3 and flew one passenger—the mayor—twenty-three miles to New York City's own Floyd Bennett Municipal Field. La Guardia knew perfectly well what he was doing (campaigning for improved regular airline service) when he traveled to Chicago by train and then bought an airline ticket for the return journey. It was a nice ploy, but it did not have the effect of diverting commercial traffic to what was then the city's lone airport. The place did not really take off, so to speak, until World War II.

Floyd Bennett himself was a pilot who attained fame in 1926 when he flew Admiral Richard Byrd's aircraft across the North Pole. The municipal airport named in his honor was built in 1930 and then enlarged a few years later, but perhaps due to its distance from Manhattan, it did not flourish as a commercial airport. During the 1930s, though, as a large facility located comparatively far to the east, it was the field of choice for numerous famous aviators and venturesome transatlantic flights. During World War II, it became a naval air station and the jumping-off place for a high percentage of the military aircraft that were flown across to Europe. After the high activity of the war years, Floyd Bennett Field slid into disuse and for a time was no more than a heliport for the NYPD. In 1972 it became part of the National Park Service's Gateway National Recreation Area, and today its enormous weedy runways are used only by

World War II PBY-5 Catalina amphibians were stationed at Floyd Bennett Field and flown in postwar years by naval reserve crews on Atlantic patrol.

Courtesy of E.B. Majors

The North American SNJ, the navy's ubiquitous trainer, was a mainstay of 1940s reserve squadrons.

radio-control model aircraft enthusiasts and its flaking hangars by a gaggle of aging aircraft restorationists that goes by the name of HARP.

HARP, for Historic Aviation Restoration Projects, is a group of fifty-odd volunteers, many of them elderly and retired, most of them airplane enthusiasts, all of them artisans (whether in the group's metalworking shop or its kitchen) who are cleaning up the World War II and postwar aircraft and 1930s hangars that still linger around the ramps and runways of the vast, overgrown and hauntingly silent field.

The spark plug that fires HARP's enthusiasm is seventy-seven-year-old Arnie Migliaccio. His roots are planted deep in Floyd Bennett Field, the scene of more historic takeoffs and landings than perhaps any airport in the country, and he is quick to reel off the names of some of the field's famous aviators: "Wrong-Way" Corrigan, Roscoe Turner, Wiley Post, Jacqueline Cochran and . . . Balbo. Who was Balbo? A suave, devilishly bearded Italian air marshal, Italo Balbo arrived at Floyd Bennett Field in July of 1933 at the head of a flight of twenty-four Savoia-Marchetti seaplanes, slab-sided, futuristic machines that resembled flying catamarans. It was a flock so huge for the era, particularly since it had already crossed the Atlantic from Italy, that RAF pilots thereafter took to calling any large formation of aircraft a "Balbo."

"I was right here when Balbo landed," Migliaccio says. "Absolutely. I was twelve. And I was here a couple of months later when another Italian gentleman tried to fly nonstop to Albania. He never made it. Crashed right into the fence behind Hangar 8." (Actually, what twelve-year-old Arnie had to have witnessed was the immolation of the Marquis Francesco de Pinedo, killed in his Bellanca without making even the first mile of the 7,500 to Baghdad, Iraq.)

Sal Pignatelli, another HARP volunteer, was a chief petty officer in a maintenance squadron at Floyd Bennett after World War II, when it was America's busiest naval air station. "There's so much history here, and it's all fading away," he muses. "When us old guys are gone . . ." Sal leaves the lament unfinished. He's a retired Aviation High School mechanics teacher and now spends his spare time working on HARP's World War II–era Consolidated PBY-5A amphibious patrol bomber that the group is patching up for display. HARP hopes to get this aircraft to the point where its engines can once again be fired up. Slow but with enormous range and endurance, PBY Catalinas once littered the ramps of Floyd Bennett, grumbling off at their typical 110-mph crawl into the sky over the Atlantic to hunt submarines, guard convoys, perform air-sea rescues and, after the war, patrol for icebergs.

HARP likes to think that it's restoring these old airplanes, that someday soon their hangar at Floyd Bennett will be another *Intrepid*-type museum. "Better than the *Intrepid*," Migliaccio insists. "Those guys have to pay the maritime unions, here nobody gets paid." But the dimensions of their task are so enormous that in fact the best they can do is repair damage (their PBY was battered by a Florida hurricane) and repaint their motley fleet in military colors. One airplane on display, a Vietnam-era surplus A-4D Skyhawk attack jet, had one of its wings sawed entirely off by the navy (it was not airworthy) to make sure no one would attempt to fly it. The wing has been coarsely riveted back into place and secured by chains and turnbuckles, and

Migliaccio putters away at its "restoration." So far, he has patched a few fuselage dents and fabricated an approximation of the airplane's original 20mm cannon. "I used electrical conduit," he says proudly. But nobody has been able to get the stilt-legged little jet's cockpit canopy open.

The National Park Service doesn't know quite what to do with its ragtag volunteers. "We're overstocked with aviation museums in this country. Every city I visit, I see one or two listed among its attractions," says John Gallagher, an NPS ranger and chief of history projects at Gateway. "I would like to see this as more of a workshop, a place where you could bring people, let them see the restorers at work, put aviation in New York City in its historical context. I can't see it becoming a bigger and better *Intrepid*."

Irving Krasner, a HARP volunteer who served as a PBY pilot in the Pacific in World War II, admits that some in the group are getting discouraged: "We have no ease of operation. No heat, no hot water. People have to bring their own tools with them. The impetus seems to have worn off. There are plenty of guys who are ambitious, but a lot of us are too old to jump up on a wing anymore. We get very little help from the Park Service, but I guess they're under budgetary constraints, too."

"We're happy to have the volunteers here, and they're happy to be here," says Gallagher. "But the happiest group of all is their wives, who get them out of the house." Meanwhile, out on the miles of Floyd Bennett runways, the only things actually getting into the air are model airplanes and gulls.

Stephan Wilkinson, a writer and former editor of Flying *magazine, could pilot any aircraft that ever landed at Floyd Bennett Field.*

 Minna's Court Street was the old Brooklyn, a placid ageless surface alive underneath with talk, with deals and casual insults, a neighborhood political machine with pizzeria and butcher-shop bosses and unwritten rules everywhere." **Jonathan Lethem**

Hattie's Indomitable Magnolia

More than one tree grows in Brooklyn

BY HELEN
ZELON

On a perfect Indian summer afternoon, under a crystalline blue sky flecked with white clouds, Arthur Shepard stands in the garden, checking the ribs he's been coaxing along since seven-thirty this morning. Near-edible cooking scents billow from his split-drum barbecue and mingle with the smells of chives and basil and new-mown grass. A tangle of a grapevine rustles nearby, and young plum and peach trees shed little shade in the sun's warmth. Far from the leafy reaches of suburban counties, this verdant patch flourishes against all odds in the heart of Bedford-Stuyvesant, where the clatter of a bus on Lafayette Avenue, followed by the shriek of sirens, serves as a reminder of the gritty surroundings.

Back in the 1960s, much of Bed-Stuy was a bombed-out ruin. Vacant, rubble-filled lots dotted its blocks, and one night an especially heartbreaking fire raged through St. Augustine's Episcopal Church, rectory and nearby houses, transforming the structures into twisted metal and piles of broken bricks. From those ruins rose the Hattie Carthan Community Garden, nearly a block square and girded by a handsome new wrought-iron fence. The unusual garden, which now hosts school groups, local gardeners, and community barbecues like the one Shepard is preparing, is the centerpiece of a larger organization called Magnolia Tree Earth Center.

Mrs. Hattie Carthan, whose warm face shines from the outsize mural on the front of MTEC's brownstone, is the patron saint and guiding spirit of the Center. Drawn by the hope of work and the prospect for a better life above the Mason-Dixon line, she had moved up north to Brooklyn as a young woman. Over long hours riding the Lafayette Avenue bus to and from work, she favored a particular tree, a rare and beautiful *Magnolia grandiflora* that she saw as a symbol, a reminder of home, now pushing its roots down into the Brooklyn soil. Years passed, the magnolia grew, she worked hard and built a life. Time finally came when urban developers sought to raze the tree and the nearby brownstones to erect new housing. That was 1969, and Hattie Carthan became a community advocate that year at the age of sixty-eight. Until her death in 1984, she was a one-

Looking forward to a stint of neighborhood gardening: Mrs. Hattie Carthan and Herbert Von King.

Courtesy of the Magnolia Tree Earth Center

woman whirlwind of charm, energy and steely will, all focused on creating opportunities for the children of Bed-Stuy.

The Earth Center grew out of her first battle, the fight to save her beloved magnolia tree and create an environmental center in the brownstones behind it. Shepard remembers that one day, when he was a little boy, Mrs. Carthan headed a big protest rally out in the street. It was part political theater and part neighborhood celebration, and the street was packed. Food, drink and music flowed freely until a phalanx of counterprotesters, led by an elderly local priest, strode toward the group. Mrs. Carthan, an indomitable force in the guise of a well-bred, proper lady, met them mid-block as the whole party held its breath and watched. "It was a sight, these two seniors gathering forces to do battle," says Shepard. "He thought we were against him, and she thought he was against us. But she was irresistible, asking, 'Wouldn't you like to help the children of Bedford-Stuyvesant?' No one could say no. She charmed them all—from this priest right up to the mayor."

Shepard's own self-effacing charms don't mask the vigor of his commitment as he works with one garden, one street tree, one child at a time. "I want to help children in the community learn about their environment, about science," he explains. "I want to keep them from going the wrong way—keep them occupied, interested and productive." The images of that afternoon victory still dance in Shepard's imagination, now thirty years later, and that experience figured large in his choice to become an MTEC horticulturist in the early 1970s: "It's all Mrs. Carthan's vision, really. We're all just carrying on her work. She got me engaged in public service. I had always thought commercially—how much money can you make from what you know?—but she showed me something different." In his early work with MTEC's Tree Corps, Shepard and a legion of neighborhood children "would march out of the Earth Center in forma-

Greening Bed-Stuy: MTEC's young volunteers prepare for an afternoon of public service.

tion, with wheelbarrows and tools, and go wherever we were needed." But beyond making the streets pretty—beyond planting trees, sending out crews and giving gardening advice—MTEC orchestrated political dialogue, rallied potential funders and promoted opportunities for economic development. And in the bargain, they taught the basics of community organizing, political advocacy and outreach to a generation of community workers.

Today, the children of that first generation of activists are at the Center, learning for themselves the power that resides in community. MTEC and its tenants all share the vision of sustaining the youth of Bedford-Stuyvesant from birth to voting booth. In that row of preserved brownstones are well-baby care, healthy-heart clinics and domestic-violence counseling services. After-school arts programs and study support for elementary-age children provide a place to connect with others and counter the isolation of latchkey afternoons. And computer skills are taught there to support the college-bound and encourage job readiness.

After a stint with the Horticultural Society of New York (where he created an innovative greenhouse program for Rikers Island inmates), Shepard returned to the Earth Center. "We deal with violence, loss, disappointment every day. The only way to keep going is to persist, to see the small successes—one person turned around, one child's life changed—as large triumphs."

Hattie Carthan's tree is now 120 years old. "You see those blooms, nothing can rival a *Magnolia grandiflora*," brags MTEC's board president, Marcia Goldman. "Mrs. Carthan understood what the tree—as an extraordinary symbol—could do for the community. She had confidence in her community, and the tree was her inspiration. At 115 years old, that's a whole lot of living, a whole lot of getting by—all the while looking gorgeous."

Helen Zelon is a writer and resident of Windsor Terrace.

Courtesy of the Magnolia Tree Earth Center

The Last Steam Engine

Pratt's keeper of the flame

BY MICHAEL
W. ROBBINS

On certain days, if you chance to pass within a dozen city blocks of Pratt Institute in the Fort Greene/Clinton Hill area, you could be forgiven for believing you were hearing a ghost ship in New York Harbor. A sonorous, powerful three-note blast fills the air, again and again, followed by some sharper, shriller piping notes. Then more of the deep blasts that stir memories—if only from flickering black-and-white newsreel footage—of the glamorous days of the great transatlantic steamships. The mighty ship whistles sound exactly like those exciting moments when the *Queen Elizabeth* or the *United States* or the *Normandie* was pulling away from its berth and departing for Europe. The sound is real—you are not hearing things. The ships are indeed gone, but the steam whistles live on.

They blow for ceremonial occasions on the Pratt campus, to observe either the New Year or the Fourth of July or the latest graduation—occasions that involve over a dozen whistles and attract hundreds of earplugged steam enthusiasts. And the reason it all sounds like the ghosts of ocean liners past is that one of the largest and loudest whistles once graced a stack of the *Normandie*, the great liner that in 1942 capsized and burned at Pier 88. That and the other whistles are in the collection and care of Conrad Milster, the chief engineer who operates Pratt's antique steam heating and generating plant. Milster says there used to be steam engines all over Brooklyn, but now the handsome 1887 engine room in his charge—a registered national historic engineering landmark—contains the last original operating steam engines in the borough.

The steam that operates the venerable but lively steam engines comes from three oil-fired boilers dating from the 1940s and '50s and is used to warm the four city blocks of buildings on the Pratt campus. Since they have to create the steam for heat, it doesn't really cost the school much to divert some of it to the three gleaming, red-enameled Ames 100-horsepower engines that generate electricity for Pratt's elevators and lighting

parts of the campus—or on special occasions to those high-decibel ceremonial whistles.

Milster is an affable sort who welcomes visitors, filmmakers and stray cats to the Engine Room, a varnished two-story space with a catwalk from which all can observe the steam engines—at least one of which is usually reciprocating furiously and silently—and the panels of period gauges and massive copper switches. He is well versed on why this is the last surviving steam

Russell Christian

plant of its kind in Brooklyn, why people like it, what it takes to keep it running and the hazards of live steam:

"Steam plants went out of favor for a number of reasons. First, most steam plants were making direct current. When most of these plants were installed, prior to 1930 or thereabouts, direct current was all that was necessary. But after World War II you had a tremendous surge in requirements for alternating current. A lot of office buildings in Manhattan used to have their own power plants. Look at a 1920s aerial photo of New York City and you'll see dozens of buildings that have this little cloud of steam coming out of them. But now you have the problem of an office building with tenants who come in and say, 'I want to put in fluorescent lighting.' And you say, 'Well, you can't, because we only have direct current.' And they say, 'Oh, okay, I'll go across the street where they have alternating current.'

"Another was, of course, the labor factor. There was a beautiful power plant in a building over in Manhattan, 165 Broadway, and they had three men on duty around the clock—an engineer, a fireman and an oiler—plus a maintenance staff during the day. So you're looking at twenty-one shifts times three people, sixty-three people on the payroll to operate that power plant, and you've got to make a hell of a lot of power to pay for that.

"It became harder to maintain this equipment because the original manufacturers went out of business. We received a letter from Skinner Engine Company—I think it was 1948—saying that if you want any spare parts for your engines you've got to order them now, because we're no longer going to carry them. Many of these plants are now at least fifty years old, the guys who installed them are no longer there, the guys who knew how to run them are no longer there, and the buildings they were put into—hospitals, hotels and breweries—have gone out of business. Nobody would put up a building today and put a steam-driven plant in it. But if you already have one, you might keep it.

"If I went to the administration now and said I need ten or twenty thousand dollars a year to keep this engine room as it is, I couldn't justify it. It's not costing anything out of pocket to preserve this steam plant—just brass polish and a couple of gallons of paint. A plant like this was designed and built to last for fifty or a hundred years. It's old technology, and it runs on old expertise. I used to work on steam-powered ships and tugs on the Hudson River. I learned it all from those old engineers. The plant does have its little quirks, and there is some trial and error involved. Mostly, it's just plain common sense. And you have to remember that you're dealing with forces that can kill you if you're careless.

"These aren't automated boilers, so the law says a man has to be on-site twenty-four hours a day. Now, a lot of the time, it's boring and mostly just observation. You walk around and check the gauges and the water levels. But occasionally there's an emergency, like the night a gasket blew on the manhole door. Usually when gaskets leak, they just hiss. But this one blew out completely and you could hear it screaming all over campus. Water and steam were coming out under a hundred and twenty pounds per square inch of pressure, at three hundred and forty degrees. That could've been a bad one. Anyone standing nearby at the time would've been scalded.

"One time I was here on the night shift and was separating some oil and water. They can get mixed together on a steam engine, but we can reuse our lubricating oil if we get the water out. So we do that by heating the oil in a big oil drum with an immersed steam coil—like a big version of one of those immersion coils that people make mugs of tea or coffee with. This time the heat control failed, and the whole thirty-five gallons of oil and water was getting *really* hot. I didn't notice, and poured in a couple gallons of cool oil that still had some water in it. When I did, the whole drum of oil just blew up and threw steaming-hot oil—like what you do french fries in—all over the engine room. I did about ten days in the hospital.

"The engine room is no longer vital to our operation, but it has achieved a historic status that justifies preserving it. Invariably, when VIPs are getting taken around the campus, they make a point to stop in. Usually they haven't the faintest idea what they're looking at, but it looks impressive to them. And it *is*. You look at the switchboard, with the symmetrical layout of the lights, and you see there's art there—an art of layout and design that the engineers had at that period. There was a little private form with a code number in back of the marble switchboard, and if you ever replaced or expanded this switchboard, you were supposed to give the number to General Electric so they could color-match the marble on your model. That was the kind of quality that went into this kind of plant.

"A lot of filmmakers want to use the power plant as a location. We get one or two filmings a year in the plant. We had a *Saturday Night Live* sequence shot here, and we've had rock videos and documentaries. For *SNL*, the place was supposed to be a sinking submarine and they had about three guys and a gal running around carrying potted plants and pulling switches on the switchboard. About ten years ago, they filmed a Chock-full-o'Nuts commercial in the office. The location scout who worked for the ad agency was a Pratt graduate, so he brought

his producer down and they looked over the office. The producer said, 'I think we want to use your office because it has built-in grime.' There was this crotchety old guy who said he didn't care what the demand for his coffee was, he wasn't going to decrease the quality to make more coffee. He had his standards and he was going to stick to them.

"I came here forty-one years ago, and I've just never left. Whether I can ever find somebody like me to take over, I don't know. I hope I do, because when I finally leave here, I'd like to leave this steam plant to an individual who would have the same long-term goals—of preserving this stuff, keeping it going and keeping it looking good."

Michael W. Robbins is a Brooklyn writer and editor with a taste for old industrial stuff.

BROOKLYN ON FILM

A Tale of Young Immigrants

A Tree Grows in Brooklyn is a film adaptation of Betty Smith's novel of the same name, published in 1943 and based on the growing-up-in-Brooklyn experiences of its author at the beginning of the twentieth century. The novel and film tell the story of the dreams and tribulations of a struggling Irish-American immigrant family living in the shadow of the Williamsburg Bridge. The story focuses on the aspirations of the daughter, Francie Nolan, for an education that will open the door to a career as a writer. The novel was an instant success, selling 300,000 copies in just six weeks, and the Twentieth Century-Fox Film Corporation paid $55,000 for the film rights.

The film was directed by Elia Kazan, the renowned stage and screen direc-

tor, and when released in 1945 it was met with widespread acclaim. This is a "Brooklyn" film shot entirely on the back lot and studios in Hollywood, and the absence of location shooting is quite noticeable to a contemporary audience. The studio-built interior sets look artificial, and the streets are far neater than in a real Williamsburg slum of the World War I years. Nevertheless, strong performances by Peggy Ann Garner, Dorothy McGuire, Joan Blondell, Lloyd Nolan, James Gleason and James Dunn, together with the fluid cinematography by cameraman Leon Shamroy, create an emotionally vibrant, realistic portrayal of the communications and miscommunications at the heart of an embattled family. James Dunn won an Academy Award for his portrayal of the father, Johnny Nolan.

The film centers on one ethnic

A Tree Grows in Brooklyn, 1945

group—Irish Americans—but the story it tells was much the same for families in all the different groups then co-existing in Brooklyn: Irish, Italian, Jewish, African-American and many others. Since this film's success, many others set in Brooklyn have addressed the same themes of aspiration, family tensions, love and loyalty. Among them: *Saturday Night Fever* (1977), *Moonstruck* (1987) and *Brighton Beach Memoirs* (1986).
–*Jon Gartenberg*

MOMA Film Stills Archive

The Boerum Hill Reservation

Mohawk ironworkers built the place

BY KEVIN BAKER

One of the great legends of New York City, a persistent tale shrouded in romance and mystery, is that the city's construction work was done mainly by Native Americans because they had some special, genetic gift for keeping their balance on the "high steel" of the new skyscrapers and bridges. The important part of the legend is true. During most of the great age of urban building in New York in the early twentieth century, a disproportionate number of the workers in high steel were indeed Indians. Working all over the United States and Canada, they were some of the best craftsmen America ever produced. Most of them were Mohawks, of the Iroquois people, and they hailed from Quebec province, upstate New York and, eventually, Brooklyn.

The legend began in 1886, when the Dominion Bridge Company built a cantilevered railroad bridge over the St. Lawrence River. The bridge traversed land owned by the Kahnawake and Akwesasne Mohawks, who in partial payment were given jobs on the project. Dominion Bridge expected the Mohawks to occupy themselves with the most menial, unskilled work on the site, such as unloading boxcars. Instead, the Indians were soon climbing all over the bridge, "as agile as goats," as Joseph Mitchell described them in his *New Yorker* essay "The Mohawks in High Steel" (1949). They seemed to love the work and even the danger, and soon a dozen or so were trained as riveters.

And what a death-defying trade this was. An old-style steel-riveting team consisted of four men. Treading carefully along a beam or girder hundreds of feet in the air, they had to work in flawless syncopation. One man, the "heater," heated the rivets in a small, mobile coal-burning forge until they were red-hot. He then flung them as far as thirty or forty feet through the air to the "sticker-in," who caught them in something that resembled a metal wastepaper basket, pulled out the temporary bolt holding the beams in place and shoved in the burning new rivet. A third man, the "bucker-up," then braced and held the rivet in place for the riveter, who banged the rivet home permanently with a cupped die and an iron maul or, later, a pneumatic hammer.

It was tough, unforgiving work, but it paid well and it enabled a man to develop a tremendous pride in himself and his craft. Soon there were seventy iron and steel riveters in the Kahnawake band alone, working throughout Canada. Then, in 1907, the collapse of the Quebec Bridge killed some thirty-five Indian workers. This tragic event, known among the Kahnawake as "the disaster," only made the young men and boys in the tribe more determined to become ironworkers. At the same time, the Mohawks prudently decided to spread out to ensure that so many of their number would not be lost in some similar accident.

By the 1910s the Kahnawakes had reached New York City, and over the next five decades they would contribute their skill, their muscle and their blood to all of the most memorable silhouettes on the area's skyline: the Empire State Building and the World Trade Center; the George Washington Bridge and the Chrysler Building; the Triborough Bridge and Rockefeller Center and the West Side Highway, and many, many more.

At night, the Mohawks went home to Brooklyn. Generally, they lived a seminomadic existence. They were prone to "booming out"—pulling up stakes, often at the drop of a hat, and driving off pell-mell to where

A father-and-son team of Mohawk construction workers, together on the high steel.

AP/Wide World

258

BROOKLYN

they heard there were jobs. In this way they managed to get around the entire continent, even riveting together the Golden Gate Bridge. While their only permanent home was the reservation land along the U.S.-Canada border, they established in the 1920s a long-term base camp in North Gowanus, Brooklyn—the neighborhood now known by the more genteel name of Boerum Hill.

It was a familiar pattern of immigration: a group drawn by an economic factor (in this case, a construction union local on Atlantic Avenue) and then attracting more of its number out of sheer companionship and familiarity—the same sort of behavior that over the years has created enclaves of Arabs, Jamaicans, Hasidic Jews, Italians, even Norwegians in the borough. At the community's height in the 1940s, some 700 Kahnawake and Akwesasne lived in a ten-square-block area, esti-

mated to be the greatest congregation of Mohawks anywhere outside a reservation. North Gowanus became known informally as "Downtown Caughnawaga," and it was very much a community. At one point the apartment building at 375 State Street had a Mohawk name next to every doorbell, and everyone's doors would generally be kept open as the families visited freely back and forth.

The ironworkers' wives took local jobs, often as store clerks and domestics. There was a Mohawk lunch counter, and local Italian groceries carried the Quaker White Enriched and Degerminated cornmeal favored by Mohawks for making boiled bread and corn soup. The riveters drank Canadian beers at the Spar Bar and Grill on Atlantic or at the Wigwam around the corner on Nevins Street, which had a big picture of the great Jim

Hundreds of Mohawks lived in North Gowanus and worked on major construction projects all over New York.

Courtesy of the Kanien'kehaka Raotitohkwa Cultural Center (both)

Thorpe on the wall and the sign "The Greatest Iron Workers in the World Pass Thru These Doors" above its entrance. And over on Pacific Street some fifty Mohawks belonged to the congregation of the Cuyler Presbyterian Church, where Reverend David Munroe Cory had translated the Gospel of St. Luke into their language and held monthly services in Mohawk-Oneida.

The Mohawk community seemed so entrenched that Joseph Mitchell, for one, thought it showed "signs of permanence." Alas, little in Brooklyn fifty years ago proved to be permanent. Gay Talese, recording the epic construction of the Verrazano Bridge, described how in 1964 many Mohawk ironworkers were still making twelve-hour trips every Friday night to their more permanent reservation homes along the St. Lawrence. These were mad, fantastic rides at reckless speeds and often fueled by alcohol. The men would arrive early Saturday morning to a joyous reception, and then, late Sunday afternoon, make the same wild trip back, reportedly leaving more of their number dead on the highway than they ever did on the great construction sites. Most of them, though, arrived only a little the worse for wear, ready to work on Monday morning.

The Verrazano Bridge was all but the last gasp. Riveting was disappearing as a method of steel construction, and rising crime rates were chasing many of the Mohawks out of their Brooklyn enclave. The last family left 375 State Street back in 1997. The Wigwam and the Spar Bar closed, as did the Atlantic Avenue union hall. Reverend Cory passed away, and Cuyler Presbyterian was converted into apartments. Even North Gowanus was no longer North Gowanus; it had become known as Boerum Hill, an increasingly gentrified neighborhood, far removed from the world of fire and iron high in the air. Only a few elderly Mohawk women were left in the area.

But like most Brooklyn stories, this one is not over

A high-altitude break: a study in balance and nerves of steel.

even after it seems to be over. For all the footloose ways of the Kahnawake, for all their rather wary, arm's-reach relationship with the city, the graves of men who died on construction jobs are still marked with crosses cut from steel girders. And because traditions die hard and the work has kept its allure, there are still Mohawks working steel construction here—though they no longer live in Boerum Hill but are scattered through other Brooklyn neighborhoods, including Bay Ridge. In the late 1990s, Mohawk men make up at least 10 percent of New York City's ironworkers, and operating out of Ironworkers Local 361 (now located in Queens), they've been putting up the steel frames of the new high-rises in downtown Brooklyn.

Their special skill in dealing with great heights remains something of a mystery. Yet it seems hard to believe any man is truly at home 500 feet above the ground, swinging red-hot iron rivets through the air. Perhaps the real key to the legendary ironworking Indians lies in the suggestion made by Kanatakta, executive director of the Kahnawake Community Cultural Centre, that it is less a question of genes, or an uncanny fearlessness, than "a question of dealing with the fear." And therein lies the truest definition of courage.

Kevin Baker is the author of Dreamland, *a novel set in Coney Island and New York of the early twentieth century.*

Moses vs. Brooklyn Heights

Where the mad builder met his match

BY JOSEPH M. McCARTHY

ome dark winter night, a grandmother will sit by the fireside in a grand old house in downtown Brooklyn and tell her assembled grandchildren about a terrible ogre who once terrified the town. She will tell this story in a brownstone that still stands on a tranquil tree-lined street in a carefully preserved nineteenth-century neighborhood. A *landmarked* neighborhood, to be precise.

It will not be a fairy tale she tells, and it will begin with a true story of a very powerful man who cared, passionately it would seem, only for the automobile and the parkways and expressways upon which it ran.

The man was named Robert Moses, and among his many public jobs (he held twelve at one time) he was chairman of the State Council of Parks and the State Power Authority, and construction coordinator for the City of New York. For over forty years, beginning in 1924, he embroidered the state with a concrete pattern of parks, dams, highways, bridges and urban development projects. He seemed inordinately fond of pavement, and in New York City his highway projects cut thriving communities off from the Hudson and East River waterfronts and the city's magnificent harbor, or sundered them without thought to their pulse or value. In his excellent biography, *The Power Broker*, Robert Caro suggests that Moses was in many ways more powerful than the governor. As head of the State Power Authority, funded by the state legislature with revenues from the dams it built, he could rarely be thwarted when his mind was set on a development scheme.

Until the early sixties, Moses suffered few setbacks. His downfall came in 1968 after a three-year effort orchestrated by Governor Nelson Rockefeller, perhaps the only man in the state who couldn't be touched by Moses' resources and power. One of the rare instances when Moses' will was thwarted occurred in Brooklyn Heights, and it was the work not of a powerful state governor but of a small group of highly motivated homeowners. Their victory over Moses and one of his expressways also led to the fruition of a new and important idea called "landmarking."

Brooklyn Heights and South Brooklyn are two of the borough's oldest neighborhoods. The Heights had grown from a tiny seventeenth-century village at the foot of Fulton Street, and South Brooklyn was an extension to the south that grew up before and after the Civil War. The communities were built when Brooklyn was prospering as a port, a manufacturing center and a railhead (rail traffic from Boston was linked by ferry across Long Island Sound to Orient Point, thence along Long Island through Brooklyn and again by ferry across to Hoboken). Mansions lined the Heights overlooking the East River, and solid row houses filled in the former farmlands to the south that came to be known as Cobble Hill and Carroll Gardens. But when Cornelius Vanderbilt moved the railhead from the Brooklyn waterfront to Hunts Point in the Bronx, downtown Brooklyn went flat. No longer a bustling center of trade, Brooklyn Heights and South Brooklyn became instead a quiet backwater suburb full of houses no one saw any need to change—until the mid-twentieth century when Robert Moses decided that the landscape of New York City should be reshaped to accommodate the automobile.

Moses' plan, first developed in the early 1930s, was to build a beautiful parkway completely around the shorelines of Brooklyn and Queens from southern Nassau County (and beyond) to the entrance to Long Island

An avid swimmer, Moses enjoyed access to the very beaches he blocked off with projects like the Verrazano Bridge (at right).

Sound in Queens on the north (and beyond). One big problem: those shorelines were not empty land but had long been built up. So Moses' parkways cut right through established communities, separating them from the waterfront that was the reason for their being there and had remained a key to their identities.

In South Brooklyn, shortly after World War II, Moses began shoving the Brooklyn-Queens Expressway through some residential neighborhoods of nineteenth-century row houses. With one particularly egregious cut, he separated most of the South Brooklyn community from Columbia Street, its waterfront main drag. The expressway, now named Interstate 287, was de-

signed to swoop down off the Gowanus Canal overpass and enter a forty-foot-deep trench, six lanes wide. That trench resulted in the destruction of as many as eight houses at the end of each of twenty blocks. It bisected and effectively destroyed an entire neighborhood. Moses planned to extend this method of entrenching

Culver Pictures; inset: Brooklyn Historical Society

the expressway (and destroying whatever neighborhood lay in its path) directly north along Hicks Street and straight through Brooklyn Heights. But at that point, his scheme ran into heavy opposition.

A resident of the Heights named Roy Richardson organized a group of wealthy homeowners to work with the Brooklyn Heights Association (BHA), resisting Moses' expressway. They argued that not only would many homes and historic Grace Church (designed by

grown up around a working-class apartment complex built on Joralemon Street by financier and philanthropist Alfred Tredway White (the first apartments with running water built for the poor in America). James persuaded Moses to bend his highway some more, saving the community.

In the early 1950s, Moses put yet another challenge to Brooklyn Heights on his agenda: to replace some deteriorating slums at its northeast corner near the

The home of Washington Roebling (left), among other landmarks, was destroyed by Moses' Brooklyn-Queens Expressway.

Richard Upjohn in 1849) be destroyed by Moses' road building, but one of New York's greatest vistas would be blocked from Brooklyn's civic center. Moses did understand wealth and power, and it was the wealth and power of this opposition that led him to detour around the Heights. At great added expense, he agreed to build cantilevered roadways projecting from the bluff below the level of the residential neighborhood.

Resistance to Moses' plan continued when Gladys James, another wealthy Heights resident, took up the cause of nearby Willowtown, a small, primarily black community on the Heights' northern edge. It had

Brooklyn Bridge on-ramp with luxury high-rise rental apartments, an area to be called Cadman Plaza. In response, the BHA and an ad hoc organization called the Community Conservation and Improvement Council proposed substituting family-sized, middle-income cooperatives for the essentially transient housing.

Many young people had moved into the magnificent old Heights housing stock in the years following World War II, and they began to realize that the ambience of the charming community could be lost not only to a rapacious urban developer (Robert Moses), but also to equally rapacious real estate developers. This

Left: Brooklyn Historical Society; right: Brooklyn Public Library-Brooklyn Collection

new challenge galvanized the community and the BHA.

At the time there were still a few freestanding mansions in the Heights, with gardens and tennis courts. Spanning a quarter to half a block, they offered —whenever they came on the market—easy opportunities for developers to profit through demolition and building rental properties. So in the early 1950s, undistinguished yellow- or white-brick apartment buildings as tall as ten stories began to appear in the Heights. Other landlords stripped the stoops from their brownstones and added extra floors to increase rental space. The BHA and its constituents could see that unless something was done quickly to preserve their "landmark" neighborhood, Brooklyn Heights would go the way of Manhattan's Upper East Side, where the flavor of the local neighborhoods had been overwhelmed by similar architecture.

Among the young residents to take up the challenge were Otis and Nancy Pearsall. They gathered around them people who took on what to them seemed a no-brainer, only to find out it wasn't. Clay Lancaster put together a survey of the architecture of the Heights (later published as *Old Brooklyn Heights, New York's First Suburb* in 1961). Others contributed time, money, imagination, legal and lobbying services, and publicity, among them *Heights Press* editor Richard Margolis, Ted Reid, Bill Fisher, Mrs. James (again!), members of the Municipal Art Society and many, many others.

They began to focus on the idea of "landmarking." Usually the term meant recognizing a unique quality in a place or an edifice. An important battlefield or a church might be set off and protected so future generations could have a firsthand experience of them. But landmarking an entire neighborhood was a relatively new concept; in 1955, Boston's famous Beacon Hill was the first to be so designated for the collective quality of its houses and streets.

A crucial turning point in public awareness of the importance of landmarking came in 1962, when plans were announced to demolish Pennsylvania Station. No longer was the interest in landmarking confined to the efforts of a small, elitist group in Brooklyn; now it was

something all New Yorkers could appreciate. Later that year, City Planning Commission chairman James Felt announced on a television panel that he would support the Brooklyn Heights effort, but said that the only workable way to implement it would be through the creation of a citywide Landmarks Preservation Commission.

It took three more years of work before all the political steps were completed for the City Council to approve and Mayor Wagner to sign the Landmarks Preservation Statute. Then, eight months after it was created, the new commission met to consider New York's first landmark neighborhood. Because the Heights had been building its case all along—with historical and architectural documentation, community support and institutional muscle—six days after its presentation the Commission voted on November 23, 1965, to create the Brooklyn Heights Historic District.

The next goal was a height limitation that would control the community's skyline. The Commission had been given the right to restrict building heights, and the community asked for a fifty-foot limit, just the height of traditional four-story row houses. In this, too, the Heights succeeded and became LH-1, the first Limited Height District. (Taller buildings in the vicinity, recently built, are either outside the designated district are or grandfathered in.)

In the years leading up to these victories in Brooklyn, Moses had begun losing favor as many of his master-builder schemes had created other enemies as effective as those in Brooklyn Heights. He was stripped of his state appointments by Governor Rockefeller in 1962 and relinquished his last chairmanship in 1968. The struggle to save Brooklyn Heights had engendered landmarking as an effective new tool in community planning. In the nearly four decades since the Landmarks Preservation Commission was established, fifty-eight historic districts have been created within New York City.

Much was lost. Much has been saved.

Joseph McCarthy is a writer, filmmaker and resident of a neighborhood split by Robert Moses' Brooklyn-Queens Expressway.

The Water

front

The waterfront made Brooklyn. That's no exaggeration. In its earliest days, Brooklyn formed around the ferry landings and the water-borne commerce, fishing, and shipbuilding and it still has some sixty-five miles of coastline on the Atlantic and on New York Harbor. And Brooklyn-ites have always worked and played on the water from the wharves of Greenpoint to the sands of Coney Island.

Three events in recent history have shaped our sense of Brooklyn's waterfront: the end of ferry service to other parts of Greater New York in 1942, the closing of the Brooklyn Navy Yard in 1966 and the changeover in ocean cargo handling that occurred in the 1960s when bulk shipping gave way to containerization.

But waterfronts are resilient: Coney and Brighton still boast the great beaches, and plans are afoot for continued revitalization of the Navy Yard. The city, state and Port Authority have at last agreed to open the historic stretch of waterfront from Atlantic Avenue to DUMBO for recreational uses. Ocean freight, especially cocoa, still moves at the Red Hook Marine Terminal. And the cleaner water in the harbor means that fishing is a here-and-now reality, and swimming is on the horizon. Gulls and ship whistles are still part of Brooklyn's waterfront sound. Above it all, we've got that great Atlantic coastal light...

Previous spread: East River,
down under the Manhattan Bridge.

Previous spread: Michael Kamber; this page: Michael W. Robbins

Canal Dreams

Venice in Gowanus? Why not?

BY PATRICIA CURTIS

Buddy Scotto is not a politician in the exact sense of holding elected office. Tall and affable, wearing a dark suit and tie even in 90-degree weather, he looks like a funeral director. In fact, he *is* a funeral director. The Scotto Funeral Home in Carroll Gardens, where he makes his living, is a big, handsome, beautifully landscaped building, old and interdenominational despite its location in a heavily Catholic neighborhood.

But Scotto himself is more: a rainmaker, a mover and shaker and, to some, a troublemaker. Community pols woo him because an endorsement from Scotto is highly prized. And, in turn, Scotto is not unmindful of each debt—he'll use it to press for something his neighborhood needs: a playground, a day care center, low-cost housing for the elderly—he's probably had a hand in most of the improvements in Carroll Gardens over the last thirty years.

Buddy Scotto's most optimistic dream has been the rehabilitation and beautification of the Gowanus Canal. A clear stream, maybe with ducks on it, the banks lined with houses, cafés, little parks—that's what he has in mind. "If San Antonio can have its River Walk, why can't we?" he asks. As recently as 1997, if anyone had suggested that the fetid, garbage-strewn stretch of slack water that extends some two miles through Carroll Gardens could ever be reclaimed, the reply would have been cynical indeed: "A river walk along the Gowanus Canal? Yeah, right!"

The canal has had its ups and downs. In 1636, ten years before Breuckelen officially became a town, an enterprising Dutch settler bought a tract of land from the Gouwane tribe of Mohawks. Extending north and east from Gowanus Bay, the land included a small creek that flowed into the bay, the water rising and falling with the tide. For many years the Dutch populated the bucolic area, which came to be known as South Brooklyn.

But with its advantageous position on New York Harbor, the farmland eventually became a busy seaport with crowded residences of the immigrant poor who worked in

Dreamer and activist Scotto pushed hard to bring the Gowanus Canal back to life.

Wibke Reimann

There's Something in the Water...

Leonard Thomas, the bridge operator in charge, raises the three drawbridges on the Gowanus Canal at Carroll, Union and Third Streets to allow boats to pass. He has spent a lot of time looking at the canal.

"Before it was cleaned up, people used to throw anything in there," Thomas says. "Garbage, old furniture, broken-down shopping carts—you name it. And every so often I'd come to work and there, stuck in the muck, would be an old refrigerator. Also parts of cars—doors or fenders—that sort of thing.

"Dead animals? Dogs, cats, rats, of course. And yes, once a human body." Thomas says he heard that the man had died of a drug overdose and fell in.

"One summer day, the smell was so bad I had to call my supervisor and ask to go off duty," Thomas recalls. "But now the water's clean and even at low tide there's no bad smell. We even have a family of ducks swimming around under the Carroll Street Bridge." –P.C.

the factories and warehouses. In 1884, Gowanus Creek was enlarged into a canal so that factories could load their goods onto ships at their very doorsteps.

The canal also carried the sewage and garbage of the entire community for several generations. The water became strikingly polluted, and early in the twentieth century an effort was made to clean up the canal. A tunnel was built, leading from Buttermilk Channel on the East River and equipped with a flushing propeller that kept fresh water moving through the canal, but after several decades the propeller broke and the canal again filled with industrial waste, garbage, old tires and whatever else people threw into it.

That was the condition of the canal when Salvatore John Scotto di Fasano, known as Buddy, came home to Brooklyn from the army after the Korean War. For many years, South Brooklyn had been largely Italian. Buddy's father had arrived in 1911, worked hard and prospered in the wine importing business. When Prohibition wiped that out, Mr. Scotto di Fasano, undaunted, built some movie theaters, at which young Buddy spent many a Saturday afternoon as an usher.

When the theaters suffered during the Depression, Mr. Scotto di Fasano branched out into the funeral business. Buddy's mother, more fluent in English than her husband, studied, took the exams and became one of the first female licensed funeral directors in New York. Their only son, the returning soldier, was expected to step into the business. But now he had seen a bit of the world and was entertaining the idea of an army career. The elder Scottos were horrified. "Over our dead bodies," they said, in effect. So the good Italian son learned the funeral business, married, stayed in the neighborhood and looked around for some fun—and some challenges. He joined and worked within the existing civic organizations to get improvements for his neighborhood. Then one day he looked at the Gowanus Canal in a different light.

Carroll Gardens residents had been complaining for years about the canal, but local politicians, believing that cleaning up the water would entail a twenty-year commitment, preferred to campaign on projects that would show quicker results. So Scotto took the first steps in what became a decades-long struggle. He became a founder of the Independent Neighborhood Democrats. Since he sought no political position for himself, the local business, religious and cultural groups trusted him and welcomed his efforts. Neighbors joined him in organizing the Carroll Gardens Association, the Congress of Italian Americans and, eventually, the Gowanus Canal Community Development Corporation. Starting with the issue of public health, Scotto persuaded two professors at the New York Technical College to study the condition of the Gowanus water. Not surprisingly, they found that the canal was full of viruses and bacteria—typhus, typhoid and a virulent strain of cholera. With this information, Scotto went to the community's elected officials. "If nothing is done about this situation," he announced, "I'll send a copy of the health report to every voter in the district." That persuaded the local Democrats and Republicans, each afraid the other would get the credit, to join together in pressing Mayor John Lindsay for a sewage treatment plant. "Unfortunately, you have to work one side against the other," says Scotto. "That's the way things get done."

Plans were drawn up, but seven years later, in 1975, the area's sewage-treatment plant still had not been built. Maybe federal funds could be secured . . . Scotto appealed to friends with clout in Washington, and one day he got a phone call from an appointee of Vice President Nelson Rockefeller, asking him to come to the White House to make his case for the plant.

Scotto was thrilled. "Imagine, the boy from Carroll Gardens being asked to come to the White House! I told my friends about it, and one of them, Jack Newfield, then editor of *The Village Voice* and a man more worldly and cynical than I was, gave me a bit of advice: 'Take a witness,' he said. 'Don't trust those Republicans.' So what better witness could I take than a priest? Father George Voiland agreed to go with me. But there was a moment on the plane that I'll never forget. Father Voiland suddenly turned to me and asked, 'Buddy, did you verify that call from the White House? Are you sure it wasn't just some prank?'

"I'm sure I turned pale," Scotto recalls. "I was so focused on the need for that sewage treatment plant that it had never occurred to me that maybe this was all some terrible practical joke. I sweated all the way to the White House gates. But the guard checked and yes, Buddy Scotto was expected." The meeting was a success, federal funds finally came available and the plant was built. Sewage that formerly emptied into the Gowanus Canal was diverted to the new treatment plant.

The next step in reviving the canal was to get the flushing propeller repaired so that water from Buttermilk Channel could circulate. Some of Scotto's friends in the Reform Liberal Democrats were pressuring him to run for political office, and to get them off his back he registered as a Republican—only to find his name submitted as a Republican candidate for the New York State Senate. This bombshell had the expected effect on the local Dems. How to get Buddy Scotto back into the Democratic fold? Some key Democratic officeholders secured money to repair the broken flushing propeller, piggybacked on a bill for senior citizen housing.

The propeller began working in 1999, the water began to flow out toward Gowanus Bay, the terrible smells dissipated and marine life began returning. Fish and crabs have actually been seen.

"It took local grassroots organizations to prod them into doing what they should have done twenty years ago," Scotto comments dryly. His dream for the Gowanus Canal has been opposed by some groups who still imagine Brooklyn returning to its status as a manufacturing mecca and want the Gowanus Canal to remain an industrial/commercial site. "That simply isn't going to happen," says Scotto. "Every major city in the country is in the throes of a changing economy, from industrial to a high-tech service economy—restaurants, stores, hotels,

In 1999, children scattered rose petals to celebrate the cleanup.

entertainment and the like. The Gowanus Canal restoration isn't just about Brooklyn—there's a lesson in it for the rest of the country."

Patricia Curtis is an enthusiastic resident of Brooklyn who likes to write about animals and local scenes.

Russell Kaye

Lyric Gowanus

BY SEAN KELLY

It is not widely known (if at all) that before undertaking his classic verse epic "The Bridge" ("O harp and altar, of the fury fused"), poet Hart Crane had sought inspiration in another, humbler Brooklyn landmark: the Gowanus Canal.

In the 1840s, Gowanus Creek was transformed into a commercial waterway, connecting Upper New York Bay to the industrial heart of Brooklyn. By 1900, waste matter spilled from the many enterprises that lined its banks—coal yards, gas houses, paint factories, paper mills— had turned the canal into a reeking cesspool so discolored that the locals nicknamed it "Lavender Lake."

Today, no longer of much commercial use, the Gowanus has finally been flushed and is in the process of becoming a picturesque tourist attraction. As is evident from the first stanza, Crane's passionately incoherent dithyramb can be dated to the early 1920s, when the mob ruled the Red Hook waterfront.

Hart Crane

Sean Kelly is not now and never has been Hart Crane—nor any other crane. He is the author of How to Be Irish (Even If You Already Are), Saints Preserve Us *and* Mr. Potato Head.

O GOWANUS

How many Dons, drilled, riddled through the vest,
The Siegel's scuttled foes, concrete-galoshed,
And in thy velvet aqua deliquesced,
Stain the bay-watered feet of Liberty

Sulcation not well-deep, nor church door-wide,
Brackish backwater, concave corridor,
(When sentences inverted are, we find,
Seems any prose like poetry the more) . . .

Who, from the docked longshore Atlantic swell
Unlocked, cargoes downtown the sea dark wine—
(When verbs are used as substantives within,
Substantially more bardic seems the line),

I think of vulgar boatmen barging in
Thy slow, lentiginous, mephitic stream,
(The more obscure the phraseology,
The more profound the verses always seem.)

And Thee, Thy surface purple as a bruise,
Pranked where blind fishsnouts sunder diesel-wake
Prisms, sect Red Hook, sluicing septic flux,
Retracting still thy Indian-given name.

O seeping Stygian ditch! O seamen's rut!
Keltoid topsoil incision, trench-mouthed portal—
Thy transient manufactories will pass—
Only the poet's gasworks are Immortal.

Brian Merlis Collection; inset: Hart Crane Papers, Rare Book and Manuscript Library, Columbia University

There's Something About the Gowanus

Water changes everything. That must be it. This waterway transforms the character of a whole neighborhood. It defines the streets around it, and it alters the high pale Atlantic light that reflects upward, catching the clouds, the muted hues of the industrial walls and knots of dark hardware, and the resilient mongrel trees that rise stubbornly from its banks. All right, the canal is only a commercial ditch. And yet it always springs a surprise when you clatter across one of its bridges: A wash of Dutch light. A glimpse of coastal objects: pilings, gulls, a barge, a lone boat, even ducks and fish. A vein of Brooklyn history, the Gowanus actually inspires painters, poets, photographers, strollers. And dreamers.

PHOTOGRAPHS
BY RUSSELL KAYE

The Bridges

Because the Gowanus Canal crosses several busy streets, drawbridges are needed to accommodate the barges and tugboats that still ply its waters. The Union Street Bridge (at right) is a conventional modern drawbridge, while the wood-decked Carroll Street Bridge (below), an 1889 engineering landmark, is a cable-operated retractile bridge, one of just four such "swing" bridges still operational in America.

Moving Water

The barge traffic and the pollution—plus an unmistakable rotten smell—had for decades forestalled any thought of recreational uses or residential development along the canal. But a short time after the Butler Street pump began propelling fresher water from the Buttermilk Channel down the length of the canal, the smell was gone. Within months, visitors were noting the presence of schools of lively fish roiling the water.

Brooklyn's Fertile Coast

Confessions of an urban fisherman

BY PETER KAMINSKY

On windy November afternoons, I have watched white-caps and sea foam scudding across the harbor from the Jersey shore as I cast my fly line against the ancient pilings on the Bay Ridge flats. There are flounder here in the spring, fluke in the summer, and all through the fall season bluefish, weakfish and the greatest prize of all: striped bass. I have even seen blue crabs, plump and meaty, crawling over the sandy bottom of Gowanus Creek. Peering down into its windowpane-clear depths, I have seen mussels and oysters in twenty feet of water. There are fish and shellfish all around Brooklyn.

Between the Verrazano Narrows and Norton Point, raucous gulls dive and hit the water, taking their pick of the baitfish that get penned in by larger predators just a stone's throw (or short cast) from Toys R Us. On past Coney Island and Brighton Beach, Russian immigrant anglers cast their lines from the sands into the rich waters at the outflow of Jamaica Bay. On the footbridge between Atlantic Beach and Sheepshead Bay, Russians, Koreans, Greeks and Italians line up with their bait buckets as they sip beer and smoke cigarettes until ungodly hours. Their conversation is the universal fisherman's gab about good luck yesterday, bad luck today, better luck to come, punctuated by lustfully appreciative comments on the miniskirted young ladies who stroll the bridge with their beaus.

At the foot of the Sheepshead Bay Bridge, a dozen or so party boats line the quay: *Helen H, Betty IV, Atomic.* Their full-throated mates entice passing anglers with promises of "heated rails, free coffee, free cartoons" and secret shoals full of reckless game fish. Across the bay the final thin finger of the Rockaways extends toward Breezy Point, and I have stood there along the curving bayside beach well past midnight, casting my popping big lure into the tidal slick, its surface illuminated by the reflection of the Coney parachute jump and lights of the Brooklyn shore. I count the blues and stripers I have

Brooklyn Coastal Fish

1. False albacore
2. Bluefish
3. Blackfish
4. Flounder
5. Herring (alewife)
6. Whiting
7. Fluke
8. Striped bass
9. Weakfish

caught there as Brooklyn fish, for, with Coney Island as my polestar, it seems to me they are as much a part of Brooklyn as I am.

I am a Brooklyn fisherman. I have been one for nearly thirty years. With hundreds of miles of snaking coastline, sandy shallows and fast-running tides, offshore Brooklyn is a fertile fishing ground. Best of all, its waters are close by when one doesn't feel like the long trek to the trout streams upstate or the crowded Hamptons. I have only to walk to the bottom of my street, where Buttermilk Channel separates Cobble Hill from Governors Island, and in the right season, with a little luck, I can be catching fish within sight of my old brownstone—which was built 150 years ago by a gentleman named Degraw who lent his name to one of the prettier tree-lined streets in my neighborhood. I can imagine his wife looking out over the fields that led down to the water, summoning her children home. "Dinner's ready," she might have called, and without intervening traffic her voice would carry to the water's edge where her children would no doubt have protested, "Just one more, Mom."

I have taken my own daughter, Lucy, fishing in the waters of the harbor right off Brooklyn Heights. There is something magical, almost mystical, about passing under a high steel bridge on the East River in a small boat looking for fish. Often, I will end my angling year with a trip to these harbor waters. I have spent two Christmas eves with trout tackle, catching small stripers on flies on the tidal flats over near Ellis Island. I always take a January warm front as a gift from Poseidon by way of a divine hint to cast one more.

During one such warm front a few years ago, Lucy and I joined Joe Shastay, a pioneer harbor fisherman, for an evening's angling. The signboard at the Watchtower showed 60 degrees—not bad for January. The tide was incoming, which meant the water would be warmer than the outgoing tide because the ocean had not yet cooled down to its winter temperature. When the water reached 43 degrees, baitfish started to slash across the surface of Wallabout Creek near the Williamsburg Bridge. Their nervous haste was a sure sign of larger fish pursuing them. Lucy cast her spinning rod downstream into the running tide. *Thwank!* A fish hit. Lucy struck back. Her rod bent, she pulled back and then reeled down to recover line. After a five-minute struggle, a twenty-three-inch striped bass surrendered. A tag had been clipped to its fin. We removed it and released the fish back into the river. We returned the tag to the local scientists who had placed it there as part of their fishery study. Then, in a special year-end lottery of tag retrievers, Lucy was awarded a hundred dollars. In a lifetime of fishing, I can truthfully say that's the only time I or any of my blood relatives have turned a profit on a fishing trip.

Peter Kaminsky writes frequently on fishing and dining for many national magazines.

Russell Christian

The Boardwalk Cafés of Brighton Beach

By Minda Novek

Brighton Beach: the official name may have been borrowed from an English resort, but this place is known now as "Little Odessa." The prevailing language here is Russian, but the émigrés who have made the place their own over the past two decades are from all

over the former Soviet Union: from Uzbekistan, Georgia, Moldova and, mostly, Ukraine.

You can shop or eat or go nightclubbing on Brighton Beach Avenue, but my friends and I always head for the cafés that dot the boardwalk between Fourth and Sixth Streets. A cool breeze off the ocean adds the smells of the briny Atlantic to those of the gastronomic wonders being passed all around us. There are dough-wrapped pelmeni and vareniki (a little like ravioli), caviar, lobster, snails, giant herring, smoked mackerel, borscht (in red, orange and green), chicken "crapes," stuffed quail "in the nest" and duck salad. The home fries come with shiitake or chanterelles. There are cappuccino and kvas, a homemade drink. Champagne is even possible, but

bottles of vodka are the most common sight.

A friend and I first came here on a September evening for an Indian summer swim. As the sky grew dark over the Atlantic, we watched the moon's reflection glow in the water around us. Back toward the boardwalk, the lights of the cafés looked so inviting that we decided to dress and go there for dinner.

Between the first warm weekend of spring and the last one of autumn, I've spent hours at those tables, watching the boats and the bathers, the gulls careening in the sky. The fresh air spices the food and cools the drinks. It sets the tone for a procession of dressed-up, dressed-down and un-dressed strollers on the boardwalk. A shaded pavilion borders the beach, and elderly American Jews—from an earlier, pre-Russian community—gather there to talk, play chess and people-watch.

Day or night, the outdoor cafés are always bustling. Many of the wait staff don't favor English, and our arrival has often been met with a distinctly brusque response—though friendliness and an appreciation of the food usually lighten things up.

Sometimes we end the day shopping along the avenue. Or we head down the boardwalk to the popcorn, hip-hop precinct of Coney Island. Or we walk east to the boardwalk's end and the fishing boats of Sheepshead Bay. Pleasures in both directions, but for me they do not compare with the cafés of Brighton Beach.

Minda Novek is a Brooklyn dancer, performing artist, filmmaker, and writer.

Ted Hardin

The Once and Future Lundy's

Brooklyn's primal seafood restaurant rises again

BY NICK VIORST

Sunday dinner at F.W.I. Lundy Brothers Seafood Restaurant and Clam Bar in Sheepshead Bay was long a Brooklyn tradition. It's a colorful primal memory shared by a large number of Brooklynites and no wonder. On a busy day in the late 1930s, Lundy's would commonly serve 5,000 full meals, and the pace of dining rose to a fever pitch every Mother's Day. On some festive evenings, it must have seemed that every family celebration in the borough was being held at Lundy's.

But the restaurant was not without its idiosyncrasies: there was no maître d' and no reservations system, so securing a table was an exercise in patience and intimidation for would-be diners. The sheer numbers of tables and customers also made it a tough place to work. Roland Hill, a waiter for seven years during the 1930s, recalls that transporting the heaping trays of food through the cavernous rooms could be an exhausting affair.

Lundy's achieved its enormous popularity almost immediately upon its grand opening in 1934. In that

Irving Lundy opened his Spanish Mission–style restaurant on Emmons Avenue in 1934.

Brooklyn Historical Society

Lundy's Now and Again

The restaurant that today bears the Lundy's moniker is not quite the same old Lundy's. It occupies the same Mission-style building on Emmons Avenue and sports the old trademark and the old oyster bar, but the painstakingly crafted cuisine and frantic energy of Irving's original grand establishment now irrevocably belong to the past.

Still, once beyond the expected grumbling of purists and old-timers, the fact is that the resurrected Lundy's offers a first-rate dining experience. This Lundy's is one New York institution that isn't coasting on its famous name.

Lundy's kitchens still (or rather, again) issue hefty portions of fresh, tasty and unpretentious seafood at unintimidating prices. The menu boasts impressive re-creations of many of Irving's specialties, from the walnut-size biscuits to red clam chowder and the popular broiled lobster. To these old reliables the new ownership has added a range of more elaborate dishes and some definitely contemporary offerings like blackened catfish and wood-oven goat-cheese pizza.

On weekends, the cavernous dining room hums with vitality. Wisecracking waiters take and deliver orders with admirable efficiency. This may not be the old Lundy's, but it does the legacy proud. And, thankfully, they've added a maître d', thus eliminating the old Lundy's hassle of finding a table on your own. –*Nick Viorst*

Roland Hill, a longtime waiter at the old Lundy's.

Depression year, the glory days of Sheepshead Bay were long behind. Gone for two decades was the Sheepshead Bay Racetrack, which since the 1870s had entertained guests from the tony Manhattan Beach hotels nearby. Gone, too, was the Sheepshead Bay Speedway, billed in its day as the fastest auto track in the world. And gone were the casinos and fine hotels that had made this distant corner of Brooklyn a haunt for Vanderbilts, Whitneys and other personalities of the Gilded Age. Yet the seafood places along the water were a stable and steady draw. A Lundy's had actually existed since 1926, perched on a rickety wooden pier projecting into Sheepshead Bay with magnificent views of the Atlantic. The restaurant's third-generation-Dutch founder, Frederick William Irving Lundy, had opened it as an adjunct to his family's thriving fish-selling operation. But while the eatery did a brisk business, it was merely a minor prelude to the remarkable establishment that would take its place.

The new Lundy's building rose on the site of the old Bayside Hotel at the corner of Emmons and Ocean Avenues, across the street from the water's edge. The original 1926 eatery had, like all the buildings along the piers, been condemned as part of an early 1930s neighborhood renewal project, but the highly ambitious Irving Lundy was ready to make a grand gesture. The architectural style he selected for his restaurant's reincarnation was Spanish Mission, a look then associated more with private mansions than with commercial establishments. With a red tile roof, sand-colored stucco walls, stained-glass windows, arched ceilings and wrought-iron grillwork, the new Lundy's was stylish and *big*: the two-story structure occupied a full city block and featured two kitchens, multiple dining areas including a patio, a clam bar and a liquor bar. The cost of the construction ran $600,000, no small price tag in the depths of the Great Depression, but Lundy's timing proved perfect. Sheepshead Bay had been losing its society luster, the surrounding blocks of Flatbush, Coney Island and Midwood were being settled by upwardly mobile middle-income Italian and Jewish families. And these same families now flocked to the flashy new restaurant, which served up classy dining at reasonable prices in surroundings of marble, carved wood, wrought iron and even stained glass. Almost at once, Lundy's outshone every other restaurant in its environs, not only the wooden-shack seafood joints clustered around Sheepshead Bay but such venerable neighborhood establishments as Villepigue's and Tappen's.

The menu at Lundy's featured an impressive and, to many first-time visitors, unfamiliar array of treats from both land and sea: lobster (broiled or boiled), oysters (broiled or on the half-shell), clams, shrimp, chowder, fresh fish (purchased from the local purveyors), chicken, steak and plenty of side dishes. Some folks came just for Lundy's miniature biscuits, served piping hot, others for desserts like fresh pies (especially blueberry) and Breyers ice cream. But the true specialty of the

The original old, *old* Lundy's of the 1920s was little more than a seafood shack on a Sheepshead Bay dock.

house, the meal for which Lundy's quickly became renowned, was the Shore Dinner, a formidable combination of shrimp, clam, oyster or crab cocktail, steamed clams, half a lobster, half a chicken, potatoes, vegetables, coffee and dessert—all for one low price of about $5 in the postwar years.

Dining at Lundy's was replete with its own rituals, from the wearing of lobster bibs (which Irving Lundy is credited with inventing) to the after-dinner cleanup in finger bowls brought by the wait staff. Perhaps the most memorable ritual involved the basic act of securing a table. Even on the busiest days, when lines formed down Emmons Avenue, the matter of finding a seat was simply left up to the hungry diners. They would elbow their way into the vast hall, find a family nearing the end of their meal and then hover territorially nearby. Predictably, mad scrambles often erupted when a table was relinquished.

Roland Hill had moved north to Brooklyn from his native South Carolina to seek work and found a full-time job at Lundy's after some summer stints there. He ended up staying seven years and later rose to the vice presidency of the Hotel and Dining Room Workers Union local. To Hill, prime credit for the satisfaction that so many Lundy's diners enjoyed—and that kept them coming back for more—went right to Irving Lundy himself. "Lundy was a fanatic about his food, about the freshness and quality. And he was a fanatic about the service," Hill recalls. But Hill would not shortchange the considerable contributions of the waiters themselves. "Imagine working in that building, with no air-conditioning, the kitchen on Eighteenth Street and you have a station on Ocean Avenue. Waiters would sweat so much, they'd have to repeatedly change into new jackets. A normal weekend shift often ran as many as twelve or even fourteen hours."

Gruff Irving Lundy drove his employees hard and was not above summarily dismissing anyone who failed, even once, to follow his orders. "All the time you tolerated Lundy's," Hill says, "you knew it was a plantation atmosphere, and you knew Lundy was the plantation boss."

Hill's words are double-edged. In those years, Irving Lundy insisted on hiring only blacks for his wait staff. From the captains on down to the busboys, the 200 or so frontline employees were African-American. As was the tradition in many of the finer New York establishments, the staff dressed in crisply starched uniforms and were encouraged to develop personal relationships with the regular customers; the idea was to convey a sort of "Southern" atmosphere. And by and large, as Hill acknowledges, neither waiters nor customers at the time questioned the convention.

Brian Merlis Collection

LUNDY'S FAMOUS BISCUITS

Yield: about 14 biscuits.

Ingredients:
1½ cups plus 3 tablespoons of all-purpose flour
1 tablespoon baking powder
1 tablespoon sugar
½ teaspoon salt
4 tablespoons unsalted butter
4 tablespoons shortening
½ cup milk

Preheat oven to 375 F degrees.

　　Sift the flour, baking powder, sugar and salt into a large bowl. Stir well. Cut the butter and shortening into small pieces and add to the flour mixture. Using your hands or a pastry blender, crumble the fat into the flour mixture until the butter and shortening are pea-size pieces and the mixture resembles coarse cornmeal. Add the milk and mix the dough just until it comes together; be careful not to overmix.

　　Knead the dough gently on a lightly floured work surface. Roll out the dough ½ inch thick; this is a crucial step in making successful biscuits. If you roll the dough out too thin, the biscuits will be dry and overcooked. If you roll it out too thick, they won't cook properly. Using a 2-inch biscuit cutter, or a 2-inch-wide glass, cut out the biscuits and place on an ungreased baking sheet. Roll out the scraps ½ inch thick and cut any additional biscuits.

　　Bake for 14 to 15 minutes, or until the biscuits are golden brown.

　　Serve hot.

(from Lundy's Reminiscences and Recipes *by Robert Cornfield and Kathy Gunst, HarperCollins, New York, 1998)*

Hill regarded his job with a mixture of relief and pride. Relief because, given the generally dire state of the nation's economy, finding any sort of job if you were black was fortunate. And pride because Lundy's was, after all, a classy place to work and it paid well. In an effort to head off any labor organizing on his premises,

Irving Lundy had a practice of paying his employees above union scale, so Hill and his colleagues tended to keep to themselves any grumbling about their boss's rigorous standards. Says Hill, "You didn't kick over the traces because of the necessity of keeping the job."

And there were other satisfactions, too. Although Lundy's did not discriminate against black diners, rarely did they visit the restaurant, if only because so few black families at the time had the means to afford it. Occasionally, though, a black doctor or dentist and his family would walk through the door. Hill remembers, "It was a kind of triumph for us to have our people come in and we tried to give them a little extra service."

Lundy's outlasted the Depression, as well as World War II. It thrived through the 1950s and '60s, providing fine meals and fond memories for generations of Brooklynites. Little changed in the way the restaurant did business (although the tradition of the all-black staff had ended by the time of the civil rights struggles of the sixties). But even as Lundy's carried on, its surroundings were changing. Little by little, the middle-class neighborhood residents who had made up the bulk of its customer base were relocating to the suburbs in Long Island and New Jersey. By the 1970s, Lundy's was no longer profitable. And in 1979, just months after Irving Lundy's death, the restaurant—to the great dismay of generations of loyalists—closed its doors.

Lundy's, however, turned out to be one Brooklyn institution that would not die. In 1995, after sixteen years during which the majestic building stood empty and crumbling, and four years after the city granted it landmark status, Lundy's resurfaced under a new family of owners. Although it now occupies but a portion of the original building on Emmons Avenue, with seating for "only" 800 diners, the old style, the old charm and an impressive approximation of the old cuisine are back. Today, Lundy's is again leading a revival of Sheepshead Bay, and New Yorkers may once again savor the ample delights of a Lundy's Shore Dinner.

Nick Viorst, once a Brooklyn resident and book publisher, comes from a long line of food writers.

Down to the Sea in Party Boats

They're still landing mackerel in Sheepshead Bay

BY YI SHUN LAI

One side of Emmons Avenue, in Sheepshead Bay, Brooklyn, is all storefronts: Loehmann's discount fashion outlet occupies the most obvious space, with Lundy's renascent restaurant and clam bar coming in a close second. But the main reason to visit Sheepshead Bay still lies on the other side of the street—on the water. There, moored to the docks, a dozen or so fishing boats stand ready to take anyone who wishes out onto the Atlantic for a few hours or even a whole day of fishing. This corner of Brooklyn has, in effect, been a fishing village since the early 1800s.

Kevin Bradshaw's boat, the *Dorothy B VIII*, is one of the busiest of the so-called "party" or "head" boats (for "fishing parties" or charging anglers "by the head"). A ninety-foot cruiser, it goes out twice every day during the summer season for half-day fishing and once a day in the fall and winter for full-day trips. Families, couples and people just out for a good time on the water come for Kevin's summertime cruises to Jamaica Bay and half-day fishing trips to Rockaway Inlet. But in the wintertime, when the deep-sea fishing is at its best, Kevin gets the "real" fishermen—people who will go as far out as Sea Bright, New Jersey, in any kind of weather to catch their share of sea bass, porgies, blackfish or mackerel.

Three generations ago, Kevin's grandfather, a housepainter in Hell's Kitchen, was diagnosed with lead poisoning. The family doctor suggested regular trips to the ocean—maybe the fresh sea air would flush out his system. So from 1914 on, the Bradshaws packed up each weekend and went out to Sheepshead Bay to spend some time on the *Dorothy B*, which was named for the only daughter among their four children.

"My grandfather often took his neighbors out with him on the boat," says Kevin, "and sometimes the neighbors would give him money by way of thanking him. Somewhere along the way, a lightbulb went off in my grandfather's head: Hey! We could make money this

Fun and seafood aboard one of Sheepshead Bay's party boats.

Brooklyn Public Library-Brooklyn Collection

way! From that point on, there was no turning back. Although the older Bradshaw didn't pursue the commercial aspect of these trips much longer, his three sons went at it with gusto and traded the original *Dorothy B* for bigger and better boats. Business was so good by the early 1930s that they built their own boat, the *Dorothy B V.* "People said they were crazy to do it," says Kevin. "It was smack in the middle of the Great Depression."

The Bradshaw brothers proved the naysayers wrong. They did more business than any other party fishing boat on Sheepshead Bay during the Depression. Kevin admits that the hard times may have actually contributed to the brothers' success: because fish were so abundant in the area, people pooled their money and sent one person from each apartment house to go fishing; that person could conceivably catch enough fish to feed the entire building.

By the 1950s, when party fishing was at its most popular among New Yorkers, the Bradshaws were by far the most successful. How did they do it? "Sheer customer service," says Kevin. "My uncles and father ran the only boat that made sure no one went home empty-handed. If the customer didn't catch anything, the three brothers gave away the fish that they'd caught themselves."

It helped, too, that the Bradshaw boys were famous for going out to sea in weather that other sea captains wouldn't touch. "They were three tough guys," says Kevin, remembering one such foul-weather day. "They had these twenty-five people lined up on the dock, egging them on: 'Hey! You chicken or what? You yellow?' And my uncles and my dad stood there with their arms crossed, and they were saying, 'No way, guys, we're not going out in that!'" The crowd got louder, though, and the Bradshaw boys, true to their reputation as great customer-service men, finally gave in and took all twenty-five fishermen out.

"There were so many cod out there that my father and my uncles made a killing," says Kevin. "It was great, great cod fishing." And the twenty-five men who had begged so vociferously to be taken out onto the water? "Oh, they were begging to be brought back to shore. It was so bad that twelve of the men who were regulars,

men who showed up faithfully every week to go out, never showed up again."

Now in his fifties, Kevin was working on the boat as a deckhand by the time he was five. "I got seasick easy," he says. "There were days when my dad would have to carry me off the boat. I swore I'd never touch the water again." But come the following weekend he was back on the boat, happy to be fishing and out on the water. "I always loved fishing," he says, "but I never really noticed the other stuff you could do on the water, like bird-watching. When I was a kid, my father would point out these birds on the water. We'd call them loony birds, or helldivers, and they were all the same to me until I took a group of birders out. I learned there were all these different birds. Not knowing that, not realizing that, is like walking through life with your eyes closed."

Kevin takes schoolchildren on cruises during the summer in a partnership with the New York Aquarium and runs bird-watching cruises to Jamaica Bay, a critical stop-off for migratory birds that borders Sheepshead Bay. But he's not sure that he'll be able to hang on to the business for very much longer—fishing regulations and limits on the number of fish customers can catch and take home have taken their toll. "When a customer catches twenty-five fish and has to throw back all of them because they're a half-inch smaller than the regulations say they can be, it takes the fun out of fishing and the life out of the business," says Kevin's wife, DeeDee, who is also the business manager of the *Dorothy B VIII.*

Kevin and DeeDee have sent their two daughters in directions that will take them away from the Sheepshead Bay seafaring life or, at least, into careers that are steadier and more secure: they are both attorneys. "My eldest daughter has her captain's license, and she helped us to run the boat a couple of summers," says Kevin, wistfully. "If I were sure that this kind of life could provide for her, I'd happily give her the business. Truth is, I can't really be sure that it would."

Yi Shun Lai is a skier, bicyclist, fisherperson and writer who lives in Astoria, Queens.

The Floating Opera of Red Hook

A stage, a home, a waterfront museum

BY JANET
REITMAN

Red Hook is the loneliest neighborhood in Brooklyn. It's cut off from the rest of South Brooklyn by the Gowanus Expressway, the subways never reached it and it's on a peninsula—not on the way to anywhere else. Never redeveloped after the postwar decline of shipbuilding, shipping and warehousing that once made Red Hook a bustling waterfront, it remains quiet and lonely. So, these days, it takes a certain type of person to live there. "You have to be able to accept the isolation," explains David Sharps, a Red Hook resident who grew up in the Appalachian foothills of rural Maryland and is accustomed to solitude.

Sharps is different from most urban homesteaders. Trained as a clown by avant-garde French performer Jacques Le Coq, he is captain and caretaker of the Hudson River Waterfront Museum located at the tip of Red Hook's waterfront on the whimsically titled "Garden Pier." The museum's major artifact is, in fact, the museum itself: an eighty-five-year-old barge that Sharps calls the "largest piece of floating wood in New York City."

Homesteading in Red Hook, entertainer David Sharps and family live aboard their barge museum.

Michael Kamber

It also happens to be a year-round home for Sharps, his wife and two young daughters. "It's a very *alternative* way of existence," Sharps, a boyish-looking forty-something, explains one particularly grim November afternoon as the cold wind whips around the wooden hull. "It can get a little rocky sometimes, but we're used to it—most of the time. We're definitely closer to the elements here."

The barge has been a fixture in Red Hook since 1994. Drawing on the tradition of riverfront "show-boats" of the late 1800s, Sharps uses the barge as a performing arts home for area musicians and diverse entertainers who more or less defy easy categorization.

The vessel is listed on the national historic register as one of the only surviving wooden examples of the barge era, which in New York extended from the opening of the Erie Canal in 1825 until the mid-1960s. In their heyday, around 1900, freight barges were commonplace on the Brooklyn waterfront, transporting cargoes from oil to coffee all around the harbor, the East River and the Hudson River. Today, trucks do that kind of heavy lifting, and barges have been abandoned to rot, most passing their last days mired in many layers of mud in backwaters along the New Jersey and Staten Island shores. "New York had the only harbor big enough to have these barges for large cargo. There used to be a line of piers and tens of thousands of people working here in Red Hook. The waterfront was the center of the city's commerce," Sharps says, surveying the nearby shoreline, now empty of commercial craft. A few gulls skid to an awkward landing in the wake of a passing tugboat. "People today don't even realize they're on an island."

Wearing jeans, work boots and a green flannel shirt, Sharps has the look of a deckhand or lumberjack. Once the weather has turned cold, he spends a lot of time tending a large woodstove—the sole heating source for his barnlike kitchen, which doubles as an office and general meeting room. Sharps fell in love with the sea in the mid-1970s, after moving to Florida to try becoming a professional golfer. Instead, he found a job on a cruise ship and spent the next several years entertaining tourists from the Caribbean to the Baltic Sea. Moving to Paris with no money, he was walking along the Seine when he noticed people living in moored barges. Needing a place to live, he asked around and soon found a home. "It was great," he says. "After living on cruise ships, I had a barge on the Seine for two hundred dollars a month."

Moving back to the United States in 1985, Sharps passed through New York and once again found himself drawn to the river: "I had no idea there was any kind of water culture in New York until I was jogging along the West Side Highway one day and saw the boats at the Seventy-Ninth Street Basin." Inquiring, he was told there was nothing available and directed instead to look across the river in New Jersey. He found his current vessel in the Jersey mudflats and bought it for only $500 in 1986.

At least 300 tons of mud lay in the hold of his barge. It hadn't been seaworthy for at least fifteen years. Sharps set to work in hip waders, mixing the mud with water into a slurry, then pumping it out. It was an arduous, two-year-long process that Sharps completed entirely on his own. "Tell people you spend your time pumping mud," he says, smiling. "Even my best friends wouldn't come out to see me more than once." Once the mud was removed, Sharps caulked the seams to prevent further leakage—though even now there are still small holes that have to be constantly monitored.

In fact, making sure the barge stays afloat is a nonstop task. "I'm constantly aware of what's floating in the harbor that might be problematic," Sharps says. A floating log, for example, is enough to cause damage. There are loose or frayed lines that need repair, a host of possible leaks, problematic deck seams, and pumps and switches that might get fouled. "There's always a problem, always something that has to be dealt with."

Kicked out from the Hudson River piers of New Jersey by the rapid development of the "Gold Coast," Sharps haunted the Brooklyn borough president's office in the hopes of finding a dock for his now-floating barge. But there is little available city-owned waterfront space in Brooklyn, and what's left is in such dilapidated condition that it is often condemned. So the borough president's office suggested that Sharps contact private developer Greg O'Connell, who has emerged as a driving force behind the development of the Red Hook waterfront. O'Connell envisions Red Hook as a working waterfront with small businesses and a public walkway. Seeing Sharps' combination residence/performing-arts venue and museum as a welcome addition to this plan, O'Connell was only too glad to have the barge tie up permanently along his stretch of harbor.

"We've finally found a community that appreciates the work we do," Sharps says, "and we fill a great void in Red Hook." Indeed, the barge has been welcomed as a way to bring people—audiences—regularly into the area. Sharps revamped the enclosed deck of the barge with a stage area at one end, an audience space with rows of folding chairs in the middle and a concession area at the other end. Summers, the barge is the site of music and other performance events. On Sunday afternoons, for instance, circus and vaudeville acts perform one after another: slack-wire walkers, jugglers, clowns, comedians, magicians and sleight-of-hand artists. Saturday nights, musicians from solo guitarists to country-rockers, jazz singers to folk-music duos, perform for hours before enthusiastic audiences cooled by the harbor breezes through the opened cargo doors. Winters, there are no performances and Sharps sits at his computer, anxiously trying to raise funds for his landmark floating museum/performing-arts space/home. He's invested over $300,000 in it to date, and the upkeep is a never-ending process.

"I see myself as a caretaker rather than a homeowner," Sharps says proudly. "Maritime historic preservation is one of the things this barge is really about."

Janet Reitman is a Park Slope resident whose work has appeared in the Washington Post, The New Yorker *and, regularly,* Marie Claire.

BROOKLYN ON FILM

The Life of a Longshoreman

The defining American film about life on a tough waterfront, with its "gangster-ridden unions" (to quote playwright Arthur Miller), was certainly the 1954 Elia Kazan eight-Oscar winner *On the Waterfront.* In this classic tale of corruption and redemption, young ex-boxer and dockworker Terry Malloy (Marlon Brando) meets Edie Doyle (Eva Marie Saint in her first film), whose father and brother Joey have joined Father Barry (Karl Malden) in fighting Johnny Friendly (Lee J. Cobb) and the gangsters who control the dockworkers' union. Following the murders of Joey Doyle (who was inadvertently set up by Terry) and his mobster brother Charley, Terry agrees to defy the gangsters and testify against Johnny Friendly at the hearings of the Waterfront Crime Commission. In the end, after a severe beating by the mobsters, Terry—supported by Edie and Father Barry—leads the dockworkers away from the gangsters.

Although most of *On the Waterfront* was filmed in Hoboken, New Jersey, its real subject was the mob-run International Longshoremen's Association local on the Brooklyn waterfront. The Budd Schulberg screenplay was based on a twenty-four-part Pulitzer prize-winning investigative series by reporter Malcolm Johnson for the *New York Sun* and on the 1949 play *The Bottom of the River* by Arthur Miller, who worked briefly on the Brooklyn waterfront. Miller became interested in the fate of a young Brooklyn dockworker named Pete Panto, who vanished while

On the Waterfront, 1954.

campaigning against the gangsters who ran the ILA. Miller rewrote his play as a screenplay, *The Hook,* and although it was not produced, it was a source for *On the Waterfront.* Shortly after the film's release, the AFL-CIO expelled the ILA for corruption, and later the ILA head and other members of the Genovese crime family were indicted for racketeering on the waterfront. *—M.W.R.*

Ohlinger

HARBOR LIFE

The Wharf Rat and Shutterbug

PHOTOGRAPH AND TEXT BY DAVID PLOWDEN

My life was bound up with the waterfront. When I was a boy, my room looked out on the East River and I would go to bed at night looking at the bridges and the boats. I know that this is where my love of the waterfront got started.

I knew every tugboat captain and every ferryboat captain. When I used to listen to the ferries at night, I could tell by their whistles which was a Staten Island ferry and which was the Lackawanna or the Jersey Central ferry. But with the New York Central tugs I could even tell who was in the pilothouse by the way he blew the steam whistle. I remember we used to say, "That's Jacobson, that's old Captain Jacobson." I remember listening to him. Also, on a night that was clear, I could hear the Hudson River boats. And of course I knew all the steamship whistles.

I photographed the last great steamship, *Sagafjord,* for the last year of her life. She was a grand old lady of the sea, and I had permission from the Dalzell Towing Company, which had the contract of docking her, to go out on any one of the tugs that was working. Every time I had a spare minute, I was out on a tugboat and I made connections with all the major tugboat lines in New York. All I had to do was call up the office at 17 Whitehall Street and tell them,

"I want to go out on a tug today."

One day I went out with my first wife, Pleasance, on the Dalzell tug that undocked the *Sagafjord.* The tug captain very kindly brought us back to Brooklyn Heights, where we lived at the time, but the immigration people came on board before we could get off. The captain said, "I think these people want to talk to you." Pleasance was wearing a Norwegian jacket that my mother had given her, and she had very light hair, so they thought she was coming into the country illegally. And we had no identification to prove that she was my wife or that we were citizens. They took us to their office and held us for hours while they checked. We called City Hall and the church where we had our wedding—trying to prove we were married. Finally they realized that Pleasance was not an illegal alien and told us we could go.

They had been watching the waterfront—I had no idea of it. They warned us: "Don't do this again. The next time you go out in the harbor, take something to prove you're an American citizen, because people do sneak into the country this way."

David Plowden's books of black-and-white photography include A Time of Trains, Tug Boat, The Hand of Man on America *and* Abraham Lincoln.

The Greatest View in the World

Except one night when the lights went out

BY ANNE
KOSTICK

One hot, beautiful summer night in 1977, I was having dinner with some friends after work when the Big Blackout—New York City's second—flung the entire city into darkness. Back then New York was more reviled than revived, and we needed another catastrophe like a hole in the head.

Sure, there was civil disorder, but I had a good time. Bars and restaurants partied until the ice melted. Folks were friendly to strangers in a way that occurs only during a crisis. This is not to say that the blackout didn't

have a direct personal effect on me: no electricity meant no air-conditioning, no subway service—no way home to Brooklyn. I stayed at a friend's apartment and fell asleep to the sounds of sirens chasing happy-go-lucky looters. The night passed noisily, heatedly, uneasily.

The next day was like a hangover. Still without power, the city tried to go about its business, but mostly gave up. Residents arose late from their beds and milled around on the shady sides of the street. Commuters were nowhere to be seen, of course. Most people just plain didn't know what to do, but I had my task ahead of me—getting back home to Brooklyn. I staked out a corner of Broadway and Seventy-Second Street, and eventually an MTA bus came by and took me to City Hall, stopping at every intersection to help footsore citizens get where they were going. The trip took about two hours. From City Hall, my travel options shrank to just one if I didn't want to swim. I walked across the Brooklyn Bridge.

That thirty-minute stroll is a pleasure, even when it's a necessity. Traveling east that afternoon, I turned my back on Manhattan and left the chaos behind. The air grew cooler, tanged with brine. Once back on the Brooklyn side, I headed for the Brooklyn Heights Promenade.

The Promenade is a mile-long stretch of octagon-paved elevated walkway that accompanies part of the Brooklyn waterfront, overhanging both roadways of the Brooklyn-Queens Expressway. People visit the Promenade to take pictures of the famous Manhattan skyline, not realizing that their pictures are brought to them courtesy of The Biggest Borough. Tourists snap and gawk while locals jog, walk their dogs, sit, read, lick ice-cream cones and generally take for granted one of the world's great urban spectacles.

The Promenade should have a commemorative sculpture depicting The Defeat of Robert Moses by

Russell Christian

the Well-Bred Residents of Brooklyn Heights. Without that victory, the Heights would today be chopped in two by the Expressway, as were less fortunate and less powerful neighborhoods. And without the triumphal Promenade, I would never have experienced my Singular Event. Everyone who lives in Brooklyn, of course, knows this little secret: Manhattan looks a lot better from over here than from over there. More beautiful, less devouring.

I sat down on one of the benches facing that million-dollar view, a vista that stretches from the Statue of Liberty in the harbor to the Staten Island ferry building at the south end of the island and all the way to the Chrysler Building at Forty-Second Street, with the Brooklyn Bridge in between. Helicopters were still circling over the East River. Tugboats and barges continued to plow upriver and down; ferries and sailboats crossed back and forth, off the power grid and its confinements, free to live just as if Con Ed were on-line after all.

It had taken most of the day to regain my home turf, and now dusk was coming on. The New Jersey horizon turned gold, then pink—a perfectly normal Jersey sight. Liberty gleamed out in the water. The sky became deep blue.

But one thing was different about this sunset. New York City had no lights at all. Nothing decorative atop the most famous skyscrapers: Woolworth, Empire, New York Life, Chrysler; nothing functional below. Nothing. And as the sky grew more intensely blue, the skyline began to stand out in silhouette before it, like a jagged cutout of black paper.

And then, in a moment, it was dark. Really dark. Dark like an upstate apple orchard during a new moon. Dark like you never see in the city that never remembers to turn off the lights. The constant hum of the Expressway, the helicopters and the boats seemed to recede—the city disappeared.

It had happened in a moment, and it lasted only a moment. Then someone somewhere with Con Ed, perhaps at some switching station, finished his splice and the power at last came back on. Not all at once, though. A single building at the southern tip of Manhattan sprang into blazing light. Then the building just north of it lit up. Then, with studied speed, each building in turn, a Milky Way of stars flowing smoothly north, lighting up. I held my breath without knowing it. My head swiveled to the right, following the flow of lights as they sailed up the river's edge and then disappeared around the bend at about Twenty-Third Street. The sky faded to charcoal. The city that never sleeps woke up.

I had seen the city vanish completely into the darkness and reappear so brilliantly that it lit up the sky around it, becoming again the shining postcard we all take for granted. I would not take it for granted, henceforth. The light was a gift.

I exhaled and looked around. I was, surprisingly, the only person in sight along the entire Promenade. This Singular Event was mine alone.

Thanks, Brooklyn.

Anne Kostick is a resident of Windsor Terrace and a walker in the city.

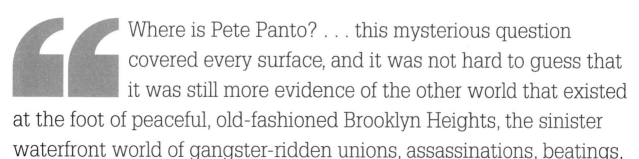

"Where is Pete Panto? . . . this mysterious question covered every surface, and it was not hard to guess that it was still more evidence of the other world that existed at the foot of peaceful, old-fashioned Brooklyn Heights, the sinister waterfront world of gangster-ridden unions, assassinations, beatings, bodies thrown into the lovely bay at night." **Arthur Miller**

Made in Brooklyn

"There's a factory someplace in Brooklyn that makes these things" is an observation that's been a commonplace for over a century, referring to practically anything from tin ceilings and cast-iron storefronts to beer, CDs and laxatives. Brooklyn has never been identified as a single-product stronghold, like Pittsburgh with its steel or New England with its textiles. Instead, in manufacturing as in so many other areas of Brooklyn life from nationalities to slang, the watchword is variety—and indeed variety that extends so widely as to reach into fringes of novelty and downright wackiness. Yes, pencils and extension cords and Linotype machines have been made in the same neighborhood, but so have penicillin and some of the best men's suits stitched up anywhere in the world. Then there's pale ale and mozzarella balls and carousel horses...

Previous spread: Bagels warm and fresh-baked daily just might be Brooklyn's favorite product.

Previous spread: Ted Hardin; this page: Picture Collection, New York Public Library

The Best Cheesecake in the Galaxy

Junior's serves up a legend

BY MARGARET
A. DALY

Hard fluorescent light bangs on the vinyl banquettes and brass detailing, bearing down on cheesecake maker, monger, philosopher Alan Rosen. The place is noisy, and it's not just the strong light and orange upholstery. It's the constant clank of cup to saucer, fork to plate, and the three dozen or so patrons uttering fragments into the air. The main dining room of Junior's restaurant and delicatessen is a cavernous space that nags warmly in Brooklynese: "You like the chicken salad, this I know. But how about saving some room for a cup of coffee and a piece of the best cheesecake in the galaxy?"

It's a very loud room and Alan Rosen is its center. This is his Algonquin and the cheesecakes in the pastry case, his viciously delicious circle. "We're not a graham-cracker house," he says, shaking his head, his face contorted almost into a sneer. "A *pie* has a crust. A cheesecake should be a cheese *cake*." Hence, the sponge cake bottom layer of the famous Junior's cheesecake.

Diets out the window: Junior's bakes a thousand cheesecakes every day in Downtown Brooklyn.

Cheesecakes were not yet a featured attraction when Harry Rosen opened Junior's in 1950 at DeKalb and Flatbush.

Rosen is a third-generation cheesecake man. His grandfather, Harry Rosen, opened Junior's in 1950 at DeKalb Avenue and Flatbush Avenue Extension on the edge of Downtown Brooklyn. Harry Rosen knew he needed to offer something distinctive to make his restaurant stand out. He sampled cheesecakes from all over the city seeking that characteristic that would make his own cheesecake special—lots of cheese and a sponge bottom.

Alan's father, Walter, and his uncle Marvin were conscripted—happily and willingly, but conscripted nonetheless—into the business as it grew. Alan, who also works with his brother Kevin, was drawn by the "glamour" of long hours, hard labor and the constant pressure of getting food from kitchen to table. "I loved when my father would knock on my bedroom door at four or five in the morning on days we didn't have

school," he recalls. "My father didn't come to Little League games or school plays. If we wanted to see him, we had to come to the restaurant." Alan's first job was the tedious task of separating hundreds of doilies for cheesecake platters with his clumsy small-boy's hands. He's broken his share of dishes—but he knows how to make a cheesecake.

Junior's got to be legendary because Harry Rosen wanted it to be. He could see there were easier, cheaper ways to make cheesecake: gelatin, cornstarch, chemicals and enzymes can be added to the batter to make it creamier without using so much cream cheese, thereby increasing the volume and profit margin. "But we can't do that," says Alan emphatically. "Everyone has an eye on us."

The cheesecake was always what distinguished Junior's from other downtown lunch counters, but it

Brooklyn Historical Society

received its knighted status when *New York* magazine dubbed it the "best cheesecake in New York" in 1974. And Rosen has not changed it since then.

Rosen charges into the bakery—the cheesecake sanctuary—and suddenly he's like a peacock in full display mode. He spreads his arms wide, embracing the entire kitchen, and puffs up his chest. "You see this?" He pries open a hot oven to expose row after row of pans baking nothing. "We dry the pans so no moisture seeps into the cheesecake." He snaps the oven door shut. This is a finicky, i-dotting, t-crossing operation. "Who does this?" he demands in the loud, edgy way that is Brooklyn's charm and pride. "No one does this" is the obvious answer. "This is what we do. Why would we change it?" he argues persuasively with no one at all.

The bakery is massive. At 6,000 square feet, it's about twice the size of the average suburban home. It's bigger than the restaurant itself, which sprawls forty feet down Flatbush and another forty down DeKalb. It's big-

ger than most restaurants' entire space. Tall carts layered with tray upon tray of rising buns are arranged at one end of the kitchen, waiting for the ovens. Giant pastry mixers mark off different sections. The floor is swept clean but for the errant spatter of flour. Most of the dozen workers on the morning shift are Dominican and Puerto Rican men who concentrate on their tasks in zen-like silence. One is checking the progress of the buns. Another is gracefully painting layer cakes with pretty, buttery icing. Several of the workers are engaged in cheesecake production.

Two men are slowly and precisely cutting the light sponge cake into half-inch layers that will cover the bottom of the pan and form the base of the cheesecake. Another team is greasing pans. Still another man is scraping pans clean and preparing them for the next shift. In a year they will crack a million eggs and beat over 500,000 pounds of cream cheese. The work seems endless. A thousand cheesecakes—300 of those shipped

Anatomy of a Great Cheesecake

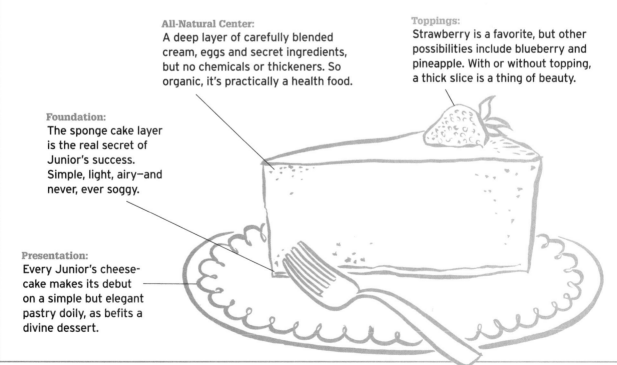

All-Natural Center:
A deep layer of carefully blended cream, eggs and secret ingredients, but no chemicals or thickeners. So organic, it's practically a health food.

Toppings:
Strawberry is a favorite, but other possibilities include blueberry and pineapple. With or without topping, a thick slice is a thing of beauty.

Foundation:
The sponge cake layer is the real secret of Junior's success. Simple, light, airy—and never, ever soggy.

Presentation:
Every Junior's cheesecake makes its debut on a simple but elegant pastry doily, as befits a divine dessert.

Russell Christian

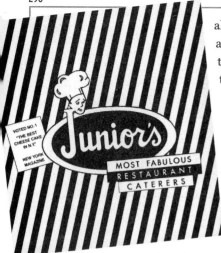

all across the globe—are baked daily and they are all exactly the same. *Exactly*.

Rosen opens another oven and peers in on pans of golden cream, all of them identical right down to the swirl in the center. "Do you see that?" he asks, holding the oven open and gazing proudly as if at a newborn in a hospital nursery. "They all look the same." He nods and smiles. "Nobody does that. I guarantee you, we make cheesecake the same way we made it in 1960." He closes the oven door quietly in order not to disturb the incubation.

The cheesecake-making is all by hand, all craft. But the beauty is not in the imprimatur of each hand that shaped it, but in carefully integrating mass production with devotion to perfection in creating each cheesecake in the exact image of the original that Harry Rosen christened "Junior's cheesecake." It's why we like a studio recording rather than a live version of our favorite song; we know it will always sound the same no matter how many times we play it or what changes the artist may make to his music.

And there has been tremendous change all around Junior's. Downtown Brooklyn used to be a family destination, with A&S Department Store sharing the block with May's and Korvettes. Thirty-five years ago, Flatbush was a busy strip of off-Broadway theaters and music venues. In the 1970s and 1980s, crime became a commonplace; a favorite Christmas Eve tradition among teens was to break shop windows after the shoppers had gone home. Now, still every bit as busy, Downtown Brooklyn is a haphazard collection of stores that sell expensive sneakers, knockoff handbags and electronics. In between those stores are street vendors infusing the air with incense, merchants hawking African-American

virtue in paintings and colorful fabrics. Most of the businesses are owned and operated by immigrants and seem to change hands frequently. Representatives from business groups, the adjacent Metrotech office development and even the borough president's office keep trying to remake downtown. But Junior's, with its vertical sign and bright red front extending a city block west and north, seems impervious to change whether good or bad.

Junior's cheesecake is no longer a mere dessert. It is a symbol—a shout from Brooklyn heard round the world. People pay big bucks to have a Junior's cheesecake shipped in for a party. It's also a message board. During the 1995 criminal trial of O.J. Simpson in Los Angeles, Junior's retaliated against a perceived bad call by Judge Ito by sending him a cheesecake that read "Brooklyn to Ito: Bite Me." Brooklyn-born Mayor Rudy Giuliani wagered a Junior's cheesecake in a bet with the mayor of Atlanta over whose town would be victorious in the 1999 World Series. If the Yankees lost the series, Giuliani promised a cheesecake. The Yankees prevailed, but Alan Rosen sent a cheesecake to Atlanta anyway to let Georgians know exactly what they lacked.

Rosen is a compulsive evangelist about the cheesecake he fervently believes in. In the mid-1990s, he began to appear on the television shopping channel QVC. In one twenty-four-hour period of extolling the virtues of the sponge-bottom cakes, he sold 26,000 special heart-shaped cheesecakes for Valentine's Day. One caller, caught up in Rosen's infectious enthusiasm, confided on the program that she had gotten engaged in front of Junior's. "We bought a cheesecake and right outside my boyfriend told me to open the box. Inside a dollop of whipped cream was my engagement ring."

"Junior's cheesecake is the most identifiable product from New York," says Rosen, as committed to upholding the past as he is in charting the future. "We have to do what we do. We just have to."

Margaret A. Daly is the author of Brooklyn Eats *and a veteran writer on food, health and fitness.*

Courtesy of Junior's

The Domino Effect

Domino Sugar's presence on the Williamsburg waterfront traces back to 1857, when the Havemeyer family moved their sugar refining business across the East River from lower Manhattan for more efficient transport of raw materials. Brothers William and Frederick C. Havemeyer had emigrated from England and in 1807 started a sugar refinery on Vandam Street.

The gaunt cluster of industrial buildings at South Third and Kent Avenue, built in 1882, is still in operation with raw sugar being offloaded from ships directly into the plant and refined sugar emerging in the familiar yellow Domino brand boxes. It is the last surviving example of an industry that boomed in the decades following the Civil War. In those years, most of the sugar refined in America was processed around New York Harbor, with over a dozen refineries in Brooklyn—many of them on the Williamsburg and Greenpoint waterfront.

The sugar refining industry was dominated by Domino—although that brand was not established until around 1920, when the Havemeyer family's American Sugar Refining Company took to marketing domino-like sugar cubes. The Havemeyers' first plant in Williamsburg had a daily production capacity of 300,000 pounds of refined sugar and gradually grew until it was producing a million pounds a day. When the existing buildings were erected after a fire in 1882 destroyed the original factory, American Sugar's capacity rose to three million pounds per day. At the same time, the sugar industry was consolidating and the Havemeyer family bought into or gained control of other refineries and formed what became known as the "Sugar Trust," following that era's familiar pattern of monopolistic industry control. There were repeated tangles with the federal government over monopolistic and unfair business practices during the early twentieth century as competition revived and the Havemeyers' company—variously named American Sugar, National Sugar, Domino and Amstar—lost market share. In 1988 the company was sold to a British sweetener firm, Tate & Lyle, although the big "Domino" sign continues to glow on the East River. Since then, the big refinery has been racked by bitter labor disputes, with hundreds of members of the International Longshoremen's Association being on strike and locked out by Tate & Lyle, a corporation with a history of union-busting. —*Genia Gould*

Brooklyn Public Library-Brooklyn Collection

Where Do Carousels Come From?

Would you believe a factory in East New York?

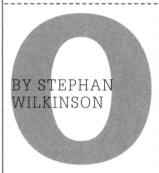

BY STEPHAN
WILKINSON

On the wall of Marvin Sylvor's cluttered office above a former door-parts warehouse in a Karachi-grim industrial section of East New York is a cartoon. It shows a roomful of Philosophy 101 students. All but one are assiduously reading textbooks titled *Plato*. The lone exception has a box of Play-Doh in front of him and over his head is a balloon lettered "Uh-ohh..."

"That's me," says Sylvor, a lapsed industrial-design student who became the country's preeminent manufacturer of custom amusement ride carousels. "I went to Pratt, but it was much too serious. I remember one classroom exercise that involved measuring precisely the angle of the point on the tip of a fork. Now, I know that angle's important"—Sylvor smiles—"but it's not *that* important."

Instead of turning out precisely angled domestic implements, Sylvor started Fabricon Carousel Company. The merry-go-rounds it creates are riotous collections of intensely colored cherubs and jesters, gaily painted panels, lights, mirrors, gimcracks, phantasmagorical Art Deco ornamentation and riding animals that range from traditional caparisoned horses to fanciful saddled frogs and a kangaroo drawn by a four-year-old. And in the case of one recent commission for the City of Nashville, a Sylvor carousel caricatures not only the Everly Brothers but also a highly regarded Nashville rabbi and a local hospital famed for establishing the first medevac helicopter service.

The Nashville carousel, which opened in 1998, was designed by artist Red Grooms. "He told me he'd always wanted to be a carny," Sylvor says, "and because he came from Nashville he wanted to establish a carnival there called Redville. The mayor said, 'We can't do a whole carnival. How about a carousel?'" For $1,300,000, Sylvor's company built Nashville a one-of-a-kind carousel, casting in fiberglass the figures designed by Grooms and paid for by proud Nashvillites bankrolling a riverfront development project.

Many of Sylvor's contracts take him even farther from Brooklyn—fifty-four Fabricon carousels are currently cranking throughout the United States as well as in Saudi Arabia, Singapore, Hong Kong, Bolivia and Brazil. But a recent project for a shopping mall in Dubai, in the United Arab Emirates, was the only carousel that Sylvor didn't himself travel to erect. "It was a disaster," he admits. "They couldn't get it to run, they were yelling that the royal family was coming to the opening...the guy we sent to be in charge was terrified that the Arabs were going to cut his hands off and throw him in some dungeon. He ran away. Came back to Brooklyn frightened to death."

It's not easy. "You spend a year building a carousel, and then you've got boxes and boxes of parts and figures and you ship them to São Paulo, and you can only hope they get there in good shape," Sylvor says with a shudder. "Then you go down there and start putting things together, and you pray that everything goes okay. Things might run fine here, in our factory, but you put them in another environment and you just don't know.

"But then it runs, and they bring in two hundred kids, and the carousel is full of people loving it and laughing, and I'm standing there going, 'Tell me again, how does this little miracle happen?' I'm always amazed when you go back a year later and it's still running, and people are happy and it's actually making money."

Champing at the bit: unpainted fiberglass horses, meticulously carved to order for customers around the world.

Sylvor is too modest. He knows perfectly well how to make a carousel run. For his own carousels, he oversaw the development of a reliable, modern version of the cranky operating mechanism that rarely rose above its nineteenth-century roots. "The big problem with those old machines was maintenance, particularly lubrication," he explains. "The old machines were put into amusement parks, and those guys just repaired them every day. Now you need to put one in a shopping mall with union maintenance people who don't even want to pick up a broom." So Sylvor developed a simple, reliable electric drive mechanism with greaseless bushings, electronic controllers and individual mini-motors driving the obligatory bobbing horses—or tigers, ostriches, camels, giraffes or rabbis.

So, obviously Sylvor was the kind of kid who took apart alarm clocks and hot-rodded his car? "No. Never! I have absolutely no mechanical intuition. I remember I had some little car and a job as a teenager working in a gas station in the Bronx, pumping gas, and one time my car wouldn't run. I tried the spark plugs, the points, the few things I knew anything about, and the thing was just

Stanley Greenberg

As the leader in custom carousel work, Fabricon does not limit itself to traditional figures of horses.

out of gas. I had the overalls, I worked in a gas station, but I couldn't put my car back together. It was humiliating.

"But in Brooklyn there are resources everywhere," Marvin says. "There are machine shops right next door, my metal shop is down the street, there's a bearing distributor up the street, the guy who sells us motors and gearboxes is right here . . . Brooklyn is an incredible place to find little crafts companies, parts companies."

It's also appropriate that Fabricon is in Brooklyn, for the carousel as Americans know it—flamboyant and Disneyish rather than Euro-realistic and classic—had

its beginnings in the hands of engineer William Mangels, who built many of the rides at Coney Island. Another carousel landmark is not far away. "Arguably the rarest carousel in the world is in Queens, in Forest Park," Marvin says. "It was done by a guy named Daniel Muller, who was the only classically trained sculptor to work on carousels. He made twelve of them, and this is the only one left in its entirety, running." Running, Marvin is too modest to add, because he himself totally restored it, as Fabricon's first project, in 1983.

Sylvor began his career by creating ornamental art—

Stanley Greenberg

cartoony fiberglass sculpture—for stores, restaurants, "anyplace that needed some kind of fun ambience," he says. "I got an assignment in the early 1980s to do some stuff for the vertical mall in Herald Square, where every floor was supposed to represent a different part of New York. The fifth floor was to be Central Park, and somebody said, 'You know, there's a carousel in Central Park, can you do one for up here?' I said, 'Yeah, we can do that. I'll get somebody else to build the machinery.'"

Then the South Street Seaport called, wanting a carousel, "and I said to myself, 'Maybe this is a business. Maybe all of a sudden we're experts.'" But Marvin quickly found himself dealing with endless problems posed by his machinery suppliers—ill-fitting parts, late deliveries, bungled orders—and decided that if he was going to be in the carousel business, he'd better learn to make his own machinery.

Fabricon is not the only carousel manufacturer in the country, but it's the only one that does custom work. "We lose seventy to eighty percent of our potential business to a big company called Chance," Sylvor explains. "They do three hundred million dollars in business a year, but they make only stock carousels and rides. They cannot *veer*. We can veer. Our path is called veer. Tell us what you want, what you would like on your carousel. That's what we can do."

Fabricon frequently gets calls from enthusiastic individuals who think it would be way cool to have a personal carousel like Michael Jackson's. "Until we tell them what it costs," Sylvor says. A basic Fabricon carousel, twenty-two feet in diameter with two rows of stock horses, can be had for $150,000, but most larger, custom-designed rides come in at $500,000 or more. Sylvor can build one as big as sixty feet across in his East New York shop. "That's why we're here. I couldn't find affordable space anywhere else that was big enough, without columns, to set up a carousel that wide. East New York was an industrial area that was being redeveloped. Also there are a lot of agencies trying to get work here for people who don't want to spend two hours and three dollars a day on transportation."

Carousels are the most expensive of small amusement park rides (other than roller coasters and the like) to make. A typical mass-produced ride with six whirling teacups or little looping airplanes costs fifty thousand dollars or so. "A good carousel is thirty horses, and each one is four or five thousand dollars, forget the pole, the brasswork, the stirrups," says Sylvor. "That's a hundred and fifty thousand, and you don't have a carousel yet." Barbra Streisand's solution was to buy a single Fabricon horse. "We get lots of requests for individual animals, just as sculpture," Marvin says. "We charge four thousand, sometimes less. Depends how we feel. We did some for a lady in Florida for twelve hundred. She's a nice lady, and everything she owned was destroyed by Hurricane Andrew. We're helping her rebuild."

Sylvor's business itself is as cyclical as a hurricane. In 1997, Fabricon built five carousels. In 1999, it began the year with nine contracts and every one fell through. "My ex-wife never could understand it," Marvin muses. "Some years we'd make a lot of money, some years not. But she came from that mind-set where you were supposed to make the same amount of money each week. I don't know the difference. I've never had another job."

At the suggestion that he doesn't actually have "a job" yet, the man who might otherwise be designing forks whoops, "That's right! I'm still playing around . . ."

Stephan Wilkinson is the kind of guy who took apart clocks and hot-rodded cars and found time to edit both Flying *and* Car and Driver *magazines, and to write hundreds of magazine articles.*

Burn high your fires, foundry chimneys! cast black shadows at nightfall! cast red and yellow light over the tops of the houses!" **Walt Whitman**

The Ansonia Clockworks

Who knew Father Time lived for half a century in Brooklyn? Well, at least in the form of Ansonia Clock Company, which occupied an entire city block of South Park Slope. Time, however, was not on Ansonia's side. The watch and clock manufacturing company went out of business in 1929.

Still, clock collectors all over the world covet the figurine cases, swing clocks and other unusual novelties produced by the company. In the Brooklyn heyday of Ansonia, a regional newspaper proudly proclaimed in 1924 that "in watches and clocks Brooklyn is one of the great leaders. There are no other clock factories near Greater New York which in any way approximate the Ansonia plant. Perhaps there are other firms of like size in the country, but they are not near New York and they are not in Brooklyn."

One of the first large companies to locate in downtown Brooklyn, Ansonia manufactured a line of products that included inexpensive watches and brass clocks (10,000 watches a day was the reported output in 1924, when there were 1,500 Ansonia employees). All the internal elements and external casings were produced entirely in the Brooklyn plant.

When the company wound down and stopped in 1929, it sold its equipment and machinery to a clock-making concern in Russia. Many of the Ansonia workmen spent several months training laborers in the production of watches and clocks. It is believed that the Russian factory may still be in production

today since mechanical timepieces are still being produced there.

Ansonia Clock Company traces its beginnings to Bristol, Connecticut, in 1841, when it was a brass clock manufacturing company formed by Theodore Terry, the nephew of a man who introduced the production of cheap clocks in the first decade of the nineteenth century, and businessman Franklin C. Andrews. Terry & Andrews prospered, producing thirty-hour weight-driven clocks as well as thirty-hour and eight-day spring-driven models. In 1850, the business underwent leadership changes and was relocated to a village west of New Haven called Ansonia (after businessman Anson Phelps, who became a principal in the firm).

The company joined forces with Henry Davies, a Brooklyn businessman who was influential in bringing the clockworks to Park Slope. Before long, Ansonia was offering 314 different clocks for sale and reaping considerable profits.

After 1929, the four remaining stately buildings of the Brooklyn factory housed many different industries. Then, in 1978, a lasting legacy was ensured when the building were refurbished into residential cooperative apartments with a pleasant courtyard that is reputed to offer reprieve from the hustle and bustle of the city streets. When it went residential it served as an important centerpiece for the renaissance of the Park Slope South neighborhood.—*Genia Gould*

The Essential Knish

Mrs. Stahl baked the best

BY MARGARET
A. DALY

Nobody ever had to tell Pat Murphy, now Pat Singer, where to get knishes. Although knish stands were ubiquitous in the 1950s in Brighton Beach, a mostly Jewish seaside neighborhood of small houses built just an arm's length apart, Mrs. Stahl's is the only one that remains—and the only one that people really remember.

Each summer Pat and her sister left their Jewish mother and Irish father behind in Queens to enjoy the cool breezes and the sandy playground at their grandmother's house in Brighton Beach. And nearly every summer day the two girls walked hand in hand to Mrs. Stahl's Knishes. As they approached, Pat could smell the potato, onion and doughy bread overtaking the salty air and pushing past the scent of fresh laundry hung out to dry between the apartments that rose above the Brighton Beach Avenue shops.

Inside Mrs. Stahl's store was all commotion. A crowd—mostly women—swarmed the counter, calling out orders in Yiddish and English, while others bustled about the store exchanging neighborhood news. "There were accents everywhere. It was loud in there, but we made our way through the crowd," Pat recalls. The counter stretched along the left side, and the entire rear wall was an oven. "We'd watch wide-eyed as the knishes came out of the oven. You could never see them being made; that was done in the back."

Pat and her sister ordered their knishes—Pat's favorite is the grainy kasha-filled—and wandered back out to the street. As traffic at the busy corner buzzed past, the girls savored their knishes. "We'd peel back the wax paper just a little bit and take that first bite. It was so good. I think the first bite was the best." The girls stepped lightly along the sidewalk, maneuvering through throngs of people to the beach.

It was on that beach, rather than in the stand at the corner of Coney Island and Brighton Beach Avenues, that Mrs. Stahl got started. In the midst of the Great Depression, Mrs. Stahl—a kindly Jewish mother, clad in a threadbare, dark wool frock—baked dozens and

Mrs. Stahl's successors in Brighton Beach still serve 'em up her way—baked, not fried.

Michael Kamber

Mozzarella Like No Other

In a ramshackle shop on lower Court Street, Joe Caputo makes mozzarella fresh every day and often several times a day. Each morning before the shop opens at eight A.M., Caputo plunges his hands into a cauldron of scalding-hot water and a mixture of curds and whey. He pulls out a taffy-like substance—the curd minus the whey—and then twists it into a ball before dropping it into a pan. He quickly repeats the process until, in about ten minutes, he has formed a mountain of fresh mozzarella.

Sometimes he pulls out small round balls of mozzarella called bocconcini. Sometimes he braids the curd to give the cheese a handsome finish. Making it right, however, takes a certain amount of sensitivity, instinct and a willingness to risk getting burned by the scalding water. Caputo, who opened the store a year and a half after he migrated to Brooklyn from Mola di Bari in 1974, works with his sons Frank and Vito. Frank knows how to make cheese, "but my father"—he shrugs his shoulders—"my father is the one who really knows."

Some of the mozzarella is made with cow's milk and some is made with the milk of water buffalo. In Italy, before World War II, all mozzarella was made with the latter. The Nazis killed off the herd of water buffalo as they were fleeing Italy, so Italians made do with cow's milk. The herd has been replaced, and now fresh buffalo milk is shipped in daily from Italy. By today's gourmet standards, that would make the mozzarella di bufala downright exotic and Joe Caputo an artisanal cheesemaker who could be charging megabucks for his cheese if he sold it in the foodie havens of Manhattan and elsewhere. But this is Brooklyn, and Caputo's nonpareil mozzarella is taken in stride by his regular customers, who see it as just another nice feature of the neighborhood. —*M.A.D.*

dozens of potato knishes daily in her tiny kitchen. Boldly, she marched the boardwalk and the beaches of Coney Island and Brighton Beach hawking knishes in the hot sun, surely mindful that her family's survival depended on her. It was not until 1935 that she opened her soon-to-be legendary store and coaxed her adoring fans to come to her.

The knish was a staple in the Jewish diet. Les Green, the current owner of Mrs. Stahl's Knishes, says: "The knish is to Jews what pasta is to Italians, what potatoes are to the Irish." A knish (the "k" is pronounced) is a hand-sized pocket of dough traditionally filled with potato, kasha or cheese and baked. It's deceptive:

it looks and feels heavy, and can weigh a half-pound or more, but it's nutritious even by today's standards; a potato knish baked contains seven grams of protein, seven grams of fat and forty grams of carbohydrates. It has fewer than 300 calories and is loaded with enough potassium to revive even the most weary. Singer says the flaky crust is light, so that the knish is filling, but it doesn't feel like an iron weight in the stomach.

Around this simple food has grown a legend. Pat Singer is certain she met the real Mrs. Stahl when she was a kid: "I remember a gray-haired old Jewish lady who was short and chubby and nice. Always nice." Says Les Green, "Mrs. Stahl was no kid when she started this business—she was around fifty in 1935—and she was done with it long before she sold to the Weingast brothers in 1960. People who say they remember Mrs. Stahl probably remember Mrs. Stahl's daughter."

Green is protective of the pedigree entrusted to him, but knishes for him, as for Mrs. Stahl, are a serious business. The hefty, crisp, potato- or cabbage-filled baked dough *is* created from the same formula that Mrs. Stahl handed down to Morris and Sam Weingast when they bought her twenty-five-year-old business in 1960. The brothers added mushroom, kasha and spinach fillings but did not trifle with the dough recipe that was passed on to Les Green when he, in turn, bought the business in 1985. Green sells knishes wholesale all around the country. They can be bought at a markup at the fashionable specialty store Citarella on the Upper West Side of Manhattan or by mail directly. He'll ship a dozen knishes anywhere for $59. "People are obviously buying nostalgia," he says, aware that the current price is a long way from Depression food. Green has a repertoire of stories about people long gone from Brooklyn who come back to Mrs. Stahl's. Recently, one fellow took a cab from JFK Airport directly to Mrs. Stahl's to eat his first knish after seven years in the Foreign Service.

The neighborhood and the store itself have grown and evolved. Most of the European Jewish immigrants have left the Brighton Beach area and have been replaced by Russians, Puerto Ricans, Dominicans, Mexicans and African-Americans. Inside the store, the long

Brooklyn Public Library-Brooklyn Collection

counter is gone. A half-dozen tables and chairs crowd the middle of the store and a narrow counter lines the wall opposite the original counter. The ovens are no longer easily visible. As walk-in knish customers became scarce, the front of the store was leased to a Russian fast-food joint. The sign outside still says "Mrs. Stahl," but jumbled along with it is the name of the tenant, Boctoyhbin, in Cyrillic letters. And it seems that the very spirit of the Queen of Knishes has been reincarnated as an eighteen-year-old Hispanic youth who could use a shave, would rather eat greasy Chinese takeout than one more knish and is as brawny as a Jets tackle. For Chris Marujo is the one who reminds people that for the merest $1.50, it is possible to feel cared for in a commercial transaction. He easily serves up sur-vival for the locals and nostalgia for the tourists, who banter back and forth with him in English and Spanish. "I've been working here six years," he says proudly. "Yeah, I was twelve when I started."

When a customer walks up to the counter and orders a knish, Marujo is crisp and efficient: It's "yes, sir, yes, ma'am, no problem, in a second. Can I get you anything else?" He responds to the tourist/returnees' inevitable questions: "Yeah, we moved the counter a couple of years ago. Sure the knishes are the same as they've always been. She sure must have been some kind of lady—that Mrs. Stahl."

Margaret A. Daly is the author of Brooklyn Eats *and a food columnist for several newspapers.*

NOW & THEN With much of America's sugar refined in Williamsburg, candy-making is a natural for Brooklyn. Below, Barton's Bonbonniere chocolate-covered cherries take shape.

Vitagraph Pictures

Long before Hollywood, there was Brooklyn

BY JON
GARTENBERG

At the dawn of the twentieth century, when the motion picture emerged as both a business and a form of entertainment, one of the most innovative and successful American pioneers of the film industry was a Brooklyn company: the Vitagraph Company of America.

Formed in 1898 by Albert E. Smith and J. Stuart Blackton, American Vitagraph was first headquartered on Nassau Street in lower Manhattan. The company rapidly became a leading exhibitor of motion pictures in vaudeville houses, as well as a producer of actuality films (i.e., newsreels of current events), comedies and trick films. By 1905, vast changes in the motion-picture industry enlarged the marketplace. To meet the increased demand for product, Vitagraph decided to strengthen its hand in film production. In August 1905, the Vitagraph Company of America broke ground for a new studio and headquarters at East Fifteenth Street and Locust Avenue in Brooklyn.

At this new site, Vitagraph built what was described at the time as "several stages for the taking of special photographic effects." The new facility contained "a complete outfit of Cooper Hewitt Lights. The entire roof and upper part of the building is covered with a specially designed prismatic glass. This construction of glass diffuses and intensifies the rays of light so that shadows are not perceptible." This was a state-of-the-art studio.

The building of this new physical plant in Brooklyn enabled Vitagraph not only to produce more films, but also to greatly improve their quality.

The vast majority of films from this early period have disappeared through deterioration of the film stock, as well as fire and neglect. Enough Vitagraph productions do survive in film archives worldwide, however, that a comparison of the pre- to post-Brooklyn studio productions reveals a marked improvement in the quality. For example, in *The 100 to 1 Shot, or, A Run of Luck* (1906), released just before the studio's completion, several scenes show the farmer and his family inside their house, where they and their furniture cast distinct shadows on the ground. However, *A Midwinter Night's Dream, or, Little Joe's Luck* (1906), released just a few months after the studio began operation, shows the obvious improvement in lighting made possible by the studio: the interior scenes of the dining room, living room and bedroom betray no shadows.

In subject matter, Vitagraph was in the forefront among early filmmakers in producing sophisticated social dramas with such themes as farm foreclosure (*The 100 to 1 Shot*), office theft (*Foul Play, or, A False Friend*, 1907) and sexual harassment (*The Mill Girl— A Story of Factory Life*, 1907). Making dramas in the new studio had challenged Vitagraph to find ways to represent space and time in a continuous narrative flow. These three contemporary Vitagraph movies show such stylistic techniques as centering the action in the middle of the frame, composition in depth and parallel editing, i.e., the showing of two simultaneous actions occurring in distinct spaces across successive shots. Before the widely acknowledged father of American film, D.W. Griffith, had even begun working at the Biograph Co. in Manhattan in 1908, Vitagraph was already using "his" modern storytelling techniques.

Vitagraph led the way toward the introduction of multi-reel films beyond the single-reel format of about

As early as 1906, the Vitagraph Company was shooting silent feature films in its Midwood studio.

Brooklyn Historical Society

Vitagraph's studios at Fifteenth Street and Locust Avenue—now used by NBC Television.

from a large bologna. A demijohn walks around the table and fills a wineglass. The teapot steams and pours tea into a cup; phantom tongs drop lumps of sugar into the tea, and the milk pitcher tries hard but fails to empty its contents.

These object-animation films were imitated by several filmmakers in Europe and America, and numerous improvements followed. Vitagraph's object-animation films were the bridge between the stop-motion substitution films of Georges Méliès and his contemporaries and the animated cartoons of later years.

Vitagraph also presaged the modern system of studio filmmaking by developing an assembly-line technique patterned after the manufacture of automobiles. Before the studio was built, J. Stuart Blackton was virtually the sole Vitagraph filmmaker. When the company's facilities expanded in Brooklyn, others were brought in to direct; from 1906 to 1910, the number of directors increased to at least half a dozen. By September 1906 at Vitagraph, the functions of the writer, stage manager, scenery painters and actors were differentiated. By the end of 1908, about 200 people in various capacities were constantly employed. Vitagraph's own documentary, *Making Moving Pictures* (1908), opens in the company's private office, where the manuscript is being carefully considered. The studio directors enter, receive their instructions, proceed to the studio, get out the cameras and give orders about scenery, props, and so on. Then we get a view of the Vitagraph actors and actresses making up for their different characters. The studio scenes are rehearsed and photographed, showing all the necessary paraphernalia for the different effects required, as well as the rapidity with which scenes are readied and struck by the stagehands.

Vitagraph established a stock company of actors, including Florence Turner, who appeared in such films

1,000 feet (10–15 minutes) that had been the standard length of motion pictures. Vitagraph's multi-reel films were primarily based on historic figures such as Napoleon and George Washington, and were presented in a kind of "tableau" format. In 1909, Vitagraph released *The Life of Moses* in five parts, each to be shown separately. The film was reissued in 1910 with all the reels presented together as a kind of continuous story.

The startling and popular technique of "object animation" was also perfected by Vitagraph in its Brooklyn studio. In this process, inanimate objects were slightly moved with each revolution of the crank of the camera. These single-frame exposures created the illusion of the independent movement of objects without having to resort to wires or cables and without the intervention of live protagonists. One of Vitagraph's most famous films in this vein was *The Haunted Hotel* (1907). In one sequence, the protagonist traveler is terror-stricken by a series of weird incidents. Finally he seats himself at a table, and to his surprise the dishes are placed and shifted by invisible hands. A large knife mysteriously raises itself in the air and slowly cuts slice after slice

as *The Athletic American Girls* (1907) and *The Boy, the Bust, and the Bath* (1907). Initially, films were promoted by their studio names, but once the general public began identifying specific actors and actresses, the studios began to exploit their names. By the summer of 1910, Florence Turner had become known as "The Vitagraph Girl." She was probably the first actress ever to be acknowledged as "A Motion Picture Star." To exploit her popularity, she began to make personal appearances to overflow crowds, even introducing her audiences to the song "The Vitagraph Girl."

By the end of 1908, Vitagraph's facilities covered two full blocks, where three studios were in operation and two more were being erected. By 1916, Vitagraph's assets included two acres of studios and factories in Brooklyn, studios in Bay Shore, plants in Los Angeles and Paris, and a business office and rental department in London.

By 1915, much of the American production of feature films had relocated to Los Angeles. World War I also saw the curtailing of studio activities on the East Coast, due to the shortage of coal to run the physical plants. After the war, studio production increased again in the East, but Vitagraph maintained only a small operation in Brooklyn. Still, the Vitagraph studio in Brooklyn remained intact and operational until 1925, when the company's assets were sold to Warner Brothers. At that time, the Brooklyn studio facility was retrofitted for the making of Vitaphone shorts, helping to usher in the new era of sound films.

Jon Gartenberg is a film historian and archivist.

BROOKLYN ON FILM

Spike Lee Does the Right Thing

Spike Lee is the latest noteworthy contemporary film director to emerge from Brooklyn. He still maintains his production company, 40 Acres and a Mule, in the Fort Greene area and frequently returns to Brooklyn neighborhood locations when shooting his films. Many of his movies have been inspired by controversial real-life people and events, including Malcolm X, Son of Sam and the Million Man March. He has also commented through his films on the nature of the racial conflicts in the borough. In *Do the Right Thing* (1989) and *Jungle Fever* (1991), he vividly depicts the simmering tensions between African Americans and Italian Americans that erupt into racial strife and violence.

Spike Lee has also insightfully chronicled in loving detail the struggles of middle-class African-American families. One of his least seen, but most subtle and charming films in this vein is *Joe's Bed Sty Barbershop: We Cut Heads.* Made as his master's thesis while attending NYU film school, it subsequently won a prize at Sundance.

The story in this film concerns the struggle of an African-American proprietor to keep in operation his barbershop in the Bedford-Stuyvesant neighborhood following the murder of his business partner for running numbers and accumulating debts. The director recounts a day in the life of the proprietor, including his encounters with an array of prospective customers as well as his home life with his wife. The film's slow, elegant pace is accentuated by long shots from deep within the rear of the shop

Do the Right Thing, 1989.

back out toward the window-framed street, wry humor in the interaction between the proprietor and his clients, and the camera's gentle focus on hands—for cutting hair, placing bets and expressing love. Spike's father, Bill Lee, enhances the film's atmosphere with his original jazz score.
—*Jon Gartenberg*

Photofest

Growing Up and Shooting Movies

Brooklyn turns out to be a great location

INTERVIEW WITH
SPIKE LEE

Brooklyn is very rich, very fertile. The stories, the ideals, the different looks. I don't know if one image can tell the whole story of the place, because you've got a couple of million people in Brooklyn—of all ethnic and racial backgrounds. But I think maybe an accumulation of images and films can do it.

I'm a product of the New York City public schools. I went to P.S. 29 on Baltic Street. I lived in Cobble Hill, on Warren Street between Henry and Clinton. Then my parents bought a brownstone in Fort Greene, where we lived at 180 Washington Park. I also went to P.S. 8 on Middagh Street and P.S. 7 on York Street. I went to Junior High

294, and then I went to John Dewey High School in Coney Island, which was an experimental school at the time. You just got pass/fail grades and could choose your own classes, work at your own rate—all that stuff.

It was a great time to be growing up in Brooklyn, you know, when I was at that age, getting high and stuff like that. But then I think crack changed everything, and that was one of the reasons for doing *Crooklyn*. I wanted to do a film about my younger siblings, my sister Joie and my brother Cinque—a script about Brooklyn in the late sixties and early seventies. That film was very autobiographical.

Fort Greene was a tough place. Even though I lived in a brownstone, the Fort Greene projects were right across from us on Myrtle Avenue. Our house was between Myrtle and Willoughby, and all the stores, the Puerto Rican bodegas, were on Myrtle Avenue. So any time you had to go

Reuters/Corbis

On location in Park Slope, Spike Lee shoots a scene for his domestic comedy *Crooklyn*.

Tom Callan

to the store, there was a chance, you know, that you'd get shaken down for your change. And, oh yeah, it happened to me.

There's a lot of Brooklyn in our films, and we're proud of the work. We shot *She's Gotta Have It* in Brooklyn. Nola's loft in that film was a place called the Bank Street Restaurant, which used to be a bank building, right underneath the Brooklyn Bridge. It's amusing me now, all this stuff about DUMBO (Down Under the Manhattan Bridge Overpass) supposedly being the new hot spot. We shot *Do the Right Thing* in Bed-Stuy, and *Mo' Better* was shot all around here. A lot of *Jungle Fever* was shot in Bensonhurst. I shot *Clockers* in the Gowanus projects. *Crooklyn* was shot in Bed-Stuy again. And *He Got Game* was shot in Coney Island.

You have neighborhoods in Brooklyn, you know? You really don't have them to the same degree in Manhattan. When I grew up across the street from Fort Greene Park,

one of the rites of passage for all boys in Brooklyn was riding your bike down Suicide Hill—underneath the Brooklyn Bridge. I don't know the name of the street there, but we used a shot of it for the introductory scene of *She's Gotta Have It*. The shot of Mars when he's on his bike and he almost crashes into the camera—that's Suicide Hill.

It's definitely an *experience*, growing up here. I still got more stories to do in Brooklyn.

Spike Lee has produced and directed many feature films.

Spike's Home Movies

The feature films and music videos that Spike Lee has shot in or about Brooklyn.

Films:
She's Gotta Have It, 1986
Do the Right Thing, 1989
Mo' Better Blues, 1990
Jungle Fever, 1991
Crooklyn, 1994
Clockers, 1995
He Got Game, 1998
Summer of Sam, 1999

Music Videos:
Anita Baker: No One in the World, 1987
Perri Sisters: Feel So Good, 1989
Public Enemy: Fight the Power, 1989
Crooklyn Dodgers: Crooklyn, 1994
Marc Dorsey: People Make the World Go Around, 1994
Crooklyn Dodgers: Return of the Crooklyn Dodgers, 1995

NOW & THEN

Hard to believe in this era of computers, but all the type for newspapers and books like this was once set on a machine called a Linotype that produced hot-lead type. The major manufacturer of such machines was a company named Mergenthaler, located on Ryerson Street. Founded in the 1880s by a German watchmaker, Ottmar Mergenthaler, the company prospered there until 1959 when it moved to Long Island.

Brooklyn Public Library-Brooklyn Collection

Two Machines, Two Worlds

Weber's Bicycles and Sewing Machines

BY DOROTHY WEISS

Amidst the kosher food shops, Jewish bookstores, Yiddish language billboards and the more than 300 synagogues in the neighborhood of Borough Park, Weber's Bicycles and Sewing Machines is an anomaly. Its stock, unlike that of many of the shops in this modern-day shtetl, is not specifically Jewish. And—who can dispute it?—its inventory is, well, *peculiar.*

"Almost everyone who comes in eventually asks, 'Why bicycles *and* sewing machines?'" says Beri Weber, a squat, fiftyish man wearing the traditional yarmulke, side locks and beard of an orthodox Jew. Though customers are stumped, the bicycle/sewing machine combination makes perfect sense to this Weber, the third-generation owner of the shop. "It's all wheels, the first machines," he says, walking down the center aisle of the no-frills, fluorescent-lit shop, where one side is lined with bicycles with brand names such as Raleigh, Ross and Mongoose, and the other side with sewing machines: Bernina, Singer and Nelco.

The inventory at Weber's New Utrecht Avenue shop is thoroughly modern, but the business—and the reason for the unusual inventory—stretches back to the 1880s when Weber's grandfather, Albert Weber, peddled (and pedaled) his wares—early bicycles and sewing machines— through the small towns of northern Hungary.

Beri Weber, a religious man with a face as friendly as a Disney dwarf, is the father of eleven children. Like many men today in Borough Park, Weber devotes hours of his day to the study of the Talmud and prayer. When asked about the contingencies of his business, his

response is Tevye-like: "Livelihood comes from God." One can more easily imagine him peddling simple machines in peasant villages alongside his grandfather than selling high-tech, twenty-speed mountain bikes. Like the Borough Park community as a whole, Weber inhabits simultaneously the worlds of the past and the present. Memories of his father's stories and of his own childhood in the small town of Papa, Hungary, are vivid. His conversation moves easily from his life today in Brooklyn to his family's narrow escapes from the Nazis and from the Communist pogroms in postwar Hungary.

Jewish life took root in this enclave known as Borough Park when Jews escaping Nazi persecution began to settle here. In the years following World War II, Jews who survived Hitler's camps found their way to Brooklyn in order to rebuild their lives. Practically every Eastern European town that was once home to Jews is now rep-

Russell Christian

The Shtetl of Borough Park

In a swath of Brooklyn perhaps ten blocks wide and twenty long, Eastern Europe's rich Jewish life, which was nearly extinguished by the Holocaust, seems to have been reborn. To a visitor emerging from the B train's Fort Hamilton Avenue stop, it feels like entering another world: not a Sturbridge Village or a Williamsburg, Virginia, but a community at once historic and thriving, actually living by the ways of the old country.

On a Friday afternoon, girls in their best long-sleeved, ankle-length dresses and patent-leather shoes stroll arm in arm. They are dressed and bathed for the Jewish Sabbath, which begins Friday at sundown. Little boys in white shirts sporting *yarmulkes* (skullcaps) and *payess* (side locks) sit on the stoops of brick row houses, while their mothers prepare the Sabbath meal. Smells of simmering soups and roasting chickens seep from every doorway.

The men in the neighborhood appear more harried. Wearing *shtreimels* (fur-brimmed hats), *beckisches* (belted black robes) and white knee-length stockings, many are rushing home from the bathhouses where they have "purified" themselves for the Sabbath. Because all work, bathing, cooking, use of electricity and travel are proscribed on the Jewish Sabbath, all preparations must be completed before it begins.

At four o'clock, the shops along New Utrecht and Thirteenth Avenues are locked up for the Sabbath; the shopkeepers must go home to prepare. It is clear that these businesses cater to the local population: Schick's Kosher Bakery, Freedman's Groceries, Rubenstein's Shtreimels, Tauber's Beckisches. It is not only the names and specialty items that signify an ultra-Orthodox clientele. It is also the special *dishmikveh* in the local hardware store, used to ritually purify new dishes before use, and the preponderance of wig shops. Wigs or hair coverings of some kind are worn by all married women, as the code of Jewish modesty prohibits a woman from exposing her natural hair in public.

At sundown, the Sabbath begins. The sidewalks are all but deserted. –*D.G.W.*

resented on this patch of Brooklyn soil. Shtetls that were once thousands of miles apart now coalesce within only a few blocks. Neighbors, originally from disparate countries, still maintain distinctions in subtle codes of dress, language, custom and even architecture. Residents here cling to traditions in order to keep alive memories of a village, a Hasidic sect or a revered rabbi. Families boast upwards of half a dozen children, each perhaps a symbolic replacement for the millions murdered. The very pavement and air in this neighborhood seem to whisper tales of miraculous rebirth, repopulation and growth—tales of lives salvaged from the ashes of the Holocaust.

From its beginnings in turn-of-the-century Hungary, the Weber family's business was marked by patience and equanimity. Grandfather Albert, leaving his village on Sunday evenings, would ride from town to town with his wares strapped onto the back of his bicycle. "In those days there was only one model of sewing machine—the straight-stitch—and one type of bicycle," says Weber, who seems to relish the stories about his grandfather told to him by his father, Leo. "Sometimes it would take all day to convince one peasant to buy a machine. By the time he finished a sale, my grandfather would have to sleep at his customer's house because it was too dark to pedal to the next village. How many times did my grandfather sleep at a peasant's house, only to have him wake up and say, 'I thought about it, I've changed my mind...'"

Apparently, enough villagers actually purchased sewing machines and bicycles for the business to thrive. "Back then, in Hungary, if you sold one sewing machine, you'd have enough money for several months," says Weber. Albert eventually brought his son Leo into the business. By that time, in the late 1930s, father and son traveled through the Hungarian countryside in an old Chevrolet. The days of the Chevy were short-lived, however. When World War II broke out, Weber's grandfather was sent off to a concentration camp, his father to forced labor.

"When my father came back from the war my grandfather's house in Papa was occupied by a Russian officer. That was common after the war," says Weber, who was born several years later in 1948. Leo Weber's first wife and two children had been sent to a concentration camp and killed, as had his father. Hungarian Jews who had been sent to forced labor when Hungary joined the war were the few among Eastern Europe's Jews to survive the war and return to their villages. This was how Leo Weber came to pick up the pieces of the family business. Though the Communists had taken over postwar Hungary and private businesses had been confiscated, Weber's father began to buy and repair secondhand machines for resale. He managed to keep an inventory of old bicycles and sewing machines in a shed out back. It was in those years that Leo remarried and Beri Weber was born.

Weber still has clear memories of the little Hungarian town of Papa, its main road narrow and paved with cobblestones. He also remembers the villagers' fear of the NKVD, the Russian-installed branch of the KGB, and how neighbors gathered in secret—huddled around a shortwave radio—to listen to Radio Free Europe. That village was lost to Beri Weber one Friday night, when his family sat down to their Sabbath meal and a loud crowd gathered in the town square, shouting, "Out Russians! Out Russians!"

"We quickly closed our shutters, and my father went out to see what was going on," Weber remembers. "Our neighbors were instigating a small revolt. My father heard them and understood that we were in danger—that there would be a pogrom. A week later, we left, with nothing but the few small bags we could carry." That was in 1956, when the Weber family escaped via a small border town in Austria and came to America to put down new roots in Brooklyn. Once in America, the family joined an uncle who had already staked out a place within the Jewish émigré community of Borough Park.

"When my uncle came to Brooklyn in 1950, the community was very small," says Weber. "There were only two synagogues. Now we have more than three hundred." By 1961, the American dream became possible for the Webers. With $2,000 in savings plus a loan of $3,000, Weber's father, Leo, opened Weber's Bicycles and Sewing Machines in the exact same storefront it occupies today on New Utrecht Avenue.

Today, Weber leads the narrowly prescribed lifestyle of the Jews of Borough Park while conducting business on a daily basis in English, Yiddish, Hebrew, Hungarian and Polish. He is also a crackerjack mechanic and, once trained as an electronics technician, spends much of his time in the back of his shop repairing the bicycles and sewing machines he has been selling since he took over the business almost twenty years ago. All day, the metallic jangle of the shop's door chime alerts him to customer arrivals: this one wanting a bike pedal fixed, that one asking for a deal on the latest-model Bernina sewing machine. Weber is patient with each customer, allotting equal attention to serious sales and niggling requests. He gently refuses a free repair to a querulous woman who purchased a sewing machine at Weber's twenty-two years ago, and then happily agrees to special-order a unicycle for a grandfather wanting a surprise Hanukkah gift for his grandson.

"When Solomon built the Temple," Weber says, "he hired a coppersmith who was the son of a coppersmith. My grandfather started this business, and I keep on."

Dorothy Weiss, a writer with an advanced degree in Jewish studies, was born and raised in Brooklyn.

"The tugboat people are usually good for a cup of coffee, and in wintry weather, when the river is tossing surf, what joy to take refuge in a stove-heated tug cabin and thaw out with a mug of the blackest Java." **Truman Capote**

The Making of Penicillin

Is it a surprise that the developers of the anti-impotence drug Viagra—potentially the best-selling drug ever—reside in Brooklyn? The health care and research conglomerate Pfizer, Inc., boasts a 150-year sustained residence in Brooklyn. Despite the company's continued growth and expansion into the global market, its main plant, built around the company's original building, remains in the borough. The corporate philosophy espouses a loyalty: the city, they say, has treated them well.

Among its many widely pre-scribed drugs, Pfizer's number-one seller is Norvasc, an antihyperten-sive drug. Recently, the company acquired Warner-Lambert, making it one of the top drugmakers in the world. Yet Pfizer had its humble start on the cobblestone streets of Williamsburg.

In 1849, young chemist Charles Pfizer and his cousin Charles Erhart, a confectioner by trade, started the company. Both had emigrated from Germany in order to escape the revolutionary turbulence that began sweeping Europe in 1848. They pooled their respective talents in a chemicals company that would soon rival their European counterparts—at the time, virtually all the chemicals being used in America were still being produced in Europe. The very first chemical they produced was an antiparasitic compound known as Santonin. Erhart was able to mask its bad taste by combining it with confectionary chocolate drops.

The Williamsburg company produced several bulk chemicals—iodine, mercurials, borax and boric acid—and in 1880 was among the first to produce vitamin C. Then, with the advent of World War II, the U.S. govern-ment contracted with Pfizer to produce penicillin for the Allied nations. To meet the demand, the company converted an old ice plant into what would be the world's largest manufacturing facility for penicillin. With its new mass-production process, Pfizer was able to turn out quantities of this miracle antibiotic that would save the lives of countless combat casualties.

In the postwar years, penicillin revolutionized the practice of medicine and the state of public health in America and abroad, ultimately building Pfizer's repu-tation into what some have referred to as the purvey-ors of "Science for the World's Well-Being."

This Brooklyn-born company, one of the first billion-dollar international pharmaceutical companies, remains highly involved in the Williamsburg commu-nity, providing its neighbors with an elementary school as well as much-needed medications and donations to people in third-world countries such as Tanzania, Morocco and Vietnam.—*Genia Gould*

Bespoke Suits

Think of London, Milan and—Williamsburg

BY JULIAN
E. BARNES

O n the edge of Williamsburg, just over the border from Bushwick, is a dirty-yellow brick factory with exterior walls ringed in black graffiti and interior linoleum floors patched with fraying duct tape. But the aggressive shabbiness of the old building belies the elegance of its product: lined up against the faux-wood-paneled walls are rows of fine men's suits awaiting the trip to Brooks Brothers, Neiman Marcus or Saks Fifth Avenue.

This is the factory of Martin Greenfield, master clothier. He has worked in this aging building since 1947; he has owned it since 1978. He has labored at every job inside its walls, from carrying suit parts to the seamstresses to cutting the fabric, from buying the cloth to measuring the customers.

Even now, Mr. Greenfield is such a familiar presence on the factory floor that no one pays him any attention. No one glances up as he floats around the bench where a team of six sews horn buttons on sleeves or moves to the station where a man with lightning hands tacks together some of the 108 pieces of cloth that make up a suit jacket. Only the designer, making a chalk line on a lapel, looks up at him, implicitly seeking approval for a last-minute change he is making to a prototype suit. There is no one in the building, no one in the borough and perhaps no one in the country who knows men's suits better than Martin Greenfield.

"I rely on my own eyes," says Greenfield with an earnestness that softens the edge of pride and confidence. "Just like a doctor who cures any illness, I know what pill to give any suit to make it better." Presidents from Dwight Eisenhower to Bill Clinton have worn Greenfield's suits, and so have the NBA's Patrick Ewing and Marcus Camby. A signed photo from Colin Powell in Greenfield's office bears the inscription "Thanks for helping me change uniforms."

The factory makes 40,000 suits a year. With that many suits and 200 workers, this is, to be sure, mass production. But it is a mass production envisioned not by Henry Ford but by the original Adam Smith.

Williamsburg clothier Martin Greenfield with political bigwigs Colin Powell (left) and Bill Clinton.

Courtesy of Martin Greenfield

The workers are specialized artisans, not unskilled cogs. "What makes our suits so special," says Greenfield, "is that lots of things are done by hand that you cannot duplicate with a machine. How come you can't hear the engine of a Rolls-Royce? Because the bearings are still packed by hand. The same thing with these suits." There are machines in Greenfield's factory. Computers trace the patterns on thin paper with a precision that a draftsman could not match. There are a few stations where workers make hidden seams with old sewing machines. But most of the work here is done by rows of skilled people moving a needle and thread through the fabric with care.

Curiously, part of the perfection of a handmade suit, Greenfield says, comes from the imperfections. Stopping midway across the factory floor, he pauses next to one seamstress sewing buttonholes on a jacket. He picks up one of the completed garments, turns it over in his hands and points to the detailed stitches, all precise but not exact duplicates. "It is like when you write someone a thank-you note by hand," he says. "It is not perfect, but it is personal." The result of all this handwork is that wearing a suit made by Martin Greenfield is like wearing a second skin. When you move, the clothes move; when you sit, the suit sits. It is all in the draping of the fabric, and that is all in the hand-stitching.

"It is difficult to describe a suit," Greenfield says. "The important thing is, everything moves. The quality talks back to you."

The fastest-growing part of the business, according to Greenfield's son Tod, is the custom-made clothing. A suit made for Brooks Brothers will start at $900; a suit made specially for an individual customer begins at $1,100. Martin Greenfield still spends a third of the year on the road, attending trunk shows where men who want him to make them a custom suit ask him to take their measure. And when Greenfield sizes a man up, it's not just at the waist, arms and shoulder. "I remember every customer," he says, leaning forward and stabbing the desk with his finger for emphasis, then leaning back with a broad smile. "I discuss everything with them—their lifestyle. I always make sure they have the right fabric for their needs. They know I wouldn't sell them anything I wouldn't wear."

Year after year, season after season his customers come back and buy new suits. "My suits never fall apart," he says. "None of my customers need a suit. But they always buy."

Martin Greenfield was born in Czechoslovakia, and when he was a child his father wanted him to become a doctor. But other events intervened. After the Germans invaded during World War II, Martin was sent to a concentration camp where he learned to sew when he was forced to repair Gestapo uniforms. In 1947, he came to Brooklyn and made his way to Varet Street in Williamsburg, where he found the Three Gs clothing factory. It had become something of an institution in its own right, if only by virtue of the sign in Ebbets Field: "Hit the sign, win a suit." Starting on the lowest rungs of the factory, Greenfield rose from errand boy and driver to cutter and designer to vice president for manufacturing. In 1978 he bought the company.

"They say it's the American Dream," he says. "But whatever you want to call it, it is hard work."

It may have been the American Dream to rise from errand boy to owner, but there was probably no worse time to buy a suit factory. In the clothing business, it was the heyday of the cheap polyester leisure suit made with cheap overseas labor. And in Greenfield's neighborhood, things were getting worse. Arsonists burned large swaths of Bushwick. The factory workers were mugged on their way to the subway. By the time Greenfield bought the factory, the workers were moving to other neighborhoods and the businesses around him were moving to other states—even other countries. Over the next decade, the fires stopped but the situation remained bleak. One year, despite two alarm systems, the business was robbed eleven times; each time the clothes ready to ship to customers were stolen or destroyed. Greenfield's sons took to sleeping in the factory as a security measure. "I have had plenty of invitations to go to other states to work, but it is just like going away from your family," Greenfield says. "You can't leave the people you work with. Leave them alone, just for a business stake? That's not my style."

But just as fashions and styles of the past inevitably

come back, so do neighborhoods—with some work. Greenfield founded an industrial park and a business association to lobby politicians, work with the police and lure new business. In recent years crime has declined, and new businesses, like Boar's Head foods, have moved in. The neighborhood has begun to climb back.

"When you work in a neighborhood, you live there," he says. "It may not be where you go to sleep, but it is where you live all day long." Martin Greenfield is a man with faith in himself, faith in his neighborhood and faith, above all, in the power of a good suit. In the era of casual Fridays and Internet millionaires dressed in jeans, the suit may appear to be in trouble. But Green-

field says he can already see the backlash beginning. The wave of the future is custom-made clothes for young professionals who want a suit that moves when they move, a suit that drapes.

"It's just like when the sons were embarrassed by their fathers wearing leisure suits," Greenfield says. "They started buying nice clothes. And then the fathers saw that and said, 'I want a suit like that.'" At that he pauses and smiles at a half-completed suit jacket he holds in his hands: "When it is done, it is beautiful to look at."

Julian E. Barnes covers as much of Brooklyn as he can for the New York Times.

ONLY IN BROOKLYN Jehovah's Witnesses—the Watchtower Bible and Tract Society—not only hand out copies of *Awake!* but also use their renovated factory buildings on the waterfront to print millions of copies of their own version of the Bible.

The Tank Tops of New York

Mysteriously sitting atop buildings like rudimentary rocketships with their coolie-hat tops, round wooden water tanks are a ubiquitous shape on New York City's skyline. They seem a link to the past, a panorama of artifacts that no one has bothered to remove, but in fact they remain functional on most buildings. Because they fool the eye and sense of time, even the newest ones manage to look ancient.

Water tanks work: the downward flow of water from a rooftop tank creates the pressure that ensures a useful flow even at the upper levels of buildings.

The reason rooftop tanks are needed is that the water piped into the city from the upstate reservoirs provides adequate pressure only to about the fifth floor in city buildings. The redwood used by Rosenwach Company—major builders of the city's rooftop tanks for a century—keeps water cool in the summer and doesn't allow it to freeze in the winter.

Andrew Rosenwach, the fourth-generation proprietor of the family business, says his grandfather journeyed across the Brooklyn Bridge in the early 1900s and set up shop on Grand Street. In the 1960s the family relocated the plant to North Ninth Street in Williamsburg, where it continues in operation today.

While there is some new and improved wood-cutting equipment, along with innovations in the production process, construction of the tanks remains very much the same since their beginning. Like his father, Rosenwach is extremely proud to be a part of something that lends a certain character to the city. But "it hurts my neck," he says, "to observe all the tanks" as he drives along the highways of New York.

Today, a new water tank is commonly constructed in just twenty-four hours. Much like doing a puzzle, the parts are put together, piece by piece, on the roof. "For me," says Rosenwach, "watching the installation of a tank is more of a thrill than going to the circus."

Presently, only about twenty new tanks are installed in a year, at the cost of some $20,000 each. Demand for new water tanks has slowed because the tanks are so durable: if well maintained, they tend to last thirty to thirty-five years with no major problems. To survive and provide year-round work for its employees, Rosenwach began diversifying into related markets: carpentry, building restoration, roof repair, and plumbing. From its signature redwood, the company also produces outdoor furniture for both urban and rural garden landscapes around the world—including the pieces at Rockefeller Center.—*Genia Gould*

Michael Kamber

How Brooklyn Got Its Brew Back

And got a great logo in the bargain

BY STEPHEN
HINDY

How could Brooklyn really be *Brooklyn* without its own brewery? That was the question I put to my downstairs Park Slope neighbor in 1986, ten years after the last remaining great old New York breweries—Schaefer and Rheingold, both based in Brooklyn—drained their tanks and scuttled off to Pennsylvania.

Maybe it can't, replied the neighbor, Chemical Bank lending officer Thomas Potter, but what could he and I,

a former Middle East correspondent for the Associated Press, do about it? The beer business had been consolidating for the past fifty years. Anheuser-Busch, Miller and Coors ruled the land. What could a banker and a journalist do against the market power of the national brewing giants? Fugehdabboudit!

We were sitting in Tom's backyard on Eighth Street near Prospect Park, watching our kids play and drinking the home brew that I had learned to make from American diplomats stuck in bone-dry Islamic countries like Saudia Arabia and Kuwait. It was a long summer, and we were watching the Mets on their way to winning the World Series. It was a summer of dreams,

Beer baron
Steve Hindy
learned about
marketing
while driving
a beer truck
in Brooklyn.

Dennis Milbauer

and my dream was to bring brewing back to Brooklyn. It had been a major industry here well into the twentieth century, and many people still recalled the great old breweries. Plus, Brooklyn has such a strong identity— a blue-collar, rough-and-ready self-image that just seems to fit with *beer*.

So I persisted. If they could do it in northern California and Seattle, we could do it in Brooklyn. Eventually, Tom traveled to Portland, Oregon, for the 1986 microbrewers' conference. He returned such a convert that we decided to take the plunge. We began talking to bar owners, beer wholesalers, restaurateurs, retired brewers and graphic designers about our plans to begin brewing a real Brooklyn beer.

From the beginning, we received encouragement, ideas and support from our neighbors and from an incredible array of people with Brooklyn connections. John Bergmann, a brewing engineer and Brooklyn Technical High School graduate, introduced us to Bill Moeller, then the head brewer at Schmidt's of Philadelphia. A fourth-generation German-American brewmaster, Bill was about to take early retirement from Schmidt's and was looking for consulting jobs. We hired him to help us develop a recipe for a Brooklyn lager— that is, a light and slowly fermented beer. It turned out that Bill's grandfather had worked for the old Claus-Lipsius Brewery in Brooklyn at the turn of the century. Using his grandfather's notebooks, Bill was able to craft a pre-Prohibition recipe for our own Brooklyn lager, which we began brewing at an underutilized brewery in Utica, New York. That was our start, and Moeller's is the recipe we still use for our Brooklyn Lager.

For our corporate logo, I began talking to the many artists and designers who lived in our Park Slope neighborhood. At the time, our working name was Brooklyn Eagle Beer, a reference to the old Brooklyn newspaper. They came up with some exciting ideas, but I began to see the critical importance of the logo and the design. I went on a crusade to find exactly the right designer and interviewed more than twenty-five design firms while working my day job at *Newsday*. One night my wife, Ellen, overheard my grumbling about the problem and said, "Why don't you find out who the best designers are and call them up? You don't mind calling anyone, anytime." A friend referred me to the biggest names in the graphic design business—Milton Glaser, Ivan Chermayeff, Pentagram and others. I started calling and got appointments with all of them except Glaser. "Do you know who Milton is?" sniffed his receptionist. "Yes, I do, and I hear he's pretty good," I replied. After four or five calls, she sent me a press kit about Milton. After fifteen calls she caved in, sighing, "You're not going to give up, are you?"

She put Milton on the phone, I blurted out my idea, and he said, "That sounds like fun. Why don't you come in?" So the man who gave the world "I ♥ NY," *New York* magazine's logo and hundreds of other symbols became our designer.

Bronx native Glaser's first bit of advice was to forget the eagle: "Who needs an eagle? You have Brooklyn— one of the most recognizable places in the world." Armed with a well-written business plan, an experienced brewer, a great old Brooklyn recipe and one of the world's foremost graphic designers, we raised five hundred thousand dollars from friends and colleagues who bought into our dream of bringing brewing back to Brooklyn.

Sofia Collier, the very successful founder of Soho Natural Soda Co., the first of the "new age" soft drinks, lived about four houses up Eighth Street from Tom and me. One Saturday morning, she agreed to give us some "neighborly advice." Distribute your own beer, she said. Don't count on the big New York beer distributors, since they're essentially controlled by the big brewers. If you distribute yourself, you will know who your customers are and you will learn from them. (About the time we sold our first case of beer, Sofia sold her company to Seagram's for more than $15 million.)

Overcoming our fears of parking tickets, high insur-

Right top: Picture Collection, New York Public Library; right bottom: Library of Congress

The Good Old Beers

A roster of the twenty-nine most prominent now-extinct breweries of Brooklyn, with address and dates of operation. (The name in parentheses is a brand or other company name or that of a successor.)

Budweiser (Nassau),
1042 Dean Street.
1849–1914

Claus-Lipsius,
493 Bushwick Avenue.
1865–1902

Congress (Williamsburg),
197 Humboldt Street.
1855–1923

Consumers Park,
Franklin & Montgomery
Streets. 1897–1913

Diogenes,
Decatur Street & Wyckoff
Avenue. 1898–

Peter Doelger,
115 Greenpoint Avenue.
1863–1885

Edelbrau,
1 Bushwick Place.
1868–1951

Conrad Eurich (Elm),
Wyckoff & Halsey. 1889–

Excelsior (Kings),
239-269 Pulaski Street.
1896–1923

Fallert,
86 Lorimer Street.
1878–1920

Federal (Long Island),
Third Avenue & Dean
Street. 1854–1907

Frank, Cypress Avenue.
1850s–1916

Golden Horn
(Fort Hamilton), Third
Avenue & Ninety-Sixth
Street. 1897–1906

Otto Huber,
Meserole Street &
Bushwick Place. 1861–

India Wharf,
48-60 Hamilton Avenue.
1889–1934

Johnson (Leavy &
Britton)
Jay & Front Streets.
1842–1902

S. Liebmann's Sons
(Rheingold), 36 Forest
Street. 1855–1902

Meltzer Brothers,
60 Meserole Street.
1865–1917

Michel (Ebling),
Third Avenue & Bond
Street. 1907–1937

Ferdinand Muench
(Hittleman),
Bushwick Place &
Montrose Avenue.
1880–1936

New York & Brooklyn,
Scholes Street.
1888–1913

North American
(Schaefer),
1303 Greene Avenue.
1892–1946

Obermeyer & Liebmann
(Havana), Bremen & Noll
Streets. 1868–1924

Old Dutch,
Forty-Second Street
& Glenwood Road.
1934–1948

Piel Brothers
(Associated/Schaefer)
Liberty & Sheffield
Avenues. 1883–1973

F&M Schaefer,
430 Kent Avenue.
1916–1976

Joseph Schlitz (Ehret),
24 George Street.
1949–1973

Trommer/Evergreen,
Bushwick Avenue &
Conway Street.
1896–1951

Welz & Zerwick,
Myrtle & Wyckoff
Avenues. 1861–1925

Brewmaster Garrett Oliver at home among the Williamsburg facility's technoid kettles and tanks.

ance rates and worse, we took Sofia's advice, and Tom and I began peddling our beer from the back of two trucks. We sold beer all over the borough—East New York, Flatlands, everywhere. It's very satisfying work: you start in the morning with a full truck and you end the day with an empty one. It's humbling, too, as people often treat truck drivers very badly. Still, we met people like Joe Marino, second-generation owner of the American Thrifty Beverage store in the Cobble Hill neighborhood, widely considered the best beer store in the city. A relentlessly optimistic man with a giant warm smile and

a handshake like a brown bear's, Joe tried our beer, liked it and took forty-eight cases of Brooklyn Lager on our first day of delivery. A week later, he ordered forty-eight more cases. When his old friend Joe Lumuscio, the very successful Budweiser distributor in Brooklyn, laughingly called Brooklyn Lager a "fucking novelty," Joe replied: "I'm selling fifty cases a week of that 'fucking novelty!'"

Joe told us stories about the 1970s, when Schaefer and Rheingold ruled New York and Budweiser was only a struggling brand. "They used to beg me to add five cases of Budweiser to my order," he said. "You just keep

Dennis Milbauer

making a good beer and working at it. It will catch on." Thank God, Joe was right.

In 1996, Mayor Giuliani cut the ribbon to open our new brewery in Brooklyn's Williamsburg neighborhood, just a mile from the old Schaefer plant, which today houses a lumberyard, a kosher wine company and a yeshiva. Brooklyn Brewery now employs eighty people in a foundry building that once housed the old Hecla Architectural Iron Works—the company that did the ironwork on the Waldorf-Astoria and the façade of the St. Regis Hotel. Our nifty logo, with its classic "B" recalling Brooklyn's baseball glory days, has become one of Brooklyn's own icons. Our beer is sold all over the borough, in Manhattan's best restaurants—Windows on the World, the River Cafe, Chanterelle—and all along the East Coast from Boston to North Carolina. And in Peter Luger's steak house: I tried for eight years to get them to sell our beer, but they hadn't changed their beer lineup since 1970. One of the owners told me, "When you open a brewery right here in this neighborhood, we'll buy your beer." And the day after our brewery opened in Williamsburg, she called and said, "Now we'll buy your beer."

In 1994 we hired Garrett Oliver, a founder of the New York City Homebrewers Guild and a former apprentice with a head brewer at England's Samuel Smith brewery. A Queens native who had made Brooklyn his home, Garrett is a highly acclaimed brewmaster, an eloquent speaker on beer and a longtime judge at the Great American and Great British beer festivals. He took charge of our brewing operations, designed our new plant in Williamsburg and developed our newer brews—although our "black chocolate stout" is still based on one of my old home-brew recipes.

We hold neighborhood block parties adjacent to our brewery on North Eleventh Street several times a year —in May and on the Fourth of July, for example—and a Beerfest in September. The enthusiastic turnouts demonstrate again that our original hunch was correct: Brooklyn *is* a beer kind of place.

Stephen Hindy is an ex-correspondent and a founding partner of Brooklyn Brewery.

Topps Baseball Cards

The gum came first. Before World War II, the Shorin brothers started a business in Brooklyn selling gum for a penny a stick. Then, after the war, they started selling a bubble gum named Bazooka and experimented with cartoon symbols for their gum wrappings: Atom Bubble Boy and then Bazooka Joe. Kids liked them, but the Shorins were still seeking a stronger marketing edge. In 1950 they tried packaging their gum with trading cards of popular television characters like the cowboy Hopalong Cassidy.

Finally, in 1952, a Topps employee and baseball fan named Sy Berger developed a major league baseball trading card, complete with color portrait on the front and stats on the back. Baseball cards had a long history, going back to the early 1900s when they were packaged with cigarettes, but these were the first modern cards. The first major league player to have a card was Andy Pafko, an outfielder then playing for the Dodgers. He was soon followed by

PEE WEE REESE
shortstop BROOKLYN DODGERS

legions of others—and many a summer evening of collecting, flipping and trading.
—M.W.R.

Courtesy of the Topps Company

Almost Lost

Brooklyn is a place with a past. It was settled over 350 years ago, and it grew from a cluster of villages to the third-largest city in America —and a commercial and cultural power in its own right—before becoming one of the five boroughs of New York City in 1898.

Living memory, if not out-and-out nostalgia, remains a strong element of most people's perception of Brooklyn. Lurking in the minds of millions of Americans, both within Brooklyn and scattered from Long Island to California, are powerful memories: of the Dodgers, the trolleys, the street 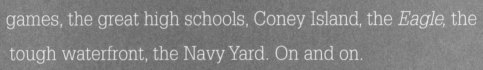 games, the great high schools, Coney Island, the *Eagle,* the tough waterfront, the Navy Yard. On and on.

But Brooklyn's past is not confined to living memory. It is palpable all around, in the streets and buildings, locations where people did things and events unfolded. A lot of the physical city has been demolished or renewed out of existence during the last dynamic century. But much more evidence of Brooklyn's past survives: you can actually go there and have a look at it, whether it's the site in Greenpoint where the Civil War *Monitor* was launched or the stage once trod by Booker T. Washington, Mark Twain and Paul Robeson.

We almost lost Brooklyn. But not quite.

Previous spread: Gateway to Green-Wood, 1865, designed by Brooklyn church architect Richard M. Upjohn.

Previous spread: Byron Collection, Museum of the City of New York; this page: Lee Stookey

The Mistake of '98?

From city to borough by just 277 votes

BY GLENN THRUSH

O n the day the City of Brooklyn officially died, January 1, 1898, the heavens above the old City Hall sopped the somber throng in a miserable, insistent torrent. It was an appropriate irony, and not just because the weather fit the mood of the crowd, but because *water* was the real issue. The six former mayors who were present to deliver Brooklyn into the grasp of Greater New York knew that lack of good water—the kind that fills pipes, toilets and teapots—had contributed mightily to the demise of their beloved independent city.

As a *city*, Brooklyn had died of thirst.

The newborn borough, beset by fifty years of water shortages and cholera outbreaks, was about to be connected to Manhattan's vast system of pristine upstate reservoirs. But that admission was not part of that day's Victorian eulogies and hand-wringing odes. Instead, Will Carleton was on the podium in the Common Council Chamber, lamenting the fact that the City of Brooklyn, "this fair comely maiden, at midnight must die." St. Clair McKelway,

the Missouri-born publisher of the powerful *Brooklyn Eagle,* had spent the better part of a decade inveighing against the New York merchants and their Brooklyn allies who pushed for consolidation. And he wasn't quite through. "Stand by Brooklyn!" he shouted to lusty applause. "If necessary, stand against the rest of Greater New York in standing by Brooklyn."

Mighty fine rhetoric for the occasion, but for years McKelway and his fellow newspapermen had run dozens of editorials and stories about Brooklyn's dire water shortage and its deteriorating quality. A year before the city died, the *Boston Standard,* an insurance industry journal, reported that fire insurance companies were considering hiking rates in the city because there wasn't

The merger was caricatured in Puck's cartoon: "Selfish Objections to a Good Match."

Brooklyn Public Library-Brooklyn Collection

enough water to put out blazes. And what water there was, was hardly drinkable. The *Standard* wrote: "The intolerable offensiveness of the water has brought complaints by the thousands from the people, and every Brooklyn newspaper has given to the subject from half a column to a column or more daily for over a fortnight." Brooklyn health department officials concluded that boiling did not improve the water ("it only cooks the smell"), and one newspaperman discovered that samples of the water "range from a dirty, muddy fluid to a gelatinous green ooze."

Politics of Consolidation

From the start, Brooklyn's outward trappings of independence had always been tempered by the reality that the colossus across the East River controlled much of the city's destiny. The authors of New York's eighteenth-century British colonial charter gave Manhattan's city fathers almost complete control over Brooklyn's commercial waterfront and ferry traffic. As a result, Brooklyn's tax base was largely residential—and a mere fraction of Manhattan's.

Moreover, as the City of Brooklyn struggled to consolidate the nearby towns into one metropolis in the 1830s, New York City's representatives in Albany fought the effort as if they were trying to suppress a rebellion. They finally conceded defeat in 1834, but they never really stopped working to annex their sister city. A half-century later, after the completion of the Brooklyn Bridge in 1883 tethered the two cities tighter than ever, a group of powerful businessmen revived the one-city movement.

The leader of that effort was a powerful Wall Street financier named Andrew Haswell Green, a kind of nineteenth-century Robert Moses with an obsessive vision of New York as the imperial capital of the commercial and cultural universe. It was that vision that impelled him to crusade against the corrupt Tweed Ring and to create Central Park and the New York Public Library. By 1890, Green had convinced the state legislature to appoint a commission—with himself as chairman—to study the consolidation question. Four years later, he sold Albany on the idea of holding a public referendum on a proposal to consolidate Manhattan, Brooklyn, the South Bronx, Queens and Staten Island into what he termed "Greater New York."

Green was probably the most thoroughly networked figure in New York at the time, with deep connections to the wealthiest, most influential men of his age. In Brooklyn, he helped organize the Brooklyn Consolidation League under the crusading Coney Island–bred reformer William Gaynor. The efforts by Green and Gaynor included the distribution of two million pieces of literature with titles like "How Taxes in Brooklyn Can Be Reduced by One-Half."

Nonetheless, Brooklyn was a problem. The core of the opposition to consolidation came from the Protestant-Republican elites in Brooklyn Heights, including shipping magnate A.A. Low, Reverend Lyman Abbott of Plymouth Church, school reformer William Maxwell and, of course, the voluble St. Clair McKelway. Their argument was simple if a little hysterical: Brooklyn was under attack by the rum-soaked, Tammany-ruled immigrant hordes of New York City. Brooklyn, wrote Mayor Fred Wurster in 1896, "is largely a New England and American city: American customs and institutions—including the public schools—are maintained free from evil influence." By the mid-1890s, that argument was almost a complete fiction. Brooklyn had its own political bosses, including the notorious Willoughby Street boss William McLaughlin.

Brooklyn was also beginning to surpass Manhattan as a magnet for Europe's huddled masses. Even by 1890, 71 percent of the city residents were immigrants or first-generation Americans, many of whom lived in the soon-to-be annexed towns of Flatlands, New Utrecht and Gravesend. Still, the notion that Brooklyn's virtue was being attacked was a powerful one. When Andrew Green awoke on November 5, 1894, the vote tally must have made it hard for him to swallow his morning tea. The pro-consolidation measure passed in Brooklyn—but only by 277 votes of the 129,211 ballots cast.

It wasn't much of a mandate, and the closeness of the vote galvanized the opposition. At that point, in early 1895, the decision could have gone either way. But three circumstances determined the outcome for good:

Here, Brooklyn is the virtuous woman and Tweed the despoiler.

The Beauties of Consolidation—Prospect Park Under Tammany Rule.

the first was Brooklyn's increasing municipal debt, which threatened to hurl the city into bankruptcy by 1900; the second was the conversion of New York State's GOP boss Thomas C. Platt to the consolidation cause; the third was an impending water catastrophe the likes of which no major U.S. city had ever seen.

Serious Thirst

The lack of clean water sources had been clear to Brooklyn's city fathers as early as 1853, when the state legislature in Albany authorized the city to conduct a survey of water sources that would provide its citizens with safer, fresher, more plentiful water than could be pumped from its inadequate system of groundwater wells. The first—and ultimately best—alternative was to link up to

Manhattan's northern streams from the Croton reservoir. No, the commission said, that would put Brooklyn in New York's thrall and strain even Manhattan's boundless resources. A proposal to siphon off water from the Bronx River was quickly dismissed as too costly.

The winning alternative was to create a system of canals and aqueducts to divert water from the area around Ridgewood, Jamaica and Hempstead to newly constructed reservoirs in Cypress Hills and Prospect Park. The idea was to gain a foothold on the vast Long Island watershed and keep expanding east. "The whole mass of the Island seems to be saturated with water," effused the city surveyor of Brooklyn in May of 1854.

The new system, completed just before the outbreak of the Civil War, pumped an additional 90,000 gallons

Brooklyn Public Library-Brooklyn Collection

Brooklyn's reservoir—on the future site of the main library—overlooked Grand Army Plaza.

296 wells examined were utterly unfit for human use. In fact, most of the samples ignited when put to the flame. At the corner of Duffield Street and Johnson Place, not far from the current MetroTech office complex, Health Commissioner E.H. Bartlett, in a memorable fit of Victorian overenthusiasm, decided to inject some of the suspicious well water under his skin. Within two hours, he was stricken with severe diarrhea that lasted half a week. A rabbit he stuck with the same needle shriveled up and died.

Enough was enough. By 1896, when most of the local headlines were occupied by the fight against consolidation, the city fathers were quietly warning that Brooklyn's water demand would exceed supply by the turn of the century. With that in mind, Alfred Tredway White, head of the City of Brooklyn's Public Works Commission, headed out to the watery Eden of eastern Suffolk County to talk watershed annexation with the locals. To say White was rebuffed is to demean the vehemence of the opposition.

As final consolidation bills were being considered in the state capital, the Long Islanders succeeded in securing a law that effectively banned any purchase of watershed land by the City of Brooklyn. New York City, by contrast, had all the water it needed and then some. Between 1866 and 1911, the city had bought up watershed rights to twelve new reservoirs in Putnam and Westchester Counties, achieving a capacity of about four million gallons a day—enough to supply Manhattan and Brooklyn with a million gallons to spare.

to the city per day—but it soon became apparent that even that wasn't nearly enough to meet the needs of the city's exploding population. In 1850, when the first water system had been contemplated, Kings County had only about 130,000 people By 1880, that number had grown to nearly 600,000. By 1896, it had doubled to 1.2 million. There simply wasn't enough water under Brooklyn or in nearby Long Island to meet the demand.

In the years following the Civil War, droughts had become an annual ordeal and many local residents still relied on private wells to supplement their municipal water. But by then the local wells were a disgusting, often deadly stopgap. Their spigots were choked with effluvia: livestock slop, human waste and industrial by-products. Disease was always common enough in the city, but the wells acted as a conduit for contagion. In 1866, on Van Brunt Street in Red Hook, 514 people died of cholera contracted from a filthy well. By 1882, city inspectors were cruising poor neighborhoods with orders to remove pump handles from the worst wells. Still, that year, two unsuspecting schoolchildren, ages six and eight, drank from a well at Throop Avenue in today's Bedford-Stuyvesant and died within days of a painful gastrointestinal ailment.

The episode prompted the health department to conduct a survey, which found that no less than 230 of the

Dreams of Secession

But romantic visions of Brooklyn as a murdered metropolis die hard. Over the last century, numerous full-blown secession movements have sprouted, flowered and withered. In the spring of 1943, as the Brooklyn Navy Yard was launching many of the U.S. Navy's most

Both pages: Library of Congress

famous ships, Brooklyn's leading lights were seriously considering declaring war on Greater New York. Although McKelway was long dead, the *Brooklyn Eagle* began devoting a significant part of its non-war coverage to State Senator Fred Morritt's secession bill—the revival of a failed 1905 secession measure. Hoping for data to bolster its claims that Brooklyn was being oppressed by its "marriage" to Manhattan, the *Eagle* contracted with the famous Princeton Surveys to study the economic and political feasibility of reestablishing the City of Brooklyn.

If the study was impartial, the *Eagle* wasn't. Brooklynites, the paper reported at the outset, "can find much in the record to support their contention that they were kidnapped by Manhattan." The results of the survey should have put the issue to rest. In two dozen single-spaced, chart-packed pages, the Princetonites concluded that there was "no evidence" that Brooklyn got less than its fair share of services and amenities.

"The facts presented," the *Eagle*'s editors responded, "can assist in determining the WISDOM of separation, but they cannot measure the real DEMAND for separation." And so it goes. On each significant anniversary, when the city at large has held "celebrations," Brooklyn has kept to its tradition of somber "observances." In 1998, while City Hall was unfurling the bunting and priming the fireworks, Brooklyn Borough President Howard Golden referred to consolidation by its Brooklyn appellation: "The Great Mistake of '98." But though history doesn't record it, at some point during the day President Golden undoubtedly turned on a faucet and helped himself to a drink of Greater New York's water.

Glenn Thrush is a writer for The Observer, Bloomberg Magazine *and other New York–area publications.*

NOW & THEN The buildings where Walt Whitman worked—the *Eagle* office, the print shop where he wrote and (below) his carpenter shop on Cumberland Street—are all long gone.

The First Big Fight

The Americans lost, but the British didn't exactly win

BY JOSEPH McCARTHY

On July 12, 1776, the freshly rebellious citizens of New York watched 150 British ships sail through the Verrazano Narrows into New York Harbor. This was no celebratory parade of "Tall Ships." This was *war*.

Counting the 130 British ships that had arrived three weeks earlier, this was the largest naval fleet ever assembled—larger than the Spanish Armada. There were more than 20 frigates with 20 to 50 guns, 2 large men-of-war with over 50 guns, and hundreds of armed cutters, transports and supply ships. On board were some 25,000 battle-seasoned British army regulars, supplemented by 5,000 Hessian mercenaries. The British had come to conquer the American rebels.

The Battle of Long Island was about to begin. Though few people know much about it, and the only story most know is of General Washington's cunning escape across the East River under cover of darkness after a disastrous defeat, others have described the battle as the most important of the American Revolution, coming as it did soon after the signing of the Declaration of Independence. Washington certainly thought it would be decisive. Surprisingly, it would be the largest engagement until the final British defeat at Yorktown.

Washington believed New York could and must be defended. Though its population of 20,000 made it smaller than Boston or Philadelphia, New York City controlled the greatest harbor in the Americas. The Hudson River divided New England from the rest of the country, and Washington didn't want the British to control it. Under Generals Charles Lee and William

Alexander—the latter was a Scottish earl also known as Lord Stirling—nine cannon batteries were built along the Hudson and around the harbor to defend the city. Five others were built along the backside of Brooklyn Heights, overlooking the Gowanus Creek.

On August 22, the first day of the invasion of Brooklyn, the frigate *Roebuck* attacked Fort Defiance on the southern tip of what is now Governors Island and destroyed it. So much for the defenses.

General William Howe, perhaps recalling his rout from Boston, felt he must take Brooklyn Heights. Also, by controlling Brooklyn, he would control the fertile pastures of Long Island, a Tory stronghold. If the Americans intended to defend the Heights, the fleet would hammer them into submission from behind. So, on August 22, the British performed the largest amphibious landing to take place before the twentieth century, moving 25,000 men ashore in less than a day. The 200 American defenders departed after firing a few shots.

At the time, the Americans had 8,000 men in Brooklyn, and shortly Washington moved another 3,000 across the river. Though he had been promised 50,000 men by the new Congress, his army in New York totaled at most 13,000 men ready for duty, of whom only about 3,000 had any military training or experience. The advantage lay with the veteran British army.

What was Washington preparing to defend? In the village of Brooklyn, nestled around the ferry landing at the foot of what is now Fulton Street, there were fewer than 250 residents and only about 2,500 in the surrounding area. Up on the Heights were the large houses owned by families like the Livingstons and the Remsens.

From the batteries at Cobble Hill (corner of Atlantic Avenue and Court Street) and above the Gowanus (Carroll and Court Streets), the American gunners saw

In bitter fighting, a vastly outnumbered Maryland regiment held off the Redcoats at the Old Stone House.

a bucolic valley at the base of what is now Park Slope, with small farms separated by stone hedgerows. The Shore Road (now approximately Fourth Avenue) skirted the edge of the wide, marshy mouth of the Gowanus Creek. Near the head of the marsh, a mill used the incoming and outgoing tides to grind the local grains. Across from it stood the Vecht-Cortelyou house, known even then as the Old Stone House because it had been built in the 1690s with fortress-like walls thick enough to stand off river pirates.

Washington was almost laughably ill-prepared to face the British forces. He had never commanded an

Brooklyn Historical Society

Battleground

One of the most important battles of the Revolutionary War occurred in Brooklyn during one long, hot week in August 1776. The British forces under General William Howe boasted a formidable armada of ships and a more than two-to-one advantage in troops, and were determined to conquer New York and destroy the American forces under the command of General George Washington. The Americans, anticipating a British move up through Brooklyn, occupied fortified positions from Red Hook to Wallabout Bay.

The British landed some 25,000 soldiers at what is now Fort Hamilton and Gravesend Bay on the morning of August 22 and advanced via Kings Highway. Sharp skirmishes were fought during the next few days. The climax of the battle occurred around midday on August 27, when a British force of about 2,000 troops tangled with a regiment of some 400 Marylanders under Major Mordecai Gist. The Marylanders, surprisingly, attacked the British at the Old Stone House at what is now Fifth Avenue and Third Street, charging again and

again. The house changed hands several times, and the Marylanders were nearly all killed, wounded or captured. But their heroic fighting stalled the British

advance for the day, and that night Washington was able to evacuate all his troops across New York Harbor—saving them to fight another day.

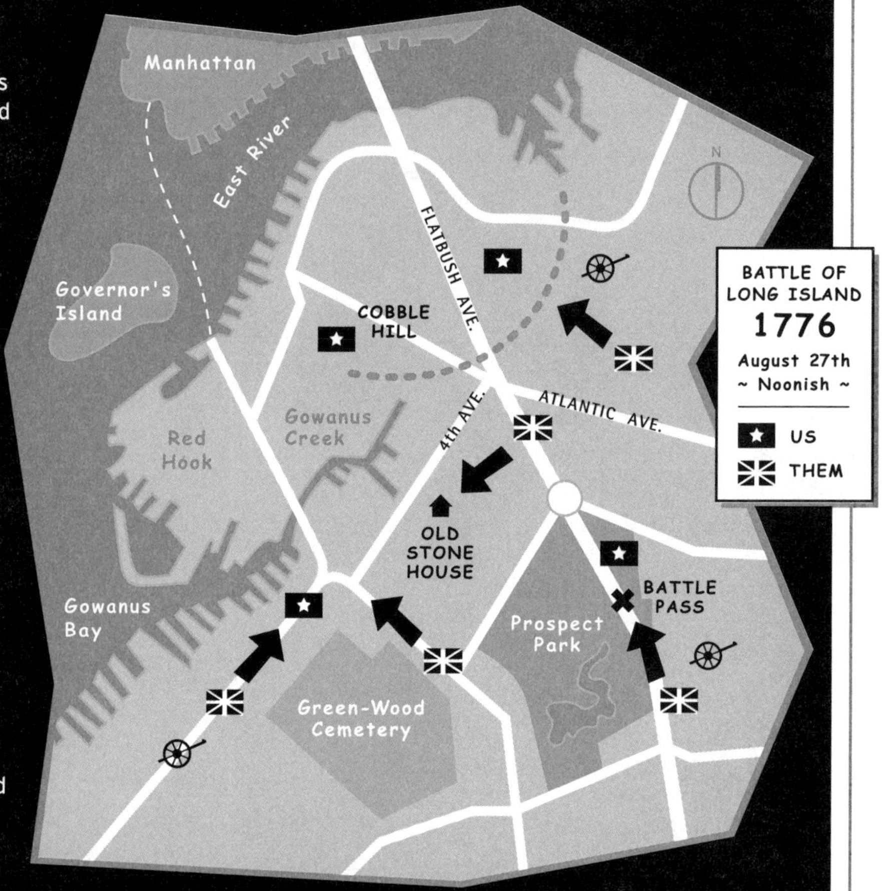

Map labels: Manhattan · East River · Governor's Island · COBBLE HILL · FLATBUSH AVE. · ATLANTIC AVE. · Gowanus Creek · Red Hook · 4th AVE. · OLD STONE HOUSE · Gowanus Bay · Green-Wood Cemetery · Prospect Park · BATTLE PASS · N

Legend: BATTLE OF LONG ISLAND 1776 · August 27th ~ Noonish ~ · ★ US · ⚑ THEM

army in the field. He made assumptions about the avenue of the British attack that would prove disastrous. He had even turned away a company of mounted soldiers who could have provided intelligence from the battlefield because he didn't know how he would feed the horses. His only advantage lay in the wind: it blew from the north, preventing the British fleet from sailing up the river behind him.

The first gunfire of the Battle of Long Island broke out across a field of watermelons just up the shore from

Red Hook, when some foraging British soldiers encountered a small group of American soldiers. The evening of August 26 was sweltering hot, and both sides coveted the melons. The battle grew as reinforcements arrived on both sides, and the sounds of the shooting echoed up the valley.

William Alexander, Lord Stirling, commanded the 2,000 men from Pennsylvania, Maryland and Delaware along Washington's right between what is now Green-Wood Cemetery and New York Harbor, some of whom

Judy Sitz

were already engaged in the fighting. While Stirling waited, and General Sullivan waited with another thousand men in the area we now know as Battle Pass in Prospect Park, the British prepared to trap the American forces.

General Grant commanded the British forces facing Lord Stirling. Stirling had known Grant during his days in London and had heard him promise in Parliament to suppress the revolt, proclaiming, "Give me five thousand good men, and I will march across the continent." Dawn came before five, and now Grant had his 5,000 men. They attacked Stirling all morning, but very slowly. Attacking Sullivan through the woods, General deHeister with 5,000 Hessians methodically drove the Americans from their battery in Battle Pass and killed them in the forest above the valley.

That same morning, a British surprise attack was brewing on the Americans' left flank. Under General Howe, Generals Clinton and Cornwallis had marched all night, first crossing what is now the Kings Highway, then marching toward the village of Brooklyn on the Jamaica Road. At nine in the morning they appeared with 14,000 soldiers, signaling their arrival (near what is now the Fulton Mall) with a cannon shot to alert Grant and deHeister, and springing the trap on the best of the American army, the 3,000 men in the valley.

Once he grasped his plight, Stirling retreated up the Shore Road toward the Heights (and Cornwallis). Releasing most of his men toward the middle of the day, he kept only a company of 400 young men from a Maryland regiment to lead an attack on the British vanguard at the Old Stone House (which still stands in a city park at Third Street and Fifth Avenue). Five times over a period of two to four hours, Stirling and his men attacked the leading elements of Cornwallis' 14,000, reforming and marching into withering fire. Twice they actually took the fortress-like house and turned the British cannon back on the invaders. Though they enjoyed enormous numerical superiority, the British troops were widely scattered. The field was confused, officers were out of touch with their troops, and since both sides wore many different uniforms in red,

blue and green, it was very difficult to identify the enemy.

The Marylanders' repeated courageous charges gave many other entrapped Americans time to escape across the Gowanus or up into the forests above the valley. They also stopped the British, who couldn't understand what was happening. The fight continued until Stirling broke off and surrendered after four that afternoon. The action of Stirling and his men, by saving the American army to fight another day, may well have saved the Revolution, although as many as 3,300 men were either lost on the field, captured or dispersed. The British buried the bodies of 256 of the 400 Marylanders in a common grave not far from the house where they fell.

Washington, who watched the engagement from the top of the Cobble Hill fort, mourned the loss of the men but was heartened by their effectiveness in halting the British. He intended to fight on. But Howe, who probably could have overwhelmed the American defenses that afternoon, chose instead to stop. His men had been marching and fighting for almost twenty-four hours.

That evening it began to rain. The weather turned cooler and the wind held from the north. Washington trusted in his defenses, which included not only heavy cannon batteries but a 600-yard-wide abatis, an open area thick with felled trees and their branches across which any attacker would have to come. He ordered 4,000 more defenders brought over from Manhattan.

But the British were masters of siege warfare, and the next day their engineers began building the trenches for cannon and men that would soon become avenues through the defenses. Only the wind was keeping the British fleet out of the East River. Throughout that day and the next, there were small firefights as the British tested the strength of the American lines. And the Americans could only watch as the British trenches grew in all directions along the battle line and larger cannons came up the Shore Road.

On August 29, Washington came to understand the desperation of his plight and called for help. Up and down the river, and across to Manhattan, men began to collect boats. That evening, as if on schedule, the winds died completely. Two regiments from Massachusetts, fishermen from the Marblehead and Salem communities, provided much of the muscle and skill needed to row and sail all the surviving American troops—as many as 11,000 of them—across the mist-shrouded river from the Brooklyn shore. The Americans left their campfires burning and kept up the regular calls of the guards as small groups of men crept away. They brought their horses, their gear and their supplies with them across the river, and spiked the cannon they had to leave behind. It is said that the last man to leave, at dawn, with the British racing down toward the beach wild with rage at their enemy's escape, was George Washington.

Never again would Washington confront the British in a set-piece battle with all his troops. Nor would he ever again fight without good intelligence. He chose his spots; he hit at the flanks of overstretched defenses; he used surprise. Though the British controlled the big cities, they made no progress in the countryside and they couldn't live off the land. The war became too costly in men and money, and the British lost their resolve. Not until Yorktown in 1781 would Washington again bring all his forces together on the enemy, and by then the positions were reversed: Cornwallis was the one trapped inside a fort, his back to the water. But the British fleet arrived too late to save him.

Joseph McCarthy is a writer, filmmaker and resident of the battle site in Cobble Hill, Brooklyn.

BROOKLYN ON FILM

The Guy from Brooklyn in World War II

Several gritty wartime dramas—among them *A Walk in the Sun* (1945) and *Guadalcanal Diary* (1943)—recount the story of ordinary American soldiers fighting Axis forces overseas: the Germans in Italy and the Japanese in the South Pacific. Such films honor the sacrifice of the average working-man in fighting for freedom. In graphic detail, the films depict gruesome war scenes and deaths, even of American soldiers. Neither film depicts any grand and glorious objectives of conquest; both deal with close-up combat on a very personal scale, for quite modest objectives.

The soldiers and marines in films like these represent diverse American combatants from city and country, small town and farm—a melting pot of religions and ethnicities. Prominent among them, there always seemed to be a protagonist from Brooklyn, usually a streetwise urban, blue-collar guy.

In these two films, in between scenes of combat, the men wait interminably for their next battle orders. Their small talk settles on longing for loved ones at home and on fond memories of their daily lives—from watching games at Ebbets Field to playing the amusements at Coney Island.

In *A Walk in the Sun*, one American soldier, played by Richard Benedict,"speaks two languages—Italian and Brooklyn." At the heart of the film, the GIs encounter two deserting Italian soldiers. Since Benedict's Brooklyn guy is the only American who can speak their language, he translates as the two are interrogated about the whereabouts of the German troops, the terrain ahead and the American soldiers' objective—a remote farmhouse controlled by German machine gunners.

A Walk In the Sun, 1945

As a nod to the ethnic makeup of Brooklyn, Benedict's character—named Franelli—converses in fluent, rapid-fire Italian with the two deserters, and discovers with great excitement that one of them is from the same region where his own "old man" was born. It's a reminder of the European immigration that populated Brooklyn earlier in the twentieth century.
—*Jon Gartenberg*

MOMA Film Stills Archive

Torch Songs

For women at the Navy Yard, welding was a political act

BY BILLIE
COHEN

Ida Pollack's and Sylvia Everett's voices grew louder and more lively with each memory they added to the ebullient pot of nostalgia they were brewing up. As lifelong friends, these gracefully aging women had many things in common apart from an afternoon spent jovially, thoughtfully and once in a while sadly in Syl's Great Neck apartment. As girls, they had grown up together in the Bronx. They had schlepped across two boroughs to attend Brooklyn College together. And they were among the first women to work in the Brooklyn Navy Yard during World War II.

When the *New York Times,* the *Sun* and *PM* hit the stands on September 14, 1941, they sported headlines like "Brooklyn Navy Yard Hires Its First Women Mechanics" and pictures of four new workers. One was Sylvia Honigman (later Everett), who had finished college the previous January and on this September day was being followed around by reporters on her first day at the Yard.

"Having women work in this man's world was such a revolutionary thing that all the newspapers covered it," Syl said proudly. Ida joined the ranks a short time later in 1942, after her husband was drafted. "It was really for a political motive," she explained. "By 'political,' I mean we took a position on what was happening with Hitler."

Along with countless others, Syl and Ida had eagerly answered America's call for women to do their part in the war. After passing a mechanical aptitude test, the young women—both were twenty-one years old when they began—went to work as skilled laborers at the Brooklyn Navy Yard, a facility that had never employed women in all of its 141-year history. "They had decided to open the doors of the man's bastion," said Syl.

Once certified by the Civil Service Commission, the women were given a choice of three trades—arc welder,

Wartime manpower shortages forced the Navy Yard to hire women mechanics.

INS/Brooklyn Public Library-Brooklyn Collection

acetylene torch burner or shipfitter—and then sent to the Yard for training. Syl and Ida both chose to be welders, as did most of the women. They started out with absolutely no experience, but today when they speak of welding, it's like listening to a musician tell how she makes a concerto out of mere breath—with art, talent, skill and pure amazement.

"Welding involves fusing two pieces of metal," Ida explained. She picked up two sheets of paper and held them at a 90-degree angle as if they were slabs of steel to be welded. "And you're adding metal to both pieces of metal by heat, using a steel rod. You have to learn to apply metal with the proper heat so that it doesn't run too fast or burn holes. We held the rod in tongs, and the tongs were attached to a lead that went to the juice, the electricity. You had to control how much heat for each particular kind of metal. You could botch it up if you used too much heat.

"And it wasn't always flat. By flat, I mean the metal is on the ground and you're welding this way." To illustrate, Ida held the papers at various angles to each other but with one sheet always flat on the table. "In the shop you can do everything, but when you're out on the ships, things are already in place. You have to learn how to do vertical welding, and you have gravity pulling the metal down. So you have to know how much heat to use to control your metal."

"It's more of a skill than she's admitting," added Syl, picking up the description. "It's called a bead when it's finished, and when it's done right, it looks like very even rings one on top of another."

"Like penmanship," said Ida.

"Yes, it's like penmanship. And if it's not that even, then it's not as strong as it should be. It's not really welded together like it should be." Syl spoke with the self-assurance of a welder whose rings were always very even.

The work they did was hard, even exhausting. They endured fifty-eight-hour weeks: ten hours Monday through Friday and then a "half day" of eight hours on Saturday. And every three months they would rotate afternoon, evening and overnight shifts. But the work was exhilarating, too. "It was a very new experience," said Syl, "but the men didn't exactly welcome us. There was a lot of hostility, a lot of sneering, a lot of sly remarks." Ida added that a woman who walked around the Yard alone would get catcalls. "You felt like you were almost being undressed."

"And you were!" roared Syl, still amused after all these years. "The first day we came to work in the shop, they had never seen a woman there. The men are standing there with these hostile looks. And the foreman is walking ahead of us with this cap on and a cigar out the side of his mouth."

"Taylor!" Ida suddenly remembered.

"Taylor. Nice man, really nice man. He's walking ahead of us and he says"—Syl affected a wise-ass Brooklynese at this point—"'Watch your language, these are teachers!'" She laughed out loud as she described an old-time tough guy with a cigar in his trap and remembered how her own language became "colorful" once she started working in the Yard. And the men, she explained, resented the women for encroaching on their territory, for being college-educated, for just being *women.*

Syl described what it was like in the shop: "For a while I was working on floor pieces in the small part of the shop where the supplies were. And men would come in for their supplies, like the rods and other things. This one guy used to come in, and I spoke to him because you try to be friendly. Not much had passed between us, and he walks in one day and wants to know if I'll go away for the weekend with him! If my mouth didn't drop to the floor! He acted like it was perfectly natural, what else is a woman good for?" She and Ida both cracked up at the audacity of the man and at the insular world of the Yard where thinking like this was completely accepted.

But it softened up after a couple years. "Oh yeah!" continued Syl. "They began to accept us because we were good. We were very good welders. We worked on the battleship *Missouri*!"

"And the aircraft carrier *Franklin Roosevelt,*" Ida added. Ida was a participant on the first day that women were allowed to work out on the ships instead of just in the shops; appropriately enough it was on Mother's Day, 1944: "There were about five of us who walked out on the

Above: Ida Pollack (center, back row) and Sylvia Honigman Everett (center, front). Right: Ida with fellow welder Joan O'Neil.

ship, and you would think we came from Mars. Every hole on the deck had a head come up! I don't know how much work was done that day, but they couldn't get used to it."

In the end they did, they had to, because the truth is, these women were good at their work. "There was this day of victory for us, for the women," Syl recalled. "In order to weld this one piece, you had to come in from both sides. Two welders came from the outside and you had to synchronize and weld at the same time so that it would be..."

"It's called twin arcs," Ida offered.

"Yes," Syl said. "And that was the day of victory because this guy who had been nasty as all hell was picked to be on one side and I was on the other. And he had to admit that it went well. And of course the foreman was watching."

That was not the only day of victory for women in the Yard. When first hired, civilian men were given the status of third-class welders and paid $1.14 an hour. The pay increased as the worker's rank increased from third to second to first class. But for the women who entered at the same time as the men, even though they all had the same level of inexperience, a new, lower category

was created—Mechanic Learner—and at half the salary. To fight this discrepancy, the women joined the Brooklyn Navy Yard Division of Industrial Union Local 22. Yard management claimed that women weren't getting equal pay because they weren't doing equal work: whereas women worked only in the shops, the men were out day after day on the ships, which was harder work.

Recounting this battle, Ida was still incredulous. "We told them, 'We're not refusing to go out on the ships. You're refusing to send us.'"

"It was a tough uphill battle," Syl said. "And it was very grudgingly that each little raise was given."

Eventually the women *did* get equal pay, and they *did* work out on the ships. Syl said she was sure the men never expected it, but the women weren't surprised at all: "We were determined. We thought, 'We're gonna win this one. We've got to.' We fought like hell, and a lot of men fought with us." Syl's first husband, who was killed on his company's last day of action at the end of the war, was one of those men.

Money wasn't the only thing the women had to fight for. Since no women had ever worked in the Yard in

Courtesy of Ida Pollack

its 141-year existence, it didn't have "heads" (a Navy term for bathrooms) set up for women. Ida remembered that the new bathrooms were installed with full floor-to-ceiling doors. "Then it was found out that some people were sleeping behind those doors," she said in a conspiratorial whisper. "It was like they had a gestapo system." So management removed the doors, leaving all the stalls exposed except one. Ida recalled how the women would all wait in line to use that one stall. Finally, the management realized they were losing a lot of working time with all the women waiting in line and put half-doors back on all the stalls.

At home, the girls' families weren't thrilled with their daughters' working arrangements, either. "I'd just graduated college, and I traveled from way up in the Bronx to the Brooklyn Navy Yard every day. I don't think my parents were delighted," said Syl. Ida, who was married during her Yard tenure but lived with her folks because her husband was overseas, had other issues to deal with: "I would come home very hungry, and I'd make myself breakfast while my father was getting ready to go to work. I'd make bacon and eggs and whatever else, and he constantly lectured me that I wasn't eating right. He irritated me—I always had to defend myself," she complained. "But one of the things that bothered me all the time was that I was earning more money than he was."

More than fifty years have passed since Ida and Syl put down their welding rods. Syl left in 1942 to get married, then moved with her husband to Boston. Ida and the rest of the women were taken off the rolls as soon as the war ended. They were told they had to leave the jobs open for the men who were returning from war. "And that was expected," explained Ida. Her voice doesn't hold even a trace of bitterness that the women who had been so important to the war effort, who had shown just how much women were capable of, were suddenly cast aside.

A few years ago, the South Street Seaport organized an exhibit at the PaineWebber Gallery to commemorate the women who had worked in the Navy Yard during World War II. One of the segments featured Ida, Syl, their friend and shipfitter Lucille Kolkin and a few other women they had worked with. "There were lots of people milling around looking at the display," Ida said with delight. "And we mentioned to some of the people next to us that the women in one of the pictures were us. They couldn't believe it!"

"The reactions were a riot," Syl said. "I think partly they couldn't believe that we were still alive!" She and Ida roared with laughter, and then Syl imitated the young people's reactions: "*That's really you? My god!*" Ida remembered that one of the young men had expressed that he felt very inefficient compared to what they had accomplished. She still recalled her words to him and repeated them in the same honest voice: "Well, it was a different time and different circumstances. You might do the same thing."

Whether or not that's true, it is a fact that these two women, and the hundreds of other female welders, burners and shipfitters at the Brooklyn Navy Yard, did indeed make history. When asked how it felt to have been such pioneers, their laughter came down a notch. "We did it innocently and inadvertently, with no intention of doing so," Ida said.

Syl agreed. "Pioneering is not what we set out to do. But that's how it worked."

Billie Cohen is a writer and the museums and radio editor for Time Out New York *magazine.*

Anchors Aweigh

During World War II, the Brooklyn Navy Yard repaired over 5,000 ships. Among the major ships built in the Yard during the twentieth century:

USS *Florida* (1910)

USS *New York* (1912)

USS *New Mexico* (1914)

USS *Arizona* (1915)

USS *Tennessee* (1916)

USS *Pensacola* (1929)

USS *New Orleans* (1933)

USS *Hull* (1934)

USS *Dale* (1935)

USS *Brooklyn* (1936)

USS *Honolulu* (1937)

USS *Helena* (1938)

USS *North Carolina* (1941)

USS *Iowa* (1942)

USS *Bennington* (1942)

USS *Missouri* (1944)

USS *Bon Homme Richard* (1944)

USS *Franklin D. Roosevelt* (1945)

USS *Oriskany* (1945)

USS *Saratoga* (1955)

USS *Independence* (1958)

USS *Constellation* (1960)

LOST TUNNEL OF ATLANTIC

Diamond in the Rough

It was—usually—a dark and stormy night when the residents along Atlantic Avenue would report hearing muffled railroad noises. What could it be? Was a ghost train or subway running somewhere nearby? Vague rumors circulated about a lost tunnel somewhere in South Brooklyn. Maybe there was something...

Illustrated by Russell Christian

Enter Bob Diamond, who's achieved notoriety as Brooklyn's "Indiana Jones." A Flatbush native, Diamond was, at twenty, a restless engineering student who could not have foreseen the strange twist of fate that would send him on an obsessive journey underground and back in time.

One night while studying, Diamond heard a radio program about rumors that a mysterious pre-Civil War railroad tunnel once existed in Brooklyn. Something about trains rumbling from the East River clear out to the far end of Long Island...

Diamond was hooked. He *had* to find out if the rumors were true. What if a long-lost tunnel ran beneath the streets? He searched through old Brooklyn city records, through libraries, through dusty documents on transportation history. Then, pay dirt! In a box of old records he found a map that pinpointed the site of an underground railroad.

THE FACTS

In the 1840s, the Brooklyn and Jamaica Railroad (precursor of the Long Island Railroad) operated a rail link from the foot of Atlantic Avenue on the East River out through Brooklyn as part of a projected line to Greenpoint, Long Island, a port for ships to Boston. Residents complained about smoke and noise from the trains, so the railroad cut and covered a 3,000-foot-long tunnel under the western end of Atlantic Avenue. The tunnel was used until 1861, but with the railroad's bankruptcy was sealed shut.

Diamond's obsessive search shifted. He had the proof. Now to find the tunnel itself! He badgered city authorities and the utility companies to let him explore the manholes along Atlantic Avenue for clues—and an entrance.

Finally they relented, and on the appointed morning Diamond arrived to find that the Brooklyn Union Gas crew had begun work an hour earlier—seeking, he believed, to discover the tunnel themselves.

In one manhole, Diamond noticed an old brick wall, and he and the crew began removing bricks and enlarging a hole. It was hot, hard, dirty work.

Diamond was lying on his stomach in the dirt, far below the surface of Atlantic Avenue, when he pulled out some cobblestones blocking a passageway. Suddenly there was only cool air before him, and utter darkness. He had found the tunnel!

His light revealed a vast, ancient-looking gallery of stone and brick. The dirt floor revealed a telltale pattern of rails and ties. Diamond's long search had ended in a startling discovery. He lay in the dirt and laughed with relief and joy.

Now, on occasional Sundays, Diamond leads groups of excited visitors down a ladder through a manhole at the corner of Atlantic Avenue and Court Street, into the long ghostly tunnel that reminds visitors more of ancient Rome than of nineteenth-century Brooklyn.

Man of the People

The first Communist on the New York City Council

BY
BRUCE
D. STUTZ

n January 1942, Peter V. Cacchione of Brooklyn took his seat in the New York City Council chambers—the first member of the Communist Party ever elected to the Council. While his election was greeted with surprise and in some cases shock ("Election of Red to Council," snarled the patrician voice of the *Brooklyn Eagle*), among Brooklyn's poor and working classes Cacchione's election was no accident.

For nearly ten years, Pete had been a force in Brooklyn politics, a kind of outer-borough Fiorello: less of a showman but no less a tireless campaigner for the rights of "the little guy" in a Depression-racked city ruled by big banking and political machinery. "He was incorrupt-

Left Politics in Brooklyn

Peter Cacchione and the Communist Party won a City Council seat in 1941—and again in 1943 and '45—but their victory didn't just come out of left field. Brooklyn had known decades of leftist politics, reaching back past the turn of the century and spanning the years of the Depression. The borough was, after all, a workers' locale, crowded with factories, shops, warehouses and wharves, and the leftist political parties of the day (including the Com-

munist Party, the Socialist Labor Party, the Socialist Party and the American Labor Party) held great direct appeal for workers and for immigrant groups— or "national groups," as they were then called. A number of major labor unions, including the Transport Workers Union, National Maritime Union and United Electrical Workers, and numerous tenant unions and "Unemployed Councils" were also active in leftist politics in Brooklyn.

ible and the people recognized it," said Simon Gershon, a Cacchione observer and editor of *The Daily Worker*.

A stocky, imposing figure, with bulldog jaw and deep-set eyes, Pete had grown up in Sayre, Pennsylvania, the son of Italian immigrants. After high school he worked for eighteen years in the railyards and foundries around his home. In this time of sometimes bitter labor disputes, Cacchione found himself blacklisted for his work in organizing workers.

In 1932 he came to New York—another penniless unemployed veteran—just as the Depression was changing the city's political landscape. A year later, the city tired of the graft and excesses of the Tammany and Jimmy Walker years and elected Fiorello La Guardia. Then, in 1936, with a quarter of the city jobless, the American Labor Party was formed. La Guardia, elected with Republican Party support, gave his support to the new party and to the election of Franklin Roosevelt. Further weakening the old Tammany political machine, a new city charter called for a city council elected by proportional representation. This meant that votes were cast in order of preference: if the first choice on a voter's ballot didn't get enough votes to win a seat, then the vote went to his or her second choice, and so on. This procedural change took away the power of the machine-controlled plurality in which the party that got the most votes simply got the most seats on the council. Finally, with fascism on the rise in Europe, opposition to Hitler became a local issue in a city full of European immigrants.

Cacchione understood these political developments and was adept at making clear to the workers and the poor how city politics affected their lot. But he was more than just another soapbox orator. Cacchione worked with the unemployment councils to prevent evictions. He led fellow veterans on Bonus Marches to Washing-

National Archives; Brooklyn Public Library-Brooklyn Collection

ton to demand veterans' pay and unemployment insurance. He led the Communist Party in its strong stand against fascism and made the connection between fascism abroad and the racism and anti-Semitism at home. Under his leadership, the Communist Party—which in the late 1930s had about 38,000 members in New York, most of them in New York City—gained a higher profile and the ear of sympathetic workers and unionists.

Si Gerson, as a reporter and then as editor of *The Daily Worker*, followed Cacchione's career and

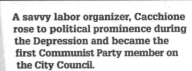

A savvy labor organizer, Cacchione rose to political prominence during the Depression and became the first Communist Party member on the City Council.

became a good friend and confidant. Now ninety years old, Gerson remembers Cacchione as a true man of the people, from his firsthand experiences as a laborer to his ardent rooting for the Brooklyn Dodgers. His favorite radio program was *The Lone Ranger*, and he'd make sure his speaking engagements never conflicted with the show's airtime. When he first won election to the

---

NOMINATING PETITION FOR COUNCILMAN

I, the undersigned, do hereby state that I am a duly qualified voter of the borough for which a nomin... is hereby made, and have registered as a voter within the said borough within the past eighteen month... residence is truly stated opposite my signature hereto and that I intend to support at the ensuing electi... nominate the following named person as a candidate of the Communist Party, for nomination for co... for at the election to be held on the 7th day of November, 1939.

Name of Candidate	Public Office	Place of Residence	
PETER V. CACCHIONE	COUNCILMAN	532 PACIFIC STREET Brooklyn, New York	131 M... Br...

And I do hereby appoint
CONSTANCE JACKSON residing at 1477 Pacific Street, Brooklyn, New York
FRANK CESTARE residing at 506 Myrtle Avenue, Brooklyn, New York
BESSIE DE JONG residing at 29 Brighton 7th Court, Brooklyn, New York
as a committee to fill vacancies in accordance with the provisions of the election law.
IN WITNESS WHEREOF I have hereunto set my hand the day and year placed opposite my sig...

Date	Name of Signer	Residence	Election District	
1. 8/13 1939	Ethel Rosenberg	111 So. 3rd St	11	County of Kings 14 A.D.
2. 8/13 1939	Sam Jagan	101 Grand St	2	County of Kings 14 A.D.
3. 8/13 1939	Stella H. Pogorsky	111 So. 3rd St.	11	County of Kings 14 A.D.
4. 8/13 1939	Anthony Mureika	17 Fillmor Pl.	9	County of Kings 14 A.D.
5. 8/13 1939	Paul Phygot	358 Wythe ave	1	County of Kings 14 A.D.

STATE OF NEW YORK
CITY OF NEW YORK } SS:
COUNTY OF KINGS

J Hrynchuk _____ being duly sworn, says: I am a duly qualified voter of the
(Name of witness to signers of petition)
State of New York and now reside at 118 So. 3rd St, _____ in the County of Kings in the
(Fill in street and house number)
City of New York, in the State of New York. I was last registered for the general elections in the year _____ from
118 So. 3rd St _____ in City of New York County of Kings in such State. I know
(Fill in street and house number where you live)
each of the voters whose names are subscribed to the above sheet of the foregoing petition containing 5 signatures
(Fill in No.)
and each of them subscribed the same in my presence and upon so subscribing declared to me that the foregoing statement, made and subscribed by him or her, was true.

John Hrynchuk
(Signature of Witness)

Sworn to before me this
SEP
1939

City Council in 1941, his comment was that it was a good year indeed: "First the Dodgers win the pennant, then this."

But Cacchione was no lone crusader. The key to his popularity was his ability to build and maintain political alliances among diverse minority interests that had been kept at odds by the political machine. His campaign literature was translated into Yiddish, Italian and Spanish. He stumped on behalf of a Black Council candidate, telling black voters that their own candidate should be first on their ballot and himself second. His alliance building, says Gerson, was never condescending and never done out of political expedience: "Pete was not just an old-fashioned spellbinder, but the soul of sincerity. He felt what they felt." It was not, for instance, politically expedient to take a stand against Mussolini, who in the mid-1930s had a great deal of support among Italian-Americans in New York. But, says Gerson, "Pete's staunchest stand, outside of his work for working men and women, was his work against fascism."

Cacchione's election didn't change him. His term coincided with the most progressive city council ever (1941 also saw the first black councilman elected, Reverend Adam Clayton Powell). He pressed for reforms in laws regarding discrimination in hiring and housing. And he even petitioned Dodgers owner Branch Rickey to break the color line and allow black players onto his ailing team. When Powell decided to run for Congress, Cacchione encouraged black leader and fellow Communist Benjamin Davis to run for City Council. Davis won, and he and Cacchione became fast friends and col-

leagues. When he introduced a resolution to declare Negro History Week, Davis ceded the floor to Cacchione to make the case to the Council.

In 1947 a Cold War backlash against Communists had begun to set in. Cacchione was still popular enough to win his seat for a third term (Jackie Robinson did play for the Dodgers that summer), but the system of proportional representation on the City Council was voted down. "The end of the ten-year experiment, which Pete considered key to maintaining a representative democracy, left him heartbroken," says Gerson. Cacchione died two days after the election, at age fifty. Gerson was chosen by the party to replace him but was prevented by the Council from being seated.

"Pete's funeral," wrote Gerson in his biography, *Pete: The Story of Peter V. Cacchione, New York's First Communist Councilman*, "was a day of civic mourning. Twelve thousand people turned out ... two thousand jamming Livingston Manor in downtown Brooklyn while ten thousand others choked the streets outside to hear the services over loudspeakers....They were trade unionists, rank and filers and leaders, community activists, black, white and Puerto Rican, and just neighbors. They were longshoremen, electricians, garment workers, clerks and artists. . . . Robert Thompson, New York Communist Party state chairman, told the mourners: 'He was so much a part of his people, the working people, that nothing could touch them without touching him.'"

Bruce D. Stutz is a writer, editor and Brooklyn resident. He is the author of Natural Lives, Modern Times.

THE BARREL SONG

After Peter Cacchione had been denied a place on the ballot in the 1939 City Council election, this campaign song was written so that voters would spell his name right when they put him in as a write-in candidate. It was sung to the tune of "Beer Barrel Polka," commonly called "Roll Out the Barrel":

Write in the ballot,
We've got the best man in town.
Write in the ballot,
A man that they couldn't keep
   down.
Write in the ballot,
Peter V. Cacchione.
Everybody write the ballot
For our victory.
Refrain: C-A-C-C-H-I-O-N-E
And don't forget to write in Peter V.
For peace without delay,
For jobs and higher pay,
C-A-C-C-H-I-O-N-E
And don't forget to write in Peter V.
For more democracy.
He'll fight for you and me. So!
(Repeat verse.)

The Late, Ornate Wallabout Market

Wallabout is the old name of a Brooklyn waterfront neighborhood and the name of the bay on the East River where in 1801 the U.S. government began building the Brooklyn Navy Yard. The name—a twist on a seventeenth-century Dutch name—was extended to the Brooklyn City produce market, built in 1890 in a surprisingly uninhibited Dutch Revival architectural style. The Wallabout Market flourished next door to the Navy Yard until 1941, when the onset of World War II prompted expansion of the Yard and the demolition of the market.

Brooklyn Public Library-Brooklyn Collection

Saving Roebling's Drawings

Barbara Millstein's Brooklyn Bridge crusade

BY BILLIE
COHEN

Never doubt the power of a rumor. A quarter-century ago, Barbara Millstein heard a rumor about thousands of architectural drawings rendered by Washington Augustus Roebling and his workers of the Brooklyn Bridge between 1870 and 1883. The rumor claimed that all of the bridge drawings had survived and were in the possession of the New York City government. At the time, Barbara Millstein had been working at the Brooklyn Museum of Art for about two years as curator of the sculpture garden. But bridges were her love. "Suspension bridges are like magic—what holds them up? Suspenders and two enormous bunches of little wires. The whole romance of the bridge is phenomenal."

And certainly the Brooklyn Bridge is the most storied of them all. Walt Whitman wrote about it, Hart Crane produced a series of long poems about it, Joseph Stella immortalized it in paintings, David McCullough devoted an entire brilliant book to the history of its building. "It's an artistic triumph," says Millstein. "And many people have tried very hard to replicate its mystique."

But back to the rumor. "I got word through a friend of mine in the Highways Division of the Department of Transportation that there was some kind of collection of drawings at New York City's carpenter shop in Williamsburg," recalls Millstein, who is still at the Brooklyn Museum of Art but is now curator of photography. "At the same time, I heard another rumor that David Hupert, a young man who was a curator for the Whitney Museum's downtown branch, was involved in

some collection with his friend Francis Valentine, a city engineer in the Buildings Department." The similarity of these two rumors drew Millstein to the DOT's outpost at 352 Kent Avenue. It was a "tiny carpenter shop with a little peaked roof right under the Williamsburg bridge," where the city's carpenters built things.

It was also the place to which Francis Valentine had been sent in 1969 to find a drawing of a particular piece of the Brooklyn Bridge that needed repair. What Valentine found were drawers full of extremely detailed architectural drawings of the bridge, some signed by Washington Roebling himself. Valentine began efforts to raise interest in what he'd found, sending notices to newspapers and museums. He made no headway until he formed an alliance with his neighbor David Hupert in 1973. Together, they began to round up funds to recover sixty-five of the drawings for a show at the Whitney, where Hubert worked. It was while Valentine and Hupert were making their selections that Barbara Millstein heard the rumors.

Millstein recalls that when she arrived at the carpenter shop, she was told that once Hupert and Valentine made their selection of drawings for the Whitney show, the rest would be discarded; the shop had no space to store them. "Oh, really . . ." was Millstein's reply. She lets out a playfully wicked little laugh when she repeats those words—because even then she had a plan. Her intention was to inform the Municipal Archives about the collection and then somehow persuade her own institution to take the drawings, especially since her higher-ups were interested in doing something for the centennial of the bridge in 1983, which was fast approaching. In the meantime, she set about convincing the Highways Division to let her catalog the papers in the shop. "The people in city government hemmed and

Established Grade

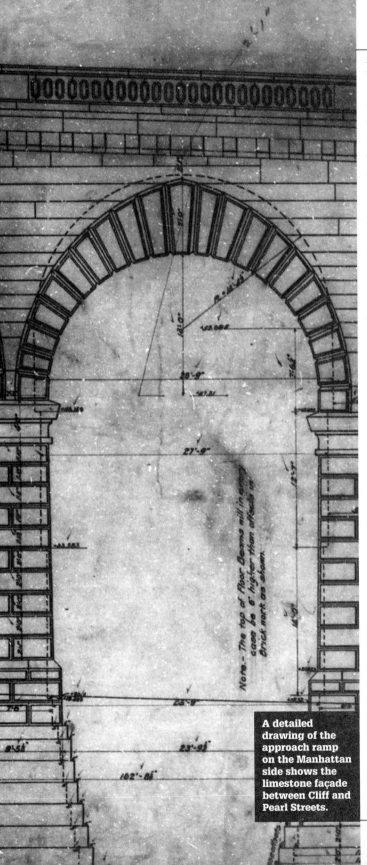

A detailed drawing of the approach ramp on the Manhattan side shows the limestone façade between Cliff and Pearl Streets.

hawed," recalls Millstein, "but they finally let me in there."

Aware of the immense task that lay before her, Millstein enlisted the help of freelancer Gail Guillette. She describes their first day on the job with a quiet sense of reverence for what they uncovered: "We began to go through these drawers, and we were overwhelmed. I thought there would be maybe a couple hundred pieces of paper. It never occurred to me that this would be an almost endless job that would take *years* to complete. It had never even passed through my mind the kind of incredible detail involved: every single facet of that bridge had its own piece of paper.

"It's sort of like being an ant," Millstein continues. "You think, 'I'll start to take it away one crumb at a time and see what I can do.'" Twenty-five years later, she laughs at her bravado back then—before she knew that the project would occupy nearly six years of her life.

Millstein and Guillette began to make some order of the drawings. They measured each one, determined what it was about and figured out whose work it was by matching the signature to the handwriting in two sign-in books for engineers and architects that they had also found. The work was endless, and the conditions were not always comfortable: "Sometimes we had to wear mittens on our hands, it was so cold in there," remembers Millstein. "But the carpenters were very sweet to us. One of them made us wooden Kleenex boxes."

During the work, she slowly recognized the historical and artistic significance of the collection. But she also realized that the Brooklyn Museum could not accommodate all 10,000 drawings. They were like a family of orphans that insisted on staying together. The Whitney had adopted some of them, but thousands still remained and no one seemed able to house them all.

Determined as ever, Millstein resorted to her backup plan: take the drawings to New York City's Municipal Archives. She was on the board there, and the man in charge of acquiring new collections, Idillio Gracia Peña, would certainly be interested. However, if the Brooklyn Museum wasn't going to take the drawings, Millstein had no official authority to remove them from the carpenter shop. She enlisted the help of Paul

Goldberger, an architectural historian who then worked at the *New York Times*. "I called him up and said, 'I have to find some way to get this material out of the Highways Division and into the Municipal Archives. It doesn't belong to Highways and it doesn't belong to the Whitney. It belongs to the city'"—her voice lowers to a solemn whisper—"'and the city has to take care of it.'" Goldberger agreed and the two met a number of times to plot their operation.

Once they received the go-ahead from the Municipal Archives, Millstein, Goldberger and Guillette sallied

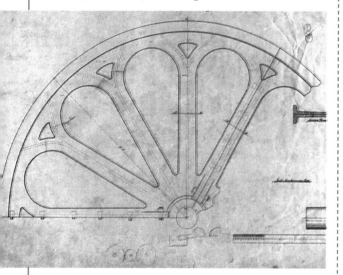

forth to the carpenter shop. "We officially knocked on the door and said, 'In the name of the people of the city of New York, we claim these drawings. We are going to take them to the Municipal Archives, where they will be kept in perpetuity for the people to consult.' The carpenters just stood aside, and the guys we got from the Municipal Archives carried out the drawers with all the 10,000 papers and put them inside the truck. We took every single drawing. And when we got them to the archives, we thought, Now what?"

Now what, indeed. Millstein and Guillette had begun the project of cataloging, but if the drawings were to be preserved for New Yorkers' use, they would have to be transferred to microfilm and microfiche. Unfortunately, the city did not have the necessary facilities. Gracia Peña had an idea—one that would get it done for

free. "We'll ask the Mormons to do it," he said. "The Mormons take pictures of everything—they're always looking for angels. We'll let them look at our papers here in the Archives if they'll do it for us." The Mormons agreed. Millstein remembers the day they came in from Salt Lake City: "This big semi rolled up in front of 31 Chambers, and a very polite guy got out and said, 'I'm parked out on Chambers Avenue and I'm here to pick up the papers.' He had all these helpers, and they came upstairs and just picked up everything and took it away." With trepidation she signed the receipt for the collection, wondering if she would ever see it again. But she did. And along with all the original papers, the Archives received microfilm and microfiche of the drawings. "The Mormons did a beautiful job," says Millstein. "And they took down the names of all the engineers and laborers who had worked on the job, looking for angels. That was okay with us."

Now Millstein could concentrate on the next project. The Brooklyn Museum had agreed to do a big exhibition celebrating the centennial of the Brooklyn Bridge in 1983. In addition to the drawings, she gathered souvenirs from the bridge's opening: spoons and lamp shades, paintings and watercolors, films and sculptures, poems and political materials. On the exhibition's opening night, she sat in awe, perched in a boat in the middle of the East River, as fireworks rained down off the bridge around her. "I felt like a queen. I never in my life was so happy."

For all her hard work, though, the satisfaction of rescuing the Roebling drawing collection pales in comparison to the glow of the treasure itself. More than anything, Millstein appreciates the magnificence of the Brooklyn Bridge and the men who built it. "We found out something about how the bridge had been made, what it took to make it, about the people who really were involved in making it. We felt that we had added something to history and added something to the city's treasures that could never have been saved otherwise."

Billie Cohen spends time with her family in Canarsie when not working as an editor of Time Out New York.

Ivan Karp: Pioneer of Urban Salvage

An artistic bent was evident early on in a youthful Ivan Karp—now a renowned collector and owner of OK Harris Gallery in Manhattan. He remembers that he was more responsive to things he saw on the street than his friends, who considered him odd for his observations. "I would remark on things like the way a car moved, or the way a building looked." This sensitivity to beauty was soon to involve Karp in a crusade to save the architectural legacy of Brooklyn buildings built between 1875 and 1919.

Largely unemployed as a young man just returned from World War II, Karp spent a good deal of his time walking around the city. One day in Brooklyn, where he was living, he observed some rubble from an old tenement building that was being demolished: "In the rubble was a carving of a cherub, with its head and parts of the body. I couldn't believe it. I looked up and saw that the building was completely festooned with ornamentation. They were knocking it off with sledgehammers and dropping it on the ground. What incredible desecration! I picked up the cherub and held it to my bosom."

Karp told his friends about this episode, and they started going around the city picking up fragments and ornaments of buildings that were being demolished. "At first we picked them up from the ground," he recalls. "Then we started going up on the buildings. We were arrested a couple of times for trespassing. Eventually I requested and got a letter from Mayor Lindsay's office saying, 'Please allow these young people to salvage what they can from these demolished buildings.'"

Karp found a receptive audience in Thomas Beakman, then the director of the Brooklyn Museum, who agreed to take the stones and carvings and store them outdoors at the rear of the museum. The collection there grew to some two thousand stones and eventually became a garden, earning Karp and his wife the status of being among the patrons of the museum.

Caryatids at the Brooklyn Museum are among treasures saved by Karp.

"Unfortunately, thirty percent of the carvings turned to dust because the museum didn't know how to take care of them and lacked sufficient funding," says Karp. He had, however, kept aside some two hundred stones, now sheltered in an arts museum in upstate New York, which he says are perfectly taken care of and beautifully displayed.

To this day Karp's architectural rescue operation continues. His most recently acquired ornament is from the 1899 Bayard-Condit building, the only Louis Sullivan–designed building in New York, whose lobby recently underwent renovation.—*Genia Gould*

Michael Kamber

Escape from Flatbush: Watching a movie from the opulent balcony of the Kings was an *experience* in the 1930s.

Saving a Palace

Time and again for the Kings

BY FRANK ANGEL

Before video rentals and cable TV, before theme parks and tenplex movie houses, the prime source of entertainment was the local movie theater. And what theaters they were! In almost every neighborhood rose grand palaces of the moving image. In Brooklyn, the Loews and RKO theater chains focused especially lavish designs on their movie houses along the busy strip where Flatbush Avenue nears Ocean Avenue. At Flatbush and Beverly Road stood one of the most opulent of all the borough's movie halls: the Kings, which opened in 1929. The great vertical Loew's sign (spelled with an apostrophe) rose nearly sixty feet and could be seen for almost a mile south and north.

In its heyday, the Kings was a teeming center of Brooklyn life. But by the mid-1970s most of the big theaters were in decline. The industry had concluded that huge single-screen theaters could not compete with other emerging forms of public entertainment. Their mammoth size, which had once made them so attractive to patrons, was the very trait that doomed them. A palatial building was not enough to wow people or lure them away from their television sets. So the movie palaces were either gutted and tortured into hybrid multiplexes, their palatial interiors partitioned, or they were closed down entirely and demolished. Some, like the Kings, by some twists of fate and back taxes, were simply closed and abandoned.

But the Loew's Kings is not yet lost, and in fact it came back to life for one shining evening of bright promise and near-tragedy in 1978.

The Kings was truly a grand place. The main lobby was flanked by massive mahogany columns that rose to the vaulted ceiling, five stories above. Stanchions marked the holding aisles where patrons would wait in line for the next stage show or movie. The entertainment often ran from noon to midnight, and it was a place for everyone. There were matinee showings for children. Teens and young adults found it well suited for courting, the subdued lighting in the boxes and alcoves conducive to private rendezvous. For adults, not only did it provide entertainment but, from the 1930s right through the mid-'50s, the newsreel was the unique "you are there" view of world events. There was even a full-size basketball court in the massive basement level; the Loews organization built employee loyalty and patron excitement by holding basketball tournaments between rival theater teams, with ushers and other staff participating. But with the pervasive spread of television sets into America's households, the communal social function of the neighborhood movie palaces faded away. The Kings, which was sold by Loews in the late 1960s, went bankrupt and, closed down, seemed fated for demolition.

Classical allusions abound among the ornate details.

But memories are long in Brooklyn, and even people who never saw a movie in the Kings share one powerful

Both pages: William Frederking

memory: their high school graduation. For years, area high schools would rent the 3,500-seat Kings Theater for commencement exercises. So when the bank that held the Kings' deed made noises about demolition, many Brooklyn high school graduates began to support a "Save the Kings" grassroots movement. The Flatbush Development Corporation, a nonprofit neighborhood support organization led by Michael Weiss, began planning ways to rescue the theater.

One idea was to persuade the City to buy the building from the bank. But to get City Hall to move on this project, there had to be a groundswell of support from local leaders and the community. But how? The answer was right there in the Kings building itself—just like the old Judy Garland movies: "We'll put on a show right here!" The idea was that if people from the community could just see the theater's unique, eye-popping opulence and beauty, that would be the catalyst to move the bureaucrats.

Early in 1978, I was among the theater industry technicians, singers, songwriters, musicians, newspaper people and those with only a desire to help signed on to the project. The doors were unlocked, and our ragtag bunch of determined "Friends of the Kings" marched into the darkened lobby to face what seemed like an impossible task: getting the theater cleaned and functional enough to stage a show—to which all of Brooklyn would be invited.

Dimmed beams of sunlight filtered through the dirty glass panels in the front of the lobby, revealing a dusty, dank interior. Evidently, stray dogs and cats had found their way into the building and had made it their home; there was plenty of sensory evidence of their presence. Someone found the switch panel and began turning on the power. Surprisingly, most of the lights worked, coming on in succession and revealing more and more of the interior. Gasps of amazement went up from the volunteers as the great lobby, fluted columns, deep red and maroon carpet and the grand staircase with its brass railings became visible. The building seemed to come alive and, despite the dirt and dust, still looked magnificent.

A Level of Detail

The next months were filled with discoveries. We found one room that contained replacement parts for every breakable item in the building, such as the various Art Deco cut-glass panels for the lighting fixtures and the porcelain faucet handles. Another room contained cases with every bulb type for every lamp fixture in the building and in all the various colors that were used. The main lighting soffit high above the orchestra floor, as well as all the proscenium area lights, was wired for three different bulb colors—red, yellow and blue. This allowed the technician to change the hues and mood in the theater. The massive lighting control panel backstage had a houselight control section with labels: "afternoon/intrm," "sunset/half," "dusk/3rd" and "night/show." We discovered that by moving the massive rheostat levers to the marked positions we could mix the three colors to create houselight colors of yellow for the intermissions and preshow, and change to a deeper yellow/orange for what we normally call "house to half." We could then turn to a deep purple/blue for an intermediate one-third level or "dusk" and finally create "night," which was barely visible deep blue light that remained on throughout the show. Evidently, the operators would go through a whole sunset sequence before the start of each show. We even found that Loews had a special blue color designed just for them. The boxes in the basement "bulb room" were stenciled "Loews Blue." Pretty impressive to have G.E. name a color for the organization.

 Westward, on the streets that lead to the park, the dusty trees of heaven droop in the sun. You can smell Brownsville's tiredness in the air like smoke." **Alfred Kazin**

When we entered the projection booth and found the light switch, our mouths dropped in awe. The booth was huge, with three projectors, a follow-spot position to one side of the projectors and a large view window in front of which were an overstuffed chair and side table. It was eerie: everything was still in place, as if it were just an intermission. There was a time schedule up on the bulletin board that said "Weekday Schedule: SAILOR WHO FELL - 105min 1 - 3 - 5 - 8 - 10. No cartoon or attr 1pm show." A chipped coffee cup sat on the small table. The booth was like a technical museum, from old tube amplifiers of the 1950s to a rack of solid-state Altec amplifiers that were used right up to the day the doors closed. There were even special 3-D motors still on the projectors and the 3-D Polaroid filters taped above the projector ports. Instead of removing equipment as it got obsolete, they evidently just added newer equipment next to the old.

As the "Friends" spent weeks crawling through the false ceilings where the fixtures were located, relamping and cleaning the chandelier pieces, it became obvious what attention to detail and design went into the operation of this theater in its prime. One discovery I made symbolized the thinking of that era. It was something I noticed while relamping one of the coves. On either side of the stage was a large cove topped by a seashell-shaped ceiling piece. The shell was lit from behind with theatrical "scoop" floodlights. I had to crawl through the top of the seashell, through a hidden door and onto a twelve-inch ledge so that I could rebulb the fixtures. This ledge was six stories above the orchestra floor. Much of the ornamentation on the walls and ceiling that gave the appearance of carved wood or marble consisted of ornamental plaster castings. As I sat there on the ledge, feet dangling in midair, I noticed that the plaster casting was applied all around the wall in the top of the cove, making the wall look like carved marble. I realized that the plasterer must have had to work up there just as I did, sitting precariously on a very small ledge, and then I noticed something surprising: the plaster appliqué work followed the curve of the wall well past the point where the audience could ever see it. So here this plaster craftsman sat on a ledge sixty feet in the air, and did he stop working

The Great Movie Palaces

For the newer generations that have no memory of these great movie palaces, it is difficult to convey their majesty. Built in the Depression years of the early 1930s, they were designed to transport patrons from the outside world of very real economic hardships into a world of stately opulence. The whole idea was to make the moviegoer forget his troubles; for fifty cents, a person could spend four hours watching a stage show and a movie on a giant screen, the day's newsreel and "selected short subjects"—all in a place that rivaled a European palace. Or at least how a patron who'd never left Brooklyn might *think* a European palace would look. —*F.A.*

William Frederking

on the plaster castings where they could no longer be seen by the audience? No. He continued his plastering so the line of the curve—visible only to *him*—would be perfect. Whoever he was, *he* could see his work and he knew when it was finished. That is craftsmanship.

A One-Night Stand

For an original musical review, *Flatbush Follies*, the Kings would open its doors just for one day and come back to life. A cast of more than fifty singers and dancers, comedians and musicians would light up the stage and people from all over Brooklyn—from the top officials including Borough President Howard Golden, the folks from BACA, Brooklyn College, Brooklyn Center and Flatbush Development to the neighborhood locals—couples in formal dress and families with kids in pajamas would all join in a Kings celebration.

On opening night, May 8, 1978, at 8 P.M., after a month of late-night rehearsals, rewrites, cuts and reedits, the marquee once more blazed with lights. Limousines lined Flatbush Avenue, and the air was electric. Inside the theater, the audience wandered the halls and lobbies, awed by the appearance of the place.

Backstage someone called "Curtain GO" and the thirty-year-old maroon velvet curtain rose to reveal singers and dancers, all with brave smiles. The spotlight in the booth turned to a wide flood to cover the dancers, and the show was on.

Although I had been there for most rehearsals, I was also the sound engineer on a show at Brooklyn Center for the Performing Arts and could not be there for the curtain. At intermission, my assistant took over so I could get to the Kings. I raced down Flatbush, and as I turned the curve, I saw five or six fire engines. I thought, "Great, a fire someplace down the block—if they don't get out of here before our show breaks, it will be chaos for the people leaving the theater." I parked, and as I ran up the block, I saw people in tuxedos and evening gowns standing out front and in the street. Others were coming out of the theater, some coughing and holding their eyes. Firemen were running into the theater with a fire hose. This fire, I finally realized, was *in* the Kings!

It seemed that the switch for the follow-spot in the projection booth was faulty. The switches and DC arcs, which make that intense light, are submerged in an oil bath to prevent dangerous arcing. Over the years this oil level had dropped, exposing the switch. When the follow-spot was turned on during the show, it arced at the switch and the oil in the bottom of the tank caught fire. The fire never went beyond the switch, but it created black noxious smoke that quickly filled the booth and then poured into the main auditorium. Even the *smell* of smoke is serious with a crowd of 3,000 people. The band stopped playing, and emcee Ed Ragowsky of Brooklyn College walked out onstage and in a shaking voice told the audience that there was no danger but everyone should all calmly walk to the nearest exit. The people did get to see most of the show; there was only one number left when the switch ignited.

Waiting for the Future

This wasn't exactly the ending anyone anticipated. The glorious reopening night at the Kings was over. But the emergency did not negate everything; there was a positive payoff. The City did buy the theater from the bank and promised not to put it on the auction block until some viable use for it could be found. They even repaired a leaking roof.

In the years since that opening night, the Kings has been rented out as a location for shooting feature films and at times has been opened for tours. Occasionally, the idea of selling it again surfaces. Once it wound up on the City's "Properties to Sell" list, and a group of local Kings supporters went to Howard Golden's office to beg that it be taken off the auction block. Golden's office responded by again removing the building from unencumbered sale.

Since then, the great Kings movie palace has remained closed, its magnificence boarded up and dark as it quietly awaits another rediscovery.

Frank Angel is director of the Brooklyn Center Cinema and a consultant to the Brooklyn Museum and the Massachusetts Museum of Contemporary Art.

The Portentous Toad

Nature rears its head

BY CARL SAFINA

In the late spring of 1964, the biggest hit song was the Beatles' "Eight Days a Week." I was a fourth grader humming that tune as I left my asphalt Catholic schoolyard, crossed the black-tarred street and headed up the concrete-and-slate sidewalks of Brooklyn. I was headed toward the pizza parlor, where that song would be among the parade of hits blasting from the jukebox as the big kids from the high school crammed the counters and flirted. I was strumming a wrought-iron picket fence with my fingers as I walked past the dented, galvanized garbage pails in front of the tenements, when the sight of a miracle stopped me dead in my tracks.

A toad.

A TOAD!

In an adult life of world travel on every continent, no sighting of an animal—not polar bear, neither elephant nor penguin—has seemed so wondrous, or struck me with such disbelief, as that toad on the Brooklyn sidewalk; one of the first wild animals I had ever seen. What was this toad doing here? How could it have gotten here? Where, among the concrete and garbage cans, had it found a home?

Home. That was the next thought: How could I get this toad home? I was an inveterate pet collector. In the backyard of the tenement we lived in, my father had two years earlier built for me (I had helped as much as I could, but I was only seven) a pigeon coop. I had a rabbit, and a turkey rescued into petdom from one of the live poultry markets that were common in Brooklyn back then. But wild animals were different: incomparably more exotic. Wild animals of any kind, be they toads or mountain lions, were the stuff of books and of wilder-

nesses. I wanted more than anything to see and know wild animals, to have some wild animal pets. I needed this toad. I burned for this toad! But something large loomed between us: The One Holy Roman Catholic and Apostolic Church. Or, more specifically, the nun who was my teacher at school. I feared her more than any living person or beast. If she detected a toad in my jacket or in a bag in my desk (and she would certainly divine any unbaptized life-form in the classroom), she would almost surely find some technicality in the cate-

chism for sending me to burn for at least eternity in the fires of hell. Or worse—those nuns knew how to hit! With a degree of supreme forebearance engendered only by my instinct for self-preservation, I left the toad behind. I was sure the super-stern nun would never understand my acquisitive love of one of the smaller members of creation. It would be up to my father now.

"I'm sorry, Carl, but there's no way that little toad could still be there. It's been hours since you saw it, and it's not going to just stay in one place. And anyway, it's been a long day and I'm tired."

I was nine years old, and I was near tears. "Can't we just look for it?"

Russell Christian

"All right," my father said wearily as he got up and reached for his jacket.

I knew he'd help. We went up the street, crossed the avenue, and traveled down several more blocks, him walking, me skipping. We got to the spot. No toad. "It was here," I said emptily, pointing to the exact garbage can in whose shadow the miraculous toad had revealed itself.

Just as my father had predicted. He had done his job and let me find out the hard way. And he knew that now I couldn't blame him for not trying. Fair enough. I began to pull the garbage cans out, scrutinizing the soot accumulated between the corners of pavement and the side of the building. My father looked uncomfortable. We were making a bit of a mess. He held his tongue, but I knew my time was short.

The glint of an eye caught mine. And the outline of the toad, pressed into a bit of silt, came into focus. "Here it is!" I yelled. I reached down and picked up the toad, showing it gleefully to my amazed father, who was already putting the trash cans back in order. We brought the toad home and put some soil into the bassinet my sister had recently outgrown, and fitted a screen over its top. We added a dish of water—my first terrarium.

In went the toad. We brought it outside so it could live next to the rabbit. The next day, after it had settled down, I watched it dig a burrow. This was wild animal behavior right in front of my eyes—a little laboratory.

I dug worms for it in a vacant lot. I learned about the way a predator orients to prey. I learned how fast an animal can strike! We read about how that long, lightning-swift tongue was attached in the front of the toad's mouth. How weird! How GREAT!

And when, a long time later, the toad finally died, I broke a rusty piece of wire from the backyard fence, placed the toad on its back and scratched its belly until the skin opened. I was amazed at how neat and orderly and colorful all the internal organs were. These weren't just guts; this was really cool plumbing. It looked so complicated. I could see that it might take a long time to learn all about this.

And still it seems so. That toad from the Brooklyn sidewalk helped open a window on the world, and my view from that window grew to include a sense of biology and evolution and the universe and deep time. But most immediately it was a window on the limitless delight and infinite interest that I suddenly realized was waiting in a wild world that still lived, lurked and hid right around me.

And to a large extent that is still my world view. I live in the suburbs now. And not only do I wonder and worry about the lives and futures of the songbirds at the feeder and the raccoons at the trash and deer at the shrubs—all of whom are struggling to adjust and exist—but I also realize that the influence of people in their cities now extends beyond Brooklyn, beyond the suburbs, beyond the farms. Our influence is felt everywhere.

Most of us live among our own species, and we call those places towns and cities. Loads of wild creatures consider those places home, too. And what a much bigger, better home it is for us all when one can recognize the call of a bluejay, or be aware of the evening flights of chimney swifts, or notice little bats swooping through moths around the streetlamp. The diversity of wildlife that still survives and sometimes thrives among us is truly a wonderful gift.

I especially find the migrations of animals, particularly the spectacular seasonal movements of birds and ocean fishes near my home on Long Island, to be among the greatest sources of energy and inspiration in my life. Their visitations and the subtle, living spectacle of them, as they come and go in our midst from hundreds or thousands of miles away, connect us to the whole wide world. Even more amazing to me is how many people don't see them. I sometimes can't help but pity these poor people—my neighbors—their seemingly meager lives. How much richer a bird feeder or a pair of binoculars would make them; these things have made all the difference for me. They're a magical window with a limitless view.

That whole world opened to me the afternoon I spotted that toad on a sidewalk in Brooklyn.

Carl Safina, director of National Audubon's Living Oceans Program, is a MacArthur Fellow and author of Song for the Blue Ocean.

NOW & THEN

It was a small ballpark by today's standards, holding about 24,000 when it opened on April 5, 1913, on Bedford Avenue. But numbers can only say so much about the home of the Dodgers and cannot capture the sense of raucous community generated there. Eight World Series were played on that field—with only one Dodger victory (over the Yankees) in 1955. It was the place where the boys of summer played their best games before they went west in 1957. And when a wrecking ball leveled Ebbets Field for an apartment complex (named for Jackie Robinson), it changed Brooklyn forever.

Michael Kamber

Weeksville, Lost and Found

Real roots in Bed-Stuy

BY TARA GEORGE

Four wooden cottages in the heart of Bedford-Stuyvesant: their white paint is peeling, the shingles on the roofs have chipped over time and the grass around them is sparse. Visible from Bergen Street through a barbed-wire fence, they look like a row of old country houses engulfed by urban sprawl.

But these nineteenth-century clapboard houses are an important monument to a period from Brooklyn's past. They are all that remain of a place known as Weeksville, one of the earliest and perhaps largest settlements of free blacks in the North. That they have survived to this day is due partly to their inconspicuousness but mainly to their serendipitous rediscovery in the 1960s by a trio of curious Brooklynites. The story of how these four historic dwellings were found and preserved is a tale of luck, perseverance and the persistent tug of history.

In 1967 James Hurley, an idealistic young man of Irish heritage, had just returned to New York after studying abroad. Combining his love of history and of education, Hurley began leading walking tours of city neighborhoods as part of a community workshop he was taking at Pratt Institute. In his Saturday morning class were two African-American friends, Delores McCollough, a court reporter, and Patricia Johnson, an employee of the city's rent-control office, both of whom had an interest in urban history and particularly in the history of blacks in Brooklyn.

One day, while doing research for one of their outings, Hurley came across a book called *Brooklyn's Eastern District* by Eugene L. Armbruster. As he flipped through its pages, he found a single paragraph mention-ing Weeksville and the location of its hub near Bergen Street and Troy Avenue. For the trio, it was an intriguing discovery. McCollough and Johnson had heard stories of Weeksville from their elders, but nobody knew exactly where it was. Suddenly, this old book from 1942 provided them with a clue.

So out they went to the area Armbruster described. What they found were about two dozen empty old shacks and, a few blocks away, up a crooked old path, four white cottages, still partially occupied. The three didn't quite

The last standing houses of the African-American Weeksville settlement as they looked before (above) and after (below) restoration in the 1980s.

Off the grid of contemporary streets, nineteenth-century Weeksville houses (center) were built along old Hunterfly Road.

Courtesy of the Society for the Preservation of Weeksville

know what to make of their find. Had they rediscovered Weeksville? Or just some run-down old homes in an out-of-the-way corner of Brooklyn? They had no way of knowing. And, surprisingly, the people who lived in the houses knew nothing about any "Weeksville."

The story may well have ended there. But not long afterward, Hurley happened upon a *New York Times* article announcing that an area in Bedford-Stuyvesant was going to be razed to make way for the construction of a massive public housing development. "I woke up in the middle of the night saying, 'Oh my God, that's Weeksville,'" recalls Hurley. The area designated for

destruction included the cluster of empty old houses that he and his two classmates had found near Troy Avenue. (The four white clapboard houses, however, were not slated for demolition.) Hurley's group felt they had to act—and act quickly. First, they had to prove that the patch of land was indeed part of Weeksville. Then they had to find a way to save what was left of it.

McCollough, who had a talent for mobilizing people, reached out to historians, community activists, anybody she could get hold of to join their cause. Johnson, who was a tireless researcher, threw herself into documenting their findings. It took some months, but with the

Born and raised in Weeksville, Mrs. Harriet Etta Lane contributed her memories to Weeksville's oral history project.

help of old maps, tax documents and census records the self-taught historians were able to back up their belief that they had found Weeksville. What's more, they were able to cobble together a much clearer picture of the settlement's past.

The community, they learned, was named for James Weeks, an African-American longshoreman who had bought a plot of land from the wealthy Lefferts family in 1838. It grew to become Brooklyn's first major free black community, large enough to support an old folks' home, an orphanage, a cemetery and a number of churches, some of which are believed to have been stops on the Underground Railroad prior to the Civil War. Weeksville endured as an African-American enclave until after the Civil War, when it served as a

refuge for those fleeing the Draft Riots on the streets of Manhattan. It survived as a community for a half-century or so. And during that time it produced Brooklyn's first African-American police officer, Moses P. Cobb, and New York State's first black woman doctor, Susan Smith-McKinney.

Their research was not sufficiently convincing in the argument that the old remnant buildings were indeed part of Weeksville, and the government remained determined to raze and build. However, thanks to some favorable news coverage, the group was given time to dig and photograph the area before it was obliterated. Hurley, an experienced aerial photographer, took to the air in a plane flown by Joseph Haynes, a subway engineer and pilot who devoted much of his time to the Weeksville cause.

At ground level, a volunteer army of Boy Scouts and children from nearby P.S. 243, which had been "Colored School 2" during the Weeksville era, went to work digging for traces of the old settlement. As the wreckers wrecked, the young diggers dug, often pulling out not much more than dirt. At times the work was demoralizing, but occasionally they unearthed buried treasure: coins, pottery, even a cannonball. Hurley is still moved by the recollection of a shy young boy with a speech impediment who was prying loose a two-inch porcelain doll with his little trowel. It filled the youngster with such pride, Hurley says, that despite his language struggles he would always be able to talk eloquently about his find.

"To me," says McCollough, "the most exciting thing about all this was the community participation. I have heard people say black folks have no history. Well, we were proving that that's not so. And our children were participating in their own history."

It became clear to the Weeksville Society, as the group had come to be called, that the four surviving Bergen Street houses should be preserved. From their research they knew that the houses lay along an ancient Indian path called the Old Hunterfly Road, which had formed Weeksville's eastern edge. So they took their case for saving those last houses to the Landmarks Preservation Commission. To their delight,

Right: Brooklyn Historical Society

on August 18, 1970, the Commission voted to designate the "Hunterfly Road Houses" at 1698 Bergen Street as historic landmarks.

It was an extraordinary victory for this group of activists, which had grown to include scholars, archaeologists and historians. Through sheer determination, they had saved a tangible piece of the past for the foreseeable future. But it was by no means the end of their struggle. Since then, they've had several setbacks. One house was burned down; another was destroyed by vandals. In 1973, U.S. Treasury agents found an illegal whiskey distillery in yet another of the houses. Thieves have stolen bits of copper plumbing. And once a house was damaged when a car crashed into it, dismantling renovations that had taken years to achieve.

Still, the Weeksville Society has persevered. Today, two of the houses have been turned into a museum, and hundreds of schoolchildren visit every year. They can listen to stories told by a professional storyteller, gaze upon a handful of relics from Weeksville's past and learn the history of the survival of those four old homes. "They're quite magical, quite sacred," says Joan Maynard, a tireless volunteer who has devoted her life to preserving the Hunterfly Road houses. "They need to be there because we've lost a lot of the fabric of the nineteenth century. They prove that not all of it was bad for blacks, that some of it was good."

Tara George is a crime-and-politics beat reporter for the New York Daily News.

NOW & THEN Today the hazards of crossing the Brooklyn Bridge in bad weather consist mainly of skidding bicycles on the walkway. But in its early days a blizzard like the big one in 1888 brought whole trains full of passengers to a standstill.

Both pages: Genevieve Naylor

**BEFORE
DUMBO**

Henri &
Brooklyn

A Great Photographer
Shoots the Waterfront

In 1946, the world-renowned photographer Henri Cartier-Bresson was at the peak of his form and, with his trademark tiny Leica, was able to transcend many photographic genres. He was about to be celebrated with a one-man show at the Museum of Modern Art when *Harper's Bazaar* brought him to New York City on assignment. Scouting locations for a photo-essay about the Brooklyn Bridge and falling madly for Brooklyn as a subject, Cartier-Bresson was joined by Genevieve Naylor, one of the magazine's leading photographers. Together, they explored what was in those days a truly working waterfront and what is now called DUMBO (Down Under the Manhattan Bridge Overpass).

While Cartier-Bresson concentrated his attention and his camera on the workmen and the buildings, Naylor concentrated on Cartier-Bresson himself—and produced these rare images of a master photographer at work.

The Last Days of the *Eagle*

When the hometown paper folded, it was like a death in the family

BY TARA GEORGE

It was a bitter winter when the staff of the *Eagle* went on strike in January 1955. Sid Frigand was a young rewrite man then, more at home weaving together the strands of a breaking news story than walking a frigid picket line in downtown Brooklyn. The placard he'd inserted in desperation inside his coat did nothing to block the biting wind in downtown Brooklyn, and the thermos of coffee his wife brought him as he paced with the others along Johnson Street did nothing to warm his soul. Frigand had the sinking realization that Old Man Schroth, as the newspaper's publisher was known, would not buckle under the demands of the Newspaper Guild for more pay. As the union's strike wore on, it was becoming more evident that the "stubborn old Dutchman" was digging in his heels and planned to close the *Eagle*. After 114 years, the newspaper that had given voice to "the Brooklyn spirit" was about to be silenced forever.

"It was a wrenching experience," recalled Frigand, who was born in Williamsburg and had joined the paper as a copyboy seven years before the strike. "Those last days were like a wake."

The *Eagle* was beloved in Brooklyn. Established in 1841 by a young Democrat (and edited for a while by poet Walt Whitman), the paper had grown over the years to become the biggest afternoon daily in the country and also the unashamed cheerleader for the city of nearly three million. It championed the building of the Brooklyn Bridge, assigned Brooklyn its label as a city of homes and churches and, as Manhattan grew ever more powerful, fought to keep Brooklyn from being bullied.

While the *Eagle* ran some international and national stories on its broadsheet pages, it was, at heart, charmingly parochial. The paper devoted most of its daily coverage to local crime and civic issues. When a reader died while abroad in France, its Paris correspondent was called upon to arrange the funeral details. Kids grew up delivering the *Eagle*, and Brooklyn families learned about their neighbors' births, deaths and marriages in the paper's pages. To make sure its readers stayed interested, the editors pushed their writers to mention as many locals in their stories as possible. "'Names, names, names,'" Frigand recalled the editors saying. "It was everybody's fifteen minutes of glory."

The paper won four Pulitzer Prizes, but by the 1950s Brooklyn itself had changed. Many of the *Eagle*'s core readers, the working-class Catholics, had prospered and moved elsewhere. African-Americans and Latinos had begun to take their place. When the *Eagle* failed to adapt to the changes surrounding it, circulation declined and so did ad revenues. In 1955, as contracts were coming up for renewal, the seven largest Manhattan newspapers gave their employees $5.80-a-week raises and the *Eagle* staffers wanted parity. Frank D. Schroth, the publisher, agreed to give the craft unions the raise but said he couldn't afford to do the same for reporters. The paper's circulation, he said, was hovering around 130,000, while its competitors were selling at least four times that. To follow the "Manhattan pattern," he said, was financially out of the question.

So the Newspaper Guild struck. Columnist Dave Anderson was then a young sportswriter covering the Dodgers. He remembers that he was packing to go to spring training when he got word of the strike and took his place on the frosty picket line. Bert Hochman was the night city editor. He, like many of the others, felt Schroth had forced the guild out onto the street for no good reason. "There was a lot of solidarity among us,"

Hochman said, "but it wasn't a happy situation. There was a growing sense that this wasn't going to end well."

If the strikers were miserable, so were some of the readers. They'd come to rely on the *Eagle* to tell them the stories of their city, and some of the columnists had extremely devoted followings. Among them was Jimmy Murphy, known for the inventive language he'd developed over a half-century of covering scholastic sports. One famous "Murphyism" included in his account of a touchdown by a player who "toted the piggie into the promised land."

With Murphy and his colleagues muted, a citizens' group decided to act. They took out advertisements in Manhattan papers, saying: "We want our *Eagle* back!" But it was to no avail. Management and the guild had reached a stalemate. On March 16, the *Eagle* finally folded. One report describes an eerie silence in the empty newsroom, save for the tapping of a bookkeeper's adding machine. At guild headquarters, strikers quietly folded up their card games and slipped away to the saloons. Most of the paper's 650 employees were now without work. Schroth issued a statement blaming the guild and saying there had been no alternative to closure. "So the Pulitzer Prize–winning paper of Whitman, Van Anden and McKelway has been silenced forever," he wrote, "and Brooklyn, the largest community in America without a voice, will indeed be doomed to be cast in Manhattan's shadow."

The final edition of January 28, 1955, was the last ever published. Its lead story was about a fifty-eight-year-old landlady who had been beaten to death. It also told of a two-year-old boy surviving an eleven-story fall, and a thief robbing a baker of $90 and making his getaway in a taxi. That day, there were thirty-six listings in the obituaries.

Frigand was heartbroken. But like many *Eagle* reporters with young families to support, he had no time to ponder the misery. He abandoned newspapering, took a job in public relations and eventually became Mayor Abe Beame's press secretary. But he's never forgotten the *Eagle* and still recalls wistfully the clatter of Underwood typewriters, the scampering copyboys and the adrenaline that drove the newsroom.

Along with the Dodgers' departure, Frigand, like many others, considered the loss of the *Eagle* to be one of the most tragic moments for Brooklyn. "There's something about a newspaper that has a living quality," he said. "The *Eagle* had character. And when it died, it was like the passing of a person."

Tara George, a reporter for the New York Daily News, *is a resident of South Brooklyn.*

Michael W. Robbins

Photo Credits:

Front Cover
top row: center, Courtesy Junior's Restaurant; right, Brooklyn Public Library—Brooklyn Collection.
middle row: left, Brooklyn Public Library—Brooklyn Collection; center, Courtesy Judith Walsh; right, Bob Day.

Back Cover
top row: center, Lee Stookey; right, Brian Merlis Collection.
middle row: Martha Cooper/City Lore.
bottom row: left, Brooklyn Historical Society; right, Ted Hardin.

Front Matter
v: Culver Pictures
viii: Everett Collection
ix: Robin Holland
x: Michael Kamber, Russell Christian
xi: Brooklyn Public Library—Brooklyn Collection
xiv: top row: left, Martha Cooper/City Lore; right, Mara Faye Lethem.
 center row: Michael Kamber; right: Ted Hardin.
 bottom row: left, Ralph Ginzburg; center, Mara Faye Lethem.
xvii: Lee Stookey
xviii: Brooklyn Historical Society

Time Line
page xx: left, The Granger Collection; bottom left, Brooklyn Historical Society; center, NYC Municipal Archives; top right, Library of Congress; bottom right, National Baseball Hall of Fame Library & Archive, Cooperstown, NY.
page xxi: top left and bottom left, Brooklyn Public Library—Brooklyn Collection; center and top right, Brooklyn Historical Society; bottom right, Lee Stookey.
page xxii: top left, Brian Merlis Collection; bottom left, Brooklyn Historical Society; top center, Library of Congress; top right and bottom right, Brooklyn Public Library—Brooklyn Collection.
page xxiii: top left and bottom right, Brooklyn Public Library—Brooklyn Collection; bottom left, Brown Brothers; center, Brian Merlis Collection; center right, Brooklyn Historical Society.
page xxiv: left center, top right, and bottom right, Brooklyn Public Library—Brooklyn Collection; left center, Photofest; center, Brian Merlis Collection.
page xxv: top left, Brooklyn Historical Society; bottom left, Brooklyn Public Library—Brooklyn Collection; top center, Michael Robbins; top right, AP/WideWorld Photos; bottom right: Brian Merlis Collection.

page xxvi: top left, Brooklyn Historical Society; bottom left, Courtesy Gold's; center, CORBIS; bottom right, Brooklyn Public Library—Brooklyn Collection.
page xxvii: top and bottom left, bottom center, Brooklyn Public Library—Brooklyn Collection; center, CORBIS; top right, NYC Municipal Archives; bottom right, AP Photo/Anthony Camerano.
page xxviii: top left, Brian Merlis Collection; top center, NYC Municipal Archives; top right, AP/WideWorld Photos; bottom left, Brooklyn Historical Society; bottom center, Michael Robbins; bottom right, Brooklyn Public Library—Brooklyn Collection.
page xxix: bottom left, Brooklyn Public Library—Brooklyn Collection; center, Everett Collection; top right, Lige Stewart/Courtesy Harry S. Truman Library; bottom center, Brooklyn Historical Society; bottom right, Photofest.
page xxx: top left, Courtesy Junior's Restaurant; all others, Brooklyn Public Library—Brooklyn Collection.
page xxxi: top left, Picture Collection, New York Public Library; center left, Photofest; bottom center, Brooklyn Historical Society; center right, AP/WideWorld; bottom right, Courtesy Kevin Burns.
page xxxii: top left, NY Daily News; bottom left, Brian Merlis Collection; center and bottom right, Michael Kamber; top right, Brooklyn Public Library—Brooklyn Collection.
page xxxiii: bottom left, CORBIS; center, Martha Swope/TimePix; center right, Brian Merlis Collection; top right, Palitz-Robbins Collection; bottom right, Owen Franken/CORBIS.
page xxxiv: center left, Courtesy Society for the Preservation of Weeksville; bottom left, Bettmann/CORBIS; top right, Suzanne Szasz/EPA/National Archives; center right, NY Daily News.
page xxxv: top left, Brooklyn Historical Society; bottom left, Michael Robbins; center, Photofest; top right, Michael Kamber; bottom right, Courtesy Borough of Brooklyn.
page xxxvi: left center, Tom Brazil; bottom center, Brooklyn Historical Society; top right, Tom Callan; bottom right, Ralph Ginzburg.
page xxxvii: top left, Palitz-Robbins Collection; bottom left, Photofest; center, Reuters/CORBIS; bottom center, Paul Warchol; top right, Tom Callan; bottom right, Courtesy BAM.
page xxxviii: bottom left, Michael Kamber; bottom center, Courtesy U.S. Supreme Court; top center, Ted Hardin; bottom right, CORBIS/UPI.
page xxxix: top left, Courtesy ABC, Inc.; bottom left, top center, bottom right, Michael Kamber; top right, Russell Kaye.

INDEX